Adapting to Rising Sea Levels

Adapting to Rising Sea Levels

Legal Challenges and Opportunities

Margaret E. Peloso

CAROLINA ACADEMIC PRESS

Durham, North Carolina

Library of Congress Cataloging-in-Publication Data

Names: Peloso, Margaret, author.
Title: Adapting to rising sea levels : legal challenges and opportunities /
  Margaret Peloso.
Description: Durham, North Carolina : Carolina Academic Press, LLC, 2017. |
  Based on author's thesis (doctoral - Duke University, 2010). | Includes
  bibliographical references and index.
Identifiers: LCCN 2016051956 | ISBN 9781611636185 (alk. paper)
Subjects: LCSH: Climatic changes--Law and legislation--United States. | Sea
  level--Government policy--United States.
Classification: LCC KF3783 .P45 2017 | DDC 346.7304/6917--dc23
LC record available at https://lccn.loc.gov/2016051956

eISBN 978-1-5310-0683-9

CAROLINA ACADEMIC PRESS, LLC
700 Kent Street
Durham, North Carolina 27701
Telephone (919) 489-7486
Fax (919) 493-5668
www.cap-press.com

Printed in the United States of America

To Mom and Dad

Contents

A Note about the Figures

The figures in this book have been printed in black and white. They can be accessed in full color at *http://www.velaw.com/AdaptingToRisingSeaLevels/* and can be downloaded for educational purposes. Unless otherwise credited, photographs are the author's own and original artwork was prepared by Laurie Duggins.

Acknowledgments

There are many people without whom this book would not have been possible. While I cannot possibly attempt to name them all here, there are a few people whose contributions I particularly want to acknowledge.

First and foremost, thank you to my family. Mom, Dad, and Tom, I truly could not have done this without you. Thank you for your support, encouragement, and the occasional "so how's the book coming?"

Thanks are also due to my colleagues at Vinson & Elkins who have provided me with a tremendous amount of research and logistical support as I prepared this book. I want to particularly acknowledge my wonderful paralegal, Deborah Raichelson, who was brave and persistent enough to proofread and cite check my entire manuscript. This book was substantially improved by her tremendous efforts. I also want to thank Jeff Kostelnik for all of the logistical support without which this book would not have many of the figures that improve its clarity.

The research that underlies the case studies in this book would not have been possible without the help of many government officials, coastal property owners, and activists who agreed to be interviewed for my research. While these people are not named individually in the book, I remain grateful to them for their time and insights.

Finally, thank you to Mike Orbach and Meg Caldwell who thought that the simultaneous pursuit of a law degree and a PhD was not only possible but also a good idea. Thank you for teaching me how to take my different skill sets and pull them together to tell a new story. Thank you also for starting me down the path of this research, which has been one of the most challenging and rewarding projects I have ever undertaken. I hope I have made you proud.

Adapting to Rising Sea Levels

Chapter 1

Introduction to Sea Level Rise

In the coming years, one of the most visible impacts of climate change will be rising seas. Since the industrial revolution, average global sea level has already risen 8 inches.[1] Sea level is projected to continue rising well into the future as a result of both increased warming of the oceans and melting of ice sheets and glaciers. The 2013 report of Intergovernmental Panel on Climate Change's ("IPCC") Working Group I—a component of the IPCC's Fifth Assessment Report—concludes that depending on future greenhouse gas ("GHG") emissions scenarios, sea levels will rise an additional 0.85 to 3.2 feet globally by 2100.[2] The Third National Climate Assessment projects that the United States will experience between 2 and 6 feet of sea level rise by the end of the century.[3]

Rising seas will have a number of important impacts on coastal zones. Chief among these impacts will be the gradual inundation of low-lying coastal areas and key infrastructure—such as major seaports—that lie within those coastal areas. In the United States, EPA has estimated that 1 meter (approximately 3 feet) of sea level rise will result in the loss of 10,000 acres of land.[4] Rising sea levels will also increase the impacts of coastal storm surges, which in combi-

---

1. UNITED STATES GLOBAL CHANGE RESEARCH PROGRAM, CLIMATE CHANGE IMPACTS IN THE UNITED STATES: THE THIRD NATIONAL CLIMATE ASSESSMENT 44 (2014) [hereinafter NCA2014].

2. IPCC, *Summary for Policymakers, in* CLIMATE CHANGE 2013: THE PHYSICAL SCIENCE BASIS. CONTRIBUTION OF WORKING GROUP I TO THE FIFTH ASSESSMENT REPORT OF THE INTERGOVERNMENTAL PANEL ON CLIMATE CHANGE 25 (2013) (noting likely ranges of sea level rise ranging from 0.26 to 0.82 m, depending on the emissions scenario considered).

3. NCA2014, *supra* note 1, at 45.

4. James G. Titus, *Chapter 7: Sea Level Rise, in* REPORT TO CONGRESS: THE POTENTIAL EFFECTS OF GLOBAL CLIMATE CHANGE ON THE UNITED STATES 123, 123 (Environmental Protection Agency 1989).

nation with sea level rise will threaten important coastal infrastructure. In addition, sea level rise can render coastal aquifers useless when they suffer from saltwater intrusion.

Collectively, these hazards pose a significant challenge not only for the United States' coastal zone but for the country as a whole. This book explores the significant legal challenges and opportunities that will arise in the face of rising sea levels. Focusing primarily on state experiences in California, North Carolina, and Texas, the book will examine how coastal management structures impact the ability of state and local governments to carry out effective measures to adapt to sea level rise. Building upon the lessons learned from these states, the book will also evaluate the legal challenges and opportunities for the private sector as it seeks to respond to rising seas.

Before proceeding to legal issues, this chapter will explain what we know about sea level rise and the impacts of climate change on storm activities—two key factors in defining the scope of the adaptation challenge.

How Do We Know That Sea Level Is Rising?

A discussion of sea level rise should begin with a basic question: how do we know that sea level is rising? The simple answer is that we know sea level is rising because of the availability of historical measurements. Historically, measurements of sea level have depended on a global network of tide gauges, which measure the height of the sea relative to the land on which they are placed.[5] While tide gauges provide an important measure of relative sea level rise, they are subject to the movement of the land on which they are placed and influenced by other factors that may limit or accelerate the rate of regional sea level rise. In addition, tide gauge distribution has historically been more dense in the northern hemisphere. As a result, tide gauges may be limited in their ability to provide global estimates of sea level rise.

---

5. *How We Observe the Ocean: Tide Gauges*, NOAA Ocean Climate Observation Program, http://oco.noaa.gov/tideGauges.html (last visited Feb. 9, 2016).

What Is Relative Sea Level Rise?

The sea level rise experienced by a coastal region is a product of the amount by which sea level increases, the movement of natural land forms, and other factors that can increase or decrease the amount of sea level rise an area actually experiences. For example, in a coastal area experiencing natural land subsidence, relative sea level rise will be greater than the rate of sea level rise because the coastal land is sinking at the same time the sea is rising.

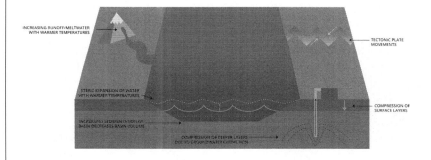

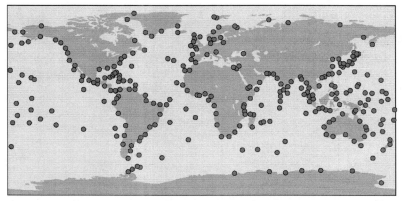

Figure 1: Global Distribution of Tide Gauges
Source: Global Sea Level Observing System (GLOSS)

Since 1992, scientists have had an additional tool available to measure sea levels: satellite altimetry. Satellite altimetry is a precise tool that measures the height of the ocean's surface using microwave radiation.[6] The satellites used to measure sea surface height cover the whole globe every 10 days. Because of their global coverage, satellite measurements of sea level rise make it possible to understand both average global and regional rates of sea level rise.[7] Satellite measurements have revealed that there is considerable regional variation in sea level rise:[8] satellite data shows that while global average sea level rise from 1993 to 2008 has averaged 0.11 inches (3 mm) per year, some regions experienced sea level rise as high as 0.4 inches (10 mm) per year and in others, sea level has actually fallen.[9]

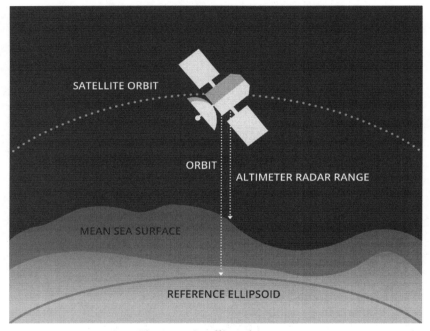

Figure 2: Satellite Altimetry

6. Anny Cazenave & William Llovel, *Contemporary Sea Level Rise*, 2010 Ann. Rev. Marine Science 145, 148.

7. *Id.* at 149.

8. *Id.*

9. *Id.* at 149, 151; Glenn A. Milne, W. Roland Gehrels, Chris W. Hughes & Mark E. Tamisiea, *Identifying the Causes of Sea Level Change*, 2 Nature Geoscience 471, 471 (2009).

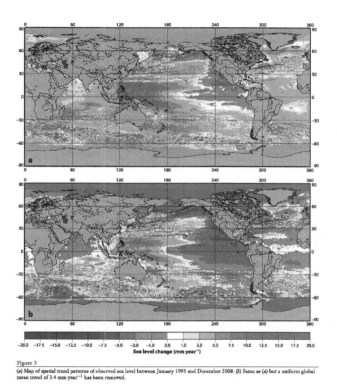

Figure 3

(*a*) Map of spatial trend patterns of observed sea level between January 1993 and December 2008. (*b*) Same as (*a*) but a uniform global mean trend of 3.4 mm year⁻¹ has been removed.

Figure 3: Satellite Altimetry Map of Sea Level Rise Differences
Reproduced with permission of *Annual Review of Marine Science*, Volume 2 © 2010 by Annual Reviews, http://www.annualreviews.org

What Causes Sea Level Rise?

There are two principal causes of sea level rise: changes in density of sea water and addition of new waters to the ocean. Addition of new waters to the ocean—principally the result of melting ice sheets and glaciers—increases the amount of water that is in the ocean. In contrast, increases in ocean temperature and decreases in ocean salinity can make ocean waters less dense, meaning that the same amount of water will take up a larger volume.

Sea Level Rise Due to Changes in the Density of Seawater

Changes in the density of seawater that lead to sea level rise are caused by both the warming of the oceans and changes in ocean salinity.[10] As global temperatures rise due to climate change, the oceans have been an important heat sink. It is estimated that the ocean has taken up over 90% of total planetary warming between 1971 and 2010,[11] and this heat uptake is thought to be resulting in slower rates of atmospheric warming than would otherwise be experienced.[12] This warming of the oceans causes sea water to expand, meaning that the same amount of water now occupies a larger volume.[13] In the ten years prior to 2003, scientists estimate that ocean thermal expansion caused 50% of sea level rise.[14] Domingues et al. find that from 1961 to 2003, heating of the surface layer of the ocean contributed 1.3 mm/yr to global sea level rise.[15] Since that time, ocean thermal expansion seems to have paused.[16] However, because the ocean continues to get warmer, scientists attribute the pause to natural variability caused by other environmental factors, as historical records of sea level rise caused by ocean warming demonstrate considerable variability over time.[17]

Scientists are only beginning to understand the role of changes in ocean salinity in causing sea level rise. The freshening of seawater—caused by the introduction of fresh water into the oceans—also causes the density of ocean water to decrease. As a result, in areas where large amounts of fresh water enter

---

10. Detlef Stammer, Anny Cazenave, Rui M. Ponte & Mark E. Tamisiea, *Causes for Contemporary Regional Sea Level Changes*, 5 Ann. Rev. Marine Science 21, 23 (2013).

11. Monika Rhein et al., *Chapter 3 Observations: Ocean* 265, *in* Intergovernmental Panel on Climate Change, Climate Change 2013: The Physical Science Basis (2013).

12. S.S. Drijfhout, A.T. Baker, S.A. Josey, A.J.G. Nurser, B. Sinha & M.A. Balmaseda, *Surface Warming Hiatus Caused by Increased Heat Uptake Across Multiple Ocean Basins*, 41 Geophysical Research Letters 7868, 7873 (2014).

13. Stammer et al., *supra* note 10, at 27.

14. A. Cazenave, K. Dominh, S. Guinehut, E. Berthier, W. Llovel, G. Ramillien, M. Ablain & G. Larnicol, *Sea Level Budget over 2003–2008: A Reevaluation from GRACE Space Gravimetry, Satellite Altimetry, and ARGO*, 63 Global Planetary Change 83, 83 (2009).

15. Catia M. Domingues, John A. Church, Neil J. White, Peter J. Gleckler, Susan E. Wijffels, Paul M. Barker & Jeff R. Dunn, *Improved Estimates of Upper-Ocean Warming and Multi-Decadal Sea Level Rise*, 453 Nature 1090 (2008).

16. Cazenave et al., *supra* note 14, at 83.

17. *Id.*; IPCC, Climate Change 2007: Working Group I: The Physical Science Basis 5.5.3 Ocean Density Change, http://www.ipcc.ch/publications_and_data/ar4/wg1/en/ch5s5-5-3. html (last visited Feb. 9, 2016).

the oceans, for example where glaciers are melting, the decrease in ocean salinity is a potentially important contributor to sea level rise. In fact, some studies have suggested that changes in ocean density caused by salinity changes will be the dominant component of sea level rise in the Arctic.[18] Conversely, seawater that is very salty has a higher density and may be able to counteract some of the sea level rise that would otherwise result from ocean warming.[19]

Sea Level Rise Caused by Melting Ice

The other major contributor to sea level rise is melting ice sheets and glaciers. Since 2003, satellite measurements of ice sheets and glaciers show that they have contributed 75–85% of sea level rise.[20] A significant influence on this rise in sea levels is the melting of terrestrial glaciers, which adds to the volume of the ocean.[21] Since 1992, one of Greenland's largest glaciers has doubled its flow speed—the rate at which the glacier moves across land—and is thinning rapidly.[22] Greenland's glaciers are losing mass because existing glacial ice is melting faster than new ice is formed by snow accumulation.[23] As of 2004, Rignot et al. projected that this melting of Greenland's glaciers results in additional sea level rise of .04 mm per year.[24] More recent studies find that the combined melting of the Greenland and Antarctic Ice Sheets contributes as much as 1.5 mm per year to rising sea levels,[25] and the melting of land ice in the Canadian Arctic Archipelago contributes a further .17 mm per year to sea level rise.[26] While many scientists consider it unlikely, the complete melting of the Greenland Ice Sheet would raise global sea levels by almost 23 feet

---

18. *See* Stammer et al., *supra* note 10, at 24.

19. *Id.*

20. Cazenave et al., *supra* note 14, at 86.

21. Cazenave & Llovel, *supra* note 6, at 154.

22. Richard B. Alley, Peter U. Clark, Philippe Huybrechts & Ian Joughin, *Ice-Sheet and Sea-Level Changes*, 310 SCIENCE 456, 458 (2005).

23. E. Rignot, D. Braaten, S.P. Gogineni, W.B. Krabill & J.R. McConnell, *Rapid Ice Discharge from Southeast Greenland Glaciers*, 31 GEOPHYSICAL RESEARCH LETTERS L10401 (2004).

24. *Id.*

25. R. Thomas, E. Frederick, J. Li., W. Krabill, S. Manizade, J. Paden, J. Sonntag, R. Swift & J. Yungel, *Accelerating Ice Loss from the Fastest Greenland and Antarctic Glaciers*, 38 GEOPHYSICAL RESEARCH LETTERS L10502 (2011).

26. Alex S. Gardner, Geir Moholdt, Bert Wouters, Gabriel J. Wolken, David O. Burgess, Martin J. Sharp, J. Graham Cogley, Carsten Braun & Claude Labine, *Sharply Increased Mass Loss from Glaciers and Ice Caps in the Canadian Arctic Archipelago*, 473 NATURE 357, 357 (2011).

Why Don't Icebergs Contribute to Sea Level Rise?

The sea already has lots of ice floating in it in the form of icebergs and sheets of sea ice. This ice is like ice in a glass of water, as it melts it doesn't cause the glass to get any fuller. As a result, the melting of sea ice and icebergs does not contribute to sea level rise. In contrast, when glaciers on land melt, it is like adding new water to the glass, causing the water level to rise.

(7 m) and the melting of the West Antarctic Ice Sheet would raise global sea levels by between 9.8 and 16.4 feet (3 to 5 m).[27]

At this time, scientists do not expect the complete melting of the ice sheets, but uncertainty over the response of ice sheets to sea levels remains a major challenge in projecting future sea level rise.[28] Ice sheets and glaciers have been melting at a rate that is faster than projected by the IPCC models.[29] This melting may be driven in part by warmer air temperatures, ice sheets being in contact with warmer ocean waters, and changing glacial dynamics.[30] Recent studies of the West Antarctic Ice Sheet conclude that the ice sheets have experienced rapid thinning over the last two decades, and that early stage collapse of the West Antarctic Ice Sheet may already be underway.[31]

---

27. Cazenave & Llovel, *supra* note 6, at 152.

28. *See* J.A. Church, P.U. Clark, A. Cazenave, J.M. Gregory, S. Jevrejeva, A. Levermann, M.A. Merrifield, G.A. Milne, R.S. Nerem, P.D. Nunn, A.J. Payne, W.T. Pfeffer, D. Stammer & A.S. Unnikrishnan, *Chapter 13 Sea Level Change* 1137, 1145, 1172–73, *in* INTERGOVERNMENTAL PANEL ON CLIMATE CHANGE, CLIMATE CHANGE 2013: THE PHYSICAL SCIENCE BASIS; J.L. Bamber & W.P. Aspinall, *An Expert Judgement Assessment of Future Sea Level Rise from the Ice Sheets*, 3 NATURE CLIMATE CHANGE 424, 425 (2013).

29. E. Rignot, I. Velicogna, M.R. van den Broeke, A. Monaghan & J. Lenaerts, *Acceleration of the Contribution of the Greenland and Antarctic Ice Sheets to Sea Level Rise*, 38 GEOPHYSICAL RESEARCH LETTERS L05503 (2013).

30. Bamber & Aspinall, *supra* note 28, at 424.

31. Fernando S. Paolo, Helen A. Fricker & Laurie Padman, *Volume Loss from Antarctic Ice Shelves is Accelerating*, 348 SCIENCE 327, 330 (2015); Ian Joughin, Benjamin E. Smith & Brooke Medley, *Marine Ice Sheet Collapse Potentially Underway for the Thwaites Glacier Basin, West Antarctica*, 344 SCIENCE 735 (2014); *see also* Robert M. DeConto & David Pollard, *Contribution of Antarctica to Past and Future Sea Level Rise*, 531 NATURE 591 (2016) (finding that Antarctica has the potential to contribute more than a meter of sea level rise by 2100 and more than 15m by 2500).

Why Is Local Sea Level Rise Different from the Global Average?

When considering the impacts of sea level rise along a particular portion of the coast, there are two important factors that may cause regional sea level rise to be different from the global average. First, rates of sea level rise are not uniform across the globe. Second, when considering impacts of sea level rise on a particular piece of land, the relevant measure is relative sea level rise, which is how much the sea is rising with respect to the land.

Scientists have concluded that spatial variation in ocean warming is the most significant contributor to the uneven amounts of sea level rise observed across the globe (as shown in Figure 3).[32] In addition, local variations in salinity can lead to local variations in sea level rise.[33] Thus variations in the changes of ocean water density in different regions are an important driver of the differences in the amount of sea level rise experienced in different parts of the world.

In addition to changes in ocean water density, larger regional phenomena can act to suppress or enhance sea level rise. For example, since the mid-1970s the West Coast of the United States has experienced slower than average coastal sea level rise with sea levels that have been nearly unchanged since the 1980s. A study by Bromirski et al. concludes that this suppression in coastal sea level rise has been caused by large-scale wind stress patterns associated with a broader climate phenomenon known as the Pacific Decadal Oscillation ("PDO").[34] Bromirski et al. also find that wind stress patterns along the West Coast appear to be changing to be more like those observed prior to 1970, and they conclude that this shift could lead to a resumption of coastal sea level rise and rates of sea level rise that are higher than the global average.[35]

Recent research has concluded that the slowing of the Gulf Stream as a result of climate change may increase the rate of sea level rise along the Atlantic Coast. The Gulf Stream is a fast-moving current that carries water along the southern U.S. Coast to Cape Hatteras and then heads out towards Bermuda. The Gulf Stream is one of the major currents that is part of Atlantic Merid-

---

32. Cazenave & Llovel, *supra* note 6, at 154.

33. *Id.* at 162.

34. Peter D. Bromirski, Arthur J. Miller, Reinhard E. Flick & Guillermo Auad, *Dynamical Suppression of Sea Level Rise Along the Pacific Coast of North America: Indications for Imminent Acceleration*, 116 J. Geophysical Research C07005 at 6 (2011).

35. *Id.* at 9.

Did You Know the Sea Is Not Flat?

While it may seem strange, the surface of the ocean is not actually flat. Instead, some areas of the sea surface will be higher than others. There are several sources of changes in sea surface height. They include:

1. variations in the topography of the ocean floor;
2. geostrophic forces (the combination of physical forces acting upon the earth that results in the uneven distribution of water);
3. large-scale ocean currents and gyres; and
4. decadal variability in large-scale climate patterns.

These differences in sea surface height are important for sea level rise for two reasons. First, some areas will experience relatively more or less sea level rise than the global average. Second, changes in broad-scale climate patterns can alter both sea surface height and the rate of sea level rise.

---

ional Overturning Circulation ("AMOC"), which is illustrated in Figure 4. Because the Gulf Stream is a fast-moving current, it tends to push water away from the shore north of Cape Hatteras, meaning that the ocean along places like New Jersey is lower than it otherwise would be and sailing out into the Atlantic is like sailing up a hill. As the Gulf Stream slows, this effect is slowed, in essence causing the ocean water to flow downhill and back towards the coastline. As a result, scientists have found that the slowing of the Gulf Stream will cause significant increases in sea level rise from Cape Hatteras, North Carolina, all the way to Newfoundland, Canada.[36] While the IPCC currently has low confidence that there has been sustained slowing of Atlantic Meridional Overturning Circulation,[37] Yin et al. project that a complete collapse of AMOC

---

36. Jianjun Yin, Michael E. Schlesinger & Ronald J. Stouffer, *Model Projections of Rapid Sea-Level Rise on the Northeast Coast of the United States*, 2 NATURE GEOSCIENCE 262, 263 (2009).

37. Rhein et al., *supra* note 11, at 282–84.

could itself cause over 3 feet (1 m) of sea level rise along the East Coast of the U.S. north of Cape Hatteras.[38]

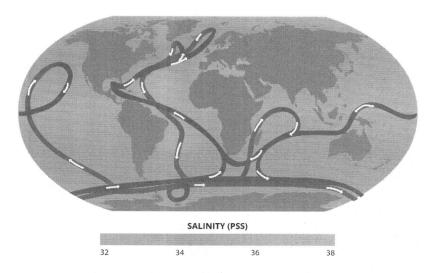

SALINITY (PSS)

32   34   36   38

Figure 4: Explanation of Atlantic Meridional Overturning Circulation and Sea Surface Height

Thermohaline circulation is the circulation of ocean waters that is driven by differences in temperature and salinity. In the North Atlantic Ocean, the formation of sea ice causes the surrounding water to become colder and saltier, increasing its density. This denser water sinks becoming part of the deep ocean currents that are sometimes referred to as the "ocean conveyor belt."

Once all the regional components contributing to the ocean's rise are factored in, there is an additional component to consider to determine impacts on land: the movement of the land itself, which can increase or lessen the impacts of sea level rise. For example, along the Mississippi River Delta, subsidence due to extraction of oil and groundwater, changes in land management practices upriver that have decreased sediment supply, and compaction of the area's peat soils are causing the delta to sink.[39] Because the land itself is falling,

_____

38. Yin et al., *supra* note 36, at 265.

39. *See generally* Alexander S. Kolker, Mead A. Allison & Sultan Hameed, *An Evaluation of Subsidence Rates and Sea-Level Variability in the Northern Gulf of Mexico*, 38 GEO-PHYSICAL RESEARCH LETTERS L21404 (2011) (discussing the role of fluid withdrawal in

the amount of relative sea level rise will be larger. In contrast, certain regions of the country that were covered by glaciers during the last ice age are still rising up in response to the removal of the weight of the glaciers—a process called glacial isostatic adjustment.[40] These regions will experience less relative sea level rise because the rise of the sea may be partially offset by the rise of coastal lands. In fact, regions that are currently covered in ice that is projected to melt in a warming climate, such as Greenland, West Antarctica, and Alaska, are expected to experience a net drop in sea levels due to the rise of land.[41]

How Much Will Sea Level Rise and When?

The 2013 report of Working Group I of the Intergovernmental Panel on Climate Change projects that by the end of the century, sea levels will rise an additional 0.85 to 3.2 feet globally, depending on future greenhouse gas emissions.[42] The 2014 National Climate Assessment concludes that, depending on future greenhouse gas emissions, the United States can expect to experience an additional 2 to 6 feet of sea level rise, with 4 feet of sea level rise being a likely upper-end estimate.[43] All models suggest that the amount of sea level rise we experience in the future is directly related to the future pathway of greenhouse gas emissions and resultant climate change: if global greenhouse gas concentrations continue to increase, the models project that we will experience additional warming of both the oceans and the atmosphere, which will lead to greater amounts of sea level rise in the future. For example, in an analysis of recent papers, Nicholls et al. concluded that if global temperatures are allowed to increase 4°C—a value that is twice the goal under the United Nations Framework Convention for Climate Change,

---

coastal subsidence); Michael D. Blum & Harry H. Roberts, *Drowning of the Mississippi Delta Due to Insufficient Sediment Supply and Global Sea Level Rise*, 2 NATURE GEOSCIENCE 488 (2009) (calculating accelerations in relative sea level rise due to sediment trapping upriver); Torbjörn E. Törnqvist, Davin J. Wallace, Joep E.A. Storms, Jakob Wallinga, Remke L. van Dam, Martijn Blaauw, Mayke S. Derksen, Cornelis J.W. Klerks, Camiel Meijneken & Els M.S. Snijders, *Mississippi Delta Subsidence Primarily Caused by Compaction of Holocene Strata*, 1 NATURE GEOSCIENCE 173 (2008) (providing estimates of subsidence rates due to compaction).

40. Mark E. Tamisiea & Jerry X. Mitrovica, *The Moving Boundaries of Sea Level Change: Understanding the Origins of Geographic Variability*, 24 OCEANOGRAPHY 24, 27–28 (2011).

41. Stammer et al., *supra* note 10, at 37.

42. IPCC, *supra* note 2, at 25.

43. NCA2014, *supra* note 1, at 45.

but seems possible given current global GHG concentrations and emissions—a "pragmatic" estimate of sea level rise by 2100 is in the range of 1.6 to 6.7 feet.[44]

Rising global temperatures are projected to result in sea level rise due to both the isostatic expansion of sea water and the melting of land ice, including the Greenland and West Antarctic Ice Sheets. As far back as 1978, Mercer argued that a 5 m rise in sea level driven by rapid deglaciation was underway.[45] Over the last century, documented sea level rise occurred at a rate of 1–2 mm per year.[46] Furthermore, the geologic record reveals that historic increases in carbon dioxide concentrations are associated with vast changes in the extent of ice cover.[47] Around 1920, the rate of sea level rise began to increase rapidly, reaching the rate observed today.[48] Gehrels et al. found that this increase in the rate of sea level rise corresponded to global temperature increases, and concluded that continuing sea level rise in the Western Atlantic may be largely attributed to global warming.[49]

How Will Climate Change Alter Hurricane Activity?

Projecting the impacts of climate change on hurricane strength and frequency is far more complicated than understanding the potential for future sea level rise. Unlike global sea levels, which are primarily controlled by atmospheric and oceanic warming, the formation and landfall of hurricanes are controlled by a greater number of factors. These factors include large-scale climatic features, such as the El Niño Southern Oscillation and the location of

---

44. Robert J. Nicholls, Natasha Marinova, Jason A. Lowe, Sally Brown, Pier Vellinga, Diogo de Gusmão, Jochen Hinkel & Richard S.J. Tol, *Sea-Level Rise and Its Possible Impacts Given a "Beyond 4°C World" in the Twenty-First Century*, 369 PHIL. TRANS. ROYAL SOC. A 161, 168 (2011).

45. *See generally* J.H. Mercer, *West Antarctic Ice Sheet and CO2 Greenhouse Effect: A Threat of Disaster*, 271 NATURE 321 (1978).

46. Alley et al., *supra* note 22, at 456; John A. Church, Neil J. White, Richard Coleman, Kurt Lambeck & Jerry X. Mitrovica, *Estimates of the Regional Distribution of Sea Level Rise Over the 1950–2000 Period*, 17 J. CLIMATE 2609, 2609 (2004).

47. Alley et al., *supra* note 22, at 456.

48. W. Roland Gehrels, Jason R. Kirby, Andreas Prokoph, Rewi N. Newnham, Eric P. Achterberg, Hywel Evans, Stuart Black & David B. Scott, *Onset of Recent Rapid Sea-Level Rise in the Western Atlantic Ocean*, 24 QUATERNARY SCIENCE REV. 2083, 2083 (2005).

49. *Id.*

the North Atlantic Oscillation,[50] as well as changes in wind shear and sea surface temperatures. Because hurricane strength and activity are controlled by several environmental variables that are not related to climate change, it is difficult to discern the contribution of climate change and rising sea surface temperatures to changes in hurricane strength and frequency.[51] In fact, the National Climate Assessment concludes that the frequency and duration of Atlantic hurricanes, as well as the frequency of category 4 and 5 hurricanes has increased since the 1980s, but that the relative contributions of human and natural causes of this change remain uncertain.[52] As discussed below, there is an emerging scientific consensus that warmer sea surface temperatures are associated with *stronger* hurricanes; the effect of increasing temperatures on the *frequency* of hurricanes depends upon the ocean basin under consideration.

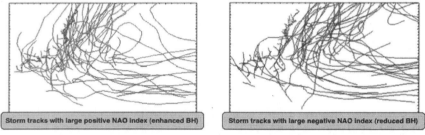

**Figure 5: Explanation of Impact of North Atlantic Oscillation
on Landfalling Hurricanes**

The North Atlantic Oscillation ("NAO") is a large-scale atmospheric circulation feature that is characterized by positive and negative phases based on the location of two pressure centers over the North Atlantic. The NAO, which can vary considerably both seasonally or multi-year time scales impacts storm tracks including those of hurricanes. Positive phases of the NAO will cause hurricanes to track closer to the U.S. East coast, while negative phases will tend to steer hurricanes out to sea.

Source: ©2017 Climatological Consulting Corporation, http://www.ccc-weather.com

---

50. The El Niño Southern Oscillation and North Atlantic Oscillation are larger pressure fronts whose movements influence both the ability of hurricanes to form and their tracks across the ocean. *See* Mark Denny, How the Ocean Works: An Introduction to Oceanography (2008).

51. *See* P.J. Webster, G.J. Holland, J.A. Curry & H.-R. Chang, *Changes in Tropical Cyclone Number, Duration, and Intensity in a Warming Environment*, 309 Science 1844, 1844 (2005).

52. NCA2014, *supra* note 1, at 41.

Warmer sea surface temperatures have been associated with increases in the intensity of tropical storms. Emanuel finds that the Power Dissipation Index, a measure of storm intensity, is positively correlated with increased sea surface temperatures and the peak potential wind speed of hurricanes increases 5% for every 1°C of warming.[53] Other studies have also found an increase in hurricane intensity that is associated with higher sea surface temperatures, and this effect is particularly significant in the North Atlantic.[54] For example, Knutson et al. project that there will be a significant increase in the frequency of category 4 and 5 storms in the North Atlantic,[55] Bender finds that the number of category 4 and 5 storms will nearly double, and the IPCC SREX report finds some models project an 80% increase in category 4 and 5 Atlantic Hurricanes.[56]

While many studies project increases in hurricane intensity due to ocean warming, there does not appear to be an increase in the number of storms that are forming. To the contrary, Gleixner et al. find that a range of models project that warmer ocean temperatures will decrease the number of storms that form, and their results suggest that in this century there will be a 22% decrease in the number of storms in the Southern Hemisphere and a 6% decrease in the number of storms in the Northern Hemisphere.[57] Overall, it appears that while the number of storms may not increase, stronger storms will make up a

---

53. Kerry Emanuel, *Increasing Destructiveness of Tropical Cyclones Over the Past 30 Years*, 436 NATURE 686 (2005).

54. *See* James B. Elsner, James P. Kossin & Thomas H. Jagger, *The Increasing Intensity of the Strongest Tropical Cyclones*, 455 NATURE 92, 93 (2008) (finding an increase in maximum lifetime wind speeds of hurricanes, and noting a particularly strong trend in the North Atlantic where sea surface temperatures have greatly increased); Webster et al., *supra* note 51, at 1846 (finding that increases in hurricane intensity are related to increased SSTs); Kerry Emanuel, Ragoth Sundararajan & John Williams, *Hurricanes and Global Warming: Results from Downscaling IPCC AR4 Simulations*, 89 BULL. AM. METEOROLOGICAL SOC. 347, 365 (2008).

55. Thomas R. Knutson, Joseph J. Sirutis, Gabriel A. Vecchi, Stephen Garner, Ming Zhao, Hyeong-Seog Kim, Morris Bender, Robert E. Tuleya, Isaac M. Held & Gabriele Villarini, *Dynamical Downscaling Projections of Twenty-First Century Atlantic Hurricane Activity: CMIP3 and CMIP5 Model-Based Scenarios*, 26 J. CLIMATE 6591, 6601 (2013).

56. M.A. Bender, T.R. Knutson, R.E. Tuleya, J.J. Sirutis, G.A. Vecchi, S.T. Garner & I.M. Held, *Modeled Impact of Anthropogenic Warming on the Frequency of Intense Atlantic Hurricanes*, 327 SCIENCE 454 (2010); IPCC, SPECIAL REPORT ON MANAGING THE RISKS OF EXTREME EVENTS AND DISASTERS TO ADVANCE CLIMATE CHANGE ADAPTATION (SREX) 162 (2012).

57. Stephanie Gleixner, Noel Kennlyside, Kevin I. Hodges, Wan-Ling Tseng & Lennart Bengtsson, *An Inter-Hemispheric Comparison of Tropical Storm Response to Global Warming*, 42 CLIMATE DYNAMICS 2147, 2152 (2014).

greater proportion of the total number of storms.[58] Holland and Bruyère examine current storm activity and conclude that there is no climate-driven effect on storm frequency, but that there are significant increases in the number of both stronger (category 4 and 5) and weaker (category 1 and 2) storms, with fewer storms of intermediate strength (category 3).[59] Overall, they suggest that the proportion of category 4 and 5 hurricanes will increase from 25% of all storms to 35%.[60] Kossin et al. examine the historical record and find a similar increase in the proportion of stronger storms, but conclude that these impacts are basin-specific noting that there have been "dramatic changes in the frequency distribution of lifetime maximum intensity (LMI) [for hurricanes] in the North Atlantic, while smaller changes are evident in the South Pacific and South Indian Oceans."[61]

Another factor that will influence the impact of future hurricanes on coastal communities is whether they make landfall or remain at sea. The future landfall of hurricanes is likely to vary regionally and will be dependent upon both long-term natural variability (e.g., the North Atlantic Oscillation) and climate-driven changes in oceanic and atmospheric circulation patterns. Hall & Yonekura model future ocean warming and its impacts on landfall, and find that warmer sea surface temperatures are projected to lead to statistically significant increases in major hurricane landfall in Texas and along the north Gulf Coast.[62] However, the East Coast is not similarly impacted in their models because changes in sea surface temperature appear to alter storm tracks and steer them away from land.[63] Barnes et al. modeled the possibility of another Hurricane Sandy making landfall under projected future conditions, and concluded that the changes projected by climate models will decrease the frequency of the steering patterns that caused Hurricane Sandy to make landfall.[64] As a re-

---

58. IPCC SREX, *supra* note 56, at 162.

59. Greg Holland & Cindy L. Bruyère, *Recent Intense Hurricane Response to Global Climate Change*, 42 CLIMATE DYNAMICS 617, 624 (2014).

60. *Id.*

61. James P. Kossin, Timothy L. Olander & Kenneth R. Knapp, *Trend Analysis with a New Global Record of Tropical Cyclone Intensity*, 26 J. CLIMATE 9960, 9973 (2013).

62. Timothy Hall & Emmi Yonekura, *North American Tropical Cyclone Landfall and SST: A Statistical Model Study*, 26 J. CLIMATE 8422, 8437 (2013).

63. *Id.*

64. Elizabeth A. Barnes, Lorenzo M. Polvani & Adam H. Sobel, *Model Projections of Atmospheric Steering of Sandy-Like Superstorms*, 110 PROCEEDINGS NAT'L ACAD. SCIENCE 15211, 15213–14 (2013).

sult, future climate conditions could make it more likely that a Sandy-like storm would travel out into the Atlantic Ocean.[65]

Because of the many factors—both climate driven and otherwise—that influence hurricane formation, the projected increase in the number of strong hurricanes is a significant concern for coastal communities. Rising sea levels will combine with those storms and intensify the impacts of coastal flooding due to storm surge.[66] And, even if storm levels were to remain constant, current patterns of coastal development will still increase societal exposure to storms as more people move into the coastal zone.[67] Further, modeling of future exposure to hurricanes in the United States indicates that a 10% increase in storm intensity will increase storm damage experienced by coastal communities by more than 50%.[68] This damage estimate does not include the often substantial damage that inland communities experience as a result of powerful hurricanes that make landfall.[69]

What Are the Impacts on the Coastal Zone?

Globally, more than 770,000 square miles of land are less than 1 meter (approximately 3 feet) above sea level.[70] While local amounts of sea level rise will vary based on the factors discussed above, all of these assets are potentially vulnerable to the range of global average sea level rise projected by the end of the century. In the United States, nearly 5 million people live within 4 feet of the local high-tide level—an amount of sea level rise the National Climate Assessment concludes is possible by the end of the century.[71] Further, the National Climate Assessment concludes that more than 5,790 square miles and $1 trillion of property and structures in the United States are at risk of inun-

---

65. *Id.*

66. For estimates of the impact of sea level rise on storm-surge flood events, *see* Robert J. Nicholls, *Analysis of Global Impacts of Sea Level Rise: A Case Study of Flooding*, 27 Physics & Chem. of the Earth 1455 (2002).

67. Roger A. Pielke, Jr., *Are There Trends in Hurricane Destruction?*, 438 Nature E11 (2005); *see also* Chapter 2.

68. Stefanie Hallegatte, *The Use of Synthetic Hurricane Tracks in Risk Analysis and Climate Change Damage Assessment*, 46 J. Applied Meteorology & Climatology 1956, 1956 (2007).

69. *Id.*

70. Milne et al., *supra* note 9, at 471.

71. NCA2014, *supra* note 1, at 45.

dation with only 2 feet of sea level rise—an amount that is possible by 2050 under high emissions scenarios.[72]

Due to the combined effects of sea level rise and storms, the National Climate Assessment estimates that the incremental annual damage to capital assets in the coastal zone along the Gulf Coast caused by climate change could reach $2.7 to $4.6 billion per year by 2030 and $8.3 to $13.2 billion per year by 2050.[73] Twenty percent of the assets included in these figures are related to the oil and gas industry,[74] raising the possibility that future sea level rise and storminess could have significant impacts on the energy industry in the United States. In addition, U.S. ports handled over $1.9 trillion in goods and over 90% of consumer goods in 2010.[75] Ports are inherently vulnerable to sea level rise due to their location directly on the coast and the fact that much of their support infrastructure is in low-lying coastal zones.[76] Given that substantial sea level rise would continue in the future even if all greenhouse gas emissions were halted today,[77] it is clear that significant investments in adaptation will be necessary to avoid disruptions to key sectors of the United States' economy.

To illustrate the extent of the potential impacts of sea level rise in the next century, Figures 6–8 highlight the areas that may be vulnerable to sea level rise along the Texas and North Carolina coasts and in the San Francisco Bay.

This inundation will also have significant environmental impacts. On sandy shorelines, Hinkel et al. find that without nourishment to counteract erosion, sea level rise will lead to the loss of 43 to 66 square miles of sandy beach by 2100.[78] The loss of beaches will impact both sandy beach ecosystems and the recreational tourism industry, which accounts for 85% of annual tourism revenues, or over $595 billion in the United States.[79]

---

72. *Id.* at 589.

73. *Id.*

74. *Id.*

75. *Id.*

76. Austin H. Becker, Michele Acciaro, Regina Asariotis, Edgard Cabrera, Laurent Cretegny, Philippe Crist, Miguel Esteban, Andrew Mather, Steve Messner, Susumu Naruse, Adolf K.Y. Ng, Stefan Rahmstorf, Michael Savonis, Dong-Wook Song, Vladimir Stenek & Adonis F. Velegrakis, *A Note on Climate Change Adaptation for Seaports: A Challenge for Global Ports, A Challenge for Global Society*, 120 Climatic Change 683, 685–86 (2013).

77. Benjamin H. Strauss, *Rapid Accumulation of Committed Sea-Level Rise from Global Warming*, 110 Proc. Nat'l Acad. of Sci. 13699, 13699 (2013).

78. Jochen Hinkel, Robert J. Nicholls, Richard S.J. Tol, Zheng B. Wang, Jacqueline M. Hamilton, Gerben Boot, Athanasios T. Vafeidis, Loraine McFadden, Andrey Ganopolski & Richard J.T. Klein, *A Global Analysis of Erosion of Sandy Beaches and Sea-Level Rise: An Application of DIVA*, 111 Global and Planetary Change 150, 154 (2013).

79. NCA2014, *supra* note 1, at 589.

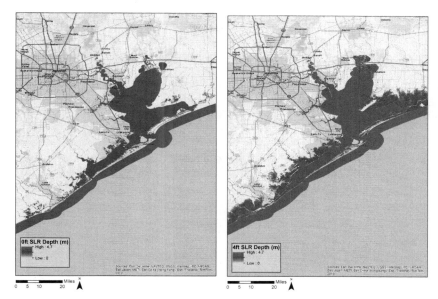

Figure 6: Map of Projected Sea Level Rise on the Texas Coast

In addition, while marshes with adequate sediment supply may be able to keep pace with slower rates of sea level rise, models project that if sea levels rise more than 1 meter by 2100, most marshes will permanently submerge.[80] Marshes play a number of important functions including purifying water, serving as breeding and hatchery grounds for fish and birds, and reducing storm surges.[81] If marshes are permanently submerged and converted to open ocean, these functions will be lost.

This chapter has explained the evidence for and causes of sea level rise. By 2100, it is likely that the United States will experience between 2 and 4 feet of sea level rise, though local levels of relative sea level rise may be more or less than this amount. Rising seas put key infrastructure and ecosystems in the United States' coastal zone at risk. These risks are potentially amplified by projected increases in the proportion of more intense hurricanes and the associated storm surges that result. Because continued sea level rise is inevitable,

---

80. Matthew L. Kirwan, Glenn R. Guntenspergen, Andrea D'Alpaos, James T. Morris, Simon M. Mudd & Stijn Temmerman, *Limits on the Adaptability of Coastal Marshes to Rising Sea Level*, 37 Geophysical Research Letters L23401 at 4 (2010).

81. United States Environmental Protection Agency, Economic Benefits of Wetlands (2015), http://nepis.epa.gov/Exe/ZyPURL.cgi?Dockey=2000D2PF.txt.

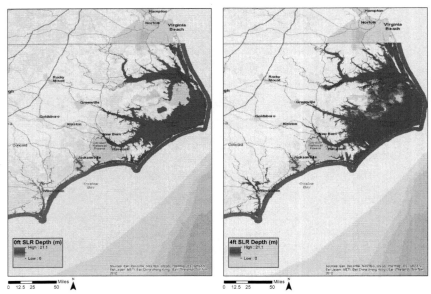

Figure 7: Map of Projected Sea Level Rise on the North Carolina Coast

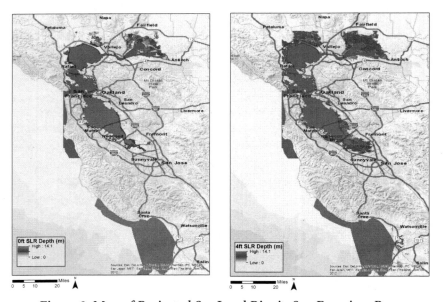

Figure 8: Map of Projected Sea Level Rise in San Francisco Bay

citizens and businesses in coastal communities will be forced to adapt. The choice becomes whether they will engage in proactive measures to reduce projected future hazard exposure due to sea level rise and storms or wait for sea levels to rise and respond to coastal inundation as it happens. Either way, the path towards adaptation will be filled with legal challenges and opportunities that are the focus of the remainder of this book.

Chapter 2

Defining Coastal Vulnerability and the Need for Coastal Management

This chapter has two primary goals. The first is to explain the concept of vulnerability and how it can be used to facilitate policymaking with respect to climate change adaptation. The second is to examine available coastal management options to respond to sea level rise and explain how each can be evaluated as part of a vulnerability framework. In addition, this chapter will explain some basic concepts in land use planning and how they can be applied to facilitate adaptation to sea level rise.

What Is Vulnerability?

The IPCC defines vulnerability as "the propensity or predisposition to be adversely affected."[1] The concept of vulnerability includes both the hazards to which a system is exposed and its capacity to withstand them. Vulnerability is a concept that has come into the literature on climate change adaptation from two different fields of research: disaster research and geography. The overarching theme in the various definitions of vulnerability that are found in the literature is a focus on identifying and reducing stressors to a system and thereby increasing its resilience.

---

1. IPCC, WGII Contribution to AR5, Glossary, http://ipcc-wg2.gov/AR5/images/uploads/WGIIAR5-Glossary_FGD.pdf.

The hazards impacts approach to vulnerability comes from social research on disasters. This approach views vulnerability as a function of the nature of physical hazards to which a system is exposed, the likelihood and frequency of hazard occurrence, the extent of exposure to the system, and the system's sensitivity.[2] This approach has come to be known as biophysical vulnerability, as it focuses primarily on the natural features of the system. This definition of vulnerability explicitly incorporates ecological definitions of resilience through its consideration of the system's sensitivity to hazards.[3] This definition also includes human agency to the extent that it impacts ecosystems. That is, biophysical vulnerability is a measure of the extent to which social interactions with nature reduce the resilience of a system.[4] Thus, the focus of the biophysical approach to vulnerability is primarily on reducing hazard exposure by avoiding interference with the ability of natural systems to recover from disturbance and self-organize in response to change.

In contrast, the concept of vulnerability in the geography literature focuses on the organization of social systems. The geographic study of vulnerability has its roots in Sen's groundbreaking work on famine.[5] In this work, Sen explores the idea of social entitlements and capacity, and he finds that famine is more the result of social structure and failures in the food distribution system than poverty itself or the inability to produce food. Most importantly, he concludes that governance, rather than food availability is the central feature driving famines.[6] This approach focuses on household level vulnerability, and led to the development of the geographer's approach to vulnerability primarily through the use of case studies, with little overarching theoretical development.[7] Under the geographer's definition, social vulnerability is all of the sys-

---

2. Nick Brooks, W. Neil Adger, & P. Mick Kelly, *The Determinants of Vulnerability and Adaptive Capacity at the National Level and the Implications for Adaptation*, 15 GLOBAL ENVTL. CHANGE 151, 152 (2005).

3. Resilience is "the capacity of a system to absorb disturbance and reorganize while undergoing change so as to still retain essentially the same function, structure, identity, and feedbacks." Carl Folke, Thomas Hahn, Per Olsson, & Jon Norberg, *Adaptive Governance of Social-Ecological Systems*, 2005 ANN. REV. ENV'T & RESOURCES 441, 443.

4. Susan L. Cutter, *Vulnerability to Environmental Hazards*, 20 PROGRESS IN HUMAN GEOGRAPHY 529, 530 (1996).

5. AMARTYA SEN, POVERTY AND FAMINES: AN ESSAY ON ENTITLEMENT AND DEPRIVATION (1982). *See* P.M. Kelly & W.N. Adger, *Theory and Practice in Assessing Vulnerability to Climate Change and Facilitating Adaptation*, 47 CLIMATIC CHANGE 325, 330 (2000).

6. SEN, *supra* note 5, at 92, 151.

7. *See* Paul McLaughlin & Thomas Dietz, *Structure, Agency, and Environment: Toward an Integrated Perspective on Vulnerability*, 18 GLOBAL ENVTL. CHANGE 99 (2008).

tem properties independent from the hazard itself that mediate the outcomes of hazard events.[8] This approach focuses explicitly on the organization of social systems and their capacity to respond to change and maintain order. In this manner, the social vulnerability approach incorporates a social definition of resilience, examining how groups of people and institutions can respond to hazards and maintain the functioning of society.[9] As I will expand upon later, this approach explicitly recognizes and studies the role of governance in enhancing societal resilience and promoting adaptation.

Overall, the vulnerability approach to climate change adaptation is one that seeks to increase the resilience of a system to climate change. That is, climate change will cause a number of disruptions along the coast including gradual inundation due to sea level rise and increased flooding and wind damage from storm events. Adaptation to these anticipated impacts should seek to reduce a community's exposure to each of these hazards. For example, a community's decision to elevate homes on stilts will reduce their vulnerability to sea level rise and storm surges because the homes will be out of the floodplain and able to withstand flooding events without being destroyed. Similarly, the adoption of stricter building codes may reduce vulnerability to hurricane events by reducing the likelihood that buildings will be badly damaged in high wind conditions.

It is important to emphasize that not all actions that enhance the resilience of coastal communities will also enhance ecological resilience. Seawalls are a prime example of the concept. The construction of a seawall reduces the vulnerability of a society to inundation, but it interferes with the landward migration of coastal habitats in response to sea level rise and therefore will result in a decline in ecological resilience.

The critical point when discussing these different approaches is that the *type* of vulnerability a society wishes to address will influence the approach counseled under the vulnerability framework. For example, there may be some places along the coast where society determines that the built infrastructure is so critical that it must be saved at all costs. In these situations, vulnerability reduction may be achieved through coastal engineering and the purchase of insurance that will cover the costs of rebuilding in the event that the engineered protections fail. While this is not optimal from an ecological standpoint, it may be that when other values are weighed against ecosystem conservation, some areas will choose

---

8. Brooks et al., *supra* note 2, at 152.

9. *See* J. Arjan Wardekker, Arie de Jong, Joost M. Knoop & Jeroen P. van der Sluijs, *Operationalising a Resilience Approach to Adapting an Urban Delta to Uncertain Climate Changes*, 77 Technological Forecasting & Soc. Change 987, 988 (2010).

Defining Adaptation, Resilience, and Vulnerability

In order to understand vulnerability as a framework to assess climate change adaptation options, there are a number of other key terms that must be defined.

Adaptation is any measure that society takes in response to experienced or anticipated future climate change. Adaptation actions can either increase or decrease exposure to climate hazards. When adaptation actions increase a society's exposure to climate hazards, this is referred to as *maladaptation*.

Vulnerability is a measure of the hazards to which a system is exposed. In the context of climate change, the goal is for adaptation measures to decrease the vulnerability of a system or community to the impacts of climate change. Therefore, a simple definition is Vulnerability = Impacts - Adaptation.

Resilience is the ability of a system to bounce back when it experiences an external stressor (e.g., a flood or storm). There are two types of resilience that are important to consider in the context of climate change adaptation. *Ecological resilience* is a measure of the ability of natural systems to withstand disruptions and self-organize to come back to a steady state. *Social resilience* is a measure of the ability of societies to create structures—whether physical, governmental, or social—that enhance their ability to recover from a disaster event.

Adaptive capacity is the ability of a society to choose between various adaptation options.

the engineer and insure approach to vulnerability reduction. Therefore, it is the critical step of framing the system for vulnerability analysis that will incorporate tradeoffs between conservation of the natural and built environments.

Figure 9: Ecological Impacts of Seawalls
In the absence of structures that prevent landward movement (e.g., seawalls, coastal roads), coastal wetlands and other important habitats will move landward in response to rising sea levels to maintain their position relative to the water. However, when seawalls or other hardened structures are built to protect coastal property, they prevent this landward movement and coastal habitats will ultimately be drowned by rising sea levels.

How Is Vulnerability Different from Other Policy Approaches?

Another useful way to understand vulnerability as an approach to policy-making is to compare it to other commonly used approaches for making decisions in the face of uncertainty. When future conditions are uncertain—as is the case with climate change where it is difficult to define both the rate and ultimate endpoint of anticipated changes—the two commonly seen approaches to decision making are the reactive approach and the precautionary approach.

The reactive approach is a classic "wait and see" policy that is politically attractive in the face of uncertainty. The reactive approach is analogous to the IPCC's concept of passive adaptation: a country does not take proactive steps to reduce its exposure to climate risks.[10] Widespread public sentiment in the United States that climate impacts are spatially and temporally distant has made it difficult to convince the general public to make near-term sacrifices to deal with climate change.[11] Far from abating societal risk, the reactive approach increases risk by allowing continued investment in high-impact zones. Furthermore, the IPCC finds the reactive approach is inefficient, particularly in addressing potentially irreversible changes, such as species loss.[12]

The reactive approach tends to decrease both adaptive capacity and resilience. By allowing policymakers and society as a whole to ignore coming problems, the reactive approach fails to equip citizens and policymakers with the information they need to make informed choices about future outcomes. As a result, the ability of society to choose among adaptation options (including no action) is severely constrained, and will often be limited to those measures that are available to respond in a time of crisis. This mode of response lowers adaptive capacity and also results in maladaptive responses to hazards that tend to increase vulnerability.[13]

At the same time, these reactive responses are also likely to decrease biophysical resilience. As explained in more detail in Chapter 3, populations tend to respond to natural disasters with determination to make their communities whole again. This desire to rebuild in exactly the same location does not ac-

10. S. Schneider, S. Semenov, A. Patwardhan, I. Burton, C.H.D. Magadza, M. Oppenheimer, A.B. Pittock, A. Rahman, J.B. Smith, A. Suarez & F. Yamin, *Assessing Key Vulnerabilities and Risk from Climate Change*, in CLIMATE CHANGE 2007: IMPACTS, ADAPTATION AND VULNERABILITY. CONTRIBUTION OF WORKING GROUP II TO THE FOURTH ASSESSMENT REPORT OF THE INTERGOVERNMENTAL PANEL ON CLIMATE CHANGE 779–810 (M.L. Parry, O.F. Canziani, J.P. Palutikof, P.J. van der Linden & C.E. Hanson eds., 2007).

11. Anthony Leiserowitz, *Communicating the Risks of Global Warming: American Risk Perceptions, Affective Images, and Interpretive Communities*, in CREATING A CLIMATE FOR CHANGE 44, 48–49 (Susanne C. Moser & Lisa Dilling eds., 2007).

12. W.N. Adger, S. Agrawala, M.M.Q. Mirza, C. Conde, K. O'Brien, J. Pulhin, R. Pulwarty, B. Smit & K. Takahashi, *Assessment of Adaptation Practices Options, Constraints and Capacity*, in CLIMATE CHANGE 2007: IMPACTS, ADAPTATION AND VULNERABILITY. CONTRIBUTION OF WORKING GROUP II TO THE FOURTH ASSESSMENT REPORT OF THE INTERGOVERNMENTAL PANEL ON CLIMATE CHANGE 717, 721 (M.L. Parry, O.F. Canziani, J.P. Palutikof, P.J. van der Linden & C.E. Hanson eds., 2007).

13. Jane C. Ingram, Guillermo Franco, Cristina Rumbaitis-del Rio & Bjian Khazai, *Post-Disaster Recovery Dilemmas: Challenges in Balancing Short-Term and Long-Term Needs for Vulnerability Reduction*, 9 ENVTL. SCIENCE & POLICY 607, 607 (2006).

count for biophysical exposures, and often does not even enhance socio-ecological resilience through the building of more robust structures.[14] Further, such rebuilding under temporary rules does not account for the impacts on ecosystems and the effect that it will have on ecological resilience.

The second commonly-employed strategy for policymaking in light of limited information is the precautionary approach. The precautionary approach requires that managers and policymakers examine projected climate change impacts and proactively protect against them. This approach encourages adaptation in the face of incomplete information and is relatively intolerant of risk. It thus encourages extensive adaptation activities and may lead to over-adaptation.[15] The precautionary approach is often politically infeasible for many of the same reasons that the reactive approach is politically attractive: while the reactive approach errs on the side of under-reacting to potential climate impacts because the general public does not believe they will be experienced in the near term, the precautionary principle errs on the side of over-adapting and therefore can run counter to public understanding of the immediacy of the threats posed by climate change.

The precautionary approach has its roots in the environmental movement and the idea that activities that may cause catastrophic environmental change should be avoided.[16] Therefore, decision making under a precautionary approach would likely focus on enhancing ecological resilience. Ironically, when the precautionary approach has been successful in the past, the general public does not tend to remember that anticipatory action averted potential disaster. Rather, people tend to respond by thinking that the risk of the averted disaster was overstated by policymakers.[17] As a result, the precautionary approach may actually erode social resilience by causing a gradual degradation of social memory of crisis response over time.[18] Further, past precautionary

---

14. As observed in Texas' recovery from Hurricane Ike, most post-disaster rebuilding is done under emergency rules, and therefore would not be required to meet tougher, post-storm construction standards that a government may adopt.

15. *See generally* Samuel Fankhauser, Joel B. Smith & Richard S.J. Tol, *Weathering Climate Change: Some Simple Rules to Guide Adaptation Decisions*, 30 ECOLOGICAL ECON. 67 (1999) (discussing efficient adaptation).

16. *See, e.g.*, Kenneth J. Arrow & Anthony C. Fisher, *Environmental Preservation, Uncertainty, and Irreversibility*, 88 Q.J. ECON. 312 (1974) (arguing that in the face of uncertainty, policies should be restrictive to avoid irreversible environmental impacts).

17. *See, e.g.*, GLYNIS M. BREAKWELL, THE PSYCHOLOGY OF RISK (2007) (explaining how a variety of social and political factors will influence the public's interpretation of hazards).

18. *See* Folke et al., *supra* note 3, at 444; Susan L. Cutter, *The Vulnerability of Science and the Science of Vulnerability*, 93 ANNALS ASS'N OF AM. GEOGRAPHERS 1 (2003) (discussing

successes may lead decision makers to put all of their focus on maintaining a system in its current state, resulting in a failure to develop the necessary capacity to absorb unexpected changes when they occur.[19]

The precautionary approach has similarly mixed effects on adaptive capacity. Because the precautionary approach is more intolerant of risk and averse to change, it is likely to preserve a larger suite of adaptation options than other approaches. However, the high degree of risk aversion embodied in the precautionary approach may actually lower adaptive capacity because it severely constrains the decision making framework that a society can use to choose among adaptation options. Because of these constraints, social adaptive capacity will be lower, and societies employing the precautionary approach may tend to over-adapt.

As summarized above, vulnerability is the degree to which natural and societal systems are unable to cope with the adverse impacts of climate change. Unlike other approaches to climate change adaptation, a socio-ecological approach to vulnerability integrates climate mitigation as a means of reducing societal exposure to risks posed by climate change and all types of climate adaptation, including measures in the natural *and* built environments.[20] Vulnerability thus captures both socio-economic and environmental values in a way that the other approaches discussed cannot.

When compared to other approaches to decision making, there are four features of the vulnerability approach that make it a worthy lens for the discussion of climate change impacts and adaptation. Vulnerability (1) empowers societies to shape their climate futures, (2) includes a range of values, (3) promotes efficiency, and (4) is a scalable tool.

The vulnerability approach recognizes important roles for both adaptation and mitigation (the reduction of GHG emissions), and thus rejects the idea, implicit in the reactive approach, that we are passive victims of climate change.[21] In this manner, it empowers societies by emphasizing that responses to climate change are the product of active societal choices. The vulnerability

---

the availability heuristic and arguing that people will not be willing to devote resources to avert disasters they haven't experienced and therefore perceive as unlikely).

19. Folke et al., *supra* note 3, at 445.

20. Brooks et al., *supra* note 2, at 152–53.

21. Remember that Vulnerability = Impacts - Adaptation, meaning that vulnerability to climate change impacts can be reduced either by decreasing greenhouse gas emissions or adopting adaptation measures. Loraine McFadden, Edmund Penning-Rowsell & Robert J. Nicholls, *Setting the Parameters: A Framework for Developing Cross-Cutting Perspectives of Vulnerability for Coastal Zone Management, in* MANAGING COASTAL VULNERABILITY 1, 5–6 (Lorraine McFadden, Robert J. Nicholls & Edmund Penning-Rowsell eds., 2007).

approach thus encourages societies to undertake active adaptation planning rather than merely respond to impacts as they happen.

Vulnerability can incorporate everything society values because it encompasses all sources of climate-induced risk.[22] In addition to mitigation, it allows decision makers to incorporate a broad range of social, economic, and environmental variables. Anywhere society perceives risk of adverse climate impacts, vulnerability analysis is possible.

Importantly, a broad vulnerability framework incorporates key ecosystem concepts, such as ecosystem resilience, into climate adaptation planning.[23] A resilience-based functionality approach allows for a dynamic systems analysis that focuses on the behavior of the system.[24] Furthermore, vulnerability as a function of ecosystem resilience is easily integrated into pre-existing management structures by emphasizing ecosystem functionality, or socio-ecological resilience, as the long-term vision for adaptation.[25]

A vulnerability approach can enhance efficiency in two ways. First, vulnerability can reduce maladaptation, or activities that *increase* exposure to climate change risks. Second, incorporating vulnerability analysis into government policies through advance planning should send a market signal that leads to efficiencies in adaptation. Because the vulnerability approach should explicitly account for tradeoffs in its evaluation of socio-ecological resilience, it is less likely to lead to over-adaptation than the precautionary principle. Conversely, recognition of the role of ecosystems and the need for advance planning to protect them means that the vulnerability approach is less susceptible to under-adaptation than the reactive approach.

Finally, the vulnerability approach has utility at multiple scales. Ideally, vulnerability analysis will be applied at the broadest possible level to inventory the risks posed by climate change and the options to reduce those risks.[26] However, decision makers often don't know what actions will reduce risk or what

---

22. *Id.*; Adger et al., *supra* note 12, at 720.

23. McFadden et al., *supra* note 21, at 5–6.

24. NOAA Coastal Services Center, Beach Nourishment: A Guide for Local Government Officials (2009).

25. McFadden et al., *supra* note 21, at 8.

26. For an example of this process at work, *see* the Global Environment Facility's implementation of the Least Developed Countries Fund under the IPCC. This process calls for the preparation of National Adaptation Programs of Action, which inventory a country's exposure and use multi-criteria analysis to prioritize concrete adaptation actions. Global Environment Facility, The Least Developed Countries Fund: Review of the Implementation of NAPAs (2014), http://www.thegef.org/gef/sites/thegef.org/files/documents/LDCF%20Implementation%20of%20NAPA.pdf.

other considerations, such as political feasibility, will narrow the range of risk-reduction options. In these cases, vulnerability can be applied within the available option range to determine an outcome that minimizes exposure to climate risk. That is, the suite of possible options can be evaluated with respect to the impacts on adaptive capacity and socio-ecological resilience to determine their vulnerability reduction outcomes.

Coastal Management Options to Respond to Sea Level Rise

Why Is the Coastal Zone a Priority Area for Climate Change Adaptation?

As detailed in the National Climate Assessment, the impacts of climate change will be felt all over the United States.[27] In addition, it is likely that full adaptation to all the impacts of climate change will be a very costly endeavor and that ultimately societies will have to choose areas to prioritize for adaptation action. This raises two important questions: (1) how should governments and communities decide where to prioritize actions that reduce vulnerability to climate hazards and (2) should the coastal zone be a priority area for climate change adaptation?

There are three major factors that a government should consider in prioritizing areas for adaptation planning: (1) what is the hazard exposure of the area and how is it changing, (2) what is the state of knowledge with respect to anticipated impacts and adaptation options, and (3) what is the natural resilience of the socio-ecological system. These factors should help a government prioritize adaptation actions by identifying areas that are most exposed to the impacts of climate change for which technical or policy solutions to reduce vulnerability are available. The third factor is a measure of overall system fragility that accounts for properties of both the socio-political system and the ecosystem. As climate change impacts are felt, there will be many systems that face increased exposure and have available technical fixes. However, adopting any adaptation measure will require the expenditure of both financial resources and political capital. Therefore, governments will not be able to address all possible targets for adaptation at once. The third factor here suggests that particular systems may have higher resilience and therefore may

---

27. NCA2014, *supra* Chapter 1 note 1, at 1.

be in less need of urgent attention from an adaptation perspective. In addition, the third factor can provide for consideration of critical infrastructure and concentrations of populations in particular regions that may require additional adaptation focus.

Crucial to any discussion about adaptation planning is understanding the basic requirements for successful adaptation. These requirements are: the need to adapt (hazard exposure), the incentive to adapt (public concern or regulation), and the ability to adapt (technical or social fix).[28] The ability to adapt will also depend upon the need to adapt being recognized while there is still sufficient time for a society to take corrective action to avoid hazards. To this end, timely recognition of the need to adapt requires access to detailed information on the potential impacts as well as the ability to process that information.[29] This suggests not only that governments have an important role to play in facilitating the development, dissemination, and discussion of information on climate change impacts, but also that to some extent the prioritization of areas for adaptation policy will be determined by the volume of information that is available regarding hazards and the willingness of governments and citizens to meaningfully engage that information and make forward-looking decisions about the desired future state of their community.

With respect to information about hazard exposure and impacts of climate change, coastal zones are a prime location in which to focus adaptation activities. As of 2005, over 23% of the world's population lived within 100 km of the coast, and this number is expected to increase to over 50% by 2030.[30] In the United States, the 2014 National Climate Assessment finds that 5 million people currently live within 4 feet of the local high tide level and that by 2100 131.2 million people are expected to live in the coastal zone.[31] Therefore, even without climate change impacts, vulnerability in the coastal zone would be increasing because the number of people exposed to baseline coastal hazards is increasing dramatically. This increase in vulnerability is magnified by the addition of climate change and other human-induced stressors on the coastal system. As of 2005, roughly ten million people each year were exposed to flooding as the result of storm surges and hurricanes.[32] By 2080, the combination

---

28. Fankhauser et al., *supra* note 15, at 69.

29. *Id.*

30. W. Neil Adger, Terry P. Hughes, Carl Folke, Stephen R. Carpenter & Johan Rockström, *Social-Ecological Resilience to Coastal Disasters*, 309 Science 1036, 1036 (2005).

31. NCA2014, *supra* Chapter 1 note 1, at 45, 591.

32. Adger et al., *supra* note 30, at 1036.

of migration to the coast, human-induced subsidence, and climate change impacts will raise this number to fifty million.[33] Around the world, people are moving to the coast and placing themselves in the path of increasing coastal hazards.

In addition, the coastal zone is home to key commercial infrastructure on which the entire economy depends. This includes ports, which are key to the distribution of goods; airports, highways, and rail systems, which are key to the transportation of people and goods; and critical energy infrastructure including oil and natural gas production and refining capacity as well as many important power plants. These operations provide two additional reasons to focus adaptation attention on the coast: First, impacts to key economic producers in the coastal zone can have far reaching economic effects, meaning that a dollar spent on coastal adaptation may avoid greater economic harms. Second, numerous key industrial players in the coastal zone will be facing their own adaptation challenges, creating opportunities for public-private partnerships and cooperative adaptation and information sharing.

Coastal areas are also a prime target for adaptation policymaking because the impacts of climate change are relatively well characterized. While there are some disagreements as to precise amounts and timing, there is scientific consensus that global sea levels will rise appreciably by 2100.[34] This is a certain impact for which adaptation measures, including both engineering and policy solutions, are already available. Therefore, governments have both sufficient knowledge of the challenges posed by sea level rise and the range of possible solutions to proceed with adaptation discussions. All that remains to be seen is whether societies have sufficient adaptive capacity to meaningfully engage this information to make informed, proactive decisions about adaptation. Because the risks and solutions in the coastal zones are so well characterized, adaptation discussions in the coastal zone may be a key component of building broader adaptive capacity to other impacts of climate change, as it will allow societies to establish a framework in which to discuss and assess such issues in the future. Therefore, adaptation in the coastal zone is doubly important not only because of the need to address rapidly increasing coastal vulnerability, but also because it provides a critical opportunity to build national adaptive capacity.

---

33. *Id.*

34. J.A. Church, P.U. Clark, A. Cazenave, J.M. Gregory, S. Jevrejeva, A. Levermann, M.A. Merrifield, G.A. Milne, R.S. Nerem, P.D. Nunn, A.J. Payne, W.T. Pfeffer, D. Stammer & A.S. Unnikrishnan, *Chapter 13 Sea Level Change* 1137, 1145, *in* INTERGOVERNMENTAL PANEL ON CLIMATE CHANGE, CLIMATE CHANGE 2013: THE PHYSICAL SCIENCE BASIS.

Tools to Decrease Coastal Vulnerability

There are five general categories into which adaptation options fall: (1) no regrets, (2) reversible, (3) safety margin, (4) soft, and (5) reduction of decision making time horizons.[35]

No regrets strategies are those that benefit society even if none of the anticipated impacts of climate change occur. Politically, these should be the easiest options to implement because they have a positive net present value and should benefit constituents in the near term. It is not necessarily the case that these strategies have low capital costs; rather, they will deliver immediate benefits. Coastal nourishment is a prime example of a no regrets strategy because even without climate change, beach nourishment creates positive current economic benefits.[36] As with beach nourishment, many of the other available policy options to respond to sea level rise and the potential for increasing storm impacts should be no regrets options. Many coastal areas experience natural long-term erosion and occasional severe storms.[37] Therefore, climate change impacts are primarily an increase over the baseline rate and intensity of these background conditions. That is, even in the absence of climate change, coastlines will continue to erode and hurricanes will continue to threaten coastal population centers. Thus, any measure aimed at responding to coastal erosion or reducing future storm damage is a no regrets measure because it reduces present vulnerability to baseline hazards.

There are many adaptation responses for the coastal zone that fall into this category: these would include construction setbacks to account for erosion, beach nourishment, erosion control structures, and building code requirements to ensure that coastal construction can withstand storms. Because all of these

---

35. Stéphane Hallegatte, *Strategies to Adapt to an Uncertain Climate Change*, 19 GLOBAL ENVTL. CHANGE 240, 244–45 (2009).

36. *See generally* Yehuda L. Klein, Jeffrey P. Osleeb & Mariano R. Viola, *Tourism-Generated Earnings in the Coastal Zone: A Regional Analysis*, 20 J. COASTAL RESEARCH 1080 (2004) (finding that continued development of tourism in the coastal zone is dependent upon the maintenance of broad, sandy beaches).

37. S. Jeffress Williams, Benjamin T. Gutierrez, James G. Titus, Stephen K. Gill, Donald R. Cahoon, E. Robert Thieler, Eric Anderson, Duncan Fitzgerald, Virginia Burkett & Jason Samenow, *Chapter 1: Sea Level Rise and Its Effects on the Coast, in* COASTAL SENSITIVITY TO SEA LEVEL RISE: A FOCUS ON THE MID-ATLANTIC REGION 11, 21–22 (U.S. Climate Change Science Program ed., 2009) (showing long-term erosion trends for the U.S. coastline). *See also* GARY GRIGGS, KIKI PATSCH & LAURET SAVOY, LIVING WITH THE CHANGING CALIFORNIA COAST 14 (2005) (72% of California's coastline consists of actively eroding sea cliffs).

PRE-NOURISHMENT

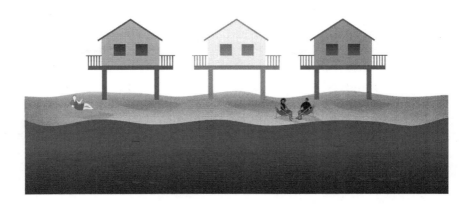

POST-NOURISHMENT

Figure 10: Erosion, Beach Nourishment and Economic Benefits

Beach nourishment creates wider, sandy beaches by placing additional sand on the beach. Larger beaches have been shown to be more attractive to tourists and nourishment can therefore have important economic benefits for entire coastal communities.

measures have high net present value they should, in theory, all be no regrets strategies. However, the case studies in Chapters 5, 6, and 7 reveal that they are not equally politically feasible. As discussed in more detail through the case studies, littoral (ocean-front) property owners are resistant to measures they

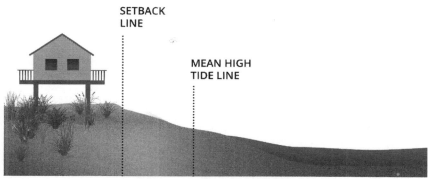

Figure 11: Coastal Setbacks

Coastal setbacks are often measured with respect to either the mean high tide line or the first line of vegetation, allowing them to be dynamic over time.

feel interfere with their private property rights, and this has led states to adopt those policy options that favor maintaining the coastline in a static position.

Reversible adaptation strategies are those that can be easily altered if the expected impacts of climate change do not occur. The hallmark of these strategies is that they do not involve an irreversible commitment of resources to adaptation measures. A potential example of a reversible strategy is the implementation of coastal setbacks that move dynamically with respect to a natural boundary (usually mean high water or the vegetation line). Such setbacks apply to the current location of the shoreline, but were the beach to be built up, a town or property owner can seek permission to build further seaward.[38]

Safety margin strategies are those that reduce vulnerability at little or no additional cost.[39] Safety margin strategies are different from no regrets strategies in that while they may have some additional cost, and still face some political resistance, they are feasible measures that governments can pursue today.

---

38. In North Carolina, if a beach is built up through natural accretion or nourishment and the vegetation line subsequently moves seaward, the local government entity governing permitting under an approved Land Use Plan can seek permission from the Coastal Resources Commission to move its setback line seaward. 15A N.C. ADMIN. CODE §§ 07H.0306(a)(8) (development setbacks are to be measured from the static line of vegetation), 07J.1200 (explaining procedures for the static line exception); Interview with Local Government Official (Dec. 1, 2009).

39. Hallegatte, *supra* note 35, at 245.

Examples of safety margin strategies at the coast include increased base flood elevation requirements and private decisions to build homes that will withstand stronger winds than would be required by the building code. Under the Federal Emergency Management Agency's rules, new construction in areas that are highly vulnerable to floods must be elevated so that the first floor is above the level of the 100-year flood elevation.[40] For an extra margin of safety, some states and local governments have flood ordinances that require elevation of an additional one to two feet above the base flood elevation. This is a clear example of a safety margin strategy because by the time the property owner is already elevating his house, adding a foot or two to the pilings is a marginal cost. With this sort of a mandated safety margin strategy, the only obstacle to implementation is convincing the appropriate level of government to adopt a flood ordinance. Such flood ordinances are widely used, and therefore, this appears to be a feasible safety margin strategy. As for private decisions to build above code, they will be influenced by the risk perceptions of the homeowner as informed by either prior experience with similar hazards or education about hazard risks as well as availability of insurance or ability to self-insure.[41] As discussed in more detail in Chapter 3, individual's risk perceptions tend to be far from reality, with personally experienced events being perceived as far larger risks than they are and other risks being under appreciated.[42] Because of the dynamics of coastal disaster response, explored in Chapter 3, private safety margin actions are unlikely to be undertaken by any but the most risk-adverse property owners or those who choose to self-insure through construction measures that mitigate potential property damages.

Soft strategies are institutional or financial tools that reduce vulnerability to climate change.[43] One example of a soft strategy is the adoption of longer planning horizons to ensure that projects can withstand future changes. In fact, some scholars suggest that long-term investments in infrastructure should already consider the impacts of climate change in order to ensure that the in-

---

40. 44 C.F.R. §9.11.

41. There is some evidence that when natural hazard insurance increases in price, some individuals will choose to undertake structural mitigation measures to reduce potential hazard losses rather than purchasing insurance. This is what some property owners have chosen to do when earthquake insurance rates increase. However, in general, the use of loss reduction measures by homeowners is very low. *See generally* Howard Kunreuther, Earthquake Insurance as a Hazard Reduction Strategy: The Case of the Homeowner (Paper Prepared for USGS Monograph on Socioeconomic Impacts of Earthquakes 1992), http://opim.wharton.upenn.edu/risk/downloads/archive/arch182.pdf.

42. *See* Chapter 3, *infra*.

43. Hallegatte, *supra* note 35, at 245.

vestments remain productive throughout their useful lifetimes.[44] For example, Boston located its coastal sewage treatment plant on higher ground so that its useful life would not be curtailed by sea level rise.[45] In theory, the National Flood Insurance Program and the Coastal Barrier Resources System should be examples of soft adaptation strategies to shape coastal development and reduce vulnerability to coastal flooding. The National Flood Insurance Program includes a number of measures to encourage property owners to take actions that reduce their individual vulnerability to flood damage, particularly through the Community Rating System. In addition, the Coastal Barrier Resources Act attempts to send a market signal to property owners that some parts of the coast are so vulnerable to flood risk that they should not be developed. As detailed in Chapter 3, neither of these programs has been particularly successful in sending market signals to influence property owner behavior. Chapter 3 explains that the inability of these programs to send market signals to property owners is partly the result of behavioral economics and risk perception, which may limit the overall utility of soft adaptation strategies targeted at individual actors. This does not mean that soft adaptation through financial mechanisms cannot be produced. In fact, the case studies presented in Chapters 5, 6, and 7 reveal that external financial incentives, such as federal grant funding, are a major driver of local government action, particularly with respect to environmental protection. Therefore, the key to success with soft financial adaptation measures lies in assuring that they are structured and targeted to actors from whom they will elicit an adaptation response.

An additional, broader example of long-range adaptation planning is the adoption of rolling easements or other forms of managed retreat. These approaches require that governments adopt planning horizons that are long enough to include the impacts of sea level rise and take actions today to reduce vulnerability by moving public and private structures landward and further away from the coastal hazard zone.

Finally, governments can adopt strategies that reduce decision making horizons. In essence, this is an attempt to institutionalize a wait-and-see policy while not making irreversible commitments that increase vulnerability in the interim. A potential example of this would be requiring that littoral owners develop their property in a manner such that improvements could be moved in the event of erosion. The California Coastal Commission has required such measures at the University of California at Santa Cruz's research facility, where

---

44. Fankhauser et al., *supra* note 15, at 70.
45. *Id.*

all of the buildings have been constructed such that they can be moved landward if necessary.[46] Shortened decision making horizons could also be achieved by increasing the rate of depreciation of coastal infrastructure to decrease the expected economic lifetimes of properties. While this approach makes sense in theory, it does not account for political lock-in on the part of owners of this infrastructure. As the case studies in Chapters 5 to 7 reveal, once development is permitted at the coast, it is essentially there forever or until it falls into the sea. As a result, the shortened time horizon adaptation measures suggested here are unlikely to be politically feasible.

Reviewing the above options, it appears that in the near term the most significant measures to reduce coastal vulnerability to sea level rise will be no regrets strategies. Over the longer term, it appears that other measures, including longer planning horizons to govern policies of retreat, will be needed. However, as subsequent chapters explore, it is not clear that such measures are politically feasible. This analysis brings us back to the importance of the role of governance in promoting social resilience. Government support of legal and political frameworks that facilitate adaptation will be crucial.[47] As the rest of this book explores, governments' most important roles will be in shaping land use planning and disaster relief policies because these are the most powerful ways of shaping the future of development at the coast in order to reduce coastal vulnerability.

---

46. Interview with Coastal Commission Staff Member (Dec. 2, 2009).
47. Adger et al., *supra* note 30, at 1038.

Chapter 3

The Role of Federal Insurance and Disaster Relief Programs

As explained in Chapter 1, one of the primary climate change hazards in the coastal zone is the potential for increased hurricane activity and larger storm surge impacts resulting from climate change. Coastal communities are already exposed to these hazards and have opportunities to reduce hazard exposure when they rebuild after disaster events and to engage in future hazard mitigation planning. However, there are a number of insurance and disaster relief programs that provide incentives for communities to rebuild as they were prior to the disaster event. In so doing, these programs can miss key opportunities to promote climate change adaptation. Further, the availability of subsidized insurance programs and disaster relief can promote *maladaptation* because they create incentives for communities to rebuild in areas that will face increasing exposure to climate change hazards in future years.

Ultimately, the most efficient way to reduce a coastal community's exposure to these hazards is to move people and structures out of the most hazard-prone areas. Subsequent chapters of this book will explore the challenges associated with relocating populations out of high-hazard areas. Before proceeding to a discussion of these legal issues, this chapter sets forth the key features of the National Flood Insurance Program, federal disaster relief programs, and state reinsurance programs in order to explain how these programs can influence incentives for coastal adaptation.

The Economics of Flood Insurance

Property insurance is intended to provide protection against catastrophic losses by spreading risk both spatially and inter-temporally. The basic economics of insurance requires that the risks insured by an individual company be randomly distributed. If insured risks are not randomly distributed, then the losses sustained by the insurer no longer conform to a normal distribution.[1] The result is that insurers are overexposed to the potential of very high losses and may not be able to maintain sufficient capitalization to cover such losses.[2] When confronted with risks for which it does not have sufficient capitalization, an insurer has two options: it may either purchase reinsurance and charge higher premiums or it may choose not to issue insurance in the area. Achieving an appropriate spreading of risk to maintain solvency is particularly challenging in the context of flood insurance because of the high degree of spatial and temporal correlation among losses when a flood occurs.[3] Private insurers will be further challenged in insuring highly correlated risks because states have the ability to regulate insurers by, for example, controlling rates and setting policy terms and solvency requirements.[4] The result is that state policy caps may limit the ability of insurers to charge policyholders for the costs associated with the purchase of reinsurance. The availability of reinsurance will also be limited by the ability of reinsurers to diversify their own risk portfolios.

Therefore, there will be situations in which the private insurance market is unable to transfer an appropriate share of risk and could become over-exposed to a hazard. In this situation, an insurer that has underwritten too many policies for risks that are spatially and temporally correlated will be subject to potential insolvency when there is a large hazard event and many policyholders attempt to collect on their policies at the same time. Flooding is a classic example of a spatially correlated risk that becomes uninsurable because of auto-correlation of losses: due to the high spatial and temporal correlation of risks, any insurer that takes on too much flood risk is in serious danger of insol-

---

1. Patricia Grossi & Howard Kunreuther, *Introduction: Needs, Stakeholders, and Government Incentives, in* Catastrophe Modeling: A New Approach to Managing Risk 3, 9 (Patricia Grossi & Howard Kunreuther eds., 2005).

2. *Id.*

3. This risk can be managed in part through the purchase of reinsurance, which I discuss in *State Insurance Regulations and Reinsurance Programs, infra.*

4. Wharton Risk Management & Decision Processes Center, Managing Large-Scale Risks in a New Era of Catastrophes 21 (2008).

What Is Reinsurance?

Reinsurance is insurance that can be purchased by a primary insurer. The primary insurer is the company that directly sells insurance to a consumer. However, if an insurer sells a large number of policies, it may have an amount of risk in its portfolio of insured assets that would cause the insurer to face insolvency if too many policyholders file claims at the same time. To protect against this, primary insurers can buy insurance on the policies they sell—the reinsurance, which allows the primary insurer to spread and diversify its own risk.

---

vency.[5] This is precisely what happened in the United States in the 1920s and 30s leading to the collapse of the private flood insurance market.[6]

Full insurance coverage, meaning that all property owners are insured, is desirable for several reasons. First, full coverage allows an insurer to spread risks over a larger spatial and temporal range, protecting against the risk of insurer insolvency discussed above. Second, insurance coverage can serve as a signal of hazard exposure to property owners if insurance rates are based on actuarially sound premiums. This latter point is particularly significant in the context of natural disaster insurance: property owners who are required to pay premiums that reflect their actual hazard exposure will not assume more hazard exposure than they personally can afford. In addition, insurance coverage increases social resilience to natural disasters because it puts property owners in a position where they are better able to recover from the impacts of natural hazards.

While insurance can enhance social resilience by making it easier for a homeowner or community to rebuild in the aftermath of a disaster, it does not necessarily reduce overall vulnerability to climate change hazards. Insurance may facilitate rebuilding that may not otherwise occur in hazard prone areas, meaning that exposure to subsequent hazard events will be increased. For example, if a hurricane causes beach erosion so significant that a brand new home could not be built on a property, but the existing home is less than 50% damaged,

---

5. Grossi & Kunreuther, *supra* note 1, at 9.

6. Jeffrey J. Pompe & James R. Rinehart, *Property Insurance for Coastal Residents: Governments' "Ill Wind"*, 13 Indep. Rev. 189, 192 (2008); The Heinz Center, Evaluation of Erosion Hazards 33 (2000).

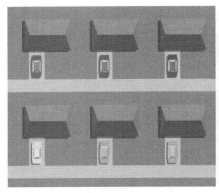 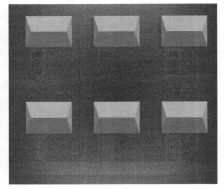

Figure 12a   **Figure 12b**

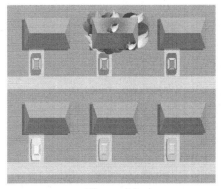

Figure 12c

Figure 12: Spatial and Temporal Correlation of Flood Risks

In a flood, if one house in the neighborhood floods, all of the others will too. This is different from a fire, where if one house burns down others might not.

most coastal states will permit rebuilding in the same location.[7] In this context, the availability of insurance coverage and disaster relief may enable some homeowners who could not otherwise rebuild to replace their homes in the exact same highly vulnerable coastal location where the initial loss occurred,

---

7. *See, e.g.*, 15A N.C. ADMIN. CODE §07J.0210 (defining a replacement, which shall be permitted under current CRC rules, proposed work to replace a damaged structure where damage was less than 50% of the market value of the structure); 31 TEX. ADMIN. CODE §15.11 (providing exemption for rebuilding for certain houses on the public beach that are less than 50% damaged).

What Does It Mean for Insurance Premiums to Be Actuarially Sound?

In the insurance field, premiums are considered to be "actuarially sound" if they reflect the actual risk of loss for a property over the period of the insurance policy. For example, consider a homeowner who wishes to purchase an insurance policy that protects against the risk of his home being lost in a fire. If the home is worth $250,000 and the insurer expects that the risk of loss in a fire is 1% in a year, the insurance premium would be set as:

$$\$250,000 * 0.01 = \$2,500/year$$

If the insurer collects a premium that is less than the expected loss of the property (the value of the property insured times the risk of loss), then the premium is not considered to be actuarially sound. If insurers collect premiums that do not reflect the risks of loss of the insured portfolio, they face the risk of financial insolvency, as there is the potential that claims by policyholders could exceed the amount of premiums collected. This is particularly true in the case of natural disaster events where many policyholders will be filing claims at the same time.

while providing no opportunity for the homeowner to use such funds to re-locate to a less hazard-prone area. While such rebuilding certainly enhances social resilience by restoring the built environment to its prior state, rebuild-ing in hazard-prone areas may not be desirable from a socio-*ecological* vul-nerability perspective. Consequently, if coastal hazard insurance is to be an effective tool in reducing socio-ecological vulnerability, insurance and other forms of disaster relief must be structured to work in tandem with local land use regulations to make sure that rebuilding occurs in a resilient and adaptive manner. There are, therefore, numerous public policy reasons that a govern-ment would want to ensure that there is a flood insurance system that is inte-grated with local land use policies such that it can decrease vulnerability to flood risks.

As mentioned above, private flood insurance has not been available in the United States since insurers suffered catastrophic losses in the Mississippi River Valley in the 1920s and 30s resulting in their insolvency. In the absence of a func-tioning private insurance market, the government has two options: (1) to pro-vide publicly backed reinsurance to assume any risk over and above what private

What Is the "Built Environment"?

When considering resilience of a coastal community to climate changes, there are two different types of resilience to consider: social and ecological. As explained in Chapter 2, social resilience can be enhanced at the expense of ecological resilience (e.g., by building seawalls) or by using natural systems to protect coastal communities (e.g., through wetland restoration and setbacks). In evaluating adaptation options, it can be helpful to distinguish between the systems we are trying to protect. Therefore the "built environment" is a term that is useful to distinguish human development, including homes, roads, and coastal infrastructure, from coastal ecosystems, such as sandy beaches and wetlands.

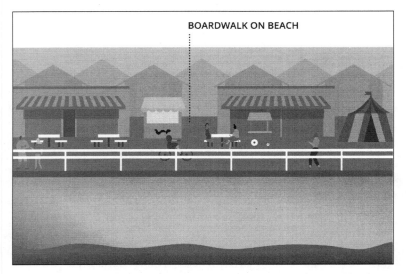

BOARDWALK ON BEACH

This distinction is particularly important when considering insurance as an adaptation strategy. Insurance covers physical structures that are part of the built environment and is a mechanism to allow physical structures to be restored to their pre-storm condition. Because insurance does not cover coastal ecosystems, it can facilitate rebuilding at the expense of these systems that would otherwise provide natural hazard protection in future events.

insurance companies are willing to bear or (2) to underwrite insurance itself. The United States is unique in that the federal government is the direct underwriter for flood insurance through the National Flood Insurance Program ("NFIP"). In addition, the federal government provides financial assistance to flood victims through disaster relief programs. While these programs do help communities recover from flood damage, they increase vulnerability in two significant ways. First, as explored in more detail below, the combination of subsidized insurance and disaster relief encourages property owners to assume more risk than they would personally want to bear, increasing exposure to coastal hazards. Second, the Federal Emergency Management Agency's ("FEMA") disaster relief policies have historically focused on expediting rebuilding and restoring communities to their pre-storm conditions. As explored below and in Chapter 7's case study of West Galveston Island, the process of restoring communities under these programs has not allowed for broad consideration of means to reduce hazard exposure while rebuilding. While new federal programs focused on climate resilience aim to encourage smarter rebuilding, the financial incentives created by the current suite of federal flood insurance and disaster response programs create significant obstacles to promoting adaptation to rising sea levels.

Government Programs Related to Hazard Insurance

This section provides an overview of the major federal government programs providing flood insurance and assistance in natural disaster recovery as well as state programs to provide insurance against other natural hazards that may be insufficiently covered by private insurance markets. This section aims to explain how these programs — which reflect conscious societal choices about disaster relief and the availability of insurance — operate in a manner that externalizes some of the risks of living in hazard-prone coastal areas to the broader tax base. In so doing, these programs have the potential to incentivize maladaptation to rising sea levels by continuing to encourage building and rebuilding in areas that may become permanently inundated or that will be subject to more severe storm surge events in the future.

Federal Flood Insurance

Introduced in 1968, the National Flood Insurance Program was intended to fill a gap in the property insurance system by providing homeowners with flood insurance to supplement their other property coverage.[8] The creation of the NFIP was a response to the fact that after a series of catastrophic flood losses early in the twentieth century, private flood insurance was not available for purchase.[9] After several decades in which private flood insurance was not available, the federal government decided to step in and fill this void by acting as an insurer of last resort.

The design of the NFIP was intended to encourage communities to adopt risk-minimizing measures, and ultimately lower the risks of flood loss.[10] The National Flood Insurance Program classifies the flood risks faced by certain communities, sets premiums for flood insurance, and requires that flood insurance be purchased to obtain a federally backed mortgage.[11] The NFIP adopts a community-based approach in which it uses flood risk mapping to classify the risk to each community and sets premiums at the community level.[12] The NFIP also gives communities the ability to adopt certain adaptation measures, such as changes to the local building code to reduce flood damage, in exchange for lower premiums through the Community Rating System. Few communities have chosen to participate in the Community Rating System because the incentives to do so are thought to be too small.[13] Even in communities that are part of the Community Rating System, local government officials report that it is extremely difficult to convince property owners to engage in flood mitigation measures because they do not perceive the risk of flooding to be high.[14]

Insurance through the NFIP covers *only* flood damage.[15] This means that to be completely protected, homeowners must purchase a general property insurance package, covering all other damages, such as fire and wind, and a flood insurance policy from the NFIP. The NFIP has attempted to make this process easier for consumers by allowing most major property insurance companies to act as third-party brokers, selling NFIP coverage.[16] However, much confu-

---

8. *See* 44 C.F.R. §59.2(a).

9. *See id.*

10. 42 U.S.C. §4022(b) (Community Rating System); *See also id.* §4012 (states must give the Director "satisfactory assurance" that they employ "adequate land use control measures" in order to be eligible for flood insurance coverage).

11. 42 U.S.C. §4012a(b).

12. *Id.* §4012.

13. WHARTON RISK MANAGEMENT & DECISION PROCESSES CENTER, *supra* note 4.

14. Interview with Local Government Official (Dec. 3, 2009).

15. This flood damage will be covered even if it is the result of erosion, but NFIP coverage does not extend to water damage caused by storms.

16. For the rules governing third party insurance brokers who sell NFIP policies, *see* 44 C.F.R. pt. 62.

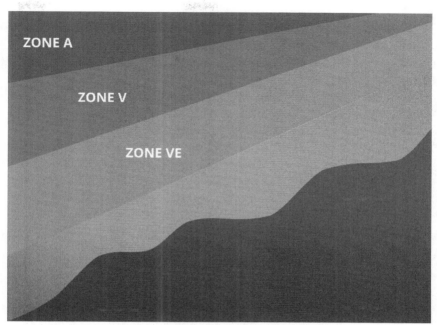

Figure 13: Flood Hazard Mapping

FEMA Flood Risk maps classify communities into zones based on flood risk. In the coastal zone the primary zones are:
Zone A: The 100-year flood plan (1% annual flood risk)
Zone V: The 100-year flood plan with additional hazards from storm waves
Zone VE: The V zone with additional risk from erosion

sion over what is covered remains. For example, if in a hurricane, the roof is ripped off a house by high winds in a storm and the house becomes damaged by rain, this damage is covered under a traditional homeowner's policy. On the other hand, if the same house is damaged by flooding due to storm surge, the loss will only be covered through federal flood insurance. As a result, it is not uncommon for hurricane victims to find themselves caught up in lengthy determinations of which source of water caused the damage. Furthermore, as homeowner's policies cover water damage from sources other than floods, many property owners do not understand that they are not covered for flood losses under a basic homeowner's policy.

Despite its good intentions, the National Flood Insurance Program has been the subject of many criticisms, including that insurance uptake rates are low, premiums tend to be highly subsidized because of improper risk projections,

> ### Grandfathering under the NFIP
>
> The National Flood Insurance Program allows for premium grand-fathering. This means that when new flood maps are released reflecting increased premiums in an area, properties that are already covered by the NFIP are allowed to keep their previous, lower premiums. Congress eliminated the premium grandfathering provisions in the Biggert-Waters Flood Insurance Reform Act of 2012, but these provisions of Biggert-Waters were repealed by the Homeowner Flood Insurance Affordability Act of 2014. This means that homeowners who are eligible for grandfathered premiums will continue to pay flood insurance rates that are much lower than what would be required to cover the flood risk to which they are exposed.

and very few communities have participated in hazard mitigation.[17] Primary among these is the fact that the NFIP is not an actuarially sound program and remains unable to collect sufficient premiums to cover the possibility of catastrophic loss.[18] The two major sources of fiscal vulnerability in the NFIP are FEMA's inability to set actuarially sound premiums and the continuation of premium subsidies and grandfathering when flood zones are reclassified.[19]

According to the Government Accountability Office ("GAO"), even FEMA's full-risk premiums fail to reach market rates that accurately reflect flood risk.[20] The GAO finds that the failure to fully capture flood risks results from FEMA's reliance on flood probability data from the 1980s and flood damage estimates that do not reflect recent experience.[21] The flood

---

17. WHARTON RISK MANAGEMENT & DECISION PROCESSES CENTER, *supra* note 4.

18. *Challenges Facing the National Flood Insurance Program: Hearing Before S. Comm. on Banking, Housing, & Urban Affairs*, 109th Cong. 1 (2005) (statement of William O. Jenkins, Jr., Director, Homeland Security and Justice Issues, U.S. Gov't Accountability Off.) [hereinafter *Jenkins Testimony re NFIP*].

19. *Id.*; U.S. GOV'T ACCOUNTABILITY OFF., FLOOD INSURANCE: FEMA'S RATE-SETTING PROCESS WARRANTS ATTENTION (2008) [hereinafter GAO, FEMA RATE SETTING].

20. GAO, FEMA RATE SETTING, *supra* note 19, at 1; *see also* U.S. FISH & WILDLIFE SERVICE, THE COASTAL BARRIER RESOURCES ACT: HARNESSING THE POWER OF MARKET FORCES TO CONSERVE AMERICA'S COASTS AND SAVE TAXPAYER'S MONEY 28 (2002) (finding that NFIP premiums in the highest risk zones are $1000–1500 per year while equivalent privately provided premiums would be $2,500–$7,500/year).

21. GAO, FEMA RATE SETTING, *supra* note 19, at 1.

mapping program traditionally based its risk maps on historical flood data, without accounting for future changes that may increase flood risks, such as increased storm intensity, and historically has failed to incorporate coastal erosion into its calculation of flood risk.[22] This approach to mapping was modified in the Biggert-Waters Flood Insurance Reform Act of 2012, which requires that flood map updates consider both projections of erosion and rising sea levels.[23] However, new limitations in FEMA's ability to raise premiums imposed by the Homeowner Flood Insurance Affordability Act of 2014 may mean that FEMA will have more accurate flood risk maps but will lack the ability to charge flood insurance premiums that accurately reflect these risks.

FEMA is currently in the process of updating its flood hazard maps across the United States.[24] In many places, these updates are long overdue: As of 2007, FEMA concluded that more than half of all flood damage occurred in areas that were not mapped as high flood risk areas.[25] Of note, San Francisco received its first-ever set of flood maps in 2010.[26] While this process of updating the flood rate maps is badly needed and represents significant progress, the GAO found that even in the map updates concluded in 2008 "a significant portion of the maps reflect data at least 15 years old, which may or may not accurately reflect actuarial risk of flooding."[27] Furthermore, flood rate map updates only apply to new construction. Each time flood rate maps are updated, existing structures are grandfathered at their old premium rates.[28] The extent of the premium subsidy from grandfathering can be significant: the GAO found that owners of pre-mapping structures tend to pay only 35% to 40% of the market premium

---

22. THE HEINZ CENTER, *supra* note 6, at 50.

23. 42 U.S.C. §4101b(b)(3). *See infra* for additional features of the Biggert-Waters Flood Insurance Reform Act of 2012.

24. *See Flood Map Revision Processes*, FEDERAL EMERGENCY MANAGEMENT AGENCY, http://www.fema.gov/flood-map-revision-processes (explaining the three mechanisms under which flood map revisions are initiated) (last visited Feb. 28, 2016).

25. *Federal Emergency Management Agency: Ongoing Challenges Facing the National Flood Insurance Program: Hearing Before S. Comm. on Banking, Housing, & Urban Affairs*, 110th Cong. 11 (2007) (statement of Orice M. Williams, Director, Financial Markets and Community Investments, Federal Emergency Management Agency) [hereinafter *Williams Testimony re NFIP*].

26. Interview with San Francisco Bay Conservation and Development Commission Official (Oct. 5, 2009).

27. GAO, FEMA RATE SETTING, *supra* note 19, at 18.

28. *Id.* at 19.

rate.[29] These grandfathered properties currently make up approximately 25% of FEMA's insurance portfolio, and in 2006 FEMA estimated that these grandfathered properties led to a premium collection shortfall of $750 million.[30]

These structural issues with FEMA's ability to collect actuarially sound premiums under the NFIP have caused the program to experience losses that far exceed its resources in the aftermath of major natural disasters. In the aftermath of Hurricanes Katrina, Rita, and Wilma in 2005, the NFIP was forced to borrow over $16.6 billion from the treasury to pay out claims.[31] Recognizing the significant debts that the NFIP had accumulated due to its failure to collect premiums that adequately reflected insured risks, Congress passed a series of reforms to the NFIP in 2012 called the Biggert-Waters Flood Insurance Reform Act. Biggert-Waters included two important provisions to correct this imbalance. First, Biggert-Waters contained a variety of measures to update flood risk mapping and cause premiums on all properties to rise to actuarially sound rates.[32] Second, Biggert-Waters required FEMA to create a plan to repay the NFIP's debt to the treasury and establish a reserve fund to protect against future losses.[33] After Biggert-Waters passage, the New York Metropolitan Area was struck by Superstorm Sandy in 2012, and Congress subsequently authorized the NFIP to borrow an additional $9.7 billion to pay out the resulting flood insurance. Collectively, the reforms to the National Flood Insurance Program do make some progress towards creating a more actuarially sound and self-sustaining flood insurance program, but significant weaknesses in the program remain. An examination of the combined impacts of these reforms clearly illustrates the important role that federal flood insurance can play in facilitating or acting as a hindrance to sea level rise adaptation.

The first significant area of attempted flood insurance reform seeks to raise flood insurance premiums to actuarially sound levels. Biggert-Waters called upon FEMA to determine the risk premium insurance rates that would be required to make flood insurance available on an actuarial basis and any lower (subsidized) premium rates that would be reasonable and encourage the purchase of flood insurance.[34] To allow premiums to rise to actuarial levels,

---

29. *Williams Testimony re NFIP, supra* note 25, at 7.

30. *Id.*

31. Rawle O. King, Congressional Research Service, National Flood Insurance Program: Background, Challenges, and Financial Status 15 (2011), http://fas.org/sgp/crs/misc/R40650.pdf.

32. *See* 42 U.S.C. §4015(h) (2012).

33. *Id.* §§4016, 4017.

34. *Id.* §4014(a)(1).

NFIP Reforms

In June 2012, Congress passed the most sweeping reforms to the National Flood Insurance Program in years. The Biggert-Waters Flood Insurance Reform Act included reforms in four key areas of the flood insurance program that were intended to improve the performance and solvency of the NFIP: (1) premium reform; (2) limitations on the availability of subsidized premiums; (3) improved flood risk mapping; and (4) establishment of a reserve fund and creation of a repayment schedule.

In September 2012, only months after Biggert-Waters became law, Superstorm Sandy hit the East Coast of the United States, causing an estimated $50 billion in damages. The coasts of New Jersey and New York were particularly hard hit during the storm. At the time, New Jersey was awaiting FEMA's release of its new flood hazard maps, which substantially delayed the rebuilding process. When the new maps were released, the public became aware of substantial increases in premiums that would result. For example in New Jersey, homeowners previously in the FEMA "A" zone who were reclassified to the "V" zone found that premiums would increase from approximately $900/year to more than $30,000/year. Almost immediately, lawmakers from New York and New Jersey began an effort to repeal key portions of Biggert-Waters.

Their efforts culminated in the Homeowner Flood Insurance Affordability Act. The Act repealed flood rate increases in Biggert-Waters that applied to properties that were uninsured as of July 6, 2012 and to properties that were purchased after July 6, 2012. The Act also requires the FEMA Administrator to allow a purchaser of a property with a current NFIP policy to assume the policy at its existing rates. This provision was intended to insulate home purchasers from premium increases until the repeal of premium increases entered into effect. The Act also restored grandfathered flood insurance premiums by eliminating the provision of Biggert-Waters that required the FEMA Administrator to raise grandfathered premiums to actuarial rates over a period of five years. The Act also required the Administrator to prepare a Draft Affordability Framework proposing programmatic and regulatory changes to address affordability issues with NFIP policies.

> ## The Problem of Severe Repetitive Loss Properties
>
> Severe repetitive loss properties are defined as properties that since 1978 have made either:
>
> (1) four or more claims exceeding $5,000 each; or
> (2) two or more claims where the total value of the claims exceeds the fair market value of the property.
>
> Severe repetitive loss properties tend to be those that are located in high-hazard areas that are subject to frequent flooding. In fact the GAO has found that while repetitive loss properties account for only 1% of the NFIP policies, they are responsible for 25–30% of all claims.[35] Severe repetitive loss properties are thus one of the central causes of financial vulnerability in the NFIP, and also are an easily identifiable class of properties that are located in high-hazard areas where efficient adaptation strategies would likely suggest relocation rather than continued rebuilding.

Biggert-Waters amended the NFIP to raise the maximum annual premium increase from 10% to 20% for most flood insurance policies.[36] Because of the large potential premium increases faced by property owners after Superstorm Sandy, the Homeowner Flood Insurance Affordability Act of 2014 lowered the maximum annual premium increase to 18%.[37]

However, the provisions requiring an analysis of insurance affordability do not apply to certain classes of properties. Subsidized premiums are not permitted for second homes, severe repetitive loss properties, properties with cumulative losses greater than their fair market value, business properties, and properties that sustained substantial damage (exceeding 50% of fair market value) or underwent substantial improvements (exceeding 50% of fair market value) after June 6, 2012.[38] Overall, the GAO estimates that elimination of these premium subsidies will eliminate subsidies for 483,000 policies nationwide, including approximately 87,000 business policies.[39] For these policies, annual

---

35. *See National Flood Insurance Program: Continued Actions Needed to Address Financial and Operational Issues: Hearing Before S. Comm. on Banking, Housing, & Urban Affairs,* 111th Cong. (2010) (statement of Orice Williams Brown, Director, Financial Markets and Community Investments, Federal Emergency Management Agency).

36. *Id.* § 4015(e)(1) (2012); *see id.* § 4015(e)(1) (2014).

37. *See id.* § 4015(e)(1) (2014).

38. 42 U.S.C. § 4014(a)(2).

39. U.S. Gov't Accountability Off., GAO-13-607, Flood Insurance: More Information Needed on Subsidized Properties 13 (2013).

premium increases of up to 25% are permitted.[40] In addition, FEMA is now prohibited from extending rate subsidies to individuals who own repetitive loss properties and refuse mitigation assistance following a major disaster.[41]

While the above-described reforms represent an important step towards achieving an actuarially sound flood insurance program, FEMA retains significant leeway to allow premium subsidies to persist where doing so would encourage the purchase of insurance. Congress's decision to continue to allow subsidized premiums is further underscored by several provisions of Biggert-Waters that were subsequently repealed. First, under the existing system, properties are grandfathered at the premium rate for the flood risk category in which the properties are mapped at the time the owners initially purchase insurance. Biggert-Waters attempted to enable NFIP premiums to rise to reflect new risk information by requiring that flood insurance rate maps ("FIRMs") be updated once every five years, and would have required that any resultant premium increase be phased in over a period of five years at the rate of 20% per year.[42] However, this provision was repealed by the Homeowner Flood Insurance Affordability Act.[43] Biggert-Waters would have also prevented the extension of subsidized premiums to properties with lapsed policies or newly purchased properties,[44] but these provisions were also repealed.[45] As a result, significant premium subsidies are likely to persist under the NFIP.

Biggert-Waters also amended the NFIP to require FEMA to develop a plan and collect additional premiums to repay the Program's substantial debts to the treasury. The Act amended the NFIP to require the establishment of a reserve fund. The reserve fund is required to maintain a balance of at least 1% of the total amount of policy exposure and is to be kept separate and remain available for the payment of future claims.[46] At his discretion, the FEMA Administrator may set a higher percentage for the reserve fund and is authorized to set additional premium amounts that are necessary to collect money for the reserve fund.[47] The Act also amended the NFIP to require the creation of a repayment plan any time FEMA must draw upon the general treasury to pay flood insurance claims. Any time a repayment plan is neces-

---

40. 42 U.S.C. §4015(e)(4).
41. *Id.* §4014(g)(2).
42. *Id.* §4015(h) (2012).
43. Pub. L. No. 113-89, §4, 128 Stat. 1020, 1022 (2014).
44. 42 U.S.C. §4014(g) (2012).
45. Pub. L. No. 113-89, §3, 128 Stat. 1020, 1021–22 (2014).
46. 42 U.S.C. §4017a(b)(1).
47. *Id.* §4017a(b)(2).

sary, FEMA must report to Congress every six months on its progress under the repayment plan.[48] The repayment plan provisions were crafted to provide for the repayment of the $17 billion that FEMA borrowed to settle claims during the 2005 hurricane season, and the borrowing cap was raised to more than $30 billion in order to facilitate the settlement of claims from Superstorm Sandy.

The final reform implemented by Biggert-Waters that will have a significant impact on future adaptation decision making was the establishment of the Technical Mapping Advisory Council ("TMAC").[49] The TMAC is a Federal Advisory Committee that is charged with reviewing flood mapping activities and making recommendations to FEMA. The TMAC is specifically charged with making recommendations on how the impacts of climate and future conditions should be incorporated into FEMA's flood hazard mapping.[50] Because FEMA's flood maps currently do not include future sea level rise risks, they will tend to systematically underestimate the hazards to which coastal property owners are exposed. However, the incorporation of such risks is likely to be particularly challenging because flood insurance policies are written on an annual basis, meaning that the time span of the policy is likely to be inconsistent with the time frame over which appreciable sea level rise occurs. That is, the annual policy is only able to convey signals about hazard exposure in a particular year as opposed to signals about longer-term risks due to increasing climate-driven hazard exposure.

Because of the structural issues that cause it to charge premiums that do not reflect actual flood risks, the NFIP has been labeled as a government subsidy of coastal behavior that leads to irresponsible coastal development that will result in increased losses of property and life.[51] The NFIP is made increasingly vulnerable by the fact that insurance purchase rates are low, and there is evidence of adverse selection in the decision to purchase flood insurance.[52] Fewer than half of all property owners who are eligible for NFIP in-

---

48. *Id.* § 4016(d).

49. *Id.* § 4101a.

50. *Id.* § 4101a(d).

51. Christine M. McMillan, Comment, *Federal Flood Insurance Policy: Making Matters Worse*, 44 Hous. L. Rev. 471, 475 (2007).

52. Michael J. Trebilcock & Ronald J. Daniels, *Rationales and Instruments for Government Intervention in Natural Disasters, in* On Risk and Disaster: Lessons from Hurricane Katrina 89, 93 (Ronald J. Daniels, Donald F. Kettl & Howard Kunreuther eds., 2006). Adverse selection is the phenomenon where only those individuals who are likely to experience insured losses choose to purchase insurance. Insurance systems that are plagued by adverse selection will not be able to maintain financial solvency because they will not have enough non-claiming policies to cover all insured losses. *See* Erik Banks, Alternative Risk Transfer 21–22 (2004).

> ### What Is Adverse Selection?
>
> Adverse Selection in insurance refers to the phenomenon that people who are more likely to need to file insurance claims are more likely to purchase insurance. In the context of flood insurance, there is evidence that people who live in higher flood hazard areas are more likely to purchase insurance policies than those exposed to lower flood risks. This has the effect of increasing the expected losses of the flood insurance program because it limits the ability of the NFIP to spread risks across a broader base of property owners and makes it more likely that those property owners who do purchase insurance will file claims against it.

surance choose to purchase it.[53] Among those property owners who are not required to purchase federal flood insurance because they do not have a federally-backed mortgage, NFIP purchase rates are less than 1%.[54] Further, the vast majority of FEMA's losses stem from a small percentage of underwritten policies that claim repetitive losses.[55] In combination, this data suggests that NFIP coverage is only significant to a particular subset of coastal property owners with very high exposure to flood hazards. Therefore, the failure to set sound premiums increases coastal vulnerability in two important ways: (1) by subsidizing the costs of high risk coastal living, it increases societal hazard exposure; and (2) by failing to collect actuarially sound premiums, the NFIP runs the risk of experiencing losses that exceed its collections—something that happened after both Hurricane Katrina and Superstorm Sandy—which must ultimately be covered by taxpayers.

In addition to the existence of subsidized premiums, which tend to encourage property owners to increase their hazard exposure, there are other aspects of the federal disaster relief program that further distort the risk signals sent to coastal property owners, thereby encouraging them to build or remain in areas with significant coastal hazard exposure. These programs are the Stafford Disaster Relief program and tax credits, which are discussed in more detail below.

---

53. *Jenkins Testimony re NFIP, supra* note 18, at 4.
54. *Williams Testimony re NFIP, supra* note 25, at 3.
55. *Id.*

Stafford Disaster Relief

The Stafford Act provides for both immediate assistance in the aftermath of a federally declared disaster and long-term assistance for community rebuilding. Stafford Disaster Relief is available to residents of an area declared a disaster area by the U.S. President upon a request by the affected state's governor.[56] The Stafford Act provides for three types of long-term disaster aid: contributions for state and local government repair of public facilities,[57] direct assistance for rebuilding or repair of private housing,[58] and funding for the repair and replacement of federal facilities.[59] Each of these programs is designed to help communities rebuild and recover from disaster events and, thus, they provide tools to enhance the resilience of the built environment. However, to the extent that long-term disaster aid under the Stafford Act permits rebuilding in high-hazard areas in a manner similar to what existed before the storm event, it is likely to foster maladaptation to rising seas and increased storminess. This section summarizes the major types of long-term disaster relief authorized by the Stafford Act and considers how they may shape coastal communities incentives to adapt to climate change.

The first major category of long-term aid available under the Stafford Act is aid for the repair of public facilities. Public facilities are defined by statute to include schools, municipal buildings, sewage treatment and collection, water supply and distribution, public power infrastructure, airports, certain streets and roads, and parks.[60] For these facilities, the Stafford Act provides that the federal government may cover at least 75% of the costs of rebuilding (the "federal share") while the balance is to be covered by the affected local government.[61] However, if a facility has been damaged in the past ten years by the same type of event and the owner has failed to implement mitigation measures, the Act requires the President to promulgate regulations reducing the federal share to not less than 25%.[62]

In order to receive assistance for the repair of public facilities, FEMA's regulations require that the state have an approved hazard mitigation plan.[63] In

---

56. 42 U.S.C. §5170.
57. *Id.* §5172(a).
58. *Id.* §5174(c).
59. *Id.* §5171.
60. *Id.* §5122(10).
61. *Id.* §5172(b).
62. *Id.*
63. 44 C.F.R. §206.226(b).

addition, if the public facility is located in a flood hazard area and does not have insurance under the NFIP, the regulations require that federal assistance be reduced to the lesser of the value of the facility on the date it was destroyed *or* the insurance proceeds that would have been available if the facility were insured.[64] FEMA's regulations further restrict the availability of federal funds to restore public facilities to exclude facilities that another federal agency has specific authority to repair or restore.[65] Disaster relief is also available under the public assistance provisions for certain non-profit facilities, including those that provide sewer services, wastewater treatment, emergency services, and medical care.[66]

When public disaster assistance is provided, FEMA's regulations permit it to require cost-effective hazard mitigation measures.[67] The regulations further grant the FEMA Administrator the authority to require relocation of a destroyed facility if the facility will be subject to "repetitive heavy damage" and the overall project is cost-effective.[68] FEMA also requires the recipients of public assistance to maintain insurance on structures that are repaired with Stafford aid.[69]

The second type of major category of long-term Stafford Act aid is individual housing assistance. The Stafford Act authorizes the President to provide assistance for rebuilding, repair, and eligible mitigation measures.[70] If the assistance provided to a homeowner is to replace a damaged structure, receipt of assistance is predicated upon the property owner's subsequent maintenance of flood insurance coverage.[71] Under the regulations implementing the Stafford program, the maximum amount of assistance provided in a single disaster event is limited to $25,000, adjusted annually by the consumer price index.[72] When assistance is needed, FEMA will determine the types of assistance available, and the property owner is expected to accept the first offer of assistance he receives.[73] According to FEMA's regulations, unwarranted refusal of the first offer of assistance can result in the forfeiture of future housing assistance.[74] FEMA's regulations specify that it can provide assistance for eligible repairs

---

64. 42 U.S.C. §5172(d).
65. 44 C.F.R. §206.226(a).
66. *Id.* §206.226(c).
67. *Id.* §206.226(e).
68. *Id.* §206.226(g).
69. *Id.* §206.252(d).
70. 42 U.S.C. §5174(c).
71. *Id.*
72. 44 C.F.R. §206.110(b).
73. *Id.* §206.110(c).
74. *Id.*

and housing replacement meeting certain criteria, including that they would not otherwise be covered by insurance.[75]

The Stafford Act also prohibits property owners from receiving flood assistance if they have previously received flood disaster assistance in an event that has occurred since 1994 that was conditioned on maintaining insurance coverage under the NFIP and they did not have flood insurance at the time of the subsequent loss.[76] FEMA's regulations make the insurance requirement more robust at the community level by limiting flood disaster assistance in a special flood hazard area to those communities that participate in the NFIP.[77] If an individual sells a property that has received flood assistance and is therefore required to maintain coverage under the NFIP, the Stafford Act requires the seller inform the buyer of their obligation to maintain flood insurance.[78] Under FEMA's implementing regulations, the seller is required to formally assign the flood insurance requirement to the purchaser.[79] In the event that a seller fails to provide the required notice, the Stafford Act allows the federal government to seek reimbursement from the seller if the buyer subsequently suffers a flood loss and seeks disaster aid.[80] The Stafford Act also imposes a general obligation on the President to ensure that benefits are not duplicated under Stafford and other disaster relief programs.[81]

The Stafford Act also authorizes the President to expend federal funds for the immediate repair of federal facilities. This authority may be exercised to repair or replace any federally owned facility if the repair or replacement is of such "urgency that it cannot reasonably be deferred" until Congress passes lending authorizing federal spending for repairs.[82] The Stafford Act authorizes agencies to transfer funds appropriated for another purpose to make the needed repairs.[83] When federal facilities are repaired using these provisions, the agencies involved in the repairs are required to evaluate the natural hazard exposure of the facility to be repaired and "take appropriate action to mitigate such hazards, including safe land use and construction practices, in accordance with standards prescribed by the President."[84]

---

75. *Id.* § 206.117(b).
76. 42 U.S.C. § 5154a.
77. 44 C.F.R. § 206.110(k)(2).
78. 42 U.S.C. § 5154a(b)(1).
79. 44 C.F.R. § 206.110(k)(3)(i)(A).
80. 42 U.S.C. § 5154a(b)(2).
81. *Id.* § 5155.
82. *Id.* § 5171.
83. *Id.*
84. *Id.* § 5171(c).

It is important to emphasize that the Stafford Act plays a key role in providing critical, immediate aid for disaster response, including assistance with emergency response services and temporary housing in impacted communities. By also providing long-term assistance, the Stafford Act reflects a societal choice to care for individuals and communities that have been the victims of natural disasters and help them to rebuild their communities. To the extent that long-term aid under Stafford helps communities to get back on their feet, it can be an important tool in enhancing social resilience in the face of climate change. However, it is important to weigh the benefits of social resilience against the incentives that long-term assistance under the Stafford program may create for maladaptation. While there is an increasing focus on incorporating resilience measures into rebuilding and requiring the purchase of flood insurance for structures that have received Stafford aid, there are still important limitations on the use and availability of federal disaster assistance that can create incentives for rebuilding in hazard-prone areas when relocation may be a better choice. A conflict arises if the overall policy goal is to promote efficient adaptation to climate change and keep coastal populations out of harms' way.

Rebuilding Tax Credits

Tax credits are available to homeowners in disaster impacted areas through favorable treatment of casualty losses: all payments received by a property owner under Stafford Disaster Relief and the NFIP are explicitly excluded from the definition of gross taxable income.[85] In addition, there are special provisions allowing for the deduction of casualty losses sustained in areas where a federal disaster is declared.[86] In a disaster area, a property owner may deduct from his taxable income the net disaster loss to the property and as much of the net casualty loss as exceeds 10% of his gross income.[87] Further, a property owner in a disaster area can elect to take the tax loss from the disaster in the year *preceding* the disaster, thus making the deducted losses available to fund rebuilding.[88]

---

85. 26 U.S.C. § 139.

86. *Id.* § 165.

87. *Id.*

88. *Id.* Note that in addition to these federal tax credits, states have a number of varying incentive programs that also encourage coastal development through preferential treatment. For a discussion of these programs *see* Kenneth J. Bagstad, Kevin Stapleton & John R. D'Agostino, *Taxes, Subsidies, and Insurance as Drivers of United States' Coastal Development*, 63 Ecological Econ. 285 (2007).

Tax incentives may thus be an additional driver of individual decisions to rebuild at the coast and encourage underinsurance. This is particularly true in cases where the property owner would choose to self-insure because the availability of tax credits dramatically reduces the cost of self-insurance. It is important to emphasize that this credit effectively amounts to an insurance subsidy: through the provision of tax credits, the government in essence provides a free insurance policy that is equal to the taxpayer's rate minus ten percent of the annual gross income. Consider a property owner with an annual gross income of $100,000 taxed at the average federal tax rate of 25%. Assume that his house is lost in a hurricane and he sustains $500,000 in damages. The deductions from his taxes result in a federal subsidy of $122,500, or 24.5% of the value of his losses.

The Impact of Disaster Relief on Property Owner Decision Making

To the extent that the above-described policies lead to the underpurchase of insurance, they signal a distortion in market behavior that could be remedied with comprehensive reform of the NFIP and federal disaster relief programs. From a policy perspective, full insurance coverage is desirable for two reasons. First, insurance coverage, if set at actuarially fair rates, sends signals to the property owner of his hazard exposure.[89] Therefore, if premiums are properly set, they should serve as a price signal to consumers and keep risk-adverse consumers from moving to natural hazard areas. Second, an insurance program is more likely to be self-sustaining if it achieves full coverage: full coverage means that risks are more likely to conform to the normal distribution and the insurer will be better able to protect its own solvency.[90] Both of these measures would reduce coastal vulnerability to the impacts of climate change. Properly set insurance premiums can reduce hazard exposure by send-

---

89. Michael S. Carolan, *One Step Forward Two Steps Back: Flood Management Policy in the United States*, 16 ENVTL. POLITICS 36, 44 (2007) (noting that a classic rationalization for flood insurance is to force the property owner to internalize risks, but this does not hold in the context of the NFIP).

90. Grossi & Kunreuther, *supra* note 1. Note that in the context of the federal government as insurer there is abundant evidence that the NFIP will not be able to rely solely on its premiums, however, this is a transfer payment and not a loss in the classic economic sense. While the cost overruns of NFIP payouts are not inherently welfare losses, we are concerned about these overruns to the extent that they represent a subsidy of unwise risk-bearing and draw funds away from other public activities.

ing price signals that limit development or rebuilding in the coastal zone. Further, ensuring the financial solvency of the National Flood Insurance Program will increase social resilience by ensuring that necessary resources for hazard recovery are available.

This section considers how the National Flood Insurance Program and accompanying policies impact the decision of where to live and whether to purchase insurance. In general, these policies induce property owners to bear more risk of flood damage than is socially optimal by limiting the costs of flood loss that are actually borne by the owner.

The ultimate goal of a well-functioning flood insurance program should be to ensure that property owners are assuming the socially efficient level of flood risk and are able to recover from the impacts of natural hazards. Under basic utility theory, this should be the level of flood risk at which the benefits that the property owner derives from living in the flood zone outweigh the losses experienced in flooding. The flood risk assumed by the property owner is socially efficient when the level of risk he bears maximizes total social utility, meaning that the full costs of flood losses are incorporated into his decision making. The most straightforward way to ensure efficient decision making with respect to risk assumption is to force the property owner to bear all of the costs of potential flood losses on his own. In this circumstance, a risk-adverse property owner may purchase insurance to gain the peace of mind of having protection but no property owner makes inefficient decisions because he is able to impose the costs of the disaster loss on other parties. In the case of coastal flooding, the ability of the property owner to transfer losses to the federal taxpayers through NFIP premium subsidies, Stafford Disaster Relief, and tax credits will lead him to assume more risk than is socially efficient.

Risk-bearing behavior will also be influenced by a number of informational asymmetries related to consumer behavior. Most importantly, consumers who have not experienced recent flooding are likely to lack or ignore flood hazard information.[91] This ignorance of hazard information means that property owners will not properly understand the risk of flood loss and they are likely to systematically undervalue flood insurance.[92] The tendency to undervalue flood insurance protection is particularly exacerbated when housing prices are low

---

91. *See* Susan L. Cutter, *The Vulnerability of Science and the Science of Vulnerability*, 93 ANNALS ASS'N OF AM. GEOGRAPHERS 1, 2 (2003) (the availability heuristic states that recent experience with, and social memory of, hazard events causes people to have biased probability estimates and think such events are more likely in the future).

92. WHARTON RISK MANAGEMENT & DECISION PROCESSES CENTER, *supra* note 4, at 129–33.

or declining, making many homeowners even more reluctant to spend money on flood insurance.[93] As a result, the peace of mind from having insurance coverage will be substantially lowered and property owners will be less likely to purchase insurance.[94] Finally, even if property owners do seek out accurate risk data, they may have difficulty finding it. While NFIP maps are supposed to be updated at least once every five years, many of them have been out-of-date.[95] Reforms to the flood mapping program under Biggert-Waters should help to address these problems and make more up-to-date flood risk information available to the public.

There are two key steps in coastal property decision making: first, a property owner must make the decision to move to or remain at the coast, and then he must decide whether to insure his property. Assuming that property owners are rational, we would expect them to choose to live in the area from which they derive the highest utility.[96] In choosing whether to live at the coast or inland, there are a number of factors that will go into a property owner's calculation of utility, including the value that the property owner derives from living at the coast and the risk of loss from natural hazards.

Overall, we would expect that property owners will choose to live at the coast any time their utility from doing so is greater than living inland. Both coastal real estate prices and population movements over the last fifty years show the high value that Americans place on living at the coast.[97] These high

---

93. Melissa Hillebrand, *Flood Coverage Not All Wet*, AM. AGENT & BROKER, Feb. 2009, at 34.

94. WHARTON RISK MANAGEMENT & DECISION PROCESSES CENTER, *supra* note 4, at 129.

95. *See* Carolan, *supra* note 89, at 44 (finding that as of 2001 over 60% of flood hazard maps were more than ten years old).

96. Many authors have argued that in the context of natural disasters and climate change it is unreasonable to assume that property owners are rational actors. I explore this more fully below. *See* WHARTON RISK MANAGEMENT & DECISION PROCESSES CENTER, *supra* note 4, at 219 (expected utility theory does not properly characterize the behavior of individuals purchasing property insurance); Howard Kunreuther & Mark Pauly, *Rules Rather Than Discretion: Lessons from Hurricane Katrina*, 33 J. RISK & UNCERTAINTY 101, 102 (2006); *see generally* John M. Gowdy, *Behavioral Economics and Climate Change Policy*, 68 J. ECON. BEHAVIOR & ORG. 632 (2008) (arguing that assuming actors are rational is a seriously flawed way to look at climate change).

97. PEW OCEANS COMMISSION, AMERICA'S LIVING OCEANS: CHARTING A COURSE FOR SEA CHANGE 6 (2003), http://www.pewtrusts.org/~/media/Assets/2003/06/02/POC_Summary.pdf; Arthur Charpentier, *Insurability of Climate Risks*, 33 THE GENEVA PAPERS 91, 103 (2008) (the value at risk in the United States' coastal zone increased 69% between 1993 and 1998).

Flood Risk Information Resources from FEMA

To help property owners understand the flood risks to which they are exposed, FEMA has created an extensive set of resources at its public outreach website, floodsmart.gov. The website provides information on flood risks, flood safety, and the availability of flood insurance policies under the NFIP.

FEMA also maintains the Map Service Center, an official online public resource for flood mapping. Through the Map Service Center's online tools, property owners can enter their addresses and explore their flood risk.

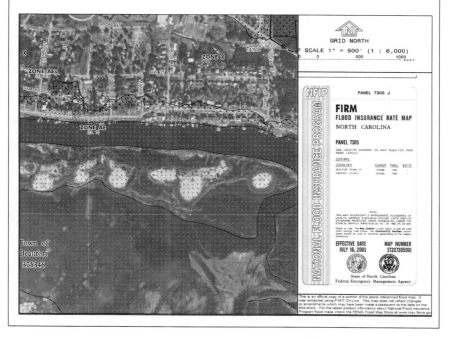

values show that property owners derive a high utility from coastal living, which they must trade off against the risks of loss from inundation, risk of loss from storm impacts, and other perceived costs of living at the coast. However, federal programs that serve to lessen the blow of losses from natural disasters can tip the balance in favor of living at the coast.

Property owners who have a much higher value for living at the coast will be willing to bear a higher risk of loss from flooding, and the risk of loss will have a significant impact on the decision of where to live. For very small loss probabilities, current population trends suggest that people will always choose to locate at the coast, meaning that signals, such as continued insurance subsidies, that lead consumers to underestimate their risk will serve to exacerbate the problem of inefficient risk-bearing on the coast. This is particularly problematic when the perceived probability of loss is not the same as the true probability of flood damage. The role of the probability of loss due to flooding and the differences in value will also have a significant impact on the decision of where to live. A property owner who systematically underestimates his risk of flood loss will correspondingly overestimate his utility from living in a flood zone.

Beyond the decision of where to live, the millions of Americans who already own property in the coastal zone must decide whether to purchase insurance through the NFIP and whether they need additional private disaster coverage. A property owner gains two major advantages from the purchase of insurance. First, the property owner is able to obtain financial indemnification for any flood loss he may experience. Second, the property owner will gain increased utility from the peace of mind of having insurance. The cost of insurance to the property owner is only the premiums that he pays to maintain the insurance coverage.

In general, the purchase of insurance will alter the value of a property: the premium cost is added for cases where the insurance is not collected, and the payout is added in the case of flood loss. In any given year, the probability of flood loss may be low. Because insurance is underwritten on an annual basis, the property owner will only purchase insurance when the peace of mind that he gains from having the insurance is greater than the difference in value from purchasing the insurance. This suggests that the perception of risk is essential to the decision to purchase insurance.[98]

When considering the efficiency of the flood insurance market, the primary concern is factors that induce consumers to go uninsured when they should purchase insurance. Tax credits and Stafford Disaster Relief both lessen the total value of the loss faced by an uninsured property owner and will therefore induce the consumer to bear a risk that he should not. Specifically, both tax credits and Stafford Disaster Relief will reduce the total value of the loss sustained by the property owner in the case of a flood loss. If the major disutility from living in the coastal zone is the risk of losing the property in

---

98. *See* Howard Kunreuther, *Disaster Mitigation and Insurance: Learning from Katrina*, 604 ANNALS AM. ACAD. POL. & SOC. SCIENCE 208, 212 (2006) (arguing that people either don't understand or willfully ignore probabilities of disaster loss).

a flood event, then these programs, which lessen the total loss suffered by the property owner, will significantly impact the decision of where to live. Both forms of relief subject the property owner to less risk from living in the coastal zone than he actually experiences. Thus, property owners will be artificially induced to live at the coast, resulting in overinvestment in coastal property.

As detailed above, the NFIP is widely recognized to heavily subsidize flood insurance premiums through direct subsidies, grandfathering, and a general failure to set actuarially sound premiums that accurately reflect flood risk. The degree of insurance subsidy therefore has the potential to lead to more than the socially efficient level of risk bearing. If insurance is cheaply available, it will increase property owners' peace of mind and encourage them to bear a risk they are unaware of. The higher the level of insurance subsidy, the more it will distort the level of risk bearing by coastal property owners.

This analysis suggests that in order to reduce coastal vulnerability by decreasing hazard exposure, reform of the National Flood Insurance Program should begin with the elimination of insurance subsidies and conditioning eligibility for other forms of federal relief on the purchase of flood insurance (or enforcing such conditions that already exist) so that these programs will not induce property owners to live at the coast or go uninsured when their true risk preferences would lead them to behave otherwise.

State Insurance Regulations and Reinsurance Programs

States play several important roles in disaster insurance and relief. States currently act as insurance regulators, and in this capacity may play a significant role in influencing the availability of insurance for privately provided insurance products. Because of their desire to maintain low insurance premiums, states are extensively involved in reinsurance markets for coastal hazards such as wind and hurricanes. Under the current system of federal flood insurance, states do not provide reinsurance, but they do have significant involvement in the system by providing additional sources of relief from flood damage, fostering development in Coastal Barrier Resources Act communities, and by exercising zoning authority in the coastal zone. Bagstad et al. provide an interesting discussion of the various sources of subsidy for coastal development given by the states.[99]

---

99. *See generally* Bagstad et al., *supra* note 88.

The Coastal Barrier Resources Act

The Coastal Barrier Resources Act ("CBRA") was an initial attempt to send a market signal to property owners in hazard prone areas: It declares that some areas are too hazard-prone to be eligible for federal funds. Communities covered by the CBRA are ineligible for NFIP insurance and Stafford Disaster Relief as well as general federal funds for infrastructure.[100] They will also be ineligible for the specific tax credits available for federally declared disaster areas, but will still be able to claim uninsured property losses as standard casualty losses on their federal income taxes.[101] However, some CBRA communities have become so developed as to be indistinguishable from neighboring communities that do not face similar restrictions.[102]

Research into what drives these patterns of development reveals that the CBRA is not a major inhibitor of coastal development. In fact, the GAO found that the most important factors limiting development in CBRA communities were (1) lack of developable land; (2) lack of accessibility of the barrier island; (3) state laws discouraging development in coastal areas; and (4) ownership of CBRA land by conservation groups.[103] In those CBRA communities where development has occurred, it is driven by commercial interest and public desire to build, local government support for development, and the availability of affordable private flood insurance.[104] In these communities state funding tends to replace the federal funding forbidden by the CBRA.[105] This result suggests that, in general, states find that their revenues from coastal development and the associated residency and tourism outweigh the costs of replacing federal funding for development and rebuilding. However, the fact that these state

---

100. 44 C.F.R. § 71.3.

101. *See supra* notes 85–88 and accompanying text.

102. David Salvesen, *The Coastal Barrier Resources Act: Has It Discouraged Coastal Development?*, 33 COASTAL MGMT. 181, 189 (2005); *see also* Rutherford H. Platt, David Salvesen & George H. Baldwin, *Rebuilding the North Carolina Coast After Hurricane Fran: Did Public Regulations Matter?*, 30 COASTAL MGMT. 249, 259–61 (2002) (noting that redevelopment in Topsail Island, a CBRA community, after Hurricane Fran was fueled by the availability of disaster relief fund and that CBRA regulations have failed to slow development).

103. U.S. GOV'T ACCOUNTABILITY OFF., GAO-07-356, COASTAL BARRIER RESOURCES SYSTEM: STATUS OF DEVELOPMENT THAT HAS OCCURRED AND FINANCIAL ASSISTANCE PROVIDED BY FEDERAL AGENCIES 1 (2007).

104. *Id.* at 4.

105. Salvesen, *supra* note 102, at 189 (finding that state policies and demand for development were more important drivers of development in CBRA communities).

subsidies are profitable in the short run does not mean that they lead to an efficient level of risk bearing.

The degree of state relief has the potential to induce property owners to bear more risk than they otherwise would. In essence, states that provide supplemental disaster relief have stepped in to fill the void left by federal government relief and, therefore, the CBRA has failed to induce the targeted change in risk-bearing behavior.[106] Note that the decision to live at the coast is once again influenced by the perceived risk of loss. As before, property owners who systematically underestimate their risk of flood loss will be more likely to move to the coast than those who correctly perceive the risks of flood loss.

There are two interesting lessons from the CBRA communities. The first is that the federal attempt to use market signals to limit development is ineffective either because consumers do not receive those market signals, property owners value property enough to pay market rates for insurance or bear the risk of living there, or states undercut the intended market signal of the CBRA through local aid. All of these explanations suggest that any modification to the National Flood Insurance Program to increase accessibility to send market signals about flood hazards must account for the potentially conflicting policies of states and adopt reforms that result in a coherent policy across levels of government to increase adaptive capacity.

Second, the CBRA communities reveal the significant role of behavioral economics in the decision to live on the coast, which is discussed in more detail below. Despite the best efforts of the federal government to signal that these areas are too risky to live in and the high private premiums charged for insurance, property owners continue to choose to live in CBRA communities. This leads to three possible conclusions: (1) CBRA homeowners systematically underestimate their risk of flood loss; (2) CBRA homeowners are properly informed of the risk, but place such a high value on living at the coast (or derive such a large revenue stream from renting their coastal property) that the short-term benefits outweigh the risks; or (3) CBRA homeowners believe that if they were to be struck by a natural disaster, the government would bail them out.[107] All of these explanations are plausible and may apply to different homeowners in these communities. What this

---

106. *Id.*

107. Raymond J. Burby, *Hurricane Katrina and the Paradoxes of Government Disaster Policy: Bringing About Wise Governmental Decisions for Hazardous Areas*, 604 ANNALS AM. ACAD. POL. & SOC. SCIENCE 171, 172 (2006); Kunreuther & Pauly, *supra* note 96, at 102, 106.

clearly reveals is the great difficulty that the federal government or private insurers will face in sending price signals to coastal homeowners that lead to a socially efficient level of risk bearing.

State Involvement in Hazard Insurance Markets

As mentioned above, states have the authority to regulate the operation of the insurance industry within their territory. State regulations typically take the form of both solvency requirements and premium regulation.[108] In general, states make the policy decision that in order to encourage constituents to purchase insurance, premiums should be kept as low as possible.[109] As explained above, state limitations on premiums may have the effect of driving insurers out of the market because they are unable to transfer enough of their risk through the purchase of reinsurance. Consequently, states wishing to maintain low insurance premiums in the face of hazard exposure run the risk that insurers will opt out of the market. To respond to this threat, states have become increasingly involved in insurance markets, both by providing direct insurance for specific coastal hazards that would otherwise be uninsured and by acting as a reinsurer for private insurance companies.

The most significant state reinsurance program is the Florida Hurricane Catastrophe Fund. After Hurricane Andrew made landfall in 1992, a number of insurers indicated their intent to stop selling policies in Florida so that they could avoid exposure to hurricane losses.[110] Finding a "compelling state interest" in maintaining an orderly system of property insurance, the state legislature intervened to provide the assurance private insurers needed to stay in the Florida market.[111] This assurance came in the form of the Florida Hurricane Catastrophe Fund, a tax-exempt trust fund that the state may use to provide reinsurance to those companies providing property insurance in Florida.[112] The fund is intended to ensure insurance availability by providing reinsurance to those companies underwriting policies in Florida.[113] In addition, the Fund created a "temporary

---

108. WHARTON RISK MANAGEMENT & DECISION PROCESSES CENTER, *supra* note 4, at 21.

109. *See id.* at 21–31.

110. David Adams, *Hurricane Season and Florida's Insurance System: Living on Borrowed Time?*, INSURANCE JOURNAL (June 3, 2013), http://www.insurancejournal.com/news/southeast/2013/06/03/294104.htm.

111. 2009 FLA. STAT. § 215.555 (2014).

112. *Id.*

113. *Id.*

emergency program" for the 2007 to 2009 hurricane seasons to alleviate problems with insurance availability due to "market disruptions."[114] The temporary emergency program extended additional amounts of reinsurance coverage to primary insurers so that homeowner's coverage would still be available.[115]

Money in the Fund primarily comes from premiums that are paid by insurance companies purchasing reinsurance.[116] In the event that these premiums do not raise enough money to cover the state's liabilities, the state also has the ability to raise money for the Fund by issuing revenue bonds.[117] By statute, the legislature is supposed to make an annual withdrawal from the Hurricane Catastrophe Fund in an amount between $10 million and 35% of the total value of the Fund to support improved hurricane preparedness.[118]

The Florida Hurricane Catastrophe Fund represents a significant intervention by the state to keep insurance premiums low. What's more, the risks that the state has assumed through the program are enormous. In 2009, the Hurricane Catastrophe Fund was estimated to have assets of $7.7 billion.[119] However, the state estimates that the Fund could need as much as $23 billion to cover future hurricane losses.[120] The consequence of this funding gap is that the state could be forced to borrow money or face bankruptcy in the event of a major hurricane.[121] The state ultimately projected a shortfall of over $18 billion for the 2009 hurricane season and sought a letter of credit from the federal government in order to avoid insolvency in the event of a major storm.[122] Florida's financial situation with respect to hurricane exposures has improved substantially since 2009 due to a lack of landfalling hurricanes. In fact, the 2015 Annual Report for the Florida Hurricane Catastrophe Fund explains that after nine seasons without a landfalling hurricane, the Fund has accumulated a $10.94 billion balance and an additional $2 billion in proceeds. However, the Annual Report concludes that the Fund "might still need to rely on emergency

---

114. *Id.* §215.555(16).

115. *Id.*

116. *Id.* §215.555(5).

117. *Id.* §215.555(6).

118. *Id.* §215.555(7).

119. *State Board of Administration of Florida: Florida Hurricane Catastrophe Fund*, Florida Legislature's Office of Program Policy Analysis & Government Accountability, http://www.oppaga.state.fl.us/profiles/4042/ (last updated May 26, 2015).

120. *Id.*

121. *See* Brandon Larrabee, *Hurricane Fund Comes Up Billions Short*, The Florida Times-Union, Apr. 15, 2009, http://jacksonville.com/news/florida/2009-02-10/story/hurricane_fund_comes_up_billions_short.

122. *Id.*

assessments and post-event bonding capabilities to pay claims if a storm or storms of sufficient size impacted Florida."[123]

In addition, Florida faces other storm risk exposure through the Citizens Property Insurance Corporation ("Citizens"), a state-backed insurance provider that writes primary policies for homeowners who can't obtain insurance in the private market.[124] Consequently, the state is doubly involved in insurance activities that subsidize the costs of living in coastal hazard zones. These activities both expose the state as a whole to insolvency and eliminate the potential for private insurance policies to communicate risks of hazard to property owners.

In addition to Florida's wind coverage through Citizens, several other hurricane-prone states maintain state wind insurance pools. These states include Alabama, Mississippi, Texas, Georgia, South Carolina, and North Carolina.[125] Wind pools are state-backed associations that provide insurance coverage for wind-storm damages in cases where such coverage is not available on the private market. Typically, a wind pool collects money to pay claims from both subsidized premiums charged to homeowners and assessments charged to insurers operating in the state. Insurers will usually be charged for the shortfall (the insurance subsidy the state is providing) as a pro rata share equal to their share of the property insurance market in the state. However, wind pools are not perfect, and they pose substantial potential liabilities for the state. As the value of property at the coast and storm hazards both increase, wind pools are sure to grow in popularity. This is significant because wind pools will impose increasing strain on the financial solvency of coastal states that employ them. Wind pools also provide subsidized insurance to coastal property owners, and will therefore have the same impact on risk perceptions discussed above.

Overall, the increasing state involvement in providing reinsurance and insurance in high-hazard areas is concerning for several reasons. First, as dis-

---

123. FLORIDA STATE BOARD OF ADMINISTRATION, FLORIDA HURRICANE CATASTROPHE FUND: ANNUAL REPORT OF AGGREGATE NET PROBABLE MAXIMUM LOSSES, FINANCING OPTIONS, AND POTENTIAL ASSESSMENTS 3 (2015), http://www.sbafla.com/fhcf/Portals/5/Reports/20150123_2015_PML_Rpt.pdf.

124. *About Us*, CITIZENS PROPERTY INSURANCE CORPORATION, https://www.citizens-fla.com/ (last visited Feb. 28, 2016).

125. *See* ALABAMA INSURANCE UNDERWRITING ASSOCIATION, https://aiua.org; MISSISSIPPI WINDSTORM UNDERWRITING ASSOCIATION, http://www.msplans.com/mwua/; *About US*, TEXAS WINDSTORM INSURANCE ASSOCIATION, http://www.twia.org/about-us; *About GUA*, GEORGIA UNDERWRITING ASSOCIATION, GEORGIA FAIR PLAN, http://georgiaunderwriting.com/informationBulletin.pdf; *About Us*, SOUTH CAROLINA WIND & HAIL UNDERWRITING ASSOCIATION, http://www.scwind.com/about.html; NORTH CAROLINA INSURANCE UNDERWRITING ASSOCIATION, http://www.ncjua-nciua.org.

cussed above, it can create significant threats to state solvency in the event of a large disaster. Second, it eliminates the possibility that the private insurance market can send property owners signals regarding the level of risk they face living in high-hazard areas. This means not only will market forces be unable to move people from the coastal zone in the face of climate change threats but also that there is an increasing potential for lock-in. The potential for lock-in comes from the fact that the above-described state programs perpetuate property owner expectations that (1) the coastal zone is a safe place to live and (2) the government will bail property owners out in the event of a natural hazard loss. Finally, if there is any entity that is truly "too big to fail" and potentially require a federal government bailout, it is a state government. The risk of requiring a federal bailout is particularly high when states assume such large potential risks because most states are legally required to maintain balanced budgets.[126] In sum, state involvement in reinsurance markets increases the exposure of both state and federal governments *and* is likely to encourage risk-assuming behavior by coastal property owners.

Local Zoning Authority

The most central role of states in reducing coastal vulnerability to flooding is in their exercise of zoning authority. Zoning authority is typically exercised at the local level and is central to the flood risk problem because it initially determines who may live in a hazard area and what sort of mitigation measures they must implement.[127] As mentioned above, the National Flood Insurance

---

126. For a summary of state balanced budget requirements, *see State Balanced Budget Requirements: Executive Summary*, National Conference of State Legislatures (Apr. 12, 1999), http://www.ncsl.org/research/fiscal-policy/state-balanced-budget-requirements.aspx.

127. Zoning authority is vested in the states through the Tenth Amendment of the Constitution, which reserves for the states all authority not explicitly granted to the federal government. U.S. Const. amend. X. By and large, states delegate their authority over zoning to local jurisdictions through state constitutions, by statute, or through the common law. Robert C. Ellickson & Vicki L. Been, Land Use Controls Cases And Materials 104-10 (3d ed. 2005). The scope of state, and consequently local government, regulatory authority is determined by the "police power," which permits the state to act to protect public health, safety, and the general welfare. *Id.* Zoning authority is simply one component of the police power, which is generally delegated to local jurisdictions. Village of Euclid v. Ambler Realty Co., 272 U.S. 365, 396–97 (1926). This delegation arises largely from the judgment that local governments are better able to determine what is in the interest of their constituents. *See generally id.* (discussing holdings of state courts that generally find municipal governments are best enabled to make judgments on behalf of and provide services to their constituents). It should be noted, however, that things are sometimes a bit differ-

Program currently contains provisions that allow communities to obtain lower flood insurance premiums upon the adoption of zoning measures that reduce the risk of flood loss.[128] However, remarkably few communities have taken advantage of this opportunity to reduce their premiums.[129]

The zoning role of states and municipalities reveals a fundamental tension between the federal and state governments resulting from the current structure of flood insurance. In general, states will derive most of the benefit from permissive coastal zoning. These benefits will be both political and economic. However, losses in these areas due to natural disasters will largely be borne by the federal government and private insurers. As states and municipalities do not have to internalize the financial risks of overly permissive zoning in the coastal zone, they will not have the proper incentives to assume the political costs of imposing restrictive zoning measures.[130]

It should, however, be noted that even if local zoning measures are permissive of coastal development, thereby increasing exposure to flood hazards, this exposure is somewhat offset by FEMA building regulations. Within special flood hazard areas, local building codes must conform to FEMA minimum standards in order for the community to maintain its eligibility for flood insurance.[131]

Most significant among these standards is FEMA's adoption of a base flood elevation, which is the height above sea level at which flooding will be experienced not more than once every one hundred years. Once base flood elevation is set, all new construction must be built above this elevation by either elevating the land or building the house on stilts.[132] The base flood elevation requirement is a significant means of reducing vulnerability, particularly when

---

ent in the coastal zone. As a result of the Coastal Zone Management Act and state-level concerns about the protection of coastal resources, many coastal states have adopted state policies that provide overarching guidance for coastal development. *See, e.g.,* CAL. PUB. RES. CODE §§ 30000 et seq.; TEX NAT. RES. CODE Chs. 61, 63; N.C. GEN. STAT. § 113A. In most states adopting such coastal management statutes, the arrangement is a partnership between the state and local governments, where state standards provide a framework for local coastal plans. *See* CAL. PUB. RES. CODE § 30001.5(e); N.C. GEN. STAT. § 113A-101.

128. 42 U.S.C. § 4022(b).

129. THE HEINZ CENTER, *supra* note 6, at 50.

130. *See* Martin F. Grace & Richard D. Phillips, *The Allocation of Governmental Regulatory Authority: Federalism and the Case of Insurance Regulation,* 74 J. RISK & INSURANCE 207, 210 (2007); *see also* John R. Nolon, *Disaster Mitigation Through Land Use Strategies,* 23 PACE ENVTL. L. REV. 959, 965 (2006) (noting the need to integrate local land use decision making with federal disaster response planning).

131. 44 C.F.R. § 59.2.

132. *Id.*

local governments are overly permissive in allowing new coastal development. For example, in Hurricane Ike the greater Galveston area experienced twelve feet of flooding. This flooding completely wiped out older, unelevated houses along the Bolivar Peninsula, while the new elevated construction along West Galveston Island was relatively undamaged.[133]

Applying Behavioral Economics to the Decision to Purchase Insurance

The NFIP has been roundly criticized for the shortcomings described above, and many scholars advocate the privatization of flood insurance. The arguments for privatization are based on the idea that actuarially sound insurance premiums have the ability to send a market signal to slow coastal development.[134] However, there is ample evidence that people tend to have a difficult time understanding their individual risks, and therefore will be likely to underpurchase insurance.[135] This tendency to underpurchase insurance is likely to be exacerbated in the private market, where insurance rates will almost certainly be higher and there is the potential that there would not be a legal mandate to obtain flood coverage. As a result, the privatization of flood insurance would increase vulnerability because property owners are likely to continue investing in the coast for the behavioral economic reasons discussed below and lower uptake rates of insurance will decrease resilience to natural hazards.

Empirical studies show that individuals tend to underestimate risks that have low probabilities.[136] As a result, in the private market, property that is at risk of suffering disaster losses will tend to be underinsured.[137] A report by the Wharton School of Business found that in coastal states, the demand for property insurance is nearly unit elastic, meaning that increases in insurance rates, which will certainly happen with privatization, will be accompanied by corresponding declines in the level of insurance coverage.[138] This is coupled with the Natural Disaster Syndrome, a label given to the propensity of individuals in hazard

---

133. Interview with Local Government Official (Nov. 16, 2009).

134. *See generally* Justin R. Pidot, Coastal Disaster Insurance in the Era of Global Warming: The Case for Relying on the Private Market (2007).

135. Kunreuther & Pauly, *supra* note 96, at 103.

136. *Id.*

137. *Id.*

138. Wharton Risk Management & Decision Processes Center, *supra* note 4, at 219.

prone areas to not adopt mitigation measures in advance of a natural disaster and instead rely upon ex post bailouts from the federal government.[139]

In addition to the Natural Disaster Syndrome, the behavior of individuals living in flood zones is influenced by what Burby calls the Safe Development Paradox.[140] Building upon the work of Kydland & Prescott, Burby argues that property owners choose to live in flood zones because they believe that if enough people choose to live in flood zones, then the government will be forced to undertake measures to protect them.[141] That is, the Safe Development Paradox explicitly recognizes a particular type of moral hazard that has arisen from our current system of flood disaster relief; because the government has consistently subsidized risk-taking behavior in the context of regional flood-ing, property owners may have a strong subjective belief that such protections will continue and that there are not great risks associated with living in a flood zone. Stafford Grants and tax credits under our current flood relief system and historic protective activities of the Army Corps, such as levee construction and beach nourishment, have reinforced the perceptions that shape the Safe De-velopment Paradox.[142]

Behavioral economics factors may thus have a significant impact on the risk tradeoffs that coastal property owners make. If property owners systematically underestimate their risk of flood loss, then many more property owners will live at the coast than would do so if their risk perceptions were accurate. That is, an artificially low perception of flood risk will reduce the expected value of flood losses leading consumers to bear risks that they would not if they knew their true risk of flood loss. If the property owner truly believes that his risk of loss is extremely low, the peace of mind he gains from purchasing insur-ance will also be substantially reduced. In fact, according to empirical research on risk perception, it appears that the peace of mind utility will likely go to zero, meaning that the property owner will perceive no benefit from the pur-chase of flood insurance.[143]

---

139. Kunreuther, *supra* note 98, at 208.

140. Burby, *supra* note 107, at 172.

141. *Id.* at 176–77.

142. Pompe & Rinehart, *supra* note 6, at 199. *See also* Kunreuther & Pauly, *supra* note 96, at 105 (showing that individuals are less likely to purchase disaster relief when they be-lieve that they can obtain alternative forms of flood relief).

143. WHARTON RISK MANAGEMENT & DECISION PROCESSES CENTER, *supra* note 4, at 129–33; Kunreuther & Pauly, *supra* note 96, at 103 (finding that individual property own-ers tend to believe their own risk of experiencing being harmed by a natural disaster is near zero).

While these behavioral factors will be in play regardless of who provides flood insurance, their impacts are likely to be particularly acute in a private insurance market. In the private market, premiums must rise to their actuarially fair levels in order for insurance companies to remain viable. If premiums rise and consumers systematically underestimate their risk of loss, they will be less inclined to purchase flood insurance. The disaster preparedness and response dynamics considered above indicate that the insurance market is likely to be unable to deliver market signals about risk to consumers because of their systematic underestimation of risk. As a result, increasing premiums to the proper value will result in lower levels of insurance coverage. This effect will be particularly severe as long as tax breaks for rebuilding and Stafford Disaster Relief continue to be available, as these programs make insurance coverage less valuable to homeowners. Therefore, in order for the privatization of flood insurance to work, the federal government will need to eliminate other forms of flood relief and maintain and enforce a statutory requirement that homeowners carry flood insurance.

Part of the reason that the requirement for insurance coverage is necessary is that many property owners will otherwise choose to forgo insurance coverage and self-insure. As mentioned above, fewer than 1% of homeowners who are eligible for, but not required to purchase, insurance from the NFIP actually buy it.[144] It is unclear what portion of property owners who do not purchase flood insurance think they are covered under other policies and what portion genuinely choose to self-insure. However, there are certainly some property owners who forgo insurance because they believe that they are better off self-insured. For example citizens in Cape Cod have objected to FEMA's proposed changes to rate maps that would require them to buy insurance because they believe, based on experience, that they are better off going uninsured.[145] Furthermore, it should be noted that many of these property owners are not fully self-insured because they are able to receive federal disaster benefits in the form of tax credits, and sometimes, Stafford Disaster Relief.

---

144. *Williams Testimony re NFIP, supra* note 25, at 3.

145. Patrick Cassidy, *Cape Coastal Coverage Bills Face Big Jump,* Cape Cod Times, June 2, 2009, http://www.capecodonline.com/apps/pbcs.dll/article?AID=/20090602/NEWS/906020321.

Opportunities to Facilitate Climate Change Adaptation

There are numerous opportunities to facilitate climate change adaptation through improved implementation of or reforms to the existing disaster relief and hazard insurance scheme described above. Over time, the use of Stafford Disaster Relief and the history of recent attempts to reform the NFIP have demonstrated the political importance of the programs. In fact, several studies have found clear relationships between the electoral competitiveness of a state, presidential election cycles, and the number of disaster declarations.[146] Therefore, the analysis that follows assumes that the current disaster relief and flood insurance system will remain in place due to its political expediency and explores opportunities for facilitating climate change adaptation within existing legal frameworks.

Using Grant Programs to Reduce Hazard Exposure

There are two significant grant programs administered under the Stafford Disaster Relief Act to encourage communities to adopt hazard mitigation measures: the Hazard Mitigation Grant Program ("HMGP") and the Pre-Disaster Mitigation ("PDM") Grant Program. HMGP funds are available to communities to implement hazard mitigation projects in the aftermath of a natural disaster.[147] In contrast, PDM funds are available to implement mitigation measures before disaster losses occur. Described in more detail below, these programs provide important opportunities to reduce the vulnerability to coastal communities to future disaster losses.

The HMGP authorizes FEMA to provide funding to state and local governments to implement eligible mitigation projects in the aftermath of a natural disaster.[148] These programs can include the acquisition of high-hazard properties for conversion to open space.[149] The goal of the program is to encourage communities that have been struck by a major disaster to recover from that

---

146. James M. Chen, *Legal Signal Processing: A Polynomial and Periodic Model of Presidential Disaster Declarations Under the Stafford Act* (2015); Andrew Reeves, *Political Disaster: Unilateral Powers, Electoral Power, and Presidential Disaster Declarations*, 73 J. POLITICS 1142, 1142 (2011).

147. 42 U.S.C. § 5170c.

148. *Id.*

149. 44 C.F.R. § 206.434.

disaster in a way that reduces risk to people and property from future disasters.[150] To this end, the program funds projects that provide long-term solutions as opposed to short-term relief.[151] An eligible project might be, for example, the elevation of a home to reduce future flood damage. In contrast, a project to sandbag a home to fight the immediate impacts of a flood would not qualify.

HMGP funding is only available to a state after the President declares a major disaster in the state.[152] In order to receive HMGP funds, state, local, and tribal governments are required to have approved mitigation plans in place.[153] A state can choose to submit either a standard mitigation plan or an enhanced mitigation plan, the latter of which allows the state to receive a greater amount of HMGP funding.[154] Among other things, a hazard mitigation plan must include (1) a risk assessment identifying the state's vulnerability to potential natural hazards and the potential losses that may result; (2) a mitigation strategy describing specific policies, programs, and mitigation activities as well as available funding; and (3) a description of the state's plan for monitoring and evaluating implementation of the plan.[155] Enhanced hazard mitigation plans must also demonstrate how they are integrated with other state and FEMA hazard mitigation initiatives as well as demonstrate the state's commitment to a comprehensive hazard mitigation program.[156] For both standard and enhanced plans, the plan must be revised and resubmitted every three years.[157] When the hazard mitigation grant applicant is a local government (rather than a state), the local hazard mitigation plan must contain the same types of information, but with a greater level of detail in several respects, including a description of key infrastructure and buildings in critical hazard areas.[158]

The amount of funds that will be available to a state or local government under the HMGP will depend upon the amount of disaster funding approved for the disaster that triggered the availability of post-disaster mitigation funds.[159] Federal HMGP funds only cover part of the costs of any proposed

---

150. FEMA, Hazard Mitigation Assistance Unified Guidance 2 (2013) [hereinafter 2013 Unified Guidance].
151. 44 C.F.R. §206.434(c)(5)(iv).
152. 42 U.S.C. §5170(a).
153. 44 C.F.R. §§201.4(a), 201.5(a)(1), 201.6(a)(1).
154. *Id.* §201.5(a).
155. *Id.* §201.4(c).
156. *Id.* §201.5(b).
157. *Id.* §§201.4(d), 201.5(c)(2).
158. *Id.* §201.6(c).
159. *Id.* §206.432.

disaster mitigation project (the so called "federal share"), and states and local governments are required to provide some level of matching funds in order to receive grants under the HMGP.[160] For disasters declared on or after June 10, 1993, the federal share under the HMGP is not to exceed 75%.[161]

The Stafford Disaster Relief Act also authorizes the Pre-Disaster Mitigation Grant Program, which provides "technical and financial assistance to States and local governments to assist in the implementation of predisaster hazard mitigation measures that are cost-effective and are designed to reduce injuries, loss of life, and damage and destruction of property...."[162] The PDM grant application process relies on applicants—states, territories, and tribal governments—submitting and ranking subapplications for specific projects submitted by state or tribal agencies or local communities within their jurisdiction.[163] In 2014, $63 million was allocated under the PDM program.[164] While over half of this amount was to be distributed evenly among states, territories, and federally recognized tribal governments, the remainder of the funds were to be distributed on a competitive basis.[165] The grants awarded through the PDM program allow FEMA to provide up to 75% of total eligible costs for a project (though "small impoverished communities" may receive up to 90% cost share),[166] up to $3 million for mitigation projects, $800,000 for new mitigation plans, and $300,000 for mitigation plan updates in 2014.[167]

In addition to the grant programs available under the Stafford Disaster Relief Act, FEMA administers the Flood Mitigation Assistance Program, which focuses on reducing repetitive-loss properties under the NFIP program. Like the PDM program, applicants—states, territories, and tribal governments— submit and rank subapplications for specific mitigation activities submitted by state or tribal agencies or local communities within their jurisdiction.[168] Properties that are the subject of a subapplication must be NFIP-insured and maintain flood insurance both throughout the completion of the mitigation activity as well as for the life of the structure.[169] Federal cost share is generally

---

160. *Id.*

161. *Id.*

162. 42 U.S.C. § 5133(b).

163. *See* FEMA, Fact Sheet: FY 2014 Pre-Disaster Mitigation (PDM) Grant Program 2–3 [hereinafter PDM Fact Sheet].

164. *Id.* at 1.

165. *Id.*

166. 2013 Unified Guidance, *supra* note 150, at 87.

167. PDM Fact Sheet, *supra* note 163, at 2.

168. 2013 Unified Guidance, *supra* note 150, at 89.

169. *Id.*

up to 75% under the program, though mitigation activities related to repetitive loss structures may be funded up to 90%, and mitigation activities related to severe repetitive loss structures may be funded up to 100%.[170] However, to receive the increased cost-share levels, the property that is the subject of the subapplication must be covered by a FEMA-approved Standard or Enhanced Mitigation Plan that includes a repetitive loss strategy.[171]

Each of these grant programs provides important opportunities for sea level rise adaptation in the form of flood hazard mitigation if state and local governments choose to take advantage of them. These programs can provide needed funds to encourage state and local governments to engage in hazard mitigation activities. Further investigation of the effectiveness of these incentives is likely needed, as state and local governments with constrained budgets and competing priorities may find that the resources required to create enhanced mitigation plans are not justified by the possibility of additional grant funding in the future. However, to the extent that state and local governments can be properly incentivized to engage in comprehensive hazard mitigation planning that incorporates local zoning and land use planning, such planning provides an important opportunity to implement adaptation measures.

The Federal Flood Risk Management Standard

On January 30, 2015, President Obama signed Executive Order 13690, which calls for the establishment of a federal flood risk management standard.[172] The Executive Order specifically notes that climate change is expected to increase losses due to flooding and says it is the policy of the United States to improve the resilience of communities to the impacts of flooding.[173] The Executive Order calls upon federal agencies to revise their current floodplain management regulations to make them consistent with the Federal Flood Risk Management Standard.[174]

The Federal Flood Risk Management Standard is an outgrowth of the federal process to facilitate long-term response to Superstorm Sandy. In the aftermath of Superstorm Sandy, President Obama signed an Executive Order creating the Hurricane Sandy Rebuilding Task Force to ensure cabinet-level

---

170. *Id.* at 90.
171. *Id.* at 89–90.
172. Exec. Order No. 13690, 80 Fed. Reg. 6425 (Feb. 4, 2015).
173. *Id.*
174. *Id.*

and government-wide coordination to assist local communities making decisions about rebuilding.[175] The Task Force produced the Hurricane Sandy Rebuilding Strategy, which recommended that the federal government establish a national flood risk standard that would be applicable to all federally funded projects.[176] As a result, the Mitigation Framework Leadership Group—an interagency working group chaired by FEMA—developed the Federal Flood Risk Management standard in 2014. Through FEMA, the Group subsequently released guidelines for the implementation of the Flood Risk Management Standard for public comment in early 2015.[177]

The Federal Flood Risk Management Standard applies to all federal actions—including direct federal activities and federally financed or assisted construction improvements—that are located in or will affect floodplains.[178] The Federal Flood Risk Management Standard encourages the use of natural features and ecosystem-based approaches for flood risk management, provides a higher vertical flood elevation to address current and future flood risks, and defines a larger flood hazard area.[179] The elevation component applies to new construction, improvements with a value of 50% or more of the existing structure, and repairs to structures that are more than 50% damaged.[180] When the elevation component applies, it will take effect as a new minimum freeboard elevation adding on 2 to 3 feet to current base flood elevations as a safety factor.[181] Under the Federal Flood Risk Management Standard, the flood hazard area may be calculated as: (1) the area lower than base flood elevation plus 2 or 3 feet (depending on the type of structure); (2) the 500-year floodplain; or (3) the "climate-informed science approach," which incorporates the best available hydraulic and climate data to project future flood vulnerabilities.[182]

The Federal Flood Risk Management Standard will not have an impact on NFIP insurance premiums.[183] However, as agencies formulate their plans to

---

175. Exec. Order No. 13632, 77 Fed. Reg. 74,341 (Dec. 14, 2012).

176. U.S. Dep't of Hous. and Urban Dev., Hurricane Sandy Rebuilding Strategy 44 (2013).

177. 80 Fed. Reg. 6530 (Feb. 5, 2015).

178. FEMA, Federal Flood Risk Management Standard 2–3 (2015), http://www.energy.gov/sites/prod/files/2015/02/f19/FederalFloodRiskManagementStandard.pdf.

179. Id. at 5.

180. Id. at 3.

181. Id. at 8.

182. Id. at 7.

183. FEMA, Implementing a Federal Flood Risk Management Standard: Listening Session, Seattle, WA (Presentation, Apr. 24, 2015), http://www.fema.gov/media-library-data/

implement the federal flood risk management standard, they will likely engage in more active flood risk analysis, which may shape federal investment decisions. To the extent that flood risk analysis shapes federal investment decisions in areas that are vulnerable to sea level rise and storm surge, it may have spillover effects in encouraging community adaptation planning.

Improving Coordination and Enforcement in Federal Programs

Perhaps the most significant opportunities for encouraging adaptation under the existing suite of federal programs will arise from improving enforcement of existing restrictions and improving coordination across federal grant and insurance programs that seek to reduce flood hazards. Successful coordination of federal programs would require that they achieve compatibility in the spatial scales and time horizons across which they work to minimize future flood hazards.

Historically, there have been documented instances that FEMA failed to enforce limitations on insurance availability under the NFIP. For example, a 1992 GAO report concluded that many homeowners in Coastal Barrier Resources Act communities obtained NFIP policies from FEMA even though CBRA prohibited the extension of the NFIP to coastal barrier resources communities.[184] In addition, it is not clear to what extent FEMA has been able to practicably enforce prohibitions of future disaster aid when property owners fail to maintain required insurance coverage. FEMA has some enforcement authorities where there do not seem to be examples of actual enforcement. For example, the Stafford Disaster Relief Act requires that recipients of disaster aid maintain insurance coverage in an amount that is at least equal to the amount of aid they received on a going-forward basis and that any future property owners also maintain this insurance.[185] The Act provides that if a property is sold and the buyer fails to maintain the required insurance due to a lack of proper notification by the seller, FEMA could seek reimbursement from the seller in the event the buyer requires disaster aid in the future for the property that should have been insured.[186] However, there do not appear

---

1430402471245-bed33bac15e7ea001e7c763d61d98228/FFRMS_Listening_Session_Briefing_March-April_2015.pdf.

184. U.S. GEN. ACCOUNTING OFF., GAO/RCED-92-115, COASTAL BARRIERS: DEVELOPMENT OCCURRING DESPITE PROHIBITIONS AGAINST FEDERAL ASSISTANCE (1992).

185. 42 U.S.C. §5154a(b)(1).

186. *Id.* §5154a(b)(2).

to be any examples of enforcement under these provisions. While any lack of enforcement of restrictions on insurance and rebuilding assistance has the potential to exacerbate the influence of these programs on property owner decision making described above, there is not a large body of evidence indicating that there are systemic issues with ineligible property owners receiving significant amounts of aid. Thus, while improved implementation and enforcement would likely be valuable in eliminating some of the perceived incentives to maladaption, it is difficult to say how significant any improvements would be.

At present, FEMA's regulations governing Stafford aid permit it to require relocation of public facilities if they will be subject to "repetitive heavy damage" and the overall project is cost-effective.[187] However, similar relocation assistance is not available under the program's provisions for individual homeowner assistance: individual homeowners will be faced with the choice of accepting disaster aid to rebuild where they are, rejecting assistance and being excluded from disaster relief in the future, or participating in a buyout under the hazard mitigation grant program if a buyout becomes available. If hazard mitigation grant funds are not available, the disaster relief system will incentivize individual homeowners to remain where they are. This approach makes little sense if FEMA determines that key public infrastructure should be relocated to avoid repeated damage. Thus, particularly in the face of rising sea levels, improved coordination between FEMA's programs that would permit communities to take advantage of federal funds to engage in meaningful hazard reduction through retreat would provide a significant opportunity to facilitate adaptation.

Another area where coordination would be beneficial would be between community land use planning, hazard mitigation planning, and coverage under the NFIP. At present, NFIP premiums follow the typical practice of writing annual policies that are renewed each year. As a result, the system is not effective in conveying long-term risks to policyholders, and the benefits of risk mitigation measures are unlikely to be realized within a single policy cycle. This means that neither individual policyholders nor local governments will have sufficient incentives to respond to any price signals insurance premiums may have by engaging in proactive mitigation measures or comprehensive land use planning that would facilitate adaptation to rising sea levels. These mismatched incentives could be addressed by writing multi-year flood insurance policies that reflect the longer-term risks associated with sea level rise and encourage comprehensive planning for flood risk mitigation.

---

187. 44 C.F.R. §206.226(g).

Long-term premiums provide an advantage in capturing the risk of loss due to sea level rise. Scientists have established that sea level rise is happening at an increasing rate, and a longer-term premium structure, where policies are written and rates are set over multiple years, could reflect the way that risks increase over time by establishing a schedule for increasing annual payments over the lifetime of the policy. While it is true that annual premiums could also increase to reflect increasing risks, annual increases do not give individual homeowners or state and local planners the same long-term view of risk, and therefore, annual premiums may not provide the proper incentives to plan for retreat.

Long-term premiums are also likely to be more effective in encouraging the adoption of risk-mitigation measures. Many flood risk-mitigation measures will be very expensive when evaluated against a premium increase for a single year. However, a longer-term premium structure can make explicit the relative impact of the mitigation measure on premiums over time. Such a longer-term view will clarify the benefits of mitigation and give the property owner or coastal community confidence that the benefits of flood hazard mitigation are more than speculative, thereby increasing the likelihood that the property owner will undertake such mitigation.

There are two possible ways that insurers could write premiums under a multi-year structure that better communicates the long-term risk of living in the coastal zone. First, insurance premiums could be subject to an increasing rate schedule reflecting increasing premium rates over time. Under this type of a system, the specific premium could still be set on an annual basis to reflect actual risk, but premiums would increase *at minimum* by a predetermined rate schedule that extended out over a period of years. This hybrid system would eliminate the risk that an insurance provider is bound to sell insurance at rates that may be too low if climate change impacts happen more quickly than projected but still signals to consumers the increasing risk of inundation and storm surge in the coastal zone. The second method of writing long-term premiums would be to attempt to calculate the risk of total loss of the property over a longer time scale, such as the projected time until the property will be inundated, and then amortize this amount over the number of years between the current underwriting period and the time of projected total loss. In order for this latter program to be solvent, it would either have to deny the ability to rebuild or reset premiums each time a property owner rebuilds after storm damage.

Implementation of this latter method could be a challenge due to the National Flood Insurance Act's annual limits on premium increases, discussed above. The statute itself contains no limitation on the ability to write multi-year premiums, and to the contrary seems to suggest some frameworks for multi-year risk-based premium increases where a community is remapped into a higher flood risk zone. However, the NFIP's ability to pursue a forward-looking multi-year pricing structure for better integration with local land use and hazard mitigation planning will likely be limited by FEMA's resources to continually update flood maps. Depending upon how the Technical Mapping Advisory Council recommends sea level rise risk be incorporated, it is possible that FEMA could create a series of forward-looking maps based on the best available science that are to be updated every five years per statute and use these as the basis of a multi-year premium structure.

The Elephant in the Room: Compulsory National, Multiperil Insurance

Climate change hazard risks are not confined to the coastal zone. While flood and hurricane risks are prominent in the aftermath of Superstorm Sandy, climate change poses a number of other natural hazard risks, including drought and wildfires. Such perils reveal that all Americans are facing increasing hazard exposure from some sort of climate-induced impacts. As explained throughout this chapter, a critical component of insurance solvency is the coverage of risks that are not spatially and temporally correlated. The spatial and temporal correlation of floods is the precise reason that private flood insurance became unavailable and the federal government stepped in with NFIP.[188] However, if federal insurance is to be successful on a going-forward basis, it must be diversified to include hazard risks that bear no correlation to one another. As explained previously, individuals tend to underinsure against natural hazards, whether that be from underbudgeting for the cost; underestimating, dismissing, or being unable to comprehend the scope of natural disaster risk; or expecting the government to step in to stem the breach.[189]

One possible solution to this problem is the creation of a compulsory national multiperil insurance policy. Such a policy is premised on the belief that insurance markets function better when there is full coverage and risks are evenly spread. The case of hazard insurance arguably provides a "special case" analogous to many of the arguments presented in the healthcare debate. Much as the Obama Administration argued that compulsory health insurance could be required because federal law guarantees that individuals receive certain min-

---

188. 44 C.F.R. §59.2.

189. *See* Cutter, *supra* note 91, at 1–2; WHARTON RISK MANAGEMENT & DECISION PROCESSES CENTER, *supra* note 4, at 129–34.

imum health services,[190] those who experience natural disasters know that they will receive federal aid in the form of Stafford relief. While there is a key difference here in that Stafford relief remains legally discretionary, the politics of disaster relief in the United States demonstrates that Stafford relief is politically compulsory. If one assumes that Stafford relief will be made available in the aftermath of each natural disaster, it is likely desirable as a matter of public policy to have full insurance coverage for natural hazards. A national, multiperil insurance program, if actuarially sound, would provide an important means to increase resiliency to climate change, make property owners whole, and minimize the vulnerability of the national treasury to increasingly severe and frequent climate-driven disasters. This section examines the Supreme Court's opinion in *National Federation of Independent Businesses v. Sibelius*, which upheld the individual mandate for health insurance and evaluates whether it provides a similar path forward for national, multiperil natural hazard insurance.

National Federation of Independent Businesses v. Sibelius[191] was a challenge to the Patient Protection and Affordable Care Act, also referred to as the Affordable Care Act ("ACA" or "Act"). One of the elements of the law challenged in the Supreme Court was the ACA's individual mandate. The individual mandate provision requires all people to maintain certain "minimum essential [health] coverage."[192] If individuals do not receive such coverage through their employers, they are to purchase coverage on the private market.[193] The Act requires anyone who does not obtain the required health coverage to make a "[s]hared responsibility payment."[194] This payment is to be collected by the IRS at the time a person files their individual income taxes.[195] The payment is assessed as a percentage of household income, with a statutory minimum level, and is not required of those who are not otherwise required to pay federal income taxes.[196] The law further specifies that the IRS is to treat the shared responsibility payment as a tax penalty,[197] and that the IRS may not use its criminal enforcement authority to collect it.[198]

In *Sibelius*, plaintiffs challenged the individual mandate as reaching beyond Congress's enumerated powers in the Constitution. The Supreme Court re-

---

190. 26 U.S.C. §5000A.
191. 132 S. Ct. 2566 (2012)
192. 26 U.S.C. §5000A.
193. *Id.* §5000A(f).
194. *Id.* §5000A(b).
195. *Id.*
196. *Id.* §5000A(c), (d), (e).
197. *Id.* §5000A(b).
198. *Id.* §5000A(g).

jected the government's preferred position—that the individual mandate was a valid exercise of the Commerce power—finding that "[c]onstruing the Commerce Clause to permit Congress to regulate individuals precisely *because* they are doing nothing would open a new and potentially vast domain to congressional authority."[199] However, the Court upheld the individual mandate as a valid exercise of Congress's power to tax.[200] The Court found that the shared responsibility payment is an exaction that "looks like a tax in many respects": (1) it is paid to the treasury by taxpayers "when they file their tax returns"; (2) "it does not apply to individuals who do not pay federal income taxes because their household income is less than the filing threshold"; (3) "for taxpayers who do owe the payment, its amount is determined by such familiar factors as taxable income, number of dependents, and joint filing status."[201] Further, the Court concluded that its own precedent supported upholding the payment of fees under the taxation power as long as they were not so punitive as to constitute unconstitutional penalties.[202]

The Supreme Court's decision in *Sibelius* can thus be read to permit national insurance programs where an individual may opt to pay a tax penalty in lieu of purchasing insurance. Key to the Supreme Court's decision was a finding that the law was neutral as to whether an individual chooses to buy insurance or pay the penalty—that is, it is not illegal to not carry health insurance. The individual can comply with the law by choosing either the penalty or insurance coverage. Thus, to the extent that *Sibelius* may be a blueprint for other nationally required insurance programs, the programs must (1) be assessed in a manner that is consistent with the regular assessment of income taxes and (2) be neutral between the purchase of insurance and the payment of a penalty. This suggests that Congress could craft a law for national multi-peril insurance. Under such a law, property owners would be required to carry insurance for flood, wind, fire, and hurricanes, as applicable, at actuarial rates, and those failing to carry such coverage would be required to pay a tax penalty.

While it thus appears *Sibelius* may provide a template for national, multi-peril insurance, it is important to evaluate whether such a program could be Constitutionally implemented in a manner that would lead to actual risk reductions. In *Sibelius* the Supreme Court finds that one of the key elements that makes the individual mandate Constitutional is that it is administered like any other income tax program, and the amount of the shared responsibility pay-

---

199. 132 S. Ct. at 2587.
200. *Id.* at 2601.
201. *Id.* at 2594.
202. *Id.* at 2599.

ment is income-dependent. If this is a central component of *any* required insurance program implemented under Congress's power to tax,[203] it could significantly undermine a national multiperil hazard insurance program. As the NFIP demonstrates, for any federally backed hazard insurance program to be fiscally sound, premiums must be set to reflect the actual hazard risks faced by the property. If insurance premiums under a federal program were tied to actuarial rates, but the non-purchase tax penalty were tied to income, it is possible that many individuals would pay significantly less under the penalty than they would if they were to purchase insurance. If this were the case, then the solvency of any multiperil insurance program would be difficult, if not impossible, to maintain.

This raises the question of whether, in the alternative, the fee paid by those choosing not to purchase insurance could be administered as a federal property tax, accounting for the hazard zone in which the property lies. While such an approach could create a system that has stronger incentives for the purchase of insurance, it is not clear that it would be Constitutionally permissible. The Tenth Amendment reserves to the states any powers not expressly committed to Congress or the executive in the Constitution.[204] This includes the regulation on land use under the state police powers.[205] Thus, any attempt to impose a property tax-based system would raise the Constitutional question of whether the tax is a valid extension of Congress's power to tax or an unconstitutional incursion into the powers of the states. The Supreme Court has not considered this issue directly, but has invalidated several federal taxes where it found that the policy aim of the tax extended beyond the federal government's enumerated powers. For example, in *United States v. Butler* the court invalidated a tax that it concluded was intended to regulate agricultural production because it concluded that such regulation was beyond the scope of Congress's power.[206]

Another significant issue may arise in a national, multiperil insurance program if the insurance program itself is administered by the federal government. The individual mandate considered in *Sibelius* allows individuals to choose between purchasing private insurance and paying the government a

---

203. Note that the NFIP is different because it arises under the Commerce power. Individuals can avoid compulsory purchasing under the NFIP by not obtaining federally backed mortgages in flood hazard zones.

204. U.S. Const. amend. X.

205. Advisory Comm. on Zoning, U.S. Dep't of Commerce, A Standard State Zoning Enabling Act Under Which Municipalities May Adopt Zoning Regulations (rev. ed. 1926).

206. 297 U.S. 1 (1936).

penalty. If a hazard insurance program were administered by the government in a manner similar to the NFIP, the choice taxpayers would face is to purchase insurance from the government or to pay the government a penalty. While the possibility of a parallel private insurance structure exists in the natural hazard space, it likely eliminates one of the major potential benefits of national, multiperil insurance. The argument for mandatory, national, multiperil insurance is premised upon the fact that Stafford Disaster Relief is likely to flow in the aftermath of any natural hazard event. Thus, the government has strong incentives to create an insurance program that is functional and solvent in order to offset the impact to the federal deficit of disaster relief. If private insurers are responsible for the market, it seems likely we will see more behavior that is analogous to that observed in state wind pooling, and a government entity will still end up bearing most of the risk.

Conclusions

As the following chapters will explore, much of the work to facilitate adaptation to rising sea levels will fall to state and local governments who have authority over land use planning. However, state and local land use planning decisions and individual property owner behaviors (including the decision to purchase property in high-hazard areas) will be shaped by the incentive structures that are created by federal disaster relief. Under the current system of federal flood insurance and disaster relief, state and local governments will have strong incentives to be highly permissive of continued coastal development and not require expensive hazard mitigation measures because many of the risks of loss can be externalized to the federal tax base as a whole. Furthermore, the current structure of federal disaster relief programs can act as a disincentive to certain types of adaptation and may be inconsistent with long-term risk mitigation. However, existing federal grant programs do provide some opportunities to those states who wish to take advantage of them to pursue hazard mitigation measures, and improved coordination of federal and state programs could create new incentives for comprehensive, long-term flood hazard mitigation that would respond to the changing risks posed by rising seas.

Chapter 4

Key Legal Principles to Understand Sea Level Rise Adaptation

The purpose of this Chapter is to explain some of the key legal concepts that shape coastal governments' responses to sea level rise in the United States. Central to all efforts to adapt to sea level rise is the need to balance the rights of the public against those of private property owners. To understand how that balancing occurs, there are five questions that we must answer:

1. Who owns what? (the public trust doctrine)
2. What is private property anyway?
3. How does the public get access to private property along the coast?
4. What happens if the government wants to use private property? (Takings)
5. What are the practical implications of all this takings stuff?

This chapter attempts to explain the key property law concepts that answer these questions in a straightforward (and at times simplified) manner. While recognizing that some parts of the currently developed coastline are too critical to regional infrastructure to seriously contemplate abandonment at this time—for example, both the San Francisco and Oakland airports are within 16 inches at high tide and 16 inches, respectively, of sea level[1]—there are not sufficient resources available to protect the entire United States coastline from

---

1. CALIFORNIA STATE ASSEMBLY SELECT COMMITTEE SEA LEVEL RISE AND THE CALIFORNIA ECONOMY, SEA-LEVEL RISE: A SLOW-MOVING EMERGENCY 8 (2014).

the impacts of storm surge and sea level rise, and significant retreat from coastal areas will be required.[2]

If one proceeds from the assumption that at least part of our coastline will ultimately be lost to the sea, the policy challenge then becomes: How should decision makers promote measures to accommodate rising seas and ultimately require retreat from areas that will become inundated? In creating and implementing sea level rise adaptation strategies, state and local policymakers must be mindful of the property rights of individuals who own property along the coast. Under the Fifth Amendment, the federal government may not take private property for public use without providing just compensation. The Fifth Amendment also applies to the states through the Fourteenth Amendment, meaning that state governments are also forbidden from taking private property without compensation.

Who Owns What? The Public Trust Doctrine

The first key question to address when thinking about the potential need to retreat in the face of rising sea levels is who owns what? Specifically, where is the boundary line between private property and public property? As the discussion below explains, this is an essential question for sea level rise adaptation because under the doctrines originating in the common law, the boundary between public and private property is *dynamic* and moves over time. This means that in the absence of any further human interventions, the gradual inundation of coastal lands by rising seas will result in a massive shift of lands from private property to public title. The special kind of title that applies to these submerged lands is called the "public trust," and it is established by a body of common law referred to as the "public trust doctrine."

The public trust doctrine is a common law doctrine, inherited from England and dating back to Roman law, stating that all submerged lands are the property of the state and held in trust for the people.[3] In the United States, the public trust consists of both the federal navigational servitude and state-level doctrines.[4] States vary in both the geographic scope of the public trust and the

---

2. *See generally* JOHN ENGLANDER, HIGH TIDE ON MAIN STREET: RISING SEA LEVEL AND THE COMING COASTAL CRISIS (2012).

3. Shively v. Bowlby, 152 U.S. 1 (1894).

4. United States v. Rio Grande Dam & Irrigation Co., 174 U.S. 690, 703 (1899) (holding that the commerce power of the federal government vests it with the authority to take all measures, even against the state, to preserve the federal navigation servitude); *Shively* 152 U.S. at 26 (noting that there is significant variation in state public trust doctrine and

specific public trust rights that they recognize. However, the federal public trust doctrine, establishes that at minimum, the public trust protects navigation, commerce, and fishing.[5] In some states, the public trust doctrine also recognizes the right to access the dry sand beach, protection of habitats, and access for scientific research, among other things.

The boundary between public trust lands and private property is a matter of state law. States can be divided into two categories (1) mean high water states and (2) mean low water states. In nearly all cases, the relevant lines for defining the limits of private title and public access are the mean high water and mean low water marks, which are the average of high and low tides over 18.6 years.[6] The first and largest category of states are those states that recognize that private title ends and state title begins at the mean high water mark.[7] Second are those states that recognize private title to the mean low water mark but find a public trust easement over the wet sand beach.[8] While the public trust property line usually defines the extent of the public's right to access the beach, New Jersey has recognized that the public trust easement extends all the way to the first line of vegetation, covering the whole dry sand beach, while the property line still lies at the mean high water mark.[9]

The Supreme Court has recognized the public trust as a special kind of title that may not be freely given away.[10] In general, the state may only grant public trust lands to private individuals when doing so will serve a higher public purpose.[11] Further, the interest in the public trust is one that the state may not abdicate.[12] This principle was established by the Supreme Court's holding in

---

finding "[g]reat caution, therefore, is necessary in applying precedents in one State to cases arising in another.").

5. Martin v. Waddell, 41 U.S. 367, 383 (1842).

6. Borax Consol. Ltd. v. Los Angeles, 296 U.S. 10, 26–27 (1935).

7. *See, e.g.*, Connecticut v. Knowles-Lombard Co., 4 Conn. Supp. 116 (1936); Georgia v. Ashmore, 224 S.E.2d 334 (Ga. 1976); Cinque Bambini P'ship v. Mississippi, 491 So.2d 508 (Miss. 1986); Purdie v. N.H. Attorney Gen., 732 A.2d 442 (N.H. 1999); People v. Steeplechase Park Co., 113 N.E. 521 (N.Y. 1916); Carolina Beach Fishing Pier, Inc. v. Town of Carolina Beach, 177 S.E.2d 513 (N.C. 1970); Oregon ex rel. Thornton v. Hay, 462 P.2d 671 (Or. 1969); Marks v. Whitney, 491 P.2d 374 (Cal. 1971).

8. *See, e.g.*, Michaelson v. Silver Beach Improvement Ass'n, 173 N.E.2d 273 (Mass. 1961).

9. Matthews v. Bay Head Improvement Ass'n, 471 A.2d 355 (N.J. 1984) (holding that the public trust right to bathe is meaningless without the accompanying right to be on the dry sand beach).

10. Illinois Cent. R.R. Co. v. Illinois, 146 U.S. 387, 452 (1892).

11. *Id.* at 453.

12. *Id.* ("The State can no more abdicate its trust over property in which the whole people are interested, like navigable waters and soils under them, ... than it can abdicate its police powers in the administration of government and the preservation of the peace.").

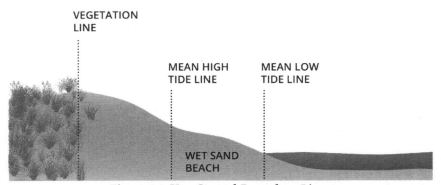

VEGETATION
LINE

MEAN HIGH
TIDE LINE

MEAN LOW
TIDE LINE

WET SAND
BEACH

Figure 14: Key Coastal Boundary Lines

Illinois Central Railroad v. Illinois.[13] In *Illinois Central,* the State of Illinois sought to have the railroad's occupation of submerged lands in Lake Michigan declared unlawful. Pursuant to a grant from the State and a City of Chicago ordinance, the railroad had occupied riparian lands along the shore of the Lake for construction of a railway and associated warehouses. The railroad constructed the railway lines pursuant to Illinois statute and a City of Chicago ordinance with some of the tracks built on pilings in the lake. The railroad then constructed a breakwater and filled the land between the breakwater and the shore, including the land under the tracks that had been built on pilings. Finally, the railroad filled in a portion of shallow land along the lake and constructed slips, wharves, and piers extending into the deeper waters of Lake Michigan. The State sought a declaration that it had "absolute title" to the submerged lands of Lake Michigan under the public trust and that as a result, the State was the only party with authority to improve the shore of the Lake for the purposes of commerce and navigation. Because it alleged that the railroad was unlawfully occupying public trust lands, the State further requested that the railroad be ordered to remove all structures it had built on State submerged lands. While the Supreme Court concluded that it did not have sufficient factual evidence before it to fully resolve all of the claims, the Court found that the key question it must answer was whether the Illinois state legislature had the authority to pass the original legislation that provided for the grant to the railroad and thereby denied the State public trust title to the lands and waters so granted.[14]

---

13. 146 U.S. 387 (1892).
14. *Id.* at 452.

Figure 15: Illinois Central
Source: Library of Congress, Prints and Photographs Division,
Detroit Publishing Company Collection, LC-DIG-det-4a06085

To resolve the question, the Court began by describing the nature of title under the public trust finding "[i]t is a title held in trust for the people of the State that they may enjoy the navigation of the waters, carry on commerce over them, and have the liberty of fishing therein freed from the obstruction or interference of private parties."[15] The Court also noted that when the public's ability to engage in navigation fishing and commerce may be enhanced by the construction of wharves, the State may grant parcels of submerged lands to private parties in order to advance these purposes.[16] However, the Court concluded that granting private parties the right to construct wharves to *enhance* the public's ability to exercise its basic rights of navigation, fishing, and commerce "is a very different doctrine from the one which would sanction the abdication of general control of the State over lands under the navigable waters of an entire harbor or bay, or of a sea or lake."[17] The Court continued that "[s]uch abdication is not consistent with the exercise of [the public] trust which requires the government of the State to preserve such waters for the use of the

15. *Id.*
16. *Id.* at 452–53.
17. *Id.* at 453.

public."[18] Therefore the Court held that the State's grant of submerged lands to the railroad was invalid because:

> The State can no more abdicate its trust over property in which the whole people are interested, like navigable waters and soils under them, so as to leave them entirely under the use and control of private parties, except in the instance of parcels mentioned for the improvement of the navigation or use of the waters, or when parcels can be disposed of without impairment of the public interest in what remains, than it can abdicate its police powers in the administration of government and the preservation of the peace.[19]

Thus, *Illinois Central* establishes two key principles arising from the public trust doctrine. First, the transfer of public trust lands to private ownership is only permissible if the state concludes that such a transfer will either enhance the public's ability to exercise its public trust rights or where doing so will not impact the public's ability to exercise its rights on remaining public trust lands. Second, the state may not abdicate its duty to defend the public trust, meaning that the state has a common law obligation to ensure that private parties use of submerged lands is consistent with the public's ability to exercise its rights under the public trust doctrine.

Common Law Background Principles Regarding Movement of the Public Trust

The common law has long recognized the dynamic nature of coastlines and the ability of littoral property lines to shift as the result of natural forces. In addition to the public trust, which is generally recognized to follow shifts in the mean high tide, the major doctrines recognizing the dynamism of the coast are the doctrines of accretion, erosion, and avulsion.[20] While all three doctrines deal with dynamic coastlines, they reflect different social values about shifting property rights and lead to different results.

---

18. *Id.*

19. *Id.*

20. *See generally* Margaret Peloso & Margaret Caldwell, *Dynamic Property Rights: The Public Trust Doctrine and Takings in a Changing Climate*, 30 STAN. ENVTL. L.J. 51, 62–63, 67–76 (2011), for a discussion of the extent to which the public trust doctrine is a *Lucas* background principle.

What Is the Common Law?

In "common law" legal systems, such as that in the United States, there are two main sources of law: statutory law and common law. Statutory law is the law that is created by the legislature and codified in statutes. At the federal level in the United States, statutory law is the law that is created by Congress, signed by the President, and codified in the United States Code.

Common law, on the other hand, is judge-made law, i.e., a set of legal principles that arise from many, many years of cases and the accumulation of judicial precedent. Because courts' decisions are guided by the legal precedent created by prior court decisions, over time, these decisions create a body of law known as the common law. There are two important features of the common law that distinguish it from statutory law. First, as compared to statutory law—which requires new legislation to be changed—the common law tends to evolve over time as judges apply it to the new facts and circumstances that are before them in individual cases. Second, while the common law establishes the background legal principles that apply in the absence of statutory law, common law principles can be superseded or amended by statutory law.

Because of the United States' status as a former British colony, common law in the United States traces its roots back to English common law.

The doctrines of accretion and erosion recognize that the coastline is always experiencing imperceptible but ultimately significant gains and losses of sediment. Over time, the mean high-tide line will shift as a result of the gain or loss of land through movement of alluvion (grains of sand or sediment).[21] Because these changes are recognized to be the result of the work of natural forces, common law doctrines recognize that property boundaries will shift to follow accretion and erosion. That is, when erosion causes once dry land to become submerged, the littoral owner is stripped of his title and the land becomes a part of the public trust.[22] Conversely, because he is subjected to the risks of

---

21. *Shively,* 152 U.S. at 35. Alluvion is a term used to refer to sediment particles that are transported and deposited by water to create accretions and erosive loss of property. *Id.*

22. *See, e.g., id.;* City of St. Paul v. Alaska, 137 P.3d 261, 265 (Alaska 2006) (Mean high tide is an ambulatory property boundary that is changed by accretion and erosion); Maryland Dep't of Nat. Res. v. Mayor and Council of Ocean City, 332 A.2d 630 (Md. 1975).

erosion, the littoral owner is usually understood to have the right to any accretions that cause previously submerged property to become dry land.[23]

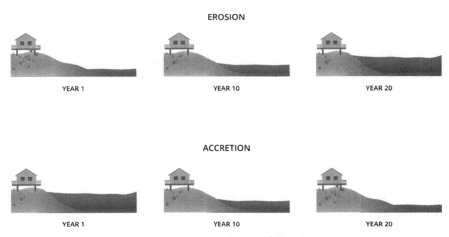

Figure 16: Accretion and Erosion

The doctrine of avulsion, on the other hand, maintains that property lines are unchanged when the gain or loss of land is sudden. For example, if a littoral owner loses his dry sand beach in a hurricane event, the common law recognizes his right to rebuild the beach.[24] For those who understand the mechanisms by which this sand is lost, this seems an odd result: an avulsive event is truly just erosion over a very rapid time scale, but the outcome with respect to property rights is completely different. While the doctrine of avulsion may make it difficult to implement policies promoting retreat by permitting the littoral property owner to rebuild his beach, it is a valuable tool for states undertaking beach nourishment projects. When a state or the Army Corps pumps sand on the beach, this is undoubtedly an avulsive event. Thus, states can

---

23. *See, e.g.*, Brannon v. Boldt, 958 So.2d 367 (Fla. Dist. Ct. App. 2007); California ex rel. State Lands Comm'n v. Superior Court, 900 P.2d 648, 664 (Cal. 1995) (finding that the general common law rule of accretion grants accreted lands to the littoral owner); Connecticut v. Knowles-Lombard Co., 4 Conn. Supp. 116 (Conn. Super. Ct. 1936). *But see* CAL. CIVIL CODE § 1014 (establishing that artificial accretions do not belong to the littoral owner).

24. *See, e.g.*, Walton Cnty. v. Stop the Beach Renourishment, Inc., 998 So.2d 1102 (Fla. 2008) (holding that under the doctrine of avulsion property owners have the right to reclaim land lost in a storm event); Mississippi v. Wiesenberg, 633 So.2d 983 (Miss. 1994); Maryland Dep't of Nat. Res. v. Ocean City, 332 A.2d 630.

greatly expand public access to beaches by creating dry sand beach below the original mean water line, as this dry sand beach will remain in the public trust.

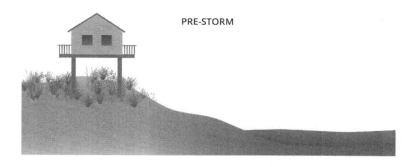

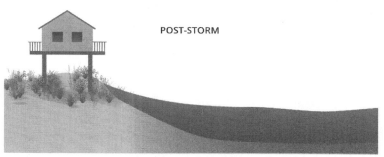

Figure 17: Avulsion

What Is Private Property Anyway?

Private property is classically described to first-year law students as a "bundle of rights."[25] The various rights that may come along with property ownership are typically referred to as "sticks" in the bundle. While there are many different types of interests that a person may have in a property, the most important is fee title, or what we would commonly refer to as ownership. Ownership of property tends to give the property owner the right to sell the land, the right to use the land as he chooses, and the right to exclude others from it.[26]

---

25. Jane B. Baron, *Rescuing the Bundle-of-Rights Metaphor in Property Law*, 82 U. Cin. L. Rev. 57 (2014).

26. J.E. Penner, *The "Bundle of Rights" Picture of Property*, 43 UCLA L. Rev. 711, 719 (1996).

A key concept in the law of property is that property rights are specific to a particular piece of property, and an owner may only exercise those rights that he actually has with respect to a particular piece of property.[27] For example, for most property, property lines do not move, and the owner would have the right to use his entire property however he chooses. However, as explained above, for properties where one of the boundaries is a body of water, the common law establishes that the geographic reach of the property owner's title will move with accretion and erosion. That is, when someone buys property along a body of water, the right to fix property lines along the water is generally not one of the "sticks" in the bundle of rights he buys. Similarly, property owner's rights will be restricted by regulations that are in place at the time they buy their property. For example, if a property owner buys a property containing wetlands that cannot be filled under environmental laws, he has not purchased the right to fill those wetlands and develop the property.[28]

The restrictions on a property owner's rights at the time of purchase that arise from the common law (and to some extent existing regulations) are referred to as "background principles."[29] Background principles draw the limits on the rights that a particular property owner has in his property—that is, they define which "sticks" are in his bundle of rights—and thus they are a key element in determining what a property owner can do with his land.

How Does the Public Get Access to Private Property Along the Coast?

To this point we have established that the line between public and private property along the shore tends to be at or below the line of the wet sand beach and that one of the key rights a property owner has is to exclude others from his property. Given these facts, how is it that the public gains access to the dry sand beach? The legal tool to grant someone the right to access property they do not own is called an easement. An easement is a right of access that does not convey title, and it is subject to the rights of the underlying owner of title to the land.[30] There are three ways in which an easement can be established—

---

27. *Id.* at 723; Baron, *supra* note 25, at 80–83.
28. *See* Palazzolo v. Rhode Island, 533 U.S. 606 (2001).
29. Lucas v. S. Carolina Coastal Council, 505 U.S. 1003, 1030 (1992).
30. EASEMENT, Black's Law Dictionary 622 (10th ed. 2014).

dedication, prescription, or custom—and each plays a role in securing the public access to the beach.

A dedicated easement is one that a property owner voluntarily gives to a third party. Typically an easement by dedication is purchased by a third party from the property owner. A dedicated easement will also sometimes be given by the property owner in order to obtain a building permit or some other kind of benefit. For example, some states require that property owners dedicate beach access in order to obtain permits. Not all dedicated easements are for access purposes: a common practice in many states is the dedication of conservation easements, where the land owner agrees not to develop a property, often in exchange for a tax benefit.[31] A dedicated easement is recorded with the deed to the property.

Prescription recognizes that a continuous, open, and hostile use of property (e.g., use of dry sand beach by the general public) can be sufficient to establish an easement over private property. There are many cases establishing that the public's continuous use of privately owned dry sand beaches can create a public easement by prescription over the dry beach.[32] A prescriptive easement may be acquired by the ongoing use of property for a statutorily required time without the permission of the landowner.[33] As with many other coastal states, California recognizes that the historic and ongoing use of private property in order to access the shoreline by the public results in the public's acquisition of an easement over the private property.[34]

Custom, in contrast, recognizes the public right to access simply because it has always existed.[35] Oregon is unique in its approach relying upon the doctrine of custom, imported from English common law.[36] Under the doctrine of custom, the court simply finds that the public has been accessing the beach in the same way since time immemorial and therefore they have a customary right to continue to do so.

---

31. *Id.*

32. Eaton v. Town of Wells, 760 A.2d 232, 248 (Me. 2000); City of Daytona Beach v. Tona-Rama, Inc., 294 So.2d 73, 78 (Fla. 1974).

33. *See, e.g., id.*

34. *See* Nollan v. Cal. Coastal Comm'n, 483 U.S. 825, 832 (1987).

35. Oregon ex rel. Thornton v. Hay, 462 P.2d 671, 676 (Or. 1969).

36. *Id.*

Rolling Easements

In the context of dynamic shorelines, there is a special type of easement that often comes up called the rolling easement. The concept of a public trust that moves with rising sea levels was first thoroughly discussed by Titus, who borrowed the term "rolling easements" from the Texas Open Beaches Act to explain this phenomenon.[37] The concept of rolling easements is becoming a popular potential tool for coastal adaptation to sea level rise.[38] Under a policy of rolling easements, coastal habitats are allowed to retreat naturally with sea level rise and human development must give way to the advance of the sea. In essence, the state prevents coastal armoring or other forms of property "protection" and the public trust is allowed to advance with rising seas. As sea levels rise, the public trust easement "rolls" inland, encompassing now dry land and imposing an obligation upon current coastal property owners to relinquish their property as it is consumed by the public trust. Because the rolling easement follows the natural movement of the public trust, a critical component of any rolling easements policy is a prohibition on permanent coastal armoring.

Rolling easements facilitate adaptation by recognizing the shift in property interest from private to public as sea levels rise. While rolling easements can provide an effective legal tool to encourage retreat when the ocean's edge shifts landward, they may be limited in their ability to prevent development *prior* to the point of land coming under tidal influence. The central concern of any climate change adaptation plan should be the reduction of vulnerability of coastal development and reduction of the risk of "coastal squeeze," or the loss of coastal habitats that are crowded out when seawalls and coastal development prevent the natural landward movement of these habitats.[39]

37. James G. Titus, *Rising Seas, Coastal Erosion, and The Takings Clause: How to Save Wetlands and Beaches Without Hurting Coastal Property Owners*, 57 MD. L. REV. 1279 (1998).

38. *Id.*

39. Robert J. Nicholls, Poh Poh Wong, Virginia Burkett, Jorge Codignotto, John Hay, Roger McLean, Sachooda Ragoonaden & Colin Woodroffe, *Chapter 6: Coastal Systems and Low-Lying Areas, in* CLIMATE CHANGE 2007: IMPACTS, ADAPTATION AND VULNERABILITY. CONTRIBUTION OF WORKING GROUP II TO THE FOURTH ASSESSMENT REPORT OF THE INTERGOVERNMENTAL PANEL ON CLIMATE CHANGE 315, 343 (M.L. Parry, O.F. Canziani, J.P. Palutikof, P.J. van der Linden & C.E. Hanson eds., 2007).

What Happens if the Government Wants to Use Private Property?

When the government wants to use private property that it does not own, it can attempt to get the property owner to sell it the property right it seeks (e.g., an easement) or it can "take" the property through a condemnation proceeding. Under the Fifth Amendment of the United States Constitution, the government is permitted to take private property, but must provide the property owner with "just compensation" for the property when it does so.[40] This Constitutional requirement has created an area of law called "takings" that examines when the government has acted in a manner that interferes with the rights of a private property owner to the extent that it must pay him. There are two major classes of takings that are applicable to the challenges associated with adapting to sea level rise—physical takings and regulatory takings[41]—each of which is discussed in more detail below.

Physical Takings

A physical taking is a permanent physical occupation of the land of another. The form of physical takings that most people are familiar with arises under the state's exercise of its power in eminent domain. Under eminent domain provisions, states are granted the authority to appropriate private land for purposes that benefit the public-at-large. Eminent domain proceedings require that the state pay any property owner whose property is taken the fair market value of the property.[42] For example, if a state wishes to build a new highway, it may exercise its powers of eminent domain to require property owners to sell their land to the state for use as part of the new highway project. While the Supreme Court remains divided on the full scope of end-uses for which eminent domain powers may be lawfully exercised under the Fifth Amendment,[43] it is settled that lands that will be subsequently used by the state for public purposes can be acquired under these procedures.

---

40. U.S. Const. amend. V. Note that the takings clause is made applicable to state governments through the Fourteenth Amendment.

41. While not yet a clearly established legal doctrine, the Supreme Court has recently expressed willingness to consider a third category of takings: the judicial taking. *See* Stop the Beach Renourishment, Inc. v. Florida Dep't of Envtl. Prot., 560 U.S. 702 (2010).

42. Olson v. United States, 292 U.S. 246, 255–56 (1934).

43. Kelo v. City of New London, 545 U.S. 469 (2005).

A physical taking need not take the entire property for payment to be required (a "compensable taking"). As long as the taking is a permanent physical occupation of a property, the property owner will be due compensation for the taking. This principle is clearly established by the Supreme Court's decision in *Loretto v. Teleprompter Manhattan CATV Corp.*[44] At the time Loretto filed suit, New York law provided that landlords must permit cable television companies to install equipment on their buildings to provide cable service. Landlords were permitted to charge cable companies for occupying space in and on the building with cable equipment, but under New York law, the rate that the landlord could charge the cable company could not exceed a fee determined to be reasonable by a state Commission, which fee the Commission set at $1. Loretto challenged the state law, claiming that the installation of cable equipment on her apartment building constituted a physical taking. In reviewing its takings case law, the Supreme Court concluded that when the action at issue involves a permanent physical occupation "our cases uniformly have found a taking to the extent of the occupation, without regard to whether the action achieves an important public benefit or has only minimal economic impact on the owner."[45] The Court thus concluded that the requirement that Loretto permit the installation of cable on her rooftop constituted a physical taking.[46]

There are numerous cases dealing with flooding and flood control devices in the context of the Takings Clause. Through these cases, it has been well established that flooding that is caused by government activities constitutes a physical taking. In *United States v. Dickinson* the Supreme Court held that flooding of private property caused by the construction of a dam by the federal government constituted the taking of a flood easement.[47] The Court held that the taking resulting from flooding is not limited to the land that is permanently flooded but will also extend to any erosion caused by that flooding stating:

> When [the government] takes property by flooding, it takes the land which it permanently floods as well as that which inevitably washes away as a result of that flooding. The mere fact that all the United States needs and physically appropriates is the land up to the new level of the river, does not determine what in nature it has taken. If the

---

44. 458 U.S. 419 (1982).
45. *Id.* at 434–35.
46. *Id.* at 438.
47. 331 U.S. 745 (1947).

Government cannot take the acreage it wants without also washing away more, that more becomes part of the taking.[48]

Dickinson also established what has come to be known as the "doctrine of stabilization." In the Supreme Court, the United States argued that Plaintiffs' suit was untimely because more than six years had passed since the dam that caused the flooding became operational. However, the Court disagreed finding that "[t]he source of the entire claim—the overflow due to rises in the level of the river—is not a single event; it is continuous. And as there is nothing in reason, so there is nothing in legal doctrine, to preclude the law from meeting such a process by postponing suit until the situation becomes stabilized."[49] Therefore, when plaintiffs wish to bring a claim for a taking of property caused by erosion or flooding, the claim does not need to be brought until the conditions have stabilized to the point where the property owner knows how much of his land has been taken.

Since *Dickinson*, there have been numerous cases holding that the government can be liable for erosion caused by navigational improvements and jetties designed to protect particular parts of the coast. In *Banks v. United States*, the Court of Federal Claims determined that erosion caused by the Army Corps' construction of jetties was a taking that required compensation.[50] In *Banks* the Court further concluded that additional erosion caused by Plaintiffs' own attempts to protect themselves from the erosion caused by the Corps' jetties was a foreseeable result of Corps' activities and, therefore, Plaintiffs were permitted to recover takings compensation not only for erosion caused by the jetties themselves but also for erosion that resulted from any attempts to protect their properties.[51] The Court further explained that the erosion Plaintiffs complained of was a physical taking (rather than a nuisance or other tortious interference with property) because it "preempt[s] the owner's right to enjoy his property for an extended period of time, rather than merely inflict[ing] an injury that reduces its value."[52]

In the context of sea level rise adaptation, physical takings are potentially significant because a state or municipality may face physical takings liability if they construct flood protections on private property. In New Jersey, there have

---

48. *Id.* at 750.
49. *Id.* at 749.
50. 69 Fed. Cl. 206 (2006).
51. *Id.* at 214.
52. *Id.* at 212 (quoting Ridge Line, Inc. v. United States, 346 F.3d 1346, 1355–56 (Fed. Cir. 2003)).

Borough of Harvey Cedars v. Karan:
New Jersey Addresses "Just Compensation" for Physical
Taking Caused by the Construction of Sand Dunes

In the aftermath of Hurricane Sandy, the New Jersey Supreme Court considered whether a municipality can be liable for takings when it takes action to protect a community from future flooding in *Borough of Harvey Cedars v. Karan*. 70 A.3d 524 (N.J. 2013). In *Karan*, the Borough exercised its power of eminent domain to take a portion of the Karan property for the construction of a dune that would complete a series of dunes protecting Long Beach, New Jersey from the impacts of future storm surges. While there was no issue as to whether a taking occurred in the case, it reached the New Jersey Supreme Court on issue of how "just compensation" for the property owners was to be calculated.

In the trial court, the Karans had been permitted to present evidence of how their property value was diminished when the dune partially obstructed their ocean view. However, the trial court did not allow the Borough to present evidence that the dune enhanced the value of the property by providing storm surge protection. The trial court concluded that the introduction of such evidence was not appropriate because the protection provided by the dunes was a general benefit for the public as a whole. The New Jersey Supreme Court reversed, concluding that "when a public project requires the partial taking of a property, 'just compensation' to the owner must be based on a consideration of all relevant factors that either decrease or increase the value of the remaining property." *Id.* at 526–27. The Court concluded that the exclusion of evidence regarding the flood protection benefits of the dunes in the determination of the takings award did not constitute just compensation and remanded the case for consideration of the same. *Id.* at 527. On remand, Karan reportedly settled with the Borough for compensation of $1 — a significant reduction from the original trial court award of $375,000. Martin Bricketto, *NJ Pushes Dune Construction as Landmark Case Settles*, Law360.com (Sept. 25, 2013, 6:31 PM ET), http://www.law360.com/articles/475651/nj-pushes-dune-construction-as-landmark-case-settles.

been a series of cases holding that the construction of sand dunes on ocean front property above the mean high tide line amounts to a physical taking.

It is also important to note that states and municipalities potentially face takings liability if they install coastal protection structures that cause erosion further down the shore. For example, a state or local government may choose to install a seawall to protect a key developed area, such as the central business district of a coastal town. However, the seawall may increase erosion experienced by those properties that lie beyond the extent of the seawall. There are numerous cases finding that when the action of a federal or state government entity results in the loss of littoral property by increasing erosion rates, that entity can be liable under the Takings Clause. For example in *United States v. Dickinson*, the Supreme Court concluded that the government was liable for land that was directly flooded as well as increased erosion rates resulting from the construction of a dam.[53] The Court concluded that when the government "takes property by flooding, it takes the land which it permanently floods as well as that which inevitably washes away as a result of that flooding."[54] Similarly, in *Banks v. United States* the Court of Federal Claims concluded that the Army Corps was liable for the taking of private property when it constructed jetties that increased the rate of erosion along nearby properties on the shore of Lake Michigan.[55] In *Banks*, the property owners had responded to the erosion that was caused by the Corps' initial jetty construction by building their own structures that were supposed to protect their properties from further erosion damage. However, as is often the case with such structures, they actually exacerbated the erosion that the property owners experienced. The Court of Federal Claims concluded that the scope of the taking for which the property owners could seek recovery included both the erosion that directly resulted from the Army Corps' jetty construction as well as the additional erosion caused by their own erosion protection structures if the property owners could demonstrate that this additional erosion was the "direct, natural, or probable result" of the Corps' jetty construction activities.[56]

---

53. 331 U.S. 745, 750 (1947).
54. *Id.*
55. 69 Fed. Cl. 206 (2006).
56. *Id.* at 214.

Regulatory Takings

The second type of takings are regulatory takings, which the Supreme Court defines as regulations that are "so onerous that its effect is tantamount ... to ouster."[57] Regulatory takings are further divided into two classes of cases: *per se* regulatory takings, which deprive the owner of all economically beneficial use of his land, and all other regulatory takings.[58] In general, when evaluating regulatory takings, the key question courts must confront is how to balance the state's constitutional exercise of its police power to protect the public health, safety, and welfare against the Fifth Amendment rights of the private property owners who will be subject to the regulation at issue.

The regulatory takings doctrine has long been recognized by U.S. courts. In 1922, the Supreme Court addressed the issue in *Pennsylvania Coal Co. v. Mahon*.[59] *Pennsylvania Coal* involved an action by a property owner to prevent the Pennsylvania Coal Company, which held the rights to mine coal under his land, from removing the support pillars of coal in the mine, which would have caused the property to subside. The issue before the Court was whether a Pennsylvania law that would prevent the removal of the support pillars in the mine was a lawful exercise of the state's police power. The Supreme Court concluded that the statute could not be sustained as a valid exercise of the state's police power and therefore constituted an unlawful taking.[60] The Court concluded that under the Constitution, the state's police power must be balanced against private property rights and "[t]he general rule at least is, that while property may be regulated to a certain extent, if regulation goes too far it will be recognized as a taking."[61]

The test for whether a regulation goes so far as to become a taking was further clarified by the Supreme Court in *Penn Central Transportation Company v. New York*.[62] The case involved a challenge to the application of New York's Landmarks Preservation Law to Grand Central Station. New York City's Land-

---

57. Lingell v. Chevron, U.S.A., Inc., 544 U.S. 528, 537 (2002); *see* Pennsylvania Coal Co. v. Mahon, 260 U.S. 393 (1922) (regulatory takings); Loretto v. Teleprompter Manhattan CATV Corp., 458 U.S. 419 (1982) (physical takings).

58. Lucas v. S. Carolina Coastal Council, 505 U.S. 1003 (1992) (establishing the doctrine of *per se* regulatory takings); Penn Central Transp. Co. v. New York, 438 U.S. 104 (1978) (establishing the factors a court should consider in determining whether a regulation goes too far and becomes a taking).

59. 260 U.S. 393 (1922).

60. *Id.* at 414.

61. *Id.* at 415.

62. 438 U.S. 104 (1978).

marks Preservation Law allowed the City to designate particular buildings as historic landmarks and impose restrictions on modifications to their exteriors or further construction on their sites. However, the Landmarks Preservation Law also permitted designated historic landmarks that had not been developed to the fullest extent permitted by the zoning code (e.g., buildings that were shorter than the maximum height allowed) to transfer their rights to build extra square footage to other buildings in the City that did not have the limitations of historical landmark status on their construction and thereby receive compensation for development rights that could no longer be exercised at the historic landmark site.[63] After Grand Central, an eight-story building, had been designated by the City as a historic landmark, Penn Central sought permission to build a 53-story office building above Grand Central and make alterations to Grand Central's façade to accommodate the new office building. The City rejected Penn Central's application to construct the office building, finding that it was inconsistent with the Landmarks Preservation Law. Rather than challenging the Commission's decision directly, Penn Central filed suit alleging that the rejection of their application to build the office tower was an unconstitutional taking of their property rights.[64]

Penn Central's takings challenge ultimately reached the Supreme Court. The Court began its analysis by noting that it has not been able to establish a "set formula" to determine when a regulatory taking has occurred and that whether just compensation will be required for an alleged regulatory taking is highly dependent upon the facts and circumstances of the case.[65] While acknowledging that regulatory takings cases are "essentially ad hoc, factual inquiries," the Court concluded that there are three key factors that have particular relevance to the regulatory takings inquiry: (1) the economic impact of the regulation on the property owner; (2) the extent to which the regulation interferes with the property owner's investment-backed expectations; and (3) the character of the governmental action.[66] In explaining these factors, the Court expressly noted that the ability of the state to issue zoning regulations—even if such regulations deprive a property of its highest and best use—is a well-established, reasonable exercise of the state's police power because such regulations are intended to benefit the public as a whole.[67] Turning to the facts of Penn Central's challenge, the Court began by noting that the parties did not dispute that

---

63. *Id.* at 110–15.
64. *Id.* at 119.
65. *Id.* at 123–24.
66. *Id.* at 124.
67. *Id.* at 125–26.

the City's objective in preserving historic structures was a permissible governmental goal or that in its current configuration Grand Central terminal would earn valuable economic returns.[68] Rather, Penn Central's claim turned upon whether the City's denial of permission to build the office tower constituted a taking of its property right to develop the space above Grand Central terminal. The Court rejected this argument finding that its takings case law required it to examine the character of the government action in relation to the parcel as a whole, not segments of the property rights that Penn Central alleged to be taken.[69] The Court further noted that the City's designation of Grand Central as a historic landmark did not interfere with the use to which Grand Central had been put for the prior 65 years as a railway terminal and therefore did not interfere with Penn Central's primary economic expectations regarding the property.[70] The Court also noted that the ability to transfer development rights that could not be exercised above Grand Central served to mitigate any economic harms that may have resulted from the building's designation as a historic landmark.[71] As a result, the Court concluded that there was no taking of Penn Central's property because the Landmark Preservation Law was "substantially related to the promotion of the general welfare," permitted reasonable and beneficial use of the landmark site, and did not impose unreasonable economic burdens on Penn Central.[72]

In the aftermath of *Penn Central*, the Court's balancing test has become the standard analysis used to determine whether a regulation will constitute a taking in most cases. However, in 1992, the Supreme Court recognized a new category of regulatory takings — *per se* regulatory taking — in *Lucas v. South Carolina Coastal Council*.[73] In *Lucas*, the Supreme Court held that some regulations can be *per se* takings because they deprive a property owner of all reasonable and beneficial uses of their property.[74] Because of the specific facts of the case, which dealt with coastal development, and the broad nature of its holding, *Lucas* is a particularly important case in the context of coastal climate change adaptation, and as explained in later chapters, does much to shape the behavior of local governments that may wish to promote retreat from the coastal zone.

---

68. *Id.* at 129.
69. *Id.* at 130–31.
70. *Id.* at 136.
71. *Id.* at 137.
72. *Id.* at 138.
73. 505 U.S. 1003 (1992).
74. *Id.* at 1019.

Figure 18: Grand Central Station, New York

David Lucas purchased two ocean-front lots in the Isle of Palms development in South Carolina in 1986 with the intent of building a single family home on each lot.[75] In 1988, before Mr. Lucas had commenced any construction on his properties, South Carolina passed its Beachfront Management Act. Among other things, the Beachfront Management Act required the South Carolina Coastal Council to establish a "baseline" determined by landwardmost points of erosion over the last 40 years. Once this baseline was established, the Beachfront Management Act prohibited the construction of any occupiable structure seaward of the baseline. When the Coastal Council established the baseline, it fell landward of Mr. Lucas' two parcels purchased in 1986 and had the effect of prohibiting any construction upon them.[76] Mr. Lucas subsequently filed suit alleging that the Beachfront Management Act deprived him of all reasonable and beneficial use of his property and therefore was a total taking.[77] The Court began by evaluating its past case law, and concluded "there are good reasons for our frequently expressed belief that when the owner of real property has been called upon to sacrifice *all* economically beneficial uses in the

---

75. *Id.* at 1006–07.
76. *Id.* at 1008–09.
77. *Id.* at 1009.

name of the common good, that is, to leave his property economically idle, he has suffered a taking."[78] However, the Court recognized an important exception to this general rule, finding that a state could avoid the need to compensate a property owner for an alleged taking if the property rights that were "taken" were not rights that the owner had in the first place.[79] That is, if a state enacts a law or regulation that merely codifies existing background principles of common law, that cannot effect a taking.[80] Importantly, the Supreme Court itself did not determine whether Mr. Lucas had actually suffered a total taking of his property that demanded compensation. Instead, it remanded the case to the South Carolina Supreme Court to determine whether South Carolina could demonstrate that there are background principles of common law that would prohibit Mr. Lucas's desired development and thus allow the state to avoid liability for a *per se* taking.[81]

Under *Lucas*, common law principles that were in existence at the time a property owner took title can serve as valid limitations on property rights and would not qualify as *per se* regulatory takings.[82] Therefore, development limitations that are rooted in the public trust or other common law doctrines will not be regulatory takings.

The Supreme Court addressed the issue of how substantially a property's value may be diminished before a *Lucas* taking occurs in *Palazzolo v. Rhode Island*.[83] Palazzolo owned a waterfront parcel in Rhode Island. Under Rhode Island law, nearly all of Palazzolo's property was designated as wetlands, and as a result, his applications for permits to develop the property were denied. After the permits were denied, Palazzolo sued, alleging that the application of Rhode Island's wetland regulations to the property resulted in a total taking of his property. Mr. Palazzolo acquired the property at issue through a holding corporation in 1959 and made several proposals to develop between 74 and 80 lots by engaging in substantial fill of the wetlands on the property. These initial applications were rejected for a lack of sufficient information and no subsequent attempts to develop the land were made for many years. In the intervening time period, Rhode Island enacted legislation creating its Coastal Resources Management Council in 1971 and the Council established regulations to carry out its authority, including those governing the fill of wetlands.

---

78. *Id.* at 1019.
79. *Id.* at 1027.
80. *Id.* at 1029.
81. *Id.* at 1031–32.
82. *Id.* at 1027.
83. 533 U.S. 606 (2001).

Lucas' lots are on either side of the square house in this photo taken in 1994.

Figure 19: Explanation of the *Lucas* Properties

Photo of the developed lot taken in 2000.
Source: William Fischel, *A Photographic Update on Lucas v. South Carolina Coastal Council: A Photographic Essay*, http://www.dartmouth.edu/~wfischel/lucasupdate.html.

In 1978, the corporate charter of the holding company through which Mr. Palazzolo purchased his property was revoked, and Mr. Palazzolo became the sole owner of the properties. In 1983, Mr. Palazzolo again sought permission to develop the parcel, asking for permission to construct a wooden bulkhead and fill the entire wetland area on the property. After this application was rejected, Palazzolo made several additional applications to fill and develop substantial portions of the wetlands on his property. When these applications were rejected, Palazzolo filed a claim alleging that the application of Rhode Island's wetland regulations to his property had resulted in a total taking without just compensation. Mr. Palazzolo asked the court to award him over $3 million in

Figure 20: Map Showing the Palazzolo Property
Source: Rhode Island Coastal Resources Management Council

damages, which was the amount an appraiser determined the property would be worth if he had been permitted to construct the proposed 74-unit development.[84] However, the record in the case also established that if Mr. Palazzolo were to develop only the upland (non-wetland) portion of his property, the property would have a value of at least $200,000. The Supreme Court agreed with the Rhode Island Supreme Court and concluded that because development of the upland property still had a value of at least $200,000, the application of Rhode Island's wetland regulations to Palazzolo's property did not constitute a total taking under *Lucas*, and should instead be evaluated under the *Penn Central* framework.[85] *Palazzolo* thus establishes that a regulation that diminishes a property's alleged value by over 90% but does not deprive the owner of *all* beneficial use of the property is not a *per se* regulatory taking under *Lucas*.

---

84. *Id.* at 616.
85. *Id.* at 631.

Exactions

An exaction is a concession that a governmental authority demands in exchange for issuance of a permit. For example, a local government may require that a property owner grant the public an easement to access the beach in connection with a permit to build a new house. While exactions can be constitutional if they bear a sufficient relationship to the costs imposed on the community by issuance of the permit, exactions that seek too great a concession from the permittee can rise to the level of unconstitutional taking. This concept is best understood through the examination of the two landmark exactions cases in the Supreme Court: *Nollan v. California Coastal Commission* and *Dolan v. City of Tigard.*[86]

The *Nollan* case arose from the Nollans' application to rebuild a house on the California coast, which required a coastal development permit from the California Coastal Commission. The Coastal Commission granted the Nollans a coastal development permit, but included in the permit a requirement that the property owners dedicate a public easement over their dry sand beach that would cover the area between the mean high tide line and the existing seawall on the property. According to the Coastal Commission, the easement was necessary because the larger house the Nollans proposed to build would impair the ability of the public to view the ocean from the street passing immediately behind the Nollans' house. The Nollans challenged the permit condition requiring a public access easement in state court. They argued that the Coastal Commission's easement requirement constituted a regulatory taking, and the case was appealed to the U.S. Supreme Court.

The Supreme Court began by noting that an access easement is a "permanent physical occupation" under its precedent in *Loretto*. The Court also noted that state regulation of land use does not amount to a taking if it substantially advances a legitimate state interest and does not deny the owner of an economically viable use of the land.[87] The Supreme Court concluded that the requirement of an easement in the absence of the permit application would have been a clear physical taking. However, the Court also noted its precedent in regulatory takings cases which establishes that land use regulations are not takings if they substantially advance legitimate state interests and do not deny the owner economically beneficial use of his land.

---

86. *Nollan*, 483 U.S. 825 (1987); *Dolan*, 512 U.S. 374 (1994).
87. *Nollan*, 483 U.S. at 830.

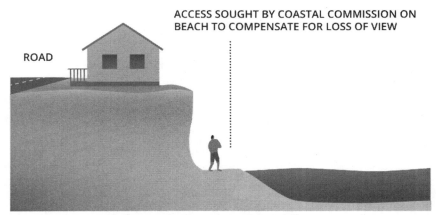

ACCESS SOUGHT BY COASTAL COMMISSION ON
BEACH TO COMPENSATE FOR LOSS OF VIEW

ROAD

Figure 21: Explanation of the *Nollan* case

In determining where the Coastal Commission's easement demand fell along this spectrum, the Court fashioned the "essential nexus" test. The Court reasoned that if the Coastal Commission could deny the development permit altogether, any conditions it might place on the issuance of the permit, including public access rights that amount to a permanent physical occupation, would be constitutional.[88] However, the Court limited the constitutionality of exactions by concluding that there must be a nexus between the permit condition and the underlying legitimate state interest (the so-called "essential nexus").[89] Turning to the facts of the *Nollan* case, the Court determined that the Coastal Commission had concluded the impact of issuing the development permit to Nollan—which permitted him to enlarge his existing house—would be that the public would no longer be able to view the ocean from the road that was landward of Nollan's property. The Majority concluded that visual access from the road and the physical access required by the beach easement the Coastal Commission sought were not comparable and therefore held that there was no essential nexus and that the Coastal Commission's condition that the Nollans dedicate an easement amounted to an unconstitutional exaction.[90]

A few years after issuing its decision in *Nollan*, the Supreme Court again considered exactions in *Dolan v. City of Tigard*. In *Dolan*, the petitioner was the owner of a hardware store who submitted an application to double the size

88. *Id.* at 831.
89. *Id.* at 836–37.
90. *Id.* at 837.

LAND FOR DRAINAGE
EASEMENT SOUGHT BY CITY

EXISTING STORE   NEW STORE   BIKE PATH SOUGHT BY CITY

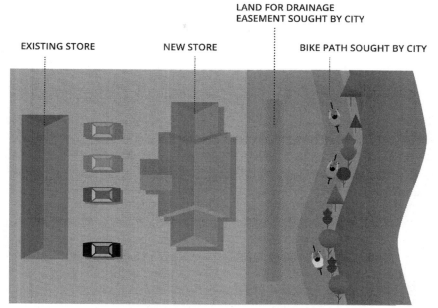

Figure 22: Explanation of the *Dolan* case

of the existing store by building a new, larger store on the lot, pave the existing gravel parking lot, and build a new structure on the location of the current store for complementary businesses. The City Planning Department
approved the permit application and included conditions required by the city's
development code. These conditions included a requirement that the City secure a greenway when the proposed development was in or adjacent to a floodplain. Following this guidance, Dolan's permit required the dedication of a
15-foot-wide strip of land as a pedestrian and bike path as well as the dedication of a drainage easement covering the portion of Dolan's property that was
within the floodplain. These conditions were to meet the city plan's objectives
of reducing development in the floodplain and reducing traffic congestion by
promoting biking and walking pathways. Dolan filed a challenge in state court
alleging that the permit conditions amounted to a taking because they were
not related to the impacts of her proposed development. The Oregon Supreme
Court concluded that both conditions had an essential nexus to the proposed
development and concluded that there was no taking.

The U.S. Supreme Court agreed to hear the *Dolan* case in order to resolve
an alleged conflict between its opinion in *Nollan* and the Oregon Supreme

Court's decision in *Dolan*. The Court found that the prevention of development in the floodplain and reduction of traffic congestion are the types of legitimate public purposes for which a state may regulate land use without affecting a taking.[91] The Court further concluded that there is an "obvious" nexus between preventing flooding and limiting development in the floodplain.[92] Once it concluded that an "essential nexus" that could justify an exaction existed, the Court then turned to the question of whether the degree of exactions required by the City had a reasonable relationship to the impacts of the development. The Court concluded that the appropriate test for the scope of exactions is that they must be "directly proportional" to the impact. The Court concluded that "[n]o precise mathematical calculation is required, but the city must make some sort of individualized determination that the required dedication is related both in nature and extent to the impact of the proposed development."[93] Considering the facts of the case, the Court concluded that there was no rough proportionality between the requirement that Dolan dedicate a greenway and any congestion impacts from the project. The Court suggested that the City's findings supporting the exaction of the greenway were constitutionally deficient because the City merely found that the bike path could offset congestion but not that it would be likely to do so.[94]

The Supreme Court most recently considered exactions in *Koontz v. St. Johns River Water Management District*, where the Court considered whether a requirement to pay mitigation fees could be an unconstitutional exaction.[95] Koontz had sought permission to develop a portion of his property that contained wetlands. Pursuant to Florida law, the St. Johns River Water Management District conditioned Koontz's ability to pursue the development upon his agreement to pay for projects to improve district-owned lands that were used for stormwater management or reduce the size of his development and dedicate a larger conservation easement to the Water Management District. The Court concluded that the Water Management District's attempt to secure payment for enhancement of its own properties was a potential "monetary exaction" that was subject to analysis under *Nollan* and *Dolan*.[96] While the Court did not reach the facts of the case to determine whether the proposed payment at issue was in fact an unconstitutional exaction, the dissent in the case raised

---

91. *Dolan*, 512 U.S. at 387–88.
92. *Id.*
93. *Id.* at 391.
94. *Id.* at 395–96.
95. 133 S. Ct. 2586 (2013).
96. *Id.* at 2601.

concerns that the ultimate implication of the holding could be that states will be limited in their ability to charge reasonable permitting fees or seek mitigation fees to offset the impacts of a proposed development.[97]

What Are the Practical Implications of All This Takings Stuff?

The most important thing to take away from the above discussion of takings is that the takings doctrine imposes real limitations on the ability of governments to promote policies of retreat in the medium- to long-run. More immediately, the limitations imposed by the takings doctrine will shape the tools that coastal governments can use to secure continuing public access in the face of rising sea levels and increase the resilience of coastal development. A few of the important policies that are implicated by takings are the use of coastal setbacks, the ability to exact easements for coastal access or shoreline protection, the ability to pursue rolling easements, and how to address seawalls that come to lie on public trust lands.

Setbacks are a key land use tool available to coastal governments to enhance short-term resilience. By requiring that a certain amount of land at the water's edge be left undeveloped, setbacks leave room for the shoreline to erode before it comes to interact with development on a property. Setbacks can thus limit the use of seawalls or other shoreline protection structures to protect new development. However setbacks are only useful to the extent that there is sufficient property to enforce the setback. As the *Lucas* case demonstrates, if the effect of a setback is to prevent any development on a property, the takings doctrine will likely preclude the permitting authority from applying its setback. While there are arguments under the test articulated in *Lucas* that the inability to build a house may not deprive the property owner of *all* beneficial use, it is unlikely that permitting authorities will be willing to assume the risk of a takings suit and deny permits where insufficient property is available to enforce a setback and permit development.

The exaction of easements also has an important role to play in facilitating adaptation to sea level rise. State and local governments may wish to exact easements either to ensure continued public access to the coast or to acquire sufficient property rights to build structures that enhance the resilience of an

---

97. *Id.* at 2606–07.

entire coastal community (e.g., a beach-long dune that will minimize the impacts of storm surge). While these exactions serve important public purposes, state and local governments seeking them will need to carefully articulate their findings to establish the essential nexus between the development and the requested exaction as well as the rough proportionality between the exaction and the impact. Successful exactions to facilitate adaptation to sea level rise will likely require detailed engineering and economic studies to support findings about the impacts of specific development activities on a community's vulnerability or public access and how the exacted easement can be used to address that impact.

For rolling easements, the takings doctrine may implicate whether states can adopt a rolling access easement over dry sand beach or if they will simply wait for the public trust property line to advance inland. Titus argues that rolling easements are an efficient means of adapting to rising sea levels because they impose no costs until sea levels actually rise, they have plenty of time to be incorporated into reasonable investment-backed expectations, and they may foster consensus on coastal development policies because developers will be forced to admit the existence of sea level rise before they can argue that they should not be subjected to rolling easements.[98]

One of the reasons that a policy of rolling easements is attractive is because it allows states to reclaim title to property without incurring liability unlawfully taking the property of the littoral owner. Caldwell and Segall argue that the public trust and other common law principles that underlie rolling easements are background principles, meaning that the movement of the public trust boundary and any easement that goes with it does not take away a right that the coastal property owner has.[99] Thus, the public trust doctrine provides a strong basis for states to claim title to newly submerged lands as mean high tide moves inland and a potential tool to continue to protect coastal habitats and public access to the shoreline.

However, if rolling easements are to be a useful tool in facilitating adaptation to sea level rise and public access, the state must obtain an easement over the current dry sand beach or use its future interest in lands that will be subject to inundation to limit current coastal development (a very tricky takings question

---

98. Titus, *supra* note 37, at 1327, 1331, 1355.

99. Meg Caldwell & Craig Holt Segall, *No Day at the Beach: Sea Level Rise, Ecosystem Loss, and Public Access Along the California Coast*, 34 ECOLOGY L.Q. 533, 551–58 (2007). *See also* Zachary C. Kleinsasser, *Public and Private Property Rights: Regulatory and Physical Takings and the Public Trust Doctrine*, 32 B.C. ENVTL. AFF. L. REV. 421, 456 (2005) (finding that the public trust doctrine "underlies a modern takings analysis").

addressed in detail elsewhere[100]). Without this extension, the persuasiveness of the efficiency argument for rolling easements is undercut, as there remains the reality that coastal development will have to be abandoned as sea levels rise. Thus, the remaining legal question potentially limiting the efficacy of rolling easements is: To what extent may the state build upon the concept of rolling easements to limit coastal development on lands currently above the mean high tide line that will be inundated by sea level rise while avoiding liability for interfering with the rights of property owners?[101] Because of the limitations imposed by the takings doctrine, any attempts to implement rolling easements over the dry sand beach or upland coastal habitats are likely to be limited to instances where the state's common law recognizes ambulatory boundaries for access easements or to the dedication or exaction of rolling easements.

Finally, state and local governments will have to confront what to do when seawalls or other coastal protection structures come to lie on submerged lands that are not part of the public trust. As sea levels rise and the shoreline recedes, shoreline protection structures that are currently located on private property will hold back the advance of the public trust by keeping some coastal lands from becoming submerged. State actions that permit property owners to hold back the advance of the dynamic property line (by allowing seawalls that come to lie on lands that would otherwise be submerged) without requiring compensation for the occupation of public-trust lands may be unlawful abdications of the state's duty as trustee as defined under *Illinois Central*. That is, the full scope of the state's duty to defend this public trust under *Illinois Central* requires not only that the state proactively assert the advance of the public trust title with rising seas but also that the state deny permits to hold back the natural advance of mean high tide or charge littoral owners rent for their occupation of land that would otherwise be part of the public trust.[102] Similarly, states will have to determine how to treat beach that is created through nourishment that turns submerged lands into uplands.

---

100. Peloso & Caldwell, *supra* note 20.

101. For an argument that coastal development restrictions should not be regulatory takings because they merely allow legislatures to make rational choices to control coastal development, *see* Marc R. Poirier, *Takings and Natural Hazards Policy: Public Choice on the Beachfront*, 46 Rutgers L. Rev. 243 (1993).

102. Note that a state may be able to permit seawalls consistent with *Illinois Central* if it charges the property owner rent for occupying land that would otherwise be subject to the public trust. However, this approach only works if the only public trust value the state is charged with protecting is access. To the extent that a state's public trust doctrine encompasses resource conservation, seawall fees may not be adequate to mitigate against the loss of ecosystem services in the public trust. Peloso & Caldwell, *supra* note 20.

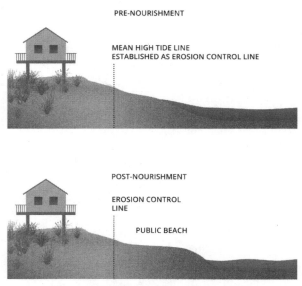

Figure 23: The Erosion Control Line

One possible approach is to deem lands created through nourishment to be public beach, either through operation of the common law or by statute. Florida has adopted the later approach under its Beach and Shore Preservation Act, which requires the establishment of an erosion control line as shown in Figure 23.[103]

Thus, there are a number of varying and important legal approaches states can use to protect the public's right to access the beach. However, the ability of all of these approaches to secure ongoing and meaningful public access to the beach will depend upon their ability to enforce the public's right, regardless of its source, as the line between public and private property shifts. While this seems simple in principle, as the state has a legal obligation to exercise its public trust duties, the reality is far more complicated.

---

103. Florida's ability to establish the erosion control line was upheld by the Supreme Court in *Stop the Beach Renourishment, Inc. v. Florida Dep't of Envtl. Prot.*, 560 U.S. 702 (2009).

Chapter 5

California

California has one of the longest coastlines of any state, and is also home to the San Francisco Bay, one of the largest and most ecologically significant estuaries along the West Coast.[1] The ocean coastline and Bay shore differ dramatically in terms of their geology, ecology, and level of development. The Bay Shoreline is an estuarine environment, historically fringed by wetlands, while much of California's ocean coastline consists of mudstone bluffs. While the California coast still has relatively undeveloped stretches, particularly in the north, the San Francisco Bay is one of the most urbanized estuaries in the world.[2] Under current projections of sea level rise, there is nearly $62 billion worth of development at risk in the San Francisco Bay area, which is twice the value of at-risk development along the ocean coastline.[3]

Both the ocean and estuarine coastlines are at risk from sea level rise. On the ocean coast, rising seas will result in increasing rates of bluff-undercutting erosion.[4] In the absence of bluff stabilization, this erosion will ultimately lead to bluff collapse and the loss of corresponding bluff top development. In addition, rising sea levels are projected to increase the amount of land that is subject to flooding during extreme high tide and flood events: for example, one

1. United States Environmental Protection Agency ("US EPA"), *Chapter 6: West Coast National Estuary Program Coastal Condition, San Francisco Estuaries Project, in* National Estuary Program Coastal Condition Report 353, 353 (2007).

2. San Francisco Bay Conservation & Development Commission, Living with a Rising Bay: Vulnerability and Adaptation in San Francisco Bay and on its Shoreline 47 (2011) [hereinafter Living with a Rising Bay].

3. Will Travis & Joseph LaClair, Draft Staff Report and Revised Preliminary Recommendation for Proposed Bay Plan Amendment 1–08 Concerning Climate Change 2 (Oct. 1, 2009).

4. Interview with Coastal Engineering Expert (Oct. 5, 2009).

Regional Inundation Extents
0 - 6 Feet Sea Level Rise

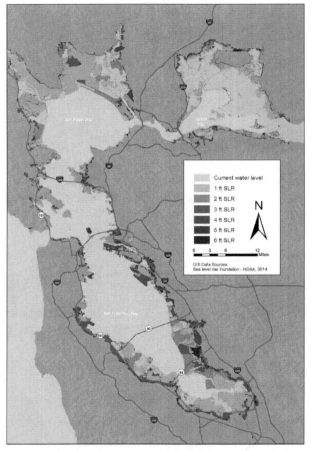

Figure 24: BCDC Sea Level Rise Map
Source: San Francisco Bay Conservation and Development Commission, www.bcdc.ca.gov/

recent study concluded that the cost of replacing coastal property at risk in a 100-year flood event in a future with 4.6 feet of sea level rise would be $100 billion.[5] In the San Francisco Bay, the San Francisco Bay Conservation and De-

---

5. MATTHEW HEBERGER, HEATHER COOLEY, PABLO HERRERA, PETER H. GLEICK & ELI MOORE, THE IMPACTS OF SEA-LEVEL RISE ON THE CALIFORNIA COAST 3, 74 (2009), http:// pacinst.org/wp-content/uploads/sites/21/2014/04/sea-level-rise.pdf.

velopment Commission ("BCDC") estimates that most areas that currently lie within the 100-year floodplain will be subject to the average monthly high tide by 2050.[6] Within the Bay, flooding is expected to impact an additional 180,000 acres of land by 2050 putting 98% more people at risk of flooding.[7] Along both the ocean and estuarine coastlines, the desire to protect shoreline development threatens both the quality of the shoreline environment and future public access to the coast. Shoreline protection projects currently cover nearly 108 miles of California's ocean coastline, which is roughly 10% of the entire coastline.[8] In the future, armoring is likely to follow trends of the recent past, which have led to an increase in the amount of the ocean shoreline covered by seawalls in the last 30 years.[9]

In the San Francisco Bay, the combination of subsidence caused by groundwater withdrawal and wetland loss will magnify the relative impacts of sea level rise. When these impacts are combined with sea level rise, BCDC acknowledges that extensive levee structures may be needed to protect pre-existing development.[10] Further, many areas of the Bay shoreline, including much of downtown San Francisco, are already protected by seawalls.

This Chapter outlines the legal frameworks governing California's ocean coastline under the Coastal Act and the Bay shore under the McAteer-Petris Act and presents two case studies of coastal development to explore the application of these acts.

Adapting to Sea Level Rise on California's Ocean Coast

Overview of the Legal Framework

Coastal management in California is governed by the California Coastal Act. Under the Coastal Act, two state agencies have primary responsibility over the coastal zone: the California Coastal Commission and the State Lands Com-

---

6. Living with a Rising Bay, *supra* note 2, at 26.

7. Travis & LaClair, *supra* note 3, at 2.

8. United States Army Corps of Engineers & Santa Cruz Redevelopment Agency, East Cliff Drive Bluff Protection and Parkway Revised Final EIS/EIR 15-3 (2006) [hereinafter Pleasure Point EIS].

9. *Id.*

10. San Francisco Bay Conservation & Development Commission, The San Francisco Bay Plan 40 (reprint 2012) (2008) [hereinafter Bay Plan].

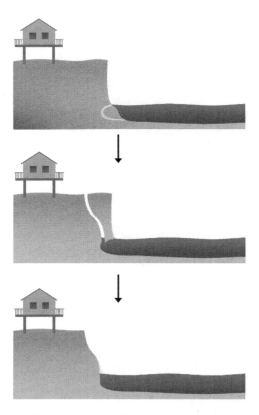

Figure 25: Bluff Undercutting Erosion

mission.[11] The Coastal Act covers a statutorily defined area reaching from three miles offshore to an inland area varying from two hundred feet in some urbanized areas to several miles in some mountainous rural areas.[12] Under the Coastal Act, the California Coastal Commission serves as the lead state permitting agency for most coastal development.[13]

The Coastal Act establishes five goals for the management of California's Coastline: (1) protect and maintain, and where possible restore and enhance, the natural and artificial resources in the coastal zone and coastal habitats; (2) assure orderly and balanced utilization and conservation of the coastal zone;

---

11. Cal. Pub. Res. Code §§ 30300–30305, 30416.

12. *See id.* Div. 20 ch. 2.5 (delimiting coastal zone boundaries for specific geographic areas).

13. *Id.* § 30300.

(3) maximize public access and recreational opportunities along the coast; (4) assure that coastal-dependent and coastal-related development are given priority over other forms of development at the coast; and (5) encourage state and local initiatives for cooperation and coordinated planning in the coastal zone.[14] To accomplish these goals, the Coastal Commission is charged to oversee a program to regulate coastal development and facilitate environmental protection and public access in the coastal zone. The Coastal Commission is to work cooperatively with local governments, and is specifically directed to provide planning and regulatory assistance to local governments in carrying out their responsibilities under the Coastal Act.[15]

Under the Coastal Act, coastal resource conservation has priority through the designation and protection of environmentally sensitive habitat areas ("ESHAs"). An ESHA is defined as "any area in which plant or animal life or their habitats are either rare or especially valuable because of their special nature or role in an ecosystem and which could be easily disturbed or degraded by human activities and developments."[16] The Coastal Act requires that ESHAs must be avoided and buffered from development impacts. Further, mitigating for avoidable impacts is not permitted.[17] While the Coastal Act provides that only "resource dependent" development, such as nature study or restoration, is allowed in ESHAs, the Commission does allow limited non-resource dependent development on ESHAs if restricting such development would affect a Fifth Amendment taking.[18]

At the core of the Coastal Act are its provisions governing coastal development and coastal resource management. These provisions provide guidance on public access, recreation, and the forms of development that are permitted in the coastal zone.[19] The Coastal Commission has primary responsibility for ensuring that these goals are met. Local governments are directed to submit Local Coastal Programs ("LCPs") to the Coastal Commission for review and approval.[20] Upon submission, the Commission will review the LCP in order to determine if it is consistent with the requirements of the Coastal Act.[21] LCPs are required to have both a land use plan ("LUP") and an implementation plan that contains the necessary provisions to achieve the goals of the

---

14. *Id.* § 30001.5.
15. *Id.* § 30336.
16. *Id.* § 30107.5.
17. Bolsa Chica Land Trust v. Superior Court, 83 Cal. Rptr. 2d 850, 862–63 (Cal. Ct. App. 1999).
18. *See* CAL. PUB. RES. CODE § 30010.
19. *Id.* Div. 20 ch. 3.
20. *Id.* § 30500.
21. *Id.* § 30512.2.

Agencies Responsible for California's Ocean Coast

There are four state-level agencies in California that have responsibility for the state's ocean coast: the Coastal Commission, the State Lands Commission, the Coastal Conservancy, and the Ocean Protection Council.

The Coastal Commission was established by a voter initiative in 1972 and made permanent by the California Coastal Act of 1976. The Coastal Commission is charged with the protection, conservation and restoration of natural and human-built resources along the coast, and works with local cities and counties to regulate land use and development activities in the coastal zone.

The Coastal Conservancy was also established by the Coastal Act of 1976, and is charged with protecting, restoring, and enhancing coastal resources and providing public access to the shore. The Coastal Conservancy is a non-regulatory agency that uses approaches such as the purchase of easements to protect coastal habitats and increase public access to the coast.

The State Lands Commission ("SLC") had jurisdiction over and management responsibility for certain public lands in the state of California. Of particular relevance in the coastal zone, the SLC holds title to all state submerged lands and is therefore the trustee under the Public Trust.

The Ocean Protection Council ("OPC") was established by the California Ocean Protection Act of 2004. The OPC is charged with coordinating the activities of ocean-related agencies in California to improve the effectiveness of their coastal protection efforts. Chief among the OPC's responsibilities is to establish a process to coordinate the collection and sharing of scientific data about the oceans across state agencies.

Coastal Act including zoning ordinances, zoning maps, and any other implementing measures that are necessary to protect sensitive coastal resource areas.[22]

---

22. *Id.* § 30108.6.

The Coastal Commission's regulations further require all LCPs to have an analysis of "potential significant adverse cumulative impacts on coastal resources and access" resulting from existing development and future development that would be allowed under the LCP.[23]

If the Commission determines the LCP is consistent with the Coastal Act, it will certify the LCP. Once the Coastal Commission certifies an LCP, it may transfer its direct permitting authority to the local area retaining original jurisdiction (over submerged lands, for example) over limited nearshore areas and some appellate jurisdiction.[24] As of 2014, the Coastal Commission reported that 73% of the LCP segments in the state have been certified, and these segments cover 87% of California's Coastline.[25] Each city or county with a certified LCP has the authority to issue Coastal Development Permits ("CDPs"), which are required for any development in the coastal zone.[26] Development is broadly defined under the Coastal Act and covers the placement of any structure in the coastal zone—including buildings, roads, pipes, and electrical transmission lines—as well as reconstruction, alteration, or demolition of structures.[27]

There are a number of measures in the Coastal Act that may impact the Coastal Commission and local governments' ability to facilitate adaptation to sea level rise. Under section 30253, permitting authorities are directed to ensure that new development minimizes risk to life and property and ensures stability and integrity of natural landforms.[28] This provision gives the Coastal Commission and local permitting agencies the ability to require setbacks that account for erosion when permitting local development. In addition, section 30233 of the Coastal Act prohibits most dredging and filling in the coastal zone, which would preclude the construction of seawalls.[29] Even in the case of certified LCPs, the Coastal Commission retains jurisdiction over the permitting of seawalls because they typically involve construction in the tidelands, submerged lands, or other public trust lands.[30] However, a major challenge for the Coastal Commission in protecting public beach access in the face of rising sea levels is an apparent inconsistency between sections 30233 and 30253 and section 30235.

---

23. CAL. CODE REGS., tit. 14, § 13511.
24. CAL. PUB. RES. CODE § 30512.
25. *Local Resources: Local Coastal Programs*, CALIFORNIA COASTAL COMMISSION, http://www.coastal.ca.gov/lcps.html (last visited Feb. 22, 2016).
26. CAL. PUB. RES. CODE § 30600(a).
27. *Id.* § 30106.
28. *Id.* § 30253.
29. *Id.* § 30233.
30. *Id.* §§ 30519, 30600–01.

As described in more detail below, sections 30233 and 30253 establish a general prohibition on armoring, while section 30235 seems to provide a right to build a seawall when a structure is "in danger."[31] In the mid-1980s, the Commission began to place provisions in all littoral development permits stating that the coastal landowner will not have the right to armor their property in the

---

The Coastal Act's Prohibition on Armoring and "Right" to Armor?

The Coastal Act contains three provisions that seem to be internally inconsistent: Section 30233, which prohibits armoring of the coast, Section 30253, which prohibits shoreline protection structures for new development, and Section 30235, which seems to create a right of armoring to protect an existing structure that is "in danger."

Section 30233 establishes a general prohibition on the placement of fill that acts as a broad prohibition on the construction of coastal protection structures, including seawalls. Section 30253 sets forth requirements that new development:

> Assure stability and structural integrity, and neither create nor contribute significantly to erosion, geologic instability, or destruction of the site or surrounding area *or in any way require the construction of protective devices that would substantially alter natural landforms along bluffs and cliffs.*

In contrast, section 30235 states:

> Revetments, breakwaters, groins, harbor channels, seawalls, cliff retaining walls, and other such construction that alters natural shoreline processes shall be permitted when required to serve coastal-dependent uses or to protect existing structures or public beaches in danger from erosion and when designed to eliminate or mitigate adverse impacts on local shoreline sand supply. Existing marine structures causing water stagnation contributing to pollution problems and fishkills should be phased out or upgraded where feasible.

(continued)

---

31. *Cf. Id.* § 30235; *id.* §§ 30233, 30253.

> ## The Coastal Act's Prohibition on Armoring and "Right" to Armor?
>
> *(continued)*
>
> Therefore the key legal question becomes the meaning of the term "existing structure," which is not defined in the Coastal Act. In the past, the Coastal Commission has, at times, indicated that "existing structure" means a structure that exists at the time the coastal protection permit is requested, suggesting section 30235 grants all littoral owners a right to defend their properties. However, the Coastal Commission's recent *Sea Level Rise Policy Guidance*—discussed in more detail below—suggests that the more appropriate interpretation is that section 30235's protections only extend to structures that were in existence at the time of the Coastal Act's passage in 1976.

future and that in the event erosion or sea level rise threatens the property, the agency reserves the right to require relocation of the structure.[32]

On August 12, 2015, the California Coastal Commission unanimously adopted the *Sea Level Rise Policy Guidance*.[33] The *Guidance* does not create any binding regulatory requirements, but sets forth the Coastal Commission's vision for how implementation of the Coastal Act can and should incorporate considerations of sea level rise. The *Guidance* finds that "[t]he potential impacts of sea level rise fall directly within the Coastal Commission's (and coastal zone local governments') planning and regulatory responsibilities under the Coastal Act."[34] To frame its approach the *Guidance* articulates twenty "funda-

32. California Coastal Commission, Sea Level Rise Policy Guidance 165 (2015), http://documents.coastal.ca.gov/assets/slr/guidance/August2015/0_Full_Adopted_Sea_Level_Rise_Policy_Guidance.pdf [hereinafter *Guidance*]; Meg Caldwell & Craig Holt Segall, *No Day at the Beach: Sea Level Rise, Ecosystem Loss, and Public Access Along the California Coast*, 34 Ecology L.Q. 533, 546, 565.

33. *See Guidance, supra* note 32.

34. *Id.* at 27.

mental guiding principles" for the incorporation of sea level rise into coastal planning and permitting.[35]

The *Guidance* envisions effecting these principles through the two key elements of Coastal Act implementation: the LCP process and Coastal Development Permits. As explained above, the LCP is the broader set of documents that govern land use planning and development controls within a particular county or municipality. The Coastal Development Permit process, on the other hand, is the process to permit individual projects and requires project-specific analysis. In both the LCP and CDP processes, the *Guidance* recommends the consideration of a range of sea-level rise scenarios in order to understand the minimum amount of sea level rise that could cause impacts, the worst-case scenario, and how impacts could change with differing amounts of sea level rise over time.[36]

The *Guidance* outlines a six-step process for incorporating sea level rise considerations into the LCP process:

1. determine relevant range of SLR projections;
2. identify potential physical SLR impacts;
3. assess potential risks to coastal resources and development;
4. identify adaptation measures and LCP policy options;
5. draft updated or new LCP for certification; and
6. implement LCP and monitor to reevaluate strategies as needed.[37]

The *Guidance* notes that most of the currently-approved LCPs were created in the 1980s and 1990s and encourages future updates to LCPs as an "essential tool" to address adaptation to sea level rise.[38] Further the *Guidance* notes that periodic updates to LCPs in the future will be important to incorporate new information on sea level rise as it becomes available, and suggests that updates every 5 to 10 years would be appropriate.[39] At the same time, the *Guidance* recognizes that availability of resources can be a significant constraint on a local government's ability to update its LCP.[40] To address this concern, the *Guidance* highlights several state-level grant programs that could be sources of funding for future LCP updates.[41]

---

35. *Id.* at 15.
36. *Id.* at 37, 75–76.
37. *Id.* at 18, 69–95.
38. *Id.* at 68.
39. *Id.* at 94.
40. *Id.* at 29.
41. *Id.*

The "Fundamental Guiding Principles" for the Coastal Commission's *Sea Level Rise Policy Guidance*

The Coastal Commission has framed its *Sea Level Rise Policy Guidance* around twenty "fundamental guiding principles" that it finds are rooted in the Coastal Act. These principles are set forth in the *Guidance* as follows:

Use Science to Guide Decisions [Coastal Act Sections 30006.5; 30335.5]

1. Acknowledge and address sea level rise as necessary in planning and permitting decisions.
2. Use the best available science to determine locally relevant and context-specific sea level rise projections for all stages of planning, project design, and permitting reviews.
3. Recognize scientific uncertainty by using scenario planning and adaptive management techniques.
4. Use a precautionary approach by planning and providing adaptive capacity for the highest amounts of possible sea level rise.
5. Design adaptation strategies according to local conditions and existing development patterns, in accordance with the Coastal Act.

Minimize Coastal Hazards through Planning and Development Standards [Coastal Act Sections 30253, 30235; 30001, 30001.5]

6. Avoid significant coastal hazard risks to new development where feasible.
7. Minimize hazard risks to new development over the life of authorized structures.
8. Minimize coastal hazard risks and resource impacts when making redevelopment decisions.
9. Account for the social and economic needs of the people of the state; assure priority for coastal-dependent and coastal-related development over other development.
10. Ensure that property owners understand and assume the risks, and mitigate the coastal resource impacts, of new development in hazardous areas.

(continued)

The "Fundamental Guiding Principles" for the Coastal Commission's *Sea Level Rise Policy Guidance*

(continued)

Maximize Protection of Public Access, Recreation, and Sensitive Coastal Resources [Coastal Act Chapter 3 policies]

11. Provide for maximum protection of coastal resources in all coastal planning and regulatory decisions.
12. Maximize natural shoreline values and processes; avoid expansion and minimize the perpetuation of shoreline armoring.
13. Recognize that sea level rise will cause the public trust boundary to move inland. Protect public trust lands and resources, including as sea level rises. New shoreline protective devices should not result in the loss of public trust lands.
14. Address other potential coastal resource impacts (wetlands, habitat, agriculture, scenic, etc.) from hazard management decisions, consistent with the Coastal Act.
15. Address the cumulative impacts and regional contexts of planning and permitting decisions.
16. Require mitigation of unavoidable coastal resource impacts related to permitting and shoreline management decisions.
17. Consider best available information on resource valuation when mitigating coastal resource impacts.

Maximize Agency Coordination and Public Participation [Coastal Act Chapter 5 policies; Sections 30006; 30320; 30339; 30500; 30503; 30711]

18. Coordinate planning and regulatory decision making with other appropriate local, state, and federal agencies; support research and monitoring efforts.
19. Consider conducting vulnerability assessments and adaptation planning at the regional level.
20. Provide for maximum public participation in planning and regulatory processes.

CALIFORNIA COASTAL COMMISSION, SEA LEVEL RISE POLICY GUIDANCE 15–16 (2015).

Approaches to Permitting and Seawall Restrictions

Because the California Coastal Commission has previously interpreted section 30235 to grant property owners the ability to build a seawall to protect property that is in danger at the time the application for the permit to build the seawall is filed, new development on California's eroding coastline presents a challenge for policy makers that wish to preserve public access to the coast. To date, the California Coastal Commission has considered two distinct approaches to this challenge: restrictions on future seawalls in Coastal Development Permits and seawall permits that are time-limited and require reauthorization.

Since the mid-1980s, the Coastal Commission has required the recipients of permits for new littoral development to waive their right to future armoring to protect their homes. For example, the permit issued to the Green Valley Corporation, discussed in more detail in the case study below, contained the following language:

> Assumption of Risk, Waiver of Liability and Indemnity Agreement. By acceptance of this permit, the Permittee acknowledges and agrees: ... (f) that the Permittee shall not construct, now or in the future, any shoreline protective device(s) for the purpose of protecting the residential development approved pursuant to coastal development permit A-3-CAP-99-023 including, but not limited to, the residence, foundations, decks, driveways, or the septic system in the event that these structures are threatened with imminent damage or destruction from waves, erosion, storm conditions, or other natural hazards in the future and by acceptance of this permit, the Permittee hereby waives any rights to construct such devices that may exist under Public Resources Code Section 30235 or City of Capitola LCP Zoning Section 17.48.090.

Some local governments have also attempted to address the balance between protecting oceanfront property and preserving public access by adopting time limitations on seawall permits. For example, in the 2013 revision to its Land Use Plan ("LUP"), the City of Solana Beach included a provision that "[a]ll permits for
(*continued*)

Approaches to Permitting and Seawall Restrictions

(*continued*)

bluff retention devices shall expire after 20 years." The Solana Beach
LUP would have required that seawall permit holders apply for a new
permit after the 20 years have passed or remove their seawall. As discussed in more detail below, this provision was ultimately revised to
be tied to the lifetime of the structure the seawall protects.

In addition, recent Coastal Commission practice has sometimes included permit language requiring removal or relocation of permitted
structures in the future if they come to be threatened by sea level rise.

The *Guidance* also sets forth five steps for addressing sea level rise in the
CDP process:

1. establish projected range of SLR;
2. determine how SLR impacts "may constrain a project site";
3. determine impact of project on coastal resources, considering impact
   of SLR on the landscape;
4. identify alternatives to avoid resource impacts and minimize risks; and
5. finalize project design and submit CDP application.[42]

The *Guidance* notes that many CDP applications already consider sea level rise
as part of their hazards analysis and that compliance with the Coastal Act requires that CDPs be properly conditioned to emphasize an adaptive approach
to future sea level rise.[43] The *Guidance* recognizes that for individual development projects, a key aspect of permit assessment and project design is the projected lifetime of the proposed development. The *Guidance* notes that some
LCPs already contain expectations for the lifetime of development, but if they
are absent, the *Guidance* recommends the following expected lifetimes be used
for permit analysis: 25 years for temporary or amenity structures, 75 to 100
years for houses, and timeframes of 100 years or more for critical infrastructure projects such as bridges or industrial facilities.[44] The *Guidance* also recommends that resource protection projects be evaluated over a 100-year

---

42. *Id.* at 20, 100–14.
43. *Id.* at 99–100.
44. *Id.* at 101.

timeframe because they should be designed to last in perpetuity.[45] The *Guidance* states that each CDP should identify potential adaptation options and consider the impacts those adaptation options will have on the project and coastal resources.[46]

The *Guidance* also contains a chapter addressing legal issues that discusses the meaning of section 30235 of the Coastal Act, the Public Trust implications of sea level rise adaptation, and takings issues. With respect to section 30235, the *Guidance* explains:

> Despite other Coastal Act provisions that could often serve as the basis for denial of shoreline protective devices ... the Coastal Commission has interpreted Section 30235 as a more specific overriding policy that requires the approval of Coastal Development Permits for construction intended to protect coastal-dependent uses or existing structures if the other requirements of Section 30235 are also satisfied.[47]

The *Guidance* then addresses the relationship between sections 30235 and 30253. It concludes that the most reasonable reading of these two provisions is that section 30235's armoring provision was intended to protect pre-Coastal Act structures.[48] The *Guidance* notes that this has been very difficult in practice because many shoreline protection structures that have been previously permitted have protected both pre- and post-Coastal Act structures due to the mixed nature of development along California's ocean coastline. In addition, the *Guidance* acknowledges that there have been some instances in the past where the Coastal Commission has relied on section 30235 to permit the construction of shoreline protection structures that only protect post-Coastal Act structures.[49] However, the *Guidance* concludes that:

> [G]oing forward, the Commission recommends the rebuttable presumption that structures built after 1976 pursuant to a coastal development permit are not "existing" as that term was originally intended relative to applications for shoreline protective devices, and that the details of any prior coastal development approvals should be fully un-

---

45. *Id.* at 102.
46. *Id.* at 111.
47. *Id.* at 164.
48. *Id.* at 165.
49. *Id.*

derstood before concluding that a development is entitled to shoreline protection under Section 30235.[50]

In defending this change in policy, the *Guidance* simply notes that there are
no appellate decisions addressing the definition of "existing structure" or the
relationship between sections 30235 and 30253.[51] However, the actual application of this change in policy could face legal challenges, particularly because
the Commission's prior actions—including the requirement of deed restrictions that constitute a "waiver" of protection rights under section 30235 in
CDPs—suggest that the Commission previously viewed the section 30235 right
to protection of structures that are "in danger" to apply to all properties.

With respect to the Public Trust, the *Guidance* notes that the state's public
trust ownership begins at the mean high tide line, and concludes that the movement of the mean high tide boundary due to sea level rise will increase the
number of conflicts over whether structures will be allowed to remain in areas
that would be seaward of the mean high tide line if shoreline protection structures were not present.[52] The *Guidance* finds that California has no case law
on this issue, but notes that a recent Ninth Circuit case found that the federal
common law permits the owner of tidelands to maintain an action in trespass
seeking the removal of shoreline protection structures.[53] While not specifically
addressed in the legal chapter, earlier portions of the *Guidance* suggest that the
state needs to recognize that sea level rise will move the public trust boundary
inland and that when the shoreline protective devices come to be located on
submerged lands, the owner of the protective structure must either seek a permit for the encroachment onto state lands or a permit to remove the protective structure.[54] In California, this permit would be issued by the State Lands
Commission, the public trustee for the tidelands.[55]

Finally, the *Guidance* briefly addresses the issue of takings. It concludes that
some of the recommendations provided in the guidance could give rise to takings issues. The *Guidance* declines to provide guidance on how to address potential takings issues because it concludes that takings inquiries are too
fact-intensive and context-specific to lend themselves to such guidance.[56] With

---

50. *Id.* at 166.

51. *Id.*

52. *Id.* at 169.

53. *Id.*

54. *Id.* at 40.

55. *See* California State Lands Comm'n Land Mgmt. Div., Application for Lease of State Lands (2015), http://www.slc.ca.gov/Forms/LMDApplication/LeaseApp.pdf.

56. *Guidance, supra* note 32, at 171.

respect to the potential for exactions (e.g., the dedication of open space to allow for upland migration of tidal habitats), the *Guidance* merely repeats the standard of *Nollan/Dolan* that an exaction must be logically connected and roughly proportional to the impact it seeks to mitigate.[57]

On the whole, the *Guidance* represents a significant step forward in articulating policies for adapting to sea level rise on California's ocean coast. However, while articulating a robust process to consider sea level rise, the *Guidance* fails to meaningfully engage with the numerous legal issues that will certainly arise. As the examples presented later in this chapter make clear, the success of the *Guidance* in promoting sea level rise adaptation will largely depend upon the willingness and ability of the Coastal Commission and local governments to craft responses to land use planning and permitting that both account for sea level rise and avoid takings issues.

While not creating binding legal mandates governing coastal climate change adaptation in California, the *Safeguarding California* plan sets forth a number of needed actions to protect coastal ecosystems that will likely serve as important policy guidance to the Coastal Commission and local governments, and is explicitly referenced as an important foundational document in the Coastal Commission's *Guidance*.[58] The Plan is firm in its stance that future development in hazard areas should be avoided, stating "[t]he state should not build or plan to build, lease, fund, or permit any significant new structures or infrastructure that will require new protection from sea-level rise, storm surges or coastal erosion during the expected life of the structure, beyond routine maintenance of existing levees or other protective measures, unless there is a compelling need."[59] To the extent that new structures requiring sea level rise protection are granted permits, the Plan directs permitting authorities to ensure that the project applicant minimizes risks through siting, design, and engineering; ensures viable funding to build, monitor, and maintain any new protections; and designs protections to account for future environmental changes and protect natural resources and coastal access.[60] The Plan also highlights the role of the OPC in facilitating a process to work with multiple stakeholders—including permitting authori-

---

57. *Id.*; Nollan v. Cal. Coastal Comm'n, 483 U.S. 825 (1987); Dolan v. City of Tigard, 512 U.S. 374 (1994).

58. California Natural Resources Agency, Safeguarding California: Reducing Climate Risk (2014), http://resources.ca.gov/docs/climate/Final_Safeguarding_CA_Plan_July_31_2014.pdf.

59. *Id.* at 179.

60. *Id.*

ties and local landowners—to improve capacity to effectively reduce sea level rise risks.[61]

The Pleasure Point Seawall, Capitola Sea Cave, and Solana Beach Seawalls

The Pleasure Point Seawall is a project completed in 2010 by the County of Santa Cruz to protect a stretch of public road along the top of a bluff just outside of the City of Santa Cruz. East Cliff Drive itself is an important community recreation area, with a number of parks along the bluff top and numerous stairwells leading down to the beach. The County maintains that East Cliff Drive itself is an important resource because it provides the public an important opportunity to view Monterey Bay.[62] Immediately off the coast of this section of East Cliff Drive lies the world-renowned Pleasure Point surfing area.

The cliff for which East Cliff Drive is named is made of soft mudstone and experiences long-term erosion of approximately one foot per year.[63] Given the undercutting erosion dynamics of the area, this erosive loss is more commonly experienced as episodic events in which as much as ten feet can be lost at one time.[64] In the early 1990s, there was a major failure of the bluff along East Cliff Drive leading to the loss of one of the lanes of the road. Because of East Cliff Drive's importance as a recreation area and the presence of utility lines below the road, the County of Santa Cruz began to explore options to permanently solve the problem of erosion along East Cliff Drive.

In 2003, the County and the U.S. Army Corps of Engineers jointly advanced a proposal to permanently armor the bluff along the East Cliff Drive. Because the project was led by the Army Corps, it came to the Coastal Commission for a determination that the project was consistent with California's Coastal Management Plan. At the time, the Army Corps estimated that the proposed seawall would cost $7 million and take six months to construct. In addition, the Corps asserted that the armoring project was necessary because 65% of the roadway between 33rd and 36th Avenues was currently failing or in imminent danger of failure.[65] While requesting that the Army Corps evaluate other alternatives to armoring, the Coastal Commission Staff ultimately recommended

---

61. *Id.* at 180.
62. CALIFORNIA COASTAL COMMISSION, STAFF REPORT: FEDERAL CONSISTENCY DETERMINATION No. CD-021-03, at 2 (2003) [hereinafter 2003 STAFF REPORT].
63. *Id.*
64. *Id.*
65. PLEASURE POINT EIS, *supra* note 8, at ES-7.

that the Commission deem the project consistent with legislative mandates because East Cliff Drive and the underlying utilities were "in danger" under the meaning of the Coastal Act.[66]

The Coastal Act grants the California Coastal Commission exclusive jurisdiction over permitting for seawalls. Section 30233 of the Act establishes a general prohibition against armoring the coast with limited exceptions for the placement of fill.[67] However, section 30235 requires that the Coastal Commission approve a seawall if it finds:

1. there is an existing structure;
2. the existing structure is in danger from erosion;
3. shoreline-altering construction is required to protect the existing or threatened structure; and
4. the required protection is designed to eliminate or mitigate its adverse effects on shoreline sand supply.[68]

The term "in danger" is not defined under the Coastal Act, and the Staff Report recommending approval of the permit concluded that "the Commission has generally interpreted 'in danger' to mean that an existing structure would be unsafe to use or otherwise occupy within the next two or three storm season cycles ... if nothing were to be done."[69] Given the threat to East Cliff Drive from erosion, the Coastal Commission Staff recommended that although the Army Corps had not performed the required alternatives analysis, the Coastal Commission still find that the project was consistent with California's Coastal Zone Management Plan and the Coastal Act.[70] Despite the Staff's recommendation, the Coastal Commission found that the proposed seawall project was not consistent with the Coastal Act, largely due to the failure of the Army Corps to perform sufficient alternatives analysis.

Following the Commission's rejection of the Army Corps' seawall proposal, Santa Cruz County decided that it might be better off gaining political sup-

---

66. 2003 Staff Report, *supra* note 62, at 2.

67. Cal. Pub. Res. Code §30233.

68. California Coastal Commission, Appeal A-3-SCO-07-015 & CDP Application 3-07-019, at 37 (2007) [hereinafter 2007 Staff Report].

69. 2003 Staff Report, *supra* note 62, at 18.

70. *Id.* at 2. Other alternatives of which the staff requested evaluation were 1) beach nourishment, 2) temporary protection measures during winter storms, and 3) adequate setbacks for new developments. *Id.* at 22. The Army Corps did evaluate acquisition of the next row of houses, but decided that in the long-run this solution was too expensive to be feasible. *Id.* at 22–23.

port for the project if it proceeded on its own.[71] Because the County was in the unique position where it could afford to fund the project without federal assistance, it asked the Army Corps to step aside.[72] The County decided to proceed with the project in the face of the initial rejection by the Coastal Commission and widespread local opposition because it felt that the consequences of not taking action in terms of lost improvements and public access were greater than the risks associated with doing the project.[73]

The proposal that the County ultimately submitted in 2007 was largely the same as the Corps' proposal in 2003, but the County spent much of the intervening time building public support for the project. The majority of public opposition to the project stemmed from two concerns: first, the public was concerned that the armoring of the bluff would result in a look that was not natural and unattractive; second, and perhaps more significantly, the local surfing community raised concerns that the armoring of the bluff would alter the dynamics of the coast and destroy the Pleasure Point surfing area.[74] Further, at the time the initial project analysis was conducted in 2003, many local residents felt that there were alternative measures that would have provided adequate protection of the bluff, but that the County dismissed these measures because it was after the most permanent solution it could obtain.[75] One of the most important aspects in building public support for the project was the need for emergency repair of the existing crib walls in the project area.[76] The County took advantage of an emergency permit for crib wall repair to demonstrate the technique that would be used on the larger seawall.[77] The County believes that this demonstration project, which allowed the public to envision what the larger seawall project would look like, was critical in gaining public acceptance of the project. In addition, it appears that between 2003 and the subsequent County application in 2007, local residents who advocated alternative approaches to protecting the shoreline came to feel that their options were armoring or nothing and consequently supported armoring to protect local property.

The Coastal Commission Staff evaluation of the 2007 County proposal found that there were still substantial issues arising from consistency between

---

71. Interview with Local Government Official (Oct. 2, 2009).

72. *Id.*

73. *Id.*

74. Interview with Nonprofit Organization Staff Member (Sept. 30, 2009); Interview with Nonprofit Organization Staff Member (Oct. 14, 2009).

75. Interview with Member, Coastal Property Owners' Association (Oct. 1, 2009).

76. *Id.*

77. *Id.*

the proposed seawall and the County's local coastal plan.[78] However, the Staff still recommended conditional approval based on the finding that the road itself was "in danger." One of the most significant elements in the Staff's recommendation was a finding that even if the Commission were to deny the permit, the bluffs would ultimately retreat to the line of private property, and at that point, individual seawall permits would be granted as a matter of right under section 30235.[79] As with the Army Corps' 2003 application, the County had rejected planned retreat as an option because of high costs.[80] The Coastal Commission Staff concurred because it found that much of urban Santa Cruz County was already armored, and that these other armored areas would need to be included in a planned retreat strategy.[81] Thus, the Commission Staff passed on an opportunity to pursue planned retreat on what was at the time the largest armored stretch of the Coast in California, based in part on a finding that even the scale of this project was too small. The project was subsequently approved by the Coastal Commission on December 13, 2007.[82] Construction of the seawall commenced in September 2009, and was completed in 2010. The complete seawall has resulted in the natural physical consequence of beach erosion, leading to the loss of a beach at high tide. Figure 26 shows a picture of the seawall under construction in September 2009 and a picture of the same stretch of coastline taken almost exactly five years later. The 2014 photo was taken several hours after high tide, and shows the lack of sandy beach.

The issue of permitting scale being too small to implement meaningful retreat is further highlighted by the efforts of local property owners in the adjacent Opal Cliffs area to obtain individual permits to protect their homes from the dangers of blufftop erosion. Opal Cliff Drive is a stretch of road following immediately down coast from East Cliff Drive with slightly more than 30 homes along the bluffs. The area has been described by coastal managers as a model of what has gone wrong with development and armoring along the California coast.[83] The homes along Opal Cliff drive have a hodgepodge of coastal defense structures including riprap, seawalls, and a few homes where defense

---

78. 2007 STAFF REPORT, *supra* note 68, at 3.

79. *Id.*

80. *Id.* at 44.

81. *Id.*

82. CALIFORNIA COASTAL COMMISSION, STAFF REPORT: REVISED FINDINGS FOR APPEAL A-3-SCO-07-015 & CDP APPLICATION 3-07-019, at 1 (2008) [hereinafter 2008 STAFF REPORT].

83. Interview with Coastal Commission Staff Member (Dec. 3, 2009).

Figure 26: The Pleasure Point
Seawall Under Construction in
2009 (*above*) and in 2014 (*left*)

structures of any kind are barred.[84] This uncoordinated mix of property defenses has led to results that are undesirable to many constituents: the defense

---

84. CALIFORNIA COASTAL COMMISSION, STAFF REPORT: COASTAL DEVELOPMENT PERMIT AMENDMENT APPLICATION NO. A-3-CAP-99-023-A1, at 4 (2009) [hereinafter GREEN VALLEY PERMIT APPLICATION].

Figure 27: Capitola Sea Cave
Source: Chad Nelsen, Surfrider Foundation

structures are unattractive; impede public access; and in the eyes of many property owners, do not provide adequate protection of bluff top homes. What's more, some private property defenses have come to have negative impacts on neighboring properties, particularly through the creation of end-effects, resulting in enhanced erosion rates at the ends of individual seawalls. These problems become particularly acute when they begin to impact properties upon which the Coastal Commission has imposed a no future armoring restriction, as was seen in the Commission's consideration of the joint permit application by Swan and Green Valley Corporation (the Capitola Sea Cave).

The Green Valley case deals with two adjacent properties along Opal Cliff Drive. The Swan property has been developed since before the passage of the Coastal Act, while the Green Valley property was more recently developed. The Swan property has previously been threatened by bluff top erosion: in the early 1990s a portion of the house had to be removed because it was falling off of the bluff.[85] Given that the Swan property was an existing property that was in danger, in 1995 the Coastal Commission granted Swan a Coastal Development Permit to construct a two hundred foot long, twenty foot high seawall at the

---

85. *Id.* at 8.

base of his bluff.[86] Continued erosion of the unarmored upper bluff caused the Swan house to be threatened again in 2003, and in 2004, Swan was granted permission to stabilize the upper bluff with concrete.[87]

In 1999, the Green Valley Corporation applied to the City of Capitola for a Coastal Development Permit to build a house on its land adjacent to the Swan property. Finding that the proposed development was consistent with the City's approved Local Coastal Plan, the City of Capitola granted Green Valley's permit. On appeal of the permit to the Coastal Commission, the Coastal Commission found that there would be substantial issues with LCP consistency because the proposed development did not meet local setback requirements from the edge of the bluff, which required that all development be at least fifty feet from the bluff edge.[88] Ultimately, the Commission approved a revised development plan in which the Green Valley house was required to have a sixty-five-foot setback.[89]

By the time that Green Valley applied for its development permit, the Commission had adopted the practice of requiring that all applicants for coastal development permits guarantee the Commission that the proposed development will not require a seawall.[90] To hold property owners to this representation, the Coastal Commission generally requires that all permit approvals include a condition that places a restriction in the property owner's deed effectively waiving the right under section 30235 to apply for a seawall in the future.[91] Knowing that this was the Commission's standard practice, Coastal Commission Staff evaluated the potential for end effects from the already-existing Swan seawall in preparing the Staff report.[92] At the time, Commission Staff concluded that there was a high likelihood that the end effects from the Swan seawall would ultimately threaten the Green Valley Property, and therefore recommended that the Commission deviate from its standard practice and not require the incorporation of a no-armoring restriction in Green Valley's deed.[93] However, the Commission ultimately decided to permit construction on the Green Valley property with the incorporation of the standard deed restriction.[94]

---

86. *Id.* at 7.
87. *Id.* at 8.
88. *Id.*
89. *Id.* at 9.
90. Interview with California Coastal Commissioner (Dec. 4, 2009).
91. *Id.*
92. Interview with Coastal Commission Staff Member (Dec. 3, 2009).
93. *Id.*
94. *Id.*

The Green Valley property was subsequently developed. Meanwhile, the end effects created by the Swan seawall had caused substantial erosion leading to the formation of a large cave behind the seawall running under the Swan property. In 2006, the cave was deemed to be at high risk of imminent failure, and coastal engineers found that the Swan house would likely be damaged if the cave collapsed.[95] As a result, Swan came back to the Coastal Commission seeking permission to fill the sea cave with concrete to stabilize his property.

The proposed project to fill the sea cave included a seawall that would cover the entirety of the Swan and Green Valley properties.[96] However, the Green Valley Property itself was not in imminent danger, so it would not qualify for armoring under section 30235.[97] As a result, Commission Staff found that only more limited filling required to protect the threatened Swan property was consistent with the Coastal Act.[98] Furthermore, Green Valley had waived any future rights that it may have had to armoring as a condition of obtaining its original coastal development permit. However, there was no proposed engineering solution that could both allow Swan to exercise his section 30235 right to protect his property while also preventing any armoring of the Green Valley property. The Staff and the Commission were thus left to struggle with how to allow Swan to protect his property without running afoul of the deed restriction the Commission had imposed upon Green Valley.

The Staff ultimately recommended that the Commission permit the filling of the cave on the Swan property and the armoring of fifteen feet of the adjacent Green Valley property to stabilize the cave.[99] An alternative proposal, advanced by the Surfrider Foundation and the Sierra Club, called for the filling of the area with erodible concrete followed by realignment of the bluff top on the Swan property so as to protect the house and allow for the removal of the armoring on the Green Valley property.[100] The Surfrider proposal thus allowed for limited hardening of the Green Valley property as an emergency measure to protect the Swan property from collapse. After a lengthy debate as to how to protect the Swan property without setting a precedent render-

---

95. GREEN VALLEY PERMIT APPLICATION, *supra* note 84, at 8, 11–12.

96. *Id.* at 2.

97. *Id.*

98. *Id.* at 2–3.

99. *Id.* at 2.

100. Memorandum from Surfrider Foundation on Proposed Special Conditions of Approval for CDP Amendment Application A-3-CAP-99-023-A1 (Swan and Green Valley Corporation Seawall) to California Coastal Commission (Oct. 5, 2009) (on file with author).

ing 30235 waivers in deed restrictions meaningless, the Commission voted to adopt the Surfrider proposal with the additional requirements that (1) Swan come back in six months with a detailed plan for bluff realignment and (2) a stipulation be placed in the permit stating that Green Valley still has no right to armor and that any concrete placed on the Green Valley property for emergency stabilization purposes will be removed during bluff realignment.[101] As of this writing, there has been no further action before the Coastal Commission regarding the permit.

Throughout their debate, numerous members of the Coastal Commission called for the development of a broader policy to deal with armoring and sea level rise in California.[102] Many of the Commissioners expressed frustrations with the current approach of confronting larger regional issues, such as sea level rise within the confines of individual permit applications.[103] Commission Staff also noted that given the Commission's lack of a policy on sea level rise, they are inevitably forced to piggyback these larger issues onto individual permit applications.[104] Such an approach leads to frustration because the Commission continues to have the same debate each time an armoring permit comes up because there is currently no other forum in which to have this discussion. The repeated analysis of large-scale sea level rise issues in individual permits wastes the time and resources of both the Commission and its Staff, and it has not proven effective in slowing the pace of armoring along the coast.[105]

Another important controversy over the permitting of seawalls along California's coast has arisen in Solana Beach. Solana Beach is a 1.7-mile-long beachside community located 20 miles north of San Diego. Single family homes have been built in Solana Beach on bluffs overlooking the beach; seawalls protect these bluff-top homes from erosion and preserve property values.

In 2013, Solana Beach adopted updates to its LCP, which included a provision to address the prevalence of seawalls in the community and their impacts on coastal resources. Solana Beach's revisions to its LCP called for all permits for "bluff retention devices" (e.g., seawalls, riprap) to have 20-year lifespans.[106] After 20 years, the LCP would have required a new coastal development per-

---

101. *Permit Amendment Application No. A-3-CAP-99-023-A1 Hearing Before California Coastal Commission* (Oct. 7, 2009).

102. *Id.*

103. *Id.*

104. Interview with Coastal Commission Staff Member (Dec. 3, 2009).

105. *Id.*

106. *See* Verified First Am. Compl. for Declaratory Relief and Pet. for Writ of Mandate, Beach & Bluff Conservancy v. City of Solana Beach, No. 37-2013-46561, 2013 WL 4805642, at ¶ 17 (Cal. Super. Aug. 20, 2013).

mit if the blufftop retention structure was to remain in place.[107] The goal of this policy was to be able to periodically reevaluate whether allowing seawalls to remain was consistent with the City's duties under the Coastal Act to protect public access and Coastal Resources. Shortly after the City adopted its LCP amendment, a local property owners group named the Beach & Bluff Conservancy filed suit against the City alleging, among other things, that the 20-year sunset provision for blufftop retention devices violated section 30235 of the Coastal Act.[108] During the pendency of the lawsuit, the Coastal Commission disapproved of the 20-year limit to seawall permits, and instead required that the permits for seawalls be tied to the lifespan of the structure they protect.[109] As amended and approved by the Coastal Commission, the City's land use plan reads as follows:

> All permits for bluff retention devices shall expire when the currently existing blufftop structure requiring protection is redeveloped…, is no longer present, or no longer requires a protective device, whichever occurs first and a new CDP must be obtained. Prior to expiration of the permit, the bluff top property owner shall apply for a coastal development permit to remove, modify, or retain the protective device.[110]

While the Commission's approved modifications to the Solana Beach LCP do not provide an explanation for the elimination of the 20-year sunset clause for seawall permits, the difficulties with the implementation of such a sunset clause are seen in the Commission's approach to permitting at the Land's End development in Pacifica Beach. On August 15, 2013, the Commission approved a Coastal Development Permit for Land's End that tied the length of the seawall authorization to the life of the structure, using language nearly identical to that included in the final Solana Beach LCP, which is quoted above.[111] Land's End sought a Coastal Development Permit to permanently authorize two sec-

---

107. *Id.*

108. *Id.* ¶¶ 31–36.

109. California Coastal Commission, Certification of City of Solana Beach LCP Land Use Plan Amendment (SOL-MAJ-1-13) 6 (2014), http://www.ci.solana--beach.ca.us/vertical/sites/%7B840804C2-F869-4904-9AE3-720581350CE7%7D/uploads/SOL-MAJ-1-13_LUPA_Certification_Letter.pdf.

110. *Id.*

111. California Coastal Commission, August 2013 Agenda, http://www.coastal.ca.gov/meetings/mtg-mm13-8.html (recording approval of the Land's End permit); California Coastal Commission, Staff Report Addendum for Th17a Application 2-10-039 (Land's End) 2 (2013), http://documents.coastal.ca.gov/reports/2013/8/Th17a-8-2013-a1.pdf.

tions of seawall constructed under emergency permits and install additional shoreline protections to protect the Land's End apartment complex.[112] In its initial report on the proposed permit, the Coastal Commission staff recommended that the armoring only be approved for 20 years and would have required a CDP amendment for the seawall to remain in place beyond 20 years.[113] In explaining its recommendation for a 20-year limit on the seawall authorization, the Staff Report stated:

> A 20-year period of development authorization ensures that the unstable situation existing at this site is reassessed before the seawall becomes a danger to the Applicants and the public. It also allows the Commission and the owners to evaluate new technology and thinking in coastline development and protection, changed blufftop or shoreline conditions, and the impacts of sea level rise.[114]

The Staff changed its initial recommendation to the language in the final permit—tying the life of the seawall to the life of the development—in an addendum to the staff report.[115] This addendum states that the applicant objected to the 20-year limitation on the seawall permit on the grounds that it constituted a regulatory taking.[116] While maintaining that the Commission has in the past used the 20-year limitation to address uncertainties about future conditions, including sea level rise, the addendum concludes "[t]here have, however, been concerns raised that a twenty-year term may not be the appropriate way to address such uncertainties, including in relation to both armoring design lifetimes and the lifetimes of development being protected by the armoring, as well as concerns that this condition could cause significant investments of staff and permittee time and resources to process additional authorizations when the twenty years is over."[117] As a result, the seawall at Land's End has a time limit that is coextensive with the lifetime of the development that allows a coastal protection structure that was initially constructed under emergency provisions to become permanent.

---

112. CALIFORNIA COASTAL COMMISSION STAFF REPORT, APPLICATION NO. 2-10-039 (LAND'S END ASSOCIATES) (2013), http://documents.coastal.ca.gov/reports/2013/8/Th17a-8-2013.pdf.

113. *Id.* at 17–18.

114. *Id.* at 38.

115. CALIFORNIA COASTAL COMMISSION, STAFF REPORT ADDENDUM FOR TH17A APPLICATION 2-10-039 (LAND'S END) (2013), *supra* note 111, at 1.

116. *Id.*

117. *Id.* at 2.

Figure 28: Land's End
© 2002–2015 Kenneth & Gabrielle Adelman, California Coastal Records Project,
www.californiacoastline.org

The above case studies make clear that there are a number of competing considerations that may pose challenges to the full implementation of the Coastal Commission's *Sea Level Rise Policy Guidance*. Because the *Guidance* is not a regulation and the Coastal Commission cannot require updates to LCPs, the interests of various coastal constituencies are likely to create political and legal constraints to implementation of the *Guidance*. Here, I will briefly address some of the concerns of coastal constituent groups before returning to an examination of the Coastal Act itself, and the limitations that may exist in the broad adoption of the Commission's recommendations in the *Guidance*.

One of the primary aims of the Coastal Act is to balance local development concerns with the larger desire of California's residents to have access to and protect the state's coasts. One of the primary reasons for the Coastal Act is because the citizens of California felt that local governments could not be trusted to responsibly manage coastal resources for the benefit of all residents of the state.[118] Left to their own devices, local coastal governments have strong incentives to permit extensive local development both to increase the local tax

---

118. Interview with Coastal Commission Member (Dec. 4, 2009).

base and to win political support. In fact, even under the current system of LCPs, it is widely believed that local coastal governments do not generally follow their own local coastal plans, particularly outside the narrow band of coastal land where permitting decisions are appealable to the Coastal Commission.[119] Thus, the system itself creates inherent tensions between local governments and the Coastal Commission. To this end, counties also report being resentful of the Coastal Commission's original jurisdiction over seawalls, which was granted in an amendment to the Coastal Act, because it bypasses the local permitting process.[120] At the same time, however, local governments recognize that political will to discuss planned retreat at the local level can be limited because the issue is large and complicated and requires significant resources.[121]

Both organized groups of property owners and NGOs also work to influence decision making at the Coastal Commission level. Property owners in general appear to feel that they are a small, underrepresented community, and that the Coastal Commission does not adequately protect their interests. They view the Coastal Commission as the most powerful agency in the state and believe that the Coastal Commission is too isolated from the political process. Property owners seem to think that the Coastal Commission proceeds on a permit-by-permit basis as a means to disempower larger associations. In fact, the Coastal Commission proceeds in this manner because it is all that they have authority to do. Particularly in the Opal Cliffs area, there is broad support amongst property owners to pursue a larger regional solution to the erosion problem. Property owners in the area believe that the appropriate solution is the extension of the Pleasure Point seawall.

On the other hand, environmental groups are encouraging long-range planning and retreat along the California Coast. As the Capitola Sea Cave Case demonstrates, the role of environmental groups in creating innovative solutions to current challenges to the Coastal Act's armoring provisions is significant. However, the Land's End approval and the *Guidance* both suggest that rather than time-limited permits that can be revisited, the Commission has favored approaches where sea level rise impacts are considered in project design. Property owners in general maintain that because the state permitted the construction, it is under an obligation to allow the property owner to protect it. Note that this is particularly problematic when houses are granted CDPs from local permitting authorities but the Commission itself issued permits for seawalls. Further, the Coastal Commission historically has appeared to accept

---

119. *Id.*; Interview with Coastal Commission Staff Member (Dec. 3, 2009).
120. Interview with Local Government Official (Oct. 2, 2009).
121. *Id.*

as a political reality that once a structure is permitted on the coast it is essentially there forever.[122]

The *Guidance* represents an important step in encouraging local governments in California to begin to engage in comprehensive planning to address sea level rise. However, the guidance itself emphasizes that it is not a new law or regulation, and therefore not binding. Even if the Coastal Commission did wish to take further steps to require comprehensive, long-range planning to address sea level rise, it is unclear how such plans would be enforceable under the current structure of the Coastal Act.[123]

The Coastal Act requires that all local governments have a local coastal plan that is approved by the Coastal Commission.[124] The Act says that these local coastal plans are to be updated once every five years, but it fails to grant anyone the authority to mandate such updates or specify any penalties for failure to update local coastal plans. As a result, once the initial local coastal plan is approved, there is essentially nothing the Commission can do to force its amendment.[125] In fact, there are some local coastal plans that are over thirty years old and have not been updated. The Coastal Commission can conduct periodic reviews of the LCPs and make recommendations for modifications to the plans. However, as with the general provisions calling for plan updates, there is no way to enforce the recommendations resulting from a periodic review.[126] The result is that many local governments have LCPs that are so outdated as to be meaningless.

This exacerbates one of the other major weaknesses of the Coastal Act, namely lack of compliance with LCPs and a limited zone of appeal to the Coastal Commission. When the Coastal Act was first passed, the Commission missed a key opportunity to create appeal zones through the designation of sensitive coastal resources, and therefore the appellate jurisdiction of the Commission is more or less confined to the first row of homes along the beach.[127] This narrow appellate jurisdiction further limits the ability of the Commission to enforce any sort of long-term planning for sea level rise because it cannot reach beyond the first row of homes to ensure that future development accommodates the potential risks of sea level rise.

---

122. Interview with Coastal Commission Member (Dec. 4, 2009).

123. *Id.*

124. Cal. Pub. Res. Code §30512.

125. Interview with Coastal Commission Member (Dec. 4, 2009); Interview with Coastal Commission Staff Member (Dec. 3, 2009); Interview with Nonprofit Organization Staff Member (Sept. 30, 2009).

126. Interview with Coastal Commission Member (Dec. 4, 2009).

127. *Id.*

If the Coastal Act is not amended, to give the Commission authority to require updates to local coastal plans, it is difficult to imagine the Commission's current case-by-case approach to seawalls being altered by the adoption of a comprehensive plan or a full set of updated LCPs that incorporate sea level rise considerations. Under the current institutional structure, the Commission will have to work to actively engage local governments and stakeholders to encourage them to voluntarily reopen their local coastal plans for consideration of the impacts of sea level rise. Absent a legal mandate that all local governments participate, local governments have a variety of potential incentives not to participate, including the argument that their adaptation actions are likely to be meaningless if there is no concerted effort to respond to sea level rise on the regional level. Thus, the Coastal Commission could have an important role to play in providing resources for local communities to come together to engage in regional planning, particularly with respect to hazard mitigation.[128]

Sea Level Rise Adaptation in the San Francisco Bay

Overview of Legal Framework

In contrast to the ocean coastline, the San Francisco Bay is managed by an entirely separate regulatory agency, the Bay Conservation and Development Commission. Passed in response to growing citizen concern that development and infill would ultimately reduce the San Francisco Bay to a mere river, the McAteer-Petris Act established the BCDC in 1965.[129] The Bay Conservation and Development Commission is a twenty-seven member commission that is charged with regulating dredging and filling of the Bay and development of the Bay shoreline.[130] BCDC's membership includes a broad variety of stakeholders, representing federal, state, and local governments as well as members of the public living in the San Francisco Bay area.[131] Under the McAteer-Petris Act,

---

128. Interview with Coastal Commission Member (Dec. 3, 2009).

129. *The McAteer-Petris Act: History*, SAN FRANCISCO BAY CONSERVATION AND DEVELOPMENT COMMISSION, http://www.bcdc.ca.gov/plans/mcateer_petris.html (last updated Feb. 26, 2010).

130. CAL. GOV'T CODE § 66632 (West 2009).

131. *Id.* § 66620.

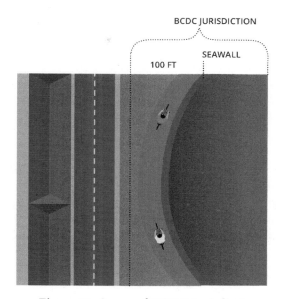

Figure 29: Scope of BCDC Jurisdiction

BCDC is granted broad authority to write its own rules governing development and fill of the Bay in the form of the Bay Plan.[132] The BCDC itself writes the Bay Plan, which then becomes the regulatory framework that governs decision making in the Bay. This great flexibility in the regulatory framework governing BCDC's actions results in a structure that is well suited to adapt to changes in the Bay's environment and protect the long-term health of the Bay.

While the McAteer-Petris Act grants BCDC broad discretion as to the basis for its regulatory activities to protect the Bay, BCDC's geographic jurisdiction is extraordinarily limited. BCDC has regulatory jurisdiction over all submerged lands in the Bay, which are owned by the State Lands Commission, and over a shoreline strip of land extending one hundred feet landward of the shoreline.[133] BCDC also has limited jurisdiction over salt ponds and wetlands along the Bay.[134]

---

132. Bay Plan, *supra* note 10, at 33, 72; Interview with BCDC Staff Member (Oct. 5, 2009).

133. Cal. Gov't Code §66632.

134. Bay Plan, *supra* note 10, at 4.

The McAteer-Petris Act further limits BCDC's jurisdiction by segmenting the Bay, designating some parts of the Bay shoreline priority use areas. Within priority use areas, BCDC may only permit those developments that constitute water-dependent uses.[135] The result is that in priority use areas, BCDC is able to exercise permitting discretion to shape coastal development.[136] In contrast, along parts of the Bay shoreline that are not priority use areas, BCDC may only deny a permit on the grounds that the proposed development fails to provide the maximum feasible public access to the shore.[137] Further, BCDC is only able to exercise its authority on a permit-by-permit basis, so its ability to engage in comprehensive planning is limited.[138] However, the BCDC has broad authority to write its own rules governing bayside development, which are set forth in the Bay Plan.

While the BCDC's landside jurisdiction is extraordinarily limited, it has led the way in encouraging municipalities along the Bay to take sea level rise into consideration and has exercised its authority to amend the Bay Plan to expressly require the consideration of climate change. Under amendments to the Bay Plan adopted on October 6, 2011, there are a number of new findings and policies that are designed to facilitate adaptation to sea level rise.[139] The Bay Plan's new findings emphasize the importance of enhancing the adaptive capacity and resilience of the Bay's ecosystem. The Bay Plan amendments also adopt the California Climate Adaptation Strategy's finding that state agencies should not plan, develop, or build any new infrastructure that will require significant protection from sea level rise. The new Bay Plan climate change policies require that a qualified engineer conduct a sea level rise risk assessment for any new project along the Bay shoreline. If the assessment determines that an area will be vulnerable to sea level rise, the only developments that the BCDC will approve are repairs to existing facilities, small projects that do not increase risks to public safety, infill developments, and those new developments that can demonstrate they are designed to be "resilient to a midcentury sea level rise projection."[140] While the requirements to demonstrate resilience to a midcentury sea level rise projection are not specified, BCDC officials have indicated that they believe there are few categories of developments that will

---

135. *Id.* at 6.
136. LIVING WITH A RISING BAY, *supra* note 2, at 7; Interview with BCDC Staff Member (Oct. 5, 2009).
137. BAY PLAN, *supra* note 10, at 6.
138. LIVING WITH A RISING BAY, *supra* note 2, at 5.
139. BCDC Res. No. 11-08.
140. *Id.* at 17.

Key Elements of the Bay Plan's Climate Change Amendment

The October 2011 Bay Plan amendment to address climate change marked a significant step toward addressing sea level rise in land use planning in the San Francisco Bay. The key elements of the Bay Plan's Climate Change Amendments include:

- an acknowledgment that landward marsh migration may be necessary to sustain marsh acreage as sea level rises and a policy calling for buffers between marshlands and development to be provided in order to facilitate such migration;
- an acknowledgment of the need to adapt to sea level rise and the potential impacts of sea level rise on key infrastructure in the Bay;
- a requirement that larger shoreline development projects include a risk assessment prepared by a qualified engineer of the 100-year flood elevation;
- a requirement that new shoreline development projects demonstrate they are "resilient to a mid-century sea level rise projection" and that projects intended to remain in place after mid-century develop an adaptive management plan to respond to sea level rise; and
- a call for the Commission along with regional, state, local, and federal entities, to develop a regional sea level rise adaptation strategy to promote resilience and protect critical developed areas along the Bay shoreline and important natural ecosystems.

meet this goal. In fact, in interviews one of the few examples that BCDC officials gave of communities that might meet this criterion were those communities that would be designed to float as the land upon which they are built becomes inundated. In addition, if a new development is projected to remain in place beyond mid-century, the developer must prepare an adaptive management plan to address long-term impacts that will arise as sea level rises. The new Bay Plan policies also call for the formulation of a regional strategy that will identify which areas should be defended from sea level rise and how they should be protected. The BCDC's rules thus take important steps towards shaping coastal development to both reduce the vulnerability of the built environment and to preserve important habitats and ecosystems.

The Redwood City Saltworks

The Redwood City Saltworks site is a commercial salt production facility owned by Cargill just outside of Redwood City, California. The site has been used for commercial salt production since 1901 and was acquired by Cargill when it purchased the Leslie Salt Company in 1978.[141] At its peak, Cargill held over 29,000 acres of land in the West Bay, and the plant on the Saltworks site alone produced over 350,000 tons of salt annually.[142] In 1974 the San Francisco Bay National Wildlife Refuge was established on Cargill's operating salt ponds, and Cargill sold 15,000 acres of its land to the refuge in 1979.[143] Since this time, Cargill has continued to sell of portions of its lands in the West Bay.[144] In 2003, Cargill donated and sold over 16,000 acres of land in the West Bay, constituting most of its remaining holdings other than the Saltworks site, to a combination of federal and state agencies so that they could undertake the South Bay Salt Ponds Restoration Project.[145] This restoration project is considered essential to both ecosystem protection and minimizing sea level rise impacts in the Bay,[146] and is currently the largest wetland restoration project on the West Coast. The Saltworks site was not included in the 2003 land sale largely because the government and Cargill could not agree on a price. Within the community, Cargill's decision to withhold the project from the sale led to the general belief that the company planned to develop the site.[147]

Confirming this belief, in 2006 DMB Associates partnered with Cargill and initiated a community outreach process regarding the potential development of the Saltworks site. This process is a normal part of the DMB de-

---

141. Memorandum from San Francisco Bay Conservation and Development Commission on Brief on the Redwood City Saltworks Project to Commissioners and Alternates (Feb. 27, 2009) [hereinafter Saltworks Memorandum], http://www.bcdc.ca.gov/meetings/commission/2009/03-05_RCSaltworks.pdf.

142. *Id.*

143. Cargill: Salt: About: San Francisco Bay Sea Salt: Cargill's Legacy—The Environmental Renaissance of San Francisco Bay, http://www.cargill.com/salt/about/san-francisco-bay-salt/environmental-renaissance/index.jsp (last visited Feb. 24, 2016).

144. Saltworks Memorandum, *supra* note 141, at 2.

145. *Id.*

146. Once established, salt marshes trap sediments and can actually elevate the Bay Shoreline, thereby mitigating the impacts of Sea Level Rise. *Climate Change & Sea Level Rise*, SOUTH BAY SALT POND RESTORATION PROJECT, http://www.southbayrestoration.org/climate// (last visited Feb. 24, 2016).

147. Interview with Local Government Official (Oct. 13, 2009).

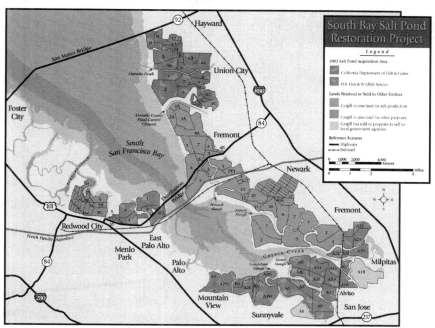

Figure 30: South Bay Salt Ponds Restoration
Source: South Bay Salt Pond Restoration Project

velopment process where they conduct extensive community outreach before submitting a plan for development.[148] These initial outreach efforts sparked

Figure 31: The Saltworks Site
© 2009 Google

---

148. Interview with DMB Official (Oct. 12, 2009).

concern from environmental groups about further development in the Bay and concerned local residents who felt that the area should remain as open space.[149] As a result, Save the Bay and several other local environmental groups sponsored a ballot measure in the fall 2008 elections dubbed Measure W. Measure W called for a requirement of a two-thirds majority in voter ratification for all future changes to the general plan expanding designations for future development areas and other designations of public space.[150] Concerned that Measure W interfered too much with the City's planning ability in other spheres but aware that the Saltworks issue would ultimately require a voter referendum, the Redwood City Council sponsored its own ballot measure, Measure V.[151] Measure V called for the adoption of an amendment to the city charter that would have required approval by the majority of voters of any future development on the Saltworks site.[152] Both of these measures were defeated in the November 2008 election, but they serve to demonstrate that there is potentially strong opposition to the Saltworks development. Further, these measures highlight an additional challenge in developing the Saltworks site: only part of the land is currently zoned for development, and the proposed build-out of the Saltworks site will require an amendment to the city's general plan.[153]

The project, however, split the environmental community because it is billed as a smart growth community. The Saltworks site is the only open infill area for major new development in the South Bay, which experiences a chronic housing shortage relative to the number of jobs in the area.[154] The proposed development would also provide key transit links through a bus to the current CalTrain station and a proposed ferry terminal.[155] As such, the development could provide the South Bay an important opportunity to reduce emissions from commuter traffic and thereby help the state to meet its obligations under AB 32.[156] Therefore, some smart growth advocates have gone so far as to argue

---

149. *Id.*

150. *Measure W: Land Use Classification City of Redwood City*, SMART VOTER (2008), http://www.smartvoter.org/2008/11/04/ca/sm/meas/W/ (last visited Feb. 24, 2016).

151. Interview with Local Government Official (Oct. 13, 2009).

152. *Measure V: Cargill Lands City of Redwood City*, SMART VOTER (2008), http://www.smartvoter.org/2008/11/04/ca/sm/meas/V/ (last visited Feb. 24, 2016).

153. Shaun Bishop, *Redwood City to Weigh Cargill Plan*, SAN JOSE MERCURY NEWS, Aug. 9, 2009, http://www.mercurynews.com/ci_13028647 (last visited Feb. 24, 2016).

154. REDWOOD CITY SALTWORKS, SALTWORKS 50/50 BALANCED PLAN: APPLICATION SUBMITTAL AND STATEMENT OF JUSTIFICATION at III-3 (2009) [hereinafter SALTWORKS 50/50 PLAN].

155. *Id.* at III-5.

156. *Id.*

The Competing 2008 Ballot Measures on the Redwood City Saltworks

Measure W was a ballot initiative by Bay-area environmental groups that was intended to require a 2/3 voter majority for any changes to the City's general plan to expand development. It read as follows:

> *Measure W*: Shall a Charter Amendment requiring two-thirds voter ratification of legislative acts approving certain land uses in area of the City designated as "Park," "Unimproved Areas (Land or Water)," "Future Development Expanding Limits of Urbanization," "Controlled Waterways (Redwood Shores Area)," or "San Francisco Bay Water" in the General Plan or designated as "Tidal Plain" or "Redwood Shores Bay Front" in the Zoning Code, with exemptions for housing obligations, takings, and vested rights, be adopted?

Measure V was a narrower measure proposed by the City council that was specifically directed to the Saltworks site. It read as follows:

> *Measure V*: Shall a Charter Amendment requiring majority voter approval for future development of the Cargill Lands, consisting of approximately 1,450 acres east of Highway 101 and south of Seaport Boulevard, with exemptions for takings and vested rights, be adopted?

---

that anything other than a full build out of the Saltworks site is irresponsible from a climate change mitigation perspective.[157]

Once the ballot measures had been defeated, DMB resumed its process and submitted a development plan for the Saltworks to the Redwood City City Council in May 2009.[158] Further confirming plans to develop the site, Cargill announced in October 2009 that it would not renew its open space contract with the city, which gave the company tax credits in exchange for its pledge to continue to preserve the Saltworks site as open space.[159] DMB's development

---

157. Peter Calthorpe, *"Saltworks" Plan—That's Smart Growth*, San Francisco Chron., June 14, 2009, at H-3.

158. Interview with DMB Official (Oct. 12, 2009).

159. *Saltworks Ends Open Space Contract*, San Mateo Daily J., Oct. 3, 2009, http://www.smdailyjournal.com/article_preview.php?id=117484 (last visited Feb. 24, 2016).

AB 32 and Transportation Emissions

California's Global Warming Solutions Act of 2006 (AB 32) adopted a broad, economy-wide approach to addressing California's greenhouse gas emissions. Among the many goals of AB 32 is the reduction of emissions from the transportation sector. The agencies that implement AB 32 set forth their plans for doing so in the *Scoping Plan*, a document required by law that must be updated every four years. The 2014 update to the *Scoping Plan* highlights California's efforts to reduce transportation emissions, which include:

- Adoption of the Low-Carbon Fuel Standard, which requires the incorporation of biofuels into gasoline and diesel supplies;
- Vehicle GHG standards and the zero emission vehicle regulations; and
- Planning strategies to reduce the number of miles people drive.

With respect to planning strategies, the 2014 *Scoping Plan* update highlights "Sustainable Community Strategies" adopted by seven Metropolitan Planning Organizations in the state.

---

proposal, called the "50-50 Balanced Plan" amounted to a plan to "develop a mini city" of 12,000 home sites on the roughly 1,200 acres of land at the Saltworks site.[160]

DMB emphasized both the smart growth features of this particular community and its history of development in an environmentally conscious manner. The company asserted that its model was to only partner with institutional landowners, such as Cargill, so that it could take its time making development plans and proceed in a way that is reflective of community desires and sensitive to the environment.[161] DMB's 50-50 Balanced Plan was the result of over 2 years of outreach, and the company stated that it entered such outreach projects with no pre-conceived ideas about what the development should look like.[162] According to the company's own statistics, more than 62% of Redwood

---

160. Shaun Bishop, *Redwood City Orders Studies of Proposal to Develop Cargill Salt Flats*, San Jose Mercury News, Aug. 11, 2009, http://www.mercurynews.com/ci_13040496?source=rss (last visited Feb. 24, 2016).

161. Interview with DMB Official (Oct. 12, 2009).

162. *Id.*

City residents supported the 50-50 Plan. However, local press reports claimed that DMB's surveys were all conducted months before the actual development plan was announced.[163]

While DMB emphasized the sustainable features of its community, it appeared to downplay the risks posed by sea level rise. Most of the proposed community was within a FEMA A-1 flood zone, and its primary means of protection would be a surrounding levee system.[164] The proposal under the 50-50 Plan would have included low-density development closer to the water, tidal marsh transitional areas, and a bayside park that DMB determined could accommodate up to 1.5 meters of sea level rise because it would be built to allow levees to be raised in the future.[165] Specifically, the levees in the community would be built with a larger than normal outside slope and a wider than normal top so that they could be raised in the future if necessary.[166] DMB stated that such levees would not only be sufficient to protect its community from sea level rise, but also that they would be essential to alleviate unrelenting flood conditions in the Redwood City area.[167] Most interestingly, at the time the 50-50 Plan was proposed, DMB appeared to take the position that the smart growth benefits were so significant that sea level rise risk need not be a meaningful factor in evaluation of the community. Rather, DMB appeared to emphasize levees merely as an incentive for approval, as they would have provided needed flood protection to existing structures within Redwood City.

In 2010, the Redwood City City Council determined that DMB's application for the 50-50 Plan was complete and the project could proceed to analysis under the California Environmental Quality Act.[168] However, as significant controversy over the project continued, DMB withdrew its permit application in 2012.[169] According to DMB's website the company is currently developing a revised plan that will confine proposed development to areas already pro-

163. Bishop, *supra* note 160.

164. Saltworks 50/50 Plan, *supra* note 154, at V-60.

165. *Id.* at V-29.

166. JMH Weiss, Inc., DMB Saltworks, Redwood City, CA, Infrastructure 5 (2009).

167. Interview with DMB Official (Oct. 12, 2009).

168. City council of Redwood City, Minutes of the Special Meeting of the City Council of Redwood City, Feb. 1, 2010, http://documents.redwoodcity.org/public weblink/0/doc/80050/Page1.aspx (last visited Feb. 24, 2016) (as of February 1, 2010 the City Council decided that the project could proceed to CEQA analysis).

169. http://www.rcsaltworks.com/ (last visited Jan. 19, 2017).

posed for such use under Redwood City's general plan and provide for restoration on most of the property.[170]

When it was considering the Saltworks proposal, it was clear that Redwood City had worked with BCDC and was aware of the threat posed by sea level rise.[171] In its role as a risk manager, the real challenge for the City is what to do to respond to the threats posed by sea level rise. It is possible that Redwood City could amend its general plan or zoning requirements to respond to the threats of sea level rise, but this is a long and tedious process for which there has not been political momentum. However, because most of the flood prone areas along the Bay are already developed, one of the most important roles of local governments like Redwood City will be in managing inundation risks and communicating them in terms that people can understand.[172] The City believes that it is likely to discuss retreat as it moves forward, but acknowledges that large issues remain in determining who will pay for retreat and where the bought out residents will go.[173]

It may well be the case that when framed to evaluate its impact on California's overall vulnerability to climate change, the mitigation benefits of putting more commuters near work will outweigh the adaptation benefits of avoiding development in a hazardous area like the Saltworks site. However, when the 50-50 Plan was under consideration, it was clear that the sensitivity of the development site to future sea level rise was not a primary consideration from the beginning of the process. Overall, the City's decision to push off the discussion of sea level rise appeared to be based on two major factors. First, as with many local governments, the City appeared to be overwhelmed by the magnitude of impacts presented in BCDC's flood maps, leading local officials to decide that it is easier to put off decision making regarding sea level rise. Second, the developer has made a conscious decision to emphasize the smart growth aspects of the project while downplaying sea level rise risks. Given the important obligations of the state under AB 32, it could have been tempting for the Council to focus on the upside of the project and avoid the relatively more politically challenging issue of responding to sea level rise.

The ultimate success of BCDC's efforts to promote measures to adapt to sea level rise in the Bay remains uncertain. BCDC's primary challenge in pro-

---

170. *Id.*
171. Interview with Local Government Official (Oct. 13, 2009).
172. *Id.*
173. *Id.*

moting adaptation to rising sea levels stems from the fact that it is an agency that was created to keep the San Francisco Bay from getting smaller and now it must deal with challenges associated with a Bay that is getting larger.[174] Further, BCDC has no meaningful landside jurisdiction beyond that which is necessary to protect public access to the Bay. While BCDC's past efforts with developers have resulted in positive relationships and public access that goes far beyond the minimum that the law requires,[175] one must ask whether these relationships can be preserved in the context of rising seas, particularly as BCDC promotes a policy of selective retreat. BCDC's aim has been to educate the public and local governments regarding the risks that the Bay Area faces as a result of sea level rise and engage in strategic planning to determine which portions of the Bay must be saved and where retreat might happen.[176] While BCDC can play an important role in bringing relevant actors to the table to have this discussion, it can do nothing on the land side to limit the value of development at risk due to sea level rise.

What's more, BCDC's current approach to bring local governments on board appears to have resulted in a form of paralysis by analysis. That is, local governments who have sat down with BCDC understand the huge amount of infrastructure that will be at risk due to sea level rise, but they are not equipped with the tools to deal with it. Local governments neither have specific legal mandates requiring them to do anything about sea level rise nor the financial or staffing resources to engage in comprehensive sea level rise planning. Therefore, any meaningful adaptation will require not only coordinated responses but also leadership from state level agencies as to how to move forward. In attempting to foster discussion about selective retreat, BCDC has attempted to assume this role. However, more needs to be done to present local governments with the risks and a range of adaptation options or other support resources at the same time. Without such resources, local governments will simply add sea level rise to the list of things to worry about in the future that are not politically expedient today. This is particularly challenging to BCDC because its land side jurisdiction does not give it the authority to require local governments to do anything. Thus, for BCDC's efforts to be successful, it will require the resources and engagement of other state agencies to adequately support local governments as they struggle with planning for sea level rise.

---

174. Interview with BCDC official (Oct. 5, 2009).
175. *Id.*
176. *Id.*

Comparing Challenges and Opportunities along the Ocean and Bay Shorelines

There are two major differences in the authority held by BCDC and the Coastal Commission that one might expect to lead to different outcomes with respect to climate change adaptation: 1) differences in territorial jurisdiction and 2) the requirement that local governments prepare local coastal plans. Based on the case studies illustrated above, it is apparent that while the different powers of BCDC and the Coastal Commission should lead to substantively different outcomes, gaps in the Coastal Act and LCP process have led to substantially similar outcomes on the ground. The Coastal Commission's inability to require LCP updates every five years or that local governments adopt particular LCP amendments has resulted in stagnation of the process. Land use planning is potentially a very powerful tool in aiding communities to reduce their vulnerability to sea level rise. However, current limitations in the Coastal Act have rendered the LCP process nearly meaningless in the absence of political will on the part of the local governments. Because of its current inability to enforce coastal land use planning requirements, the Coastal Commission finds itself in largely the same position as BCDC, relegated in large part to a leadership role where it can attempt to foster local government action by providing information on impacts and planning guidance.

It is along these lines that one of the most significant differences in the Agencies' ability to promote adaptation may emerge from their different relationships with local governments. BCDC's work has been characterized by strong relationships with local governments. This is largely a result of two significant factors: 1) BCDC has no direct regulatory authority over local governments, limiting tensions between the agency and those responsible for local land use planning, and 2) the different stances of the two agencies with respect to development. Many outsiders view the Coastal Commission's primary mission to be to limit coastal development and preserve ocean coastline in its natural state.[177] In contrast, BCDC has historically been much more pro-development. Furthermore, many of the Commissioners on the BCDC are representatives of local governments, and they are working in an environment that is largely built out. The result is that BCDC has been very successful in establishing collaborative relationships with communities and developers, while the Coastal

---

177. Interview with BCDC Official (Oct. 5, 2009).

Commission has often been viewed as an adversary.[178] These different historical relationships will certainly come into play as the two agencies attempt to bring local governments to the table to engage in sea level rise planning. However, questions remain as to whether BCDC will be able to both maintain its good relationship with the development community and local governments and enforce its new sea level rise policies.

The one unique and significant authority that the Coastal Commission retains is its jurisdiction over seawalls. This authority helps to insulate seawall requests from the usual local politics of disaster response, which would likely lead to more extensive coastal armoring. However, as the Capitola sea cave case makes clear, the Commission's interpretation of "existing" and its practice of imposing deed restrictions will surely continue to come into conflict in the future. In the long run, political pressures to allow armoring in already urbanized areas will grow stronger, and the Commission's ability to maintain its no armoring policies in these areas is in doubt.[179] Thus, without more vertical integration into the long-term land use planning process to stop current coastal development, the seawall prohibition alone will not be sufficient to promote rolling easements along the California Coast.

---

178. *Id.*
179. Interview with Coastal Commission Member (Dec. 4, 2009).

Chapter 6

North Carolina

North Carolina's Outer Banks are a series of coastal barrier islands that run from the North Carolina-Virginia border in the North down to the southern end of the state. While barrier islands are a common feature of many coastal areas, the Outer Banks are unique due to the significant distance between the barrier islands and the mainland.[1] Like all barrier islands, the Outer Banks are inherently unstable, and a combination of movement of sand by waves and currents and rising sea levels causes the Outer Banks to slowly migrate landward.[2] Today, much of the Outer Banks is protected as part of the Cape Hatteras and Cape Lookout National Seashores. North Carolina's Outer Banks remain a very popular vacation destination and as such have experienced significant development in those areas that are not set aside for conservation.

The dynamic nature of North Carolina's coast and its high desirability for recreation and tourism pose significant management challenges. Recognizing the importance of public access to the coast, North Carolina's Coastal Resources Commission ("CRC") implemented a "no hardened structures" policy in 1985. As discussed in more detail below, this policy prevents the installation of seawalls, riprap, and other hard forms of shoreline protection along North Carolina's ocean coastline. While hardened structures are prohibited, the level of development on the Outer Banks has been significant and the dynamic retreat of the Outer Banks continues. Together these phenomena have resulted in the demand for temporary erosion control structures and non-hardened forms of

---

1. *Geology of the Albemarle-Pamlico Estuarine System*, NCDENR, http://portal.ncdenr.org/web/apnep/geology (last visited Feb. 25, 2016).
2. Robert Dolan & Harry Lins, U.S. Department of the Interior & U.S. Geological Survey, The Outer Banks of North Carolina, Professional Paper No. 1177-B (2000), http://pubs.usgs.gov/pp/1177b/report.pdf; Orrin H. Pilkey et al., The North Carolina Shore and its Barrier Islands: Restless Ribbons of Sand 44–48 (1998).

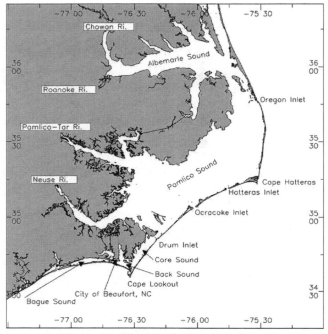

Figure 32: The North Carolina Coast
Source: http://www.nauticalcharts.noaa.gov/pdfcharts/

shoreline protection. Beach nourishment is seen as key to the future of the Outer Banks as it provides a potential way to keep the shoreline in a stable location without building seawalls. In fact, one local official claimed that beach communities that do not have systematic nourishment plans are shortsighted and may as well quit existing as communities now.[3]

In addition to the Outer Banks, North Carolina boasts an extensive estuarine shoreline. North Carolina differs from the other states evaluated in detail in this book in that it manages these two coastlines under a single authority: the Coastal Area Management Act ("CAMA"). Despite having a unified management structure for its entire coastal zone, North Carolina has developed two very different approaches to dealing with its extensive shoreline. Since the inception of North Carolina's Coastal Zone Management Program, the legislature and Division of Coastal Management have emphasized the preservation

---

3. Interview with Local Government Official (Dec. 4, 2009).

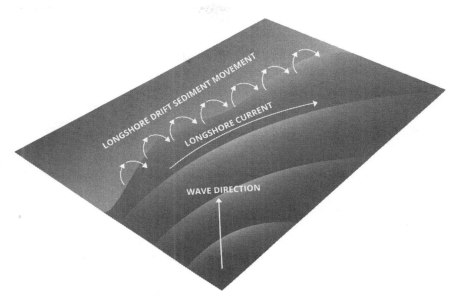

Figure 33: Littoral Transport

of public trust rights on the ocean front, particularly access to the beach.[4] However, estuarine shorelines have been managed in a manner that is much more oriented towards private property rights.[5]

On the estuarine side, the Pamlico-Albemarle Sound provides one of the most significant nursery habitats along the East Coast, and is the largest lagoonal estuarine system in the country.[6] Because of the extensive amount of low-lying land along the coastal sounds, the Division of Coastal Management estimates that North Carolina's estuaries are actually far more vulnerable to sea level rise than the ocean coastline.[7] However, the impacts of this rise and the potential for coastal squeeze of essential marsh habitat are unknown because CRC rules currently permit construction of bulkheads all along the estuarine coastline.[8] This potential for habitat loss is likely to be exacerbated by

---

4. Interview with North Carolina Division of Coastal Management ("DCM") Staff Member (Nov. 5, 2009).

5. *Id.*

6. Albemarle-Pamlico National Estuary Program. Work Plan for the Cooperative Agreement Between the U.S. Environmental Protection Agency and NC Department of Environment and Natural Resources 4 (2009), http://www.apnep.org/pages/FY2009_%20WORK PLAN.pdf.

7. Interview with DCM Staff Member (Nov. 5, 2009).

8. 15A N.C. Admin. Code §07H.1101.

Why Are Estuaries So Important?

Estuaries, including wetlands, have been recognized to provide a number of services that are important to the function of coastal ecosystems and that benefit human and natural communities ("ecosystem services"). One of the most important roles that estuaries play is as a breeding ground and home for juveniles of many aquatic species. The habitats in estuaries provide marine species with a source of food and refuge from larger predators in the early stages of their life and therefore play a key role in the long-term health of fisheries. Wetlands located in estuaries also play important roles in regulating improving water quality. Wetlands can trap sediments from upstream areas and also act to filter out nutrients from the water column. Wetlands can also play an important role in storm protection, as wetland vegetation absorbs the energy of storm surges and reduces their impact on upland communities.

---

the extensive development that took place along North Carolina's sounds during the real estate boom of the 1990s and early 2000s. The case study of the River Dunes development examines the decision-making process that led one developer to attempt to minimize the use of bulkheads. While this initial step may be a success, the case study reveals that the community as a whole will face challenges in dealing with the impacts of sea level rise.

Adaptation on North Carolina's Ocean Coast

Overview of Legal Framework

Coastal zone management in North Carolina is governed by the Coastal Area Management Act. CAMA delegates authority over coastal management to the North Carolina Division of Coastal Management ("DCM") and further grants permitting authority to the Coastal Resources Commission ("CRC").[9] CAMA was passed in 1974 because the general assembly found that "an immediate and pressing need exists to establish a comprehensive plan for the protection, preservation, orderly development, and management of the coastal

---

9. N.C. Gen. Stat. §113A-104.

area of North Carolina."[10] The most obvious difference between these two frameworks is in the state's "no hardened structures" policy. Since 1979, the state has enforced a ban on oceanfront hardening.[11] However, bulkheading has been permitted along the estuarine coast, and the state does not even have a good idea of how much of North Carolina's estuarine shoreline has been converted through the installation of hardened structures.[12]

CAMA covers all of North Carolina's coastal counties.[13] It is a cooperative program in which the state, through the Coastal Resources Commission, is responsible for designating Areas of Environmental Concern ("AECs") and minimum requirements for land use plans while local governments retain responsibility for creating and administering local land use plans that are consistent with CAMA's goals.[14] The Coastal Resources Commission is a thirteen-member body appointed by the governor with the majority of seats being designated to represent particular interests (e.g., development, local governments, natural sciences).[15] The members of the CRC are charged to act as representatives of the public and uphold the public trust.[16] In addition to the support it receives from DCM staff, the CRC is advised by the twenty member Coastal Resources Advisory Council, which is comprised of representatives including state and local government officials.[17]

The primary duties of the CRC are to shape the planning process by designating both AECs and the minimum requirements for CAMA land use plans. Once a local government prepares a land use plan, the CRC must review the land use plan and approve it if it meets CRC's minimum criteria.[18] All development within the CAMA counties should proceed in a manner that is consistent with the local government's approved land use plan. At minimum, a land use plan must state the objectives, policies, and standards of the local government that are to be followed for the use of public and private land within its jurisdiction.[19]

Under the CAMA rules, there are three types of land use plan that a local government may choose to write: a workbook plan, a core plan, or an ad-

---

10. *Id.* § 113A-102.

11. Jackson Mabry, *Sandbags: Temporary or Permanent? The Riggings Case Study*, LEGAL TIDES, Summer 2009, at 1.

12. Interview with DCM Staff Member (Nov. 5, 2009).

13. N.C. GEN. STAT. § 113A-103.

14. *Id.* § 113A-101.

15. *Id.* § 113A-104.

16. *Id.*

17. *Id.* § 113A-105.

18. *Id.* § 113A-106-08.

19. *Id.* § 113A-110.

vanced core plan.[20] The workbook plan is only available to municipalities that are creating their own plans and not located within Ocean Hazard Areas. It requires only a statement of purpose, land use map, suitability analysis, and land growth and development policies addressing the CAMA management topics and any AECs within its boundaries.[21] Core plans require a far more in-depth analysis of community concerns, existing conditions, and plans for the future, while advanced core plans are the same as core plans but exceed the CRC minimum requirements in at least two areas.[22] For a plan to obtain CRC certification, it must have all of the required elements of a core plan and be consistent with North Carolina's approved Coastal Zone Management Plan and federal laws.[23] All subsequent permitting is to be consistent with the approved CAMA land use plan.[24]

Once a CAMA land use plan is approved, it may be freely amended.[25] If a local government with an approved land use plan chooses to modify fewer than half of the policies in its land use plan, it may submit only those revised policies for certification. If more than half of the policies are amended, the CRC must newly certify the whole land use plan.[26] The only time that CAMA land use plans must be amended is when the CRC adopts new rules for CAMA land use plans. The CRC updates the rules for CAMA land use plans every five years, and local governments have six years from each set of rule updates to create a new land use plan.[27] As a result, local governments write new land use plans approximately once every five to ten years.

In addition, to its land use planning role, the CRC issues permits for all construction within AECs.[28] The backbone of CAMA permitting is the designation of areas of environmental concern. The four major classes of AEC in North Carolina are 1) estuarine and ocean ecosystem; 2) ocean hazard system; 3) public water supply; and 4) natural and cultural resource areas.[29] Permitting requirements under CAMA are triggered when the proposed activity is located within an AEC.[30] When proposed development is located within an

---

20. 15A N.C. Admin. Code §07B.0701(c).
21. Id.
22. Id. §07B.0702.
23. Id. §07B.0802.
24. N.C. Gen. Stat. §113A-111.
25. Id. §113A-110.
26. 15A N.C. Admin. Code. §07B.0901.
27. Id. §07B.0802.
28. 15A N.C. Admin. Code §07J.0201.
29. N.C. Gen. Stat. §113A-113.
30. Id. §113A-118.

AEC, development may not proceed without a CAMA permit.[31] Permits are issued by the CRC, which operates under the guidance of both state regulations and its own announced policies.[32]

Permitting within an AEC can proceed under a major permit, a minor permit, or a general permit.[33] A major permit is required for any major development, which includes projects covering more than twenty acres, construction covering more than 60,000 square feet, and any activities that require other state or federal permits.[34] Major development permits must be obtained directly from the Coastal Resources Commission.[35] Any development not meeting the thresholds of a major development and not covered under a general permit requires a minor permit.[36] Minor permits may be obtained either from the CRC or from a designated local permit officer.[37] Under CAMA, the Commission can designate certain classes of activities for which a development permit would otherwise be required to proceed under general permits.[38] General permits may be issued for development in Areas of Environmental Concern that will have insignificant impacts and do not require public review or comment.[39]

Further the CRC has designated classes of activities in AECs which are exempt from the CAMA permitting requirements.[40] There are two classes of exemptions that are likely to prove significant in terms of vulnerability reduction: 1) maintenance and repairs, and 2) beach bulldozing. Under the CAMA exemptions, maintenance and repairs can be excluded from CAMA permitting requirements when the structure to be repaired is imminently threatened, meaning that the foundation or septic system is less than twenty feet from the erosion scarp.[41] A structure more than twenty feet from the erosion scarp may also be deemed imminently threatened "when site conditions, such as a flat beach profile or accelerated erosion, tend to increase the risk of imminent damage to the structure."[42] The second important category of exemptions is beach bulldozing. A littoral owner may engage in beach bulldozing to create protec-

---

31. *Id.*
32. *Id.* § 113A-104.
33. *Id.* § 113A-118.
34. *Id.* § 113A-118(d).
35. 15A N.C. Admin. Code § 07J.0201.
36. N.C. Gen. Stat. § 113A-118(d).
37. 15A N.C. Admin. Code § 07J.0201.
38. N.C. Gen. Stat. § 113A-118.1.
39. 15A N.C. Admin. Code § 07J.1101.
40. *See id.* § 07K.0101.
41. *Id.* § 07K.0103(a).
42. *Id.*

Areas of Environmental Concern under CAMA

CAMA gives the CRC the authority to designate a wide variety of types of AECs. N.C. GEN. STAT. § 113A-113. Through regulations, the CRC has established four broad groupings that capture the 13 types of AECs that trigger CAMA permitting. 15A N.C. ADMIN. CODE § 07H.0103.

Estuarine and Ocean Systems: For the estuarine and ocean area the CRC's stated objective is "to conserve and manage estuarine waters, coastal wetlands, public trust areas, and estuarine and public trust shorelines as an interrelated group of AECs so as to safeguard and perpetuate their biological, social, economic, and aesthetic values and to ensure that development occurring within these AECs is compatible with natural characteristics so as to minimize the likelihood of significant loss of private property and public resources." *Id.* § 07H.0203.

The AECs within the estuarine and ocean system are as follows §§ 07H.0205 –.0207, .0209.

- Coastal Wetlands;
- Estuarine Waters;
- Public Trust Areas; and
- Coastal Shorelines. *Id.*

In these areas, only water-dependent uses are permitted. *Id.* § 07H.0208. The CRC may also permit development where the applicant can demonstrate that the public benefit of a project will outweigh any long-term adverse consequences of its construction. There are a set of additional requirements for development along coastal shorelines, which include a requirement that—with limited exceptions—all new development be set back at least 30 feet from the shoreline. *Id.* § 07H.0209(d)(10).

Ocean Hazard Systems: Ocean hazard areas are areas along North Carolina's Atlantic Coast that "because of their special vulnerability to erosion or other adverse effects of sand, wind, and water, uncontrolled or incompatible development could unreasonably endanger life or property." *Id.* § 07H.0301.

(continued)

Areas of Environmental Concern under CAMA

(*continued*)

The AECs within the Ocean Hazard System are as follows:

- Ocean erodible areas which have a high likelihood of "excessive erosion and significant shoreline fluctuation";
- Unvegetated beach areas, which are defined as those areas subject to high velocity flood waters; and
- Inlet hazard areas, which are defined as vulnerable due to their proximity to dynamic inlets. *Id.* §07H.0304.

In Ocean Hazard Areas, all new development must observe a setback that is determined by the size of the structure and the local erosion rate. *Id.* §07H.0306.

Public Water Supply: The public water supply category applies to areas containing "critical water supplies" which would adversely affect public health or require substantial expenditures to replace if damaged. The two types of AECs included in this category are small surface water supply watersheds and public water supply well fields. *Id.* §07H.0401.

Natural and Cultural Resource Areas: Natural and cultural resource areas are defined as "areas containing environmental, natural or cultural resources of more than local significance in which uncontrolled or incompatible development could result in major or irreversible damage to natural systems or cultural resources, scientific, educational, or associative values, or aesthetic qualities." *Id.* §07H.0501. The AECs in this category are as follows:

- Coastal areas that sustain remnant species;
- Natural areas supporting native plant and animal communities and provide habitat quality that is essentially unchanged by human activity;
- Unique coastal geologic formations;
- Significant coastal archaeological resources; and
- Significant coastal historic architectural resources. *Id.* §§07H.0505–.0507, .0509–.0510.

Figure 34: Beach Bulldozing
Source: North Carolina Coastal Federation

tive sand dunes without a CAMA permit when the following conditions are met: 1) the bulldozed beach must maintain a natural slope so as not to impede public access and the littoral owner may take no more than one foot of sand from the surface; 2) the bulldozing must stay within the bounds of the littoral owner's property unless he has permission from neighbors to extend it; 3) the material moved is all landward of the mean high water line; 4) the creation of dunes in this manner will not increase erosion on neighbors' property or impact cultural or natural resources; and 5) the bulldozing will protect either the foundation of the littoral owner's house or an on-site disposal system.[43] These two exemptions could potentially cover extensive activities to protect threatened littoral homes, thus giving the owners a false sense of security against natural hazards and making it more difficult to implement a policy of retreat.

Particularly significant in the context of coastal adaptation are the well-enumerated requirements for development in an ocean hazard area, which emphasize dune preservation for protection of property and life.[44] Most important among these requirements is the implementation of a setback in coastal hazard areas equal to thirty times the annual rate of erosion. In addition to these regulations, the Coastal Resources Commission has a no coastal hardening policy. This policy prohibits the hardening of ocean coastline when the planting of vegetation will be sufficient.[45] In practice, the CRC allows the installation of many "temporary" armoring structures, in the form of sandbag dikes.[46] As explained further below, the CRC's policies regarding

---

43. *Id.* §07K.0103(b).
44. *See id.* §07H.0301–.0305.
45. *Id.* §07M.0202.
46. *Id.* §07H.1705(a).

North Carolina's No Hardened Structures Policy

The CRC has observed a policy preventing the placement of hardened structures on North Carolina's coast since 1979. This policy was adopted into law as part of CAMA in 2003. The no hardened structures policy defines erosion control structure to mean "a breakwater, bulkhead, groin, jetty, revetment, seawall, or any similar structure." N.C. Gen. Stat. § 113A-115.1(a)(1). The statutory prohibition on the placement of these structures reads as follows:

> (b) No person shall construct a permanent erosion control structure in an ocean shoreline. The Commission shall not permit the construction of a temporary erosion control structure that consists of anything other than sandbags in an ocean shoreline. This subsection shall not apply to any of the following:

> (1) Any permanent erosion control structure that is approved pursuant to an exception set out in a rule adopted by the Commission prior to July 1, 2003.

> (2) Any permanent erosion control structure that was originally constructed prior to July 1, 1974, and that has since been in continuous use to protect an inlet that is maintained for navigation.

> (3) Any terminal groin permitted pursuant to this section. *Id.* § 113A-115.1.

---

temporary erosion control structures have been in flux over the last few years, and the ability to protect coastal properties has recently been significantly expanded.

Underlying all of this statutory law and regulatory structure are the basic principles of North Carolina common law that apply to littoral property. Following the general common law, North Carolina adheres to both the doctrines of accretion and erosion, meaning that the boundary between private property and state submerged lands shifts with gradual, imperceptible changes in the shoreline.[47] North Carolina also appears to follow the doctrine of avul-

---

47. Carolina Beach Fishing Pier, Inc. v. Carolina Beach, 177 S.E.2d 513 (N.C. 1970).

sion, recognizing that sudden shifts in the shoreline do not change the boundary of title between the littoral owner and the state: North Carolina claims title to all dry sand beach that is created through beach nourishment, and littoral owners have a limited right to replace their beaches after major storm events.[48]

However, state officials claim that it is the state's policy to assert title to all submerged lands, even when they are created in a storm event.[49] There is limited case law in North Carolina acknowledging that the doctrine of avulsion exists in common law, but none explicitly adjudicating a littoral boundary dispute resulting from an avulsive change.[50] Therefore, legal title to littoral lands after sudden shifts in the location of mean high tide appears to be murky at best.

The Riggings and Sandbags along the North Carolina Coast

In 1979, the Coastal Resources Commission enacted a rule forbidding the placement of hardened structures for erosion stabilization along North Carolina's ocean coast.[51] This "no hardened structures" policy was so successful that it was incorporated into CAMA by the legislature in 2003.[52] Under the "no hardened structures" policy the only means of erosion protection available to ocean front property owners are beach nourishment and seeking permits for the placement of temporary erosion control structures. The CRC's regulations allow property owners to apply for permits to place sandbags in front of their homes as temporary erosion control structures. Permits allow for the placement of sandbags for up to two years for structures smaller than 5,000 square feet and up to five years for larger structures.[53] The intention of the temporary erosion control structure is to give the property owner ample time to figure out a more permanent solution to the erosion threat.[54] To that end, there are three circumstances in which temporary erosion control structures may remain in place for longer than their permitted time: 1) the community is actively pursuing beach nour-

---

48. *Id.*

49. Interview with DCM Staff Member (Nov. 5, 2009).

50. *See* North Carolina v. Johnson, 179 S.E.2d 371, 383 (N.C. 1971) (citing Thompson on Real Property for the proposition that avulsive events do not create a change in title).

51. Mabry, *supra* note 11, at 1.

52. *See* N.C. GEN. STAT. §113A-115.1(b); Mabry, *supra* note 11, at 1.

53. 15A N.C. ADMIN. CODE §07H.0308(a)(2)(F).

54. Interview with Coastal Resources Commission Member (Nov. 23, 2009).

ishment, 2) the sandbags have become permanently covered with sand and support dune vegetation, or 3) the property owner obtains a variance from the CRC.[55]

Despite the time limitations on sandbags in CRC's regulations, many homes along the North Carolina coast have been protected by sandbags for decades.[56] Over the years, the CRC's general policy with respect to non-conforming sandbags has been to look the other way and continue to grant variances to homeowners.[57] Historically, the CRC has been reluctant to remove non-conforming sandbags because no one has come forward with a good permanent solution, and removal hurts both property owners who lose their homes and local governments who lose a part of their tax base.[58] As of 2010, the Division of Coastal Management estimated that there are 352 sandbagged structures along the North Carolina Coast.[59] Of these sandbag installations, it is thought that at least 150 of them illegally remain in place with neither current permits nor variances from the CRC.[60]

These sandbags can constitute a major interference with the public beach. In some places, sandbags protecting coastal homes form a continuous wall that is over six feet high.[61] As erosion along the Outer Banks continues, such sandbag walls could lead to the loss of the public beach in a manner similar to that observed with concrete seawalls. As a result, in July 2008, the Coastal Resources Commission voted to issue a removal order for non-conforming sandbags.[62] According to the CRC, the order would have required removal of all sandbags that are more than five years old, and may require removal of sandbags in as many as 250 different locations.[63]

Seeing an imminent threat to their properties, littoral owners immediately sought relief from the legislature. In May 2009 the legislature passed a bill im-

---

55. 15A N.C. Admin. Code §07H.0308(a)(2).
56. Mabry, *supra* note 11, at 1.
57. *Id.*
58. Interview with Coastal Resources Commission Member (Nov. 23, 2009).
59. *News and Events: History of the CRC's Sandbag Rules*, NCDENR Division of Coastal Management (2010).
60. Gareth McGrath, *Commission Refuses to Alter Sandbag Rules*, Star News Online, May 22, 2008, http://www.starnewsonline.com/article/20080522/ARTICLE/805220342 (last visited Feb. 25, 2016).
61. Jerry Allegood, *Time Runs Out for Sandbags on Beaches*, News & Observer, Sept. 22, 2009.
62. *Actions from July Meeting*, CRC (2008) (noting that the Commission unanimously endorsed sandbag removal enforcement based on DCM's prioritization).
63. Interview with Coastal Resources Commission Member (Nov. 23, 2009).

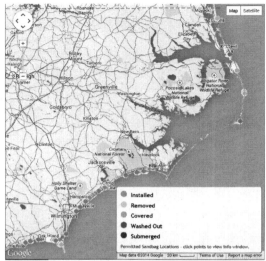

Figure 35: Sandbag Placement Along the North Carolina Coast
Source: North Carolina Division of Coastal Management

posing a one-year moratorium on the enforcement of the CRC's sandbag removal order.[64] Further, new legislation charged the CRC to conduct a study on the potential efficacy of terminal groins as an alternative means to slow erosion and protect coastal property.[65]

Released in March 2010, the Terminal Groin Study concluded that there is a significant and positive result, defined as halting erosion or causing accretion of sediments, within the first mile of shoreline from the terminal groin, and only mild increased erosion on the side opposite the terminal groin.[66] In its review of these results, the CRC concluded that the impacts of terminal groins amount to mere "noise" in the context of other inlet management activities occurring in the study areas.[67] Determining that the results of the Terminal Groin Study were inconclusive but recognizing the need to respond to the mandate of the legislature, the CRC concluded that the use of terminal groins should only be considered where all other options including relocation of threatened structures are deemed impracticable.[68] After issuing its findings

---

64. S.B. 998, General Assembly (N.C. 2009), http://www.ncga.state.nc.us/Sessions/2009/Bills/Senate/PDF/S998v2.pdf.

65. *Id.*

66. NCDENR, Terminal Groin Study Final Report (2010).

67. CRC, Terminal Groin Study Recommendations 3–4 (Apr. 1 2010).

68. *Id.* at 8.

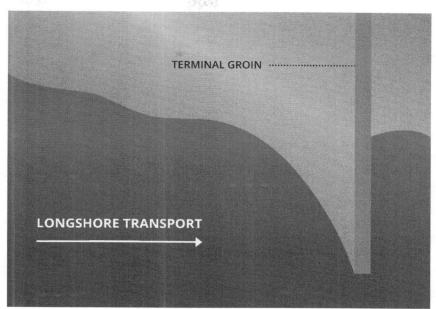

TERMINAL GROIN ··

LONGSHORE TRANSPORT
───────────────────────────▶

Figure 36: Terminal Groins

on the Terminal Groin Study, the CRC unanimously ordered the DCM to re-
sume enforcement activities against non-conforming sandbags.[69]

However, facing continuing difficulties in enforcing its sandbag rules, the
CRC adopted a series of revisions to these rules in February 2013.[70] Under the
revised rules, sandbags may be used as follows: (1) for two years to protect
buildings 5,000 square feet or smaller; (2) for five years to protect buildings
larger than 5,000 square feet; (3) for five years to protect properties located in
a community that is actively pursuing a beach nourishment project; (4) for
eight years for properties located in an Inlet Hazard Area adjacent to an inlet
for which a community is actively pursuing an inlet relocation project.[71] In addition, the rule revisions provide that existing sandbags in Inlet Hazard Areas
can receive an eight-year permit extension provided the structure protected by
the sandbags is still imminently threatened.[72]

---

69. *Meeting Minutes Sept. 15–17, 2010*, CRC.

70. *Actions from February Meeting*, CRC (2013).

71. *Sandbags for Temporary Erosion Control*, DCM, http://www.ncnhp.org/web/cm/
sandbags-for-temporary-erosion-control (last visited Feb. 25, 2016).

72. *Id.*

In 2012, North Carolina's General Assembly enacted House Bill 819, which provided that the CRC and the Division of Coastal Management of the Department of Environment and Natural Resources "shall not define rates of sea-level change for regulatory purposes prior to July 1, 2016";[73] however, counties, municipalities, and local governments were not prohibited from defining rates of sea-level change for regulatory purposes. The Bill required the CRC's Science Panel to deliver a five-year update to their 2010 report, "North Carolina Sea Level Rise Assessment," no later than March 31, 2015.[74] Furthermore, the Science Panel's 2015 report was required describe the limitations and assumptions of its models; address the full range of sea-level change hypotheses, including falling sea levels and decelerating sea rise; compare determinations of sea level based on historical calculations versus predictive models; and calculate sea level rise for at least four different regions of the coast, rather than using a single rate of sea level rise for the entire state.[75] House Bill 819 called for the report to be finalized by March 31, 2015 and presented to the legislature with public comments no later than March 1, 2016.[76] The Final Report—the *Sea Level Rise Study Update*—was unanimously adopted by the CRC in February 2016.[77] The *Sea Level Rise Study Update* relies upon the upper and lower emissions scenarios from the most recent IPCC report and the impacts of subsidence and changes in the Gulf Stream to create 30-year projections of relative sea level rise in North Carolina.[78] The *Sea Level Rise Study Update* concludes that under high emissions scenarios, sea level rise in the next 30 years will be between 6.8 and 8.1 inches, depending on location.[79] The *Study Update* concludes that the state of the science on sea level rise is rapidly evolving and recommends further updates every five years.[80]

In effect, the passage of House Bill 819 prevented the Coastal Resources Commission from adopting accelerating rates of sea level rise for planning pur-

---

73. H.B 819, General Assembly, Sess. 2011 (N.C. 2012); *see* N.C. Gen. Stat. § 113A-107.1(c) (2012).

74. 2012 N.C. Sess. Law 202 § 2(c).

75. *Id.*

76. *Id.*

77. *Meeting Minutes Feb. 9–10, 2016*, CRC, at 4–5.

78. North Carolina Coastal Resources Council, Sea Level Rise Assessment Report 2015 Update to the 2010 Report and 2012 Addendum (2015), https://ncdenr.s3.amazonaws.com/s3fs-public/Coastal%20Management/documents/PDF/Science%20Panel/2015%20NC%20SLR%20Assessment-FINAL%20REPORT%20Jan%2028%202016.pdf.

79. *Id.* at 24–25.

80. *Id.* at 25.

poses until 2016. While the Coastal Resources Commission has adopted the *Sea Level Rise Study Update*, the meeting minutes do not reflect the adoption of particular rates of sea level rise for planning purposes,[81] and the North Carolina Legislature has not yet taken further action. Therefore, it appears that North Carolina's approach to accelerating rates of sea level rise is still evolving.

House Bill 819 further provides that the CRC "shall not deny a development permit for the replacement of a single-family or duplex residential dwelling with a total floor area greater than 5,000 square feet based on failure to meet ocean hazard setback" requirements, if the dwelling was built prior to August 11, 2009, and meets other minimum setback requirements.[82] The CRC responded to this final provision by adopting a rule amendment at its July 2013 meeting.[83]

The North Carolina Legislature again addressed the issue of development in the ocean hazard area AEC in the 2015 legislative session with a specific provision in the annual appropriations bill addressing temporary erosion control structures. The legislation requires the CRC to make modifications to its rules governing the use of temporary erosion control structures, and says the rules must:

1. allow the placement of temporary erosion control structures on a property that is experiencing coastal erosion even if there are no imminently threatened structures on the property if the property is adjacent to a property where temporary erosion control structures have been placed;
2. allow the placement of contiguous temporary erosion control structures from one shoreline boundary of a property to the other shoreline boundary, regardless of proximity to an imminently threatened structure;
3. provide that the termination date of all permits for contiguous temporary erosion control structures on the same property shall be the same and shall be the latest termination date for any of the permits; and
4. provide for the replacement, repair, or modification of damaged temporary erosion control structures that are either legally placed with a current permit or legally placed with an expired permit, but the status of the permit is being litigated by the property owner.[84]

The language in the appropriations bill further required that the CRC adopt temporary rules to implement these requirements by the end of 2015 and then

---

81. *Id.*
82. 2012 N.C. Sess. Law § 3(a).
83. *Actions from July Meeting*, CRC (2013).
84. 2015-241 N.C. Sess. Law 206-07 (Erosion Control Structures § 14.6.(p)).

undertake action to implement final rules.[85] The CRC responded by approving language for temporary rules in November 2015 and deciding on provisions for final rules in February 2016.[86] As required by the statute, the rules will permit the use of sandbags to protect an eroding property *even when there is no structure on the property needing protection.*[87] This represents a significant shift from prior CRC policy and substantially expands the circumstances in which temporary erosion control structures can be permitted.

Sandbags have thus become the biggest and most politically contentious issue facing the CRC.[88] The CRC did not see sandbags as a permanent measure when they were permitted.[89] However, under current CRC policies nonconforming sandbags are likely to remain on North Carolina's beaches, particularly now that the state legislature has made it clear to the CRC that sandbags should not be their priority.[90] This is particularly true because sandbags are seen as the least bad of a bunch of unattractive alternatives.[91] People living along the North Carolina coast do not want to retreat, so until the state comes up with another option, the CRC appears to have no option other than to look the other way and tolerate the continued presence of non-conforming sandbags.[92]

This dilemma is clearly seen in the example of the Riggings Condominium complex ("Riggings") in Kure Beach. The shoreline in front of the land upon which the Riggings complex was built has been eroding since at least 1926.[93] The complex was built in 1985 and has required protective sandbags since its construction.[94] At the time that Riggings obtained its first permit for a temporary erosion control structure, the CRC rules in place allowed sandbags to remain in place for ten years.[95] When these initial ten years expired, the complex was able to obtain a permit extension on the grounds that the community was pursuing a beach nourishment project.

---

85. *Id.* §14.6.(q).

86. *Meeting Minutes Feb. 9–10, 2016*, CRC, at 8–10.

87. *Id.*

88. Interview with Coastal Resources Commission Member (Nov. 23, 2009).

89. *Id.*

90. *Id.*

91. *Id.*

92. *Id.*

93. Mabry, *supra* note 11, at 2.

94. *Id.*; Gareth McGrath, *State Regulators Deny Permit Extension for Sandbags at the Riggings*, Star News Online, Jan. 17, 2008, http://www.starnewsonline.com/article/200801 17/NEWS/283526570 (last visited Feb. 26, 2016).

95. Interview with Local Government Official (Dec. 3, 2009).

Did North Carolina Outlaw Sea Level Rise?

When House Bill 819 was being debated in North Carolina, it was widely covered in the national media as an attempt by the state to "ban sea level rise." This raises the question, did North Carolina actually ban sea level rise and if not, what did it prohibit?

Beginning with the obvious answer, sea level rise is a physical phenomenon that cannot be stopped by the act of any state legislature. As a result, the idea of banning sea level rise doesn't make any sense. The more relevant question here is whether the state legislature banned planning that accounts for sea level rise.

Here, the answer is a bit more complicated. In the simplest sense, yes, House Bill 819's passage bans planning for sea level rise. However, what the bill prevents is the adoption of a regulatory rate of sea level rise for planning purposes that accounts for accelerating sea level rise in the future. Because of the dynamic nature of the Outer Banks, North Carolina already has a set of rules requiring setbacks to account for future erosion, and these aspects of CAMA were not disturbed by House Bill 819. Therefore, to the extent that sea level rise is consistent with historic rates of rise and resulting erosion, it can still be incorporated in the CAMA process.

Finally, it is important to note that the sea level rise policy provision added to CAMA does not prevent the adoption of a sea level rise rate for planning purposes. Rather, it requires the completion of several studies and reports before CAMA may proceed and then states that any sea level rise rate must be adopted in accordance with the state administrative procedures act. N.C. GEN. STAT. § 113A-107.1. Whether CAMA will be permitted to require planning for accelerating rates of sea level rise in the future remains to be seen.

However, the beach in front of the Riggings complex boasts a hard coquina rock shelf that extends several hundred yards into the ocean. This coquina rock shelf is an important habitat for many benthic species and one of the few natural rock habitats remaining along North Carolina's coast. Consequently, the Army Corps of Engineers announced that it would nourish neither the area

Figure 37: The Riggings Complex

directly in front of Riggings nor the area upstream in terms of littoral transport in order to insure that the coquina rock would not become covered by subsequent nourishment projects.[96]

When it became clear that Riggings was not going to receive the nourishment it needed, state officials and North Carolina Congressman Mike McIntyre arranged for a proposed buyout of the complex in 2004. Under the terms of the proposed buyout, FEMA would fund the relocation of the condominiums to a parcel of vacant land across the street that the association already owned.[97] The area where the condominiums currently sit would be returned to its natural state and become dedicated public beach.[98] The FEMA grant would have provided a total of $3.6 million for the relocation.[99] While this was likely a sufficient amount in 2004 when the grant was proposed, when the Rig-

96. Interview with Local Government Official (Nov. 23, 2009).
97. *Id.*
98. *Id.*
99. Memorandum from Christine Goebel, Assistant Attorney General, to CRC Regarding Variance Request by the Riggings Homeowners Ass'n (CRC-VR-15-08), Att. B Stipulated Facts ¶ 26 (Nov. 3, 2015), https://ncdenr.s3.amazonaws.com/s3fs-public/Coastal%20 Management/documents/PDF/Coastal%20Resources%20Commission%20-%20Meeting %20Agendas%20-%20Minutes/FINAL%20Rigging%20SR%20and%20Attach%20thru%20 E.pdf.

gings owners were evaluating the proposal in 2006, they did not feel that the proffered compensation was sufficient.[100] Further, the terms of the grant required unanimous consent of all the condo owners for the relocation to proceed.[101] Because they felt that the proposed compensation was inadequate, the Riggings homeowners rejected the FEMA buyout offer in 2006.[102]

While the FEMA buyout had been pending, the CRC had granted Riggings an extension of its variance for the sandbags protecting the condominiums.[103] However, upon rejection of the FEMA buyout, this variance expired and Riggings had to seek a new variance. To issue a variance, the Coastal Resources Commission must make four findings: 1) an unnecessary hardship would result if the rules were strictly applied; 2) the hardship is the result of conditions that are unique to the property; 3) the hardship is not the result of actions taken by the applicant; and 4) the variance is "consistent with the spirit, purpose, and intent of the rules, standards, or orders; will secure public safety and welfare; and will preserve substantial justice."[104] In January of 2008, the CRC denied Riggings's variance request.[105]

Concerned that the denial of the variance would result in removal of the sandbags and loss of their property, the Riggings homeowners association challenged the CRC's variance denial in the New Hanover County Superior Court. In January 2009, the Superior Court remanded the variance denial to the CRC for further consideration, finding that the CRC had not articulated adequate grounds upon which to deny the variance request.[106] In April 2009, the CRC heard the variance request for a second time. The CRC again denied Riggings' variance request finding that the issuance of a variance would be inconsistent with the spirit of CRC's rules because there were no plans for future beach nourishment in the area.[107] The CRC's denial of the variance request was reversed by a North Carolina trial court and subsequently appealed by the CRC. In August 2013, the Appeals Court affirmed the trial court's ruling and held that the CRC had improperly denied Riggings' variance request.[108] The Ap-

---

100. Interview with Local Government Official (Nov. 23, 2009).

101. *Id.*

102. Interview with Local Government Official (Dec. 3, 2009).

103. *Meeting Minutes Aug. 25–26, 2004*, CRC.

104. N.C. Gen. Stat. § 113A-120.1.

105. *Meeting Minutes Jan. 17–18, 2008*, CRC.

106. *See* Riggings Homeowners, Inc. v. Coastal Res. Comm'n, No. 08-CVS-1069 (Feb. 18, 2009).

107. *Meeting Minutes Apr. 29, 2009*, CRC.

108. Riggings Homeowners, Inc. v. Coastal Res. Comm'n, 747 S.E.2d 301 (N.C. Ct. App. 2013).

peals Court determined that the outcome of the variance decision depends upon a balancing of the interests of the Riggings owners against the public interests of prohibition of permanent erosion control structures, aesthetic concerns, and public access.[109] In considering the public's interest in not having permanent erosion control structures, the court noted that the Riggings' variance application proposed a new beach nourishment solution that would render the sandbags unnecessary and therefore rejected the CRC's claim that the sandbags had become de facto permanent structures.[110] Overall, the court concluded that the private property interests of the Riggings owners outweighed the public interests at stake and upheld the reversal of CRC's variance denial.[111] The CRC appealed the appellate court's decision to the North Carolina Supreme Court, which divided evenly in its vote, meaning that the appellate court's decision was upheld.[112]

After the litigation, the Riggings variance request returned to the CRC for consideration at its November 2015 meeting.[113] In light of the appellate court's decision, the CRC staff recommended that the CRC find in favor of the Riggings and issue a variance for the sandbags.[114] The CRC ultimately approved the variance request with a number of conditions.[115] These conditions included a five-year limitation on the approval for the non-conforming sandbags, a requirement that the Riggings remove any visible existing sandbag debris, a requirement that new sandbag installations conform with the state's regulations, and a requirement that the Riggings homeowners association make an annual report to the CRC Executive Secretary providing an update on its progress to find a permanent alternative to the sandbags.[116]

---

109. *Id.* at 312.

110. *Id.*

111. *Id.*

112. Notice of Appeal, Riggings Homeowners Ass'n v. Coastal Res. Comm'n, No. 401A13 (N.C. Sept. 10, 2013).

113. *Meeting Agenda Nov. 2015*, CRC, https://deq.nc.gov/about/divisions/coastal-management/coastal-resources-commission/crc-meeting-agendas-minutes/nov-2015-agenda.

114. Memorandum from Christine Goebel, Assistant Attorney General, to CRC Regarding Variance Request by the Riggings Homeowners Ass'n (CRC-VR-15-08), Att. C Petitioners' and Staff's Positions (Nov. 3, 2015), https://ncdenr.s3.amazonaws.com/s3fs-public/Coastal%20Management/documents/PDF/Coastal%20Resources%20Commission%20-%20Meeting%20Agendas%20-%20Minutes/FINAL%20Rigging%20SR%20and%20Attach%20thru%20E.pdf.

115. *Meeting Minutes Nov. 17–18, 2015*, CRC, at 6.

116. *Id.*

The Riggings case serves to highlight several important features of the current situation in North Carolina and its implications for adaptation to rising sea levels. First, it is clear that many property owners will pursue every option to protect their properties before retreating in the face of rising sea levels. The ability of property owners to challenge CRC decisions through both the judicial and legislative systems creates significant obstacles to the implementation of a retreat policy in North Carolina. Continued judicial challenges of variance denials will clog the courts with expensive and time-consuming litigation. The CRC's losses in court and the willingness of the state legislature to intervene on behalf of coastal homeowners mean that the CRC could have a difficult time using its enforcement authority to require the removal of sandbags along the coast. This is particularly so in light of the Appeals Court's recent holding in the Riggings case, as it suggests that so long as property owners continue to pursue renourishment as an option—even when attempts to obtain renourishment projects in the past have been unsuccessful—reviewing courts will be inclined to view their erosion controls structures as temporary. Furthermore, it is important to note that the variance ultimately granted to the Riggings does nothing to provide a long-term solution for either the property owners or the public. Rather, the variance forestalls a real decision on the future of the Riggings community for an additional five years. While the CRC does require annual reporting on the Riggings progress in identifying an alternative solution, it is difficult to imagine what new solution the Riggings will arrive at, and it remains to be seen what a future reviewing court might require for a community to show it is "pursuing renourishment" in a manner that maintains the "temporary" status of the erosion control structures.

However, it is important to point out that Riggings is unique within the Town of Kure Beach. While the Town has opted to hold the line, the rest of its oceanfront is a story of the relative success of the CRC and CAMA rules. With the exception of Riggings, all development along Kure Beach's ocean coastline observes a sixty-foot setback from the first line of vegetation.[117] This setback combined with periodic nourishment has allowed the town to build up a formidable dune system that provides important protection during storms.[118] In fact, this program has been so successful that the town believes in the absence of accelerated erosion due to sea level rise, it would be able to hold the line for years to come.[119] However, the town's major concern is its ability to fund sufficient beach nour-

---

117. Interview with Local Government Official (Dec. 3, 2009).
118. Interview with Local Government Official (Nov. 23, 2009).
119. *Id.*

Figure 38: Kure Beach Coastline
Source: U.S. Army Corps of Engineers

ishment in the future. As with the rest of the North Carolina Coast, Kure Beach assesses a 6% room occupancy tax, of which one quarter is saved in a dedicated beach nourishment fund,[120] but there are significant concerns that this fund will not be sufficient to keep pace with nourishment needs in the future.[121]

The struggle of how to pay for beach nourishment is one that is shared by many of North Carolina's coastal communities. Typically, beach nourishment has been funded with federal funds dedicated under either the Water Resources Development Act or the Coastal Impact Assistance Program in combination with state funds from the room occupancy tax.[122] However, as sea level rise leads to increased erosion rates and state and federal budgets are otherwise strained, less funding may be available for beach nourishment projects in the future. For these communities to continue to be successful in holding the line without external funding for nourishment, they will need to come up with alternative sources of funding.

---

120. Interview with Local Government Official (Dec. 3, 2009).

121. Interview with Local Government Official (Nov. 23, 2009).

122. *See* NEW HANOVER COUNTY, NORTH CAROLINA COMPREHENSIVE PLAN 2016 61 (2016).

Figure Eight Island is an example of one coastal community that has been successful in using local assessments to help to pay for beach nourishment. On Figure Eight Island, homeowners are assessed a fee related to their distance from the beach and amount of beach frontage to pay for local beach nourishment projects.[123]

As the above example makes clear, North Carolina has been generally successful in preventing the hardening of the coast. However, as sea level rise leads to increased erosion rates and threats of coastal inundation, the "no hardened structures" policy will come under increasing challenge. North Carolina's current policy of permitting sandbags and extensive nourishment will not be sustainable into the future. While nourishment tends to impart significant economic benefits to communities that receive it, there are questions as to whether nourishment can keep pace with sea level rise.[124] Local governments may increasingly have to provide their own funding for nourishment, which may prove increasingly challenging given the view of some local property owners that the state should pay for nourishment given the large contributions that coastal homes make to the state tax base.[125] In addition, some local governments have raised concerns that even if there were to be enough money to fund necessary nourishment, there may not be a sufficient source of compatible sand to maintain extensive nourishment activities in the future.[126] The potential inability of the Outer Banks to maintain their communities with nourishment is particularly concerning given the apparent position of numerous local government officials and CRC members who are unwilling to engage in the discussion of retreat on the Outer Banks on the grounds that there is nowhere to go. While there has historically been some willingness to let coastal property go to the oceans and move houses back when there is additional space on the same lot or another free lot further back,[127] it is clear that this micro-level retreat has yet to develop into larger discussions about relocating entire communities.

---

123. Interview with Coastal Resources Commission Member (Nov. 23, 2009).
124. *Id.*
125. Interview with Local Government Official (Dec. 4, 2009).
126. Interview with Local Government Official (Nov. 23, 2009).
127. Interview with DCM Staff Member (Nov. 5, 2009).

**Money and Sand Supply: Is Beach Nourishment a
Viable Long-Term Strategy?**

One of the biggest challenges for communities choosing to use beach nourishment as a strategy to respond to rising sea levels will be the increasing frequency with which beach nourishment is necessary over time. To maintain beaches in their present locations, climate change would require more frequent nourishment because rising sea levels and stronger storm surges will tend to wash away the sand that is deposited on beaches.

Beach nourishment can be an expensive adaptation strategy. For example, in North Carolina, it has been estimated that beach nourishment costs $1.5 million/mile and must be redone every 4 years. *See* http://el.erdc.usace.army.mil/workshops/05feb-dots/session4-pilkey.pdf. An additional challenge for beach nourishment is that the quality of sandy beaches for recreation and habitat can only be preserved if nourishment is conducted with sand that is compatible with that already present on the beach. Therefore, even if communities have the financial resources to continue beach nourishment, their efforts may be constrained by the availability of compatible sand.

For example, in 2014, the Bureau of Ocean Energy Management—the federal agency with responsibility for offshore leasing—entered into a series of agreements with Atlantic coastal states to jointly survey the continental shelf and determine the volumes of sand that may be available for beach nourishment projects. At this time, the Bureau has stated that it does not know how much sand might be available on the outer continental shelf, a potentially important limitation on the use of nourishment as a strategy to respond to sea level rise.

Adaptation along North Carolina's Estuaries

Overview of Legal Framework

Because the Coastal Area Management Act applies to all of North Carolina's Coastlines, the legal framework governing adaptation along estuarine shorelines is much the same as that which applies to North Carolina's ocean coast.

The most significant difference is that the "no hardened structures" policy does not apply to the estuarine shoreline. In addition, there are a number of general permits that apply on the estuarine coast that may lead to different outcomes on the estuarine and ocean coasts.

An important class of exemption along the estuarine shoreline applies to the construction of single-family residences. Single-family homes built more than forty feet from the normal high water line are exempted from CAMA permitting requirements.[128] The single-family home exemption has the potential to result in unchecked development in vulnerable areas. The risk here is somewhat minimized, however, by the requirement that anyone constructing a home under this permit first notify the Department of Environmental and Natural Resources and allow for onsite review.[129] In addition, the exemption will only apply in eroding areas "when the local permit officer has determined that the house has been located the maximum feasible distance back on the lot but not less than forty feet."[130]

River Dunes

While the dynamic nature of the Outer Banks has long been documented and understood, historically there has been less of an understanding of what happens with estuarine shorelines, how wetlands migrate, and what coastal program regulations mean for the continued existence and ecological function of estuarine shorelines.[131] Recently there has been a push within DCM to do things differently with respect to estuarine shorelines. This approach emphasizes moving away from bulkheads, break walls, and other structures and promoting the use of living shorelines with appropriate setbacks.[132] The River Dunes development is an example of a community that has employed a living shorelines approach. The example that follows explores the factors that led River Dunes to adopt a living shoreline approach and considers its potential as a successful method of accommodating sea level rise.

At the time of its construction, the River Dunes development was the largest single investment in the history of Pamlico County.[133] The project in-

---

128. 15A N.C. Admin. Code §07K.0208(a).
129. *Id.* §07K.0208(d).
130. *Id.* §07K.0208(e).
131. Interview with DCM Staff Member (Nov. 5, 2009).
132. *Id.*
133. Wade Rawlins, *Ecofriendly Design Marks Pamlico Development*, News & Observer, Sept. 3, 2006.

volves the conversion of a 1,300-acre pine plantation into a residential community with 550 homes and a marina with an equivalent number of boat slips.[134] The development site lies north of the town of Oriental in Pamlico County, and has over 14 miles of shoreline along the Neuse River and Broad Creek.[135] When River Dunes conducted its initial site analysis, it recognized that the entire community is surrounded by primary nursery areas for fisheries, and that impacts on these primary nursery areas would have to be minimized in project development.[136]

With the goal of building an enjoyable community while preserving environmental quality, River Dunes decided to reach out to the community of knowledgeable stakeholders, including both non-profit environmental groups and state and local agencies early in the design process.[137] The River Dunes Corporation held its first stakeholder meeting in 1999 in New Bern, North Carolina to begin the process of engaging both regulators and environmental groups in the early stages of the project.[138] This process grew out of a recognition that while River Dunes had expertise in developing communities and creating infrastructure to support them, the project as a whole would benefit from conservation of environmental values, which was most readily accomplished through the engagement of other groups with expertise in these areas.[139] The resulting process identified potential impacts to primary nursery areas as the major concern arising from development of the site, and it led to changes in community design to minimize these impacts.[140] Overall, River Dunes feels that this process improved the quality of the community it is now developing.[141]

Initially River Dunes intended to follow the classic model for development of North Carolina's estuarine coast. This model would have called for the individual permitting of each of the 358 home sites along the water, with each lot containing a private home and dock.[142] However, through its initial consultations with the North Carolina Coastal Federation and state permitting officials, it became clear to River Dunes that the most significant method of

---

134. Pam Smith, *Conservation by Design: Variations on a Theme*, COASTWATCH, Winter 2005, at 6, http://ncseagrant.ncsu.edu/coastwatch/previous-issues/2005-2/winter-2005/.

135. *The Village*, RIVER DUNES, http://www.riverdunes.com/index.php?flag=masterplan (last visited Feb. 26, 2016).

136. Interview with River Dunes Official (Dec. 4, 2009).

137. *Id.*

138. *Id.*

139. *Id.*

140. *Id.*

141. *Id.*

142. *Id.*

Figure 39: River Dunes Marina

reducing impacts on the primary nursery areas in the waters surrounding the community would be to minimize the number of boat docks.[143] In the collaboration with environmental groups and state regulators, the idea of building an upland basin marina was raised.[144] Through its market research with boaters, River Dunes discovered that as long as they provided a high quality marina facility with safe harbor for large vessels, many potential buyers did not particularly care that their boat slip would not be located in their back yard.[145]

Because River Dunes is located in Pamlico County, it is required to comply with the terms of the county's land use plan, which include a minimum 75-foot setback from the water and impervious surface cover of no greater than 30%.[146] In order to accommodate this latter requirement, the residences in River Dunes have been designed as complexes of buildings, including a main house, a separate garage, and a guesthouse on the larger properties, rather than one larger house.[147] The development of the community as a whole

---

143. Interview with River Dunes Official (Dec. 2, 2009).

144. *Id.*

145. *Id.*

146. Interview with Local Government Official (Dec. 4, 2009); Pamlico County Joint CAMA Land Use Plan 27, 64 (2004).

147. Interview with River Dunes Official (Dec. 4, 2009).

is governed under a CAMA major permit, and individual homeowners do not have to obtain additional permits beyond the county building permits unless they want to put in a bulkhead or private vista dock.[148] All of the elements of the CAMA land use plan are enforced directly by the Pamlico County building inspector.

Pamlico County is the only county in North Carolina with a 75-foot setback, which is set by local ordinance.[149] The County has adopted such a large setback because prior to the adoption of the 75-foot setback, nearly every application for riparian development required a CAMA permit, and the CAMA permitting process was a drain on the County's limited resources.[150] Therefore, the County adopted the 75-foot setback requirement to streamline the permitting process by placing all development so far landward that it would not require CAMA permitting.[151] Pamlico County further restricts riparian development by requiring that a landowner have at least one hundred linear feet of riparian land and a lot size of one acre or larger.[152] Development on property that contains marshland requires an additional 50-foot setback from the marsh line under the rules of the State Division of Water Quality.[153]

While the River Dunes Community has adopted the living shorelines approach throughout much of the community, many of the currently built lots have extensive structures placed just behind the county's 75-foot setback. While this is certainly an improvement over immediately bulkheading the entire shoreline, in some places it appears that there is little, if any, room for upland migration of the wetland habitat. Thus, while the living shorelines approach will help to preserve coastal wetland habitat in its current location, this habitat is still ultimately threatened by coastal squeeze because of extensive development immediately landward of the setback. This issue could become particularly interesting in the future if these properties become threatened by sea level rise.

While the CRC's "no hardened structures" policy does not apply to the estuarine shoreline, the community itself has a set of restrictive covenants limiting the use of bulkheads. Under these covenants, any property owner wishing to install a bulkhead must obtain the prior approval of the architectural review committee in order to ensure that the proposed bulkhead won't have negative

148. *Id.*
149. Interview with Local Government Official (Dec. 4, 2009).
150. *Id.*
151. *Id.*
152. Pamlico County Flood Ordinance (on file with author).
153. Interview with Local Government Official (Dec. 4, 2009).

LIVING SHORELINE

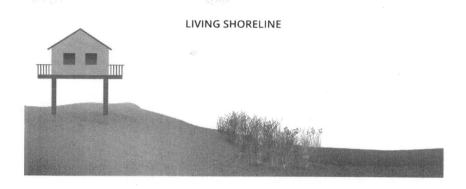

SEAWALL

Figure 40: Living Shorelines

Living shorelines focus on using natural littoral landscapes as the border between land and sea. In contrast to seawalls (bottom), the living shoreline will migrate landward as sea levels rise.

effects on neighboring properties in the community.[154] Given that individuals in the community have significant latitude in the design of their homes and location on the lot, it will likely be the case that some future property owners will need bulkheads well before others and the architectural review committee may end up mediating disputes between neighbors immediately threatened and those not wanting to be subjected to increased rates of passive erosion.

It bears emphasizing that River Dunes innovative approach was motivated not by hazard mitigation or sea level rise concerns. Rather, it was shaped by concerns about existing primary fishery nursery areas and county-imposed restrictions on coastal development. Pamlico County as a whole remains largely

---

154. *Id.*

Figure 41: Example of Living Shoreline and Setback at River Dunes

rural due to the fact that there is so much marsh land in the County that it simply will not support higher density development.[155]

Comparing Challenges and Opportunities on North Carolina's Ocean and Estuarine Coasts

Other than the no hardened structures ban, one of the most significant differences between the ocean and estuarine coastlines in North Carolina is their level of development. At this point, the parts of North Carolina's Outer Banks that are available for development are almost completely built out, with only limited opportunities for infill and redevelopment remaining.[156] This level of development is significant both because it means that there are many property owners with interests in holding the line along the ocean coast to protect their investments and also because the result is that there are not opportunities for gradual retreat by slowly moving back existing development. This means that the adoption of a policy of retreat along North Carolina's ocean coast may

---

155. *Id.*
156. Interview with Local Government Official (Dec. 4, 2009).

prove to be both politically challenging and economically infeasible. This is because littoral owners are likely to have sufficient influence over the political process to persuade local governments to maintain their current policies to hold the line with nourishment. In addition, if there is nowhere for property owners on the Outer Banks to move, a policy of retreat is likely to require that the government buy out homeowners, essentially paying them to leave. Given the high value of coastal property, it seems unlikely that local governments would have sufficient resources to buy out enough homeowners to institute meaningful retreat.[157]

In contrast, North Carolina's estuarine coastline is still largely rural. As the setback and density requirements in Pamlico County reflect, many of the long-time residents of these areas are not eager to see new, high density development. This desire to preserve the character of local estuarine communities could have the positive externality of reducing the number of new homes that are built in vulnerable environments. Given that much of the future development along North Carolina's estuarine coast will be greenfield building where there is more open space, there is still an opportunity to shape local building codes so as to reduce vulnerability to rising sea levels. For such measures to be effective, however, local governments must act now to pass a proactive set of rules that account for the potential impacts of climate change and seek to reduce vulnerability along North Carolina's coast.

The CRC has attempted to establish such proactive efforts, undertaking a study of sea level rise at the state level in 2010 with the intention of pursuing additional rulemaking to account for sea level rise in land use planning and permitting. However, these efforts have been stalled by the passage of House Bill 819 and the preparation of the *Sea Level Rise Study Update*. At this time, it remains unclear how the CRC will move forward in considering accelerating rates of sea level rise.

Furthermore, changes to the CAMA rules alone will not be sufficient to encourage effective adaptation to sea level rise. Local governments lack the resources to evaluate the science on their own or to do extensive additional planning. Therefore, the CRC and DCM must provide local governments with adequate support, including both accessible information as to the impacts of sea level rise and suggested policy measures.[158] Local governments also suggest that additional measures will be necessary to ensure that there is a coordinated

---

157. Unless, of course, the government were to reduce the amount of compensation it paid to littoral owners to reflect past regulatory givings. I explore this issue in more detail in Chapter 5.

158. Interview with DCM Staff Member (Dec. 1, 2009).

response to sea level rise. Local government officials all note that there is little incentive for them to engage in sea level rise planning, particularly a consideration of retreat, if neighboring jurisdictions do not tackle similar problems. Therefore, the CRC must be prepared to play a coordinating role to ensure that local governments will not feel that they are taking the risk of acting alone. Some local governments would like to see the CRC go even further, expressing the opinion that the CRC should take a more top down approach and specify particular elements that land use plans must have to deal with sea level rise.[159]

If the CRC wishes to proceed with comprehensive sea level rise planning, it must also be prepared to provide adequate funding to support a new round of CAMA Land Use Plan updates. With a few exceptions, local governments depend upon CAMA grants to support the creation of their land use plans.[160] In structuring this grant funding, the CRC must ensure that the land use plans it supports go beyond the rote process of consultant-driven plans, which currently dominate the land use planning process.[161] Rather, new land use plan elements that deal with sea level rise will only be useful if local governments truly engage in the planning process, and base their activity on realistic projections and assumptions.

At the end of the day, incorporating sea level rise into land use planning may not produce the kind of long-range planning and response to sea level rise that the CRC might wish to pursue. First, it is important to observe that under the current system, most land use plans lack the long-range vision to which CAMA aspires. In fact, both DCM officials and CRC members have observed that many CAMA land use plans often do the bare minimum necessary for approval. Thus, one must question whether simply adding an additional requirement to the CAMA rules will be sufficient to produce land use plans that are broad and forward-looking enough to lead to meaningful responses to the threat of rising sea levels. Furthermore, the heart of the land use plan is the community's vision of its own future. As a result, it is quite possible that even if local communities do consider sea level rise when creating their land use plans, local responses will simply preserve the status quo and focus on finding ways to maintain the coastline in its current location. Because of this feature of the CAMA land use planning process it is possible that the creation of the land use plan will be subject to internal political pressures in creating the community's vision

---

159. Interview with Local Government Official (Dec. 3, 2009).
160. Interview with DCM Staff Member (Dec. 1, 2009).
161. *Id.*

as well as external political pressures similar to those that have been at work with regard to the CRC's actions on sandbag enforcement.

Even if there is new comprehensive land use planning to account for sea level rise, there will still be a significant population along North Carolina's coastline that will continue to be subjected to the impacts of hurricanes and nor'easters and the associated storm surge. A large part of successful adaptation to these impacts will include proper building design and improved emergency management. Surviving storms, first and foremost requires that a state be able to move people out of harms' way, and this will become increasingly challenging as coastal populations grow and rising sea levels result in episodic flooding of access roads. As a result, the Division of Coastal Management began working with the Division of Emergency Management to improve emergency response planning.[162] On the development side, as long as developers adhere to the FEMA flood elevations and construct sufficiently strong foundations, they do not anticipate significant problems from flood impacts.[163] While these policies may be effective as a means of short-term storm response, they are not necessarily an appropriate response to long-term inundation, and likely serve to create more communities like Topsail Island, North Carolina, or West Galveston, Texas, where homes are literally over the water and the public is effectively denied access to the shoreline.

North Carolina's response to sea level rise is clearly continuing to evolve through a complex set of interactions between the CRC, DCM, the legislature, property owners, and the courts. Particularly given the legislature's direct requirements to increase the availability of temporary erosion control structures, North Carolina's ocean coastline seems destined for a future of increasing nourishment and the use of sandbags. Nourishment may well provide a reasonable medium term adaptation strategy for the ocean coastline, but it is likely to become increasingly challenging over time. Much uncertainty remains for the future of sea level rise planning and response in North Carolina, and the political context for adaptation planning will likely continue to evolve as the CRC continues to evaluate how to plan for sea level rise.

---

162. Interview with DCM Official (Nov. 5, 2009).
163. Interview with River Dunes Official (Dec. 4, 2009).

Chapter 7

Texas

This chapter examines coastal land use management in Texas, with a particular focus on the state of public beach access and the ability to respond to sea level rise in the aftermath of the *Severance v. Patterson* litigation.

Texas has over 367 miles of Gulf Shoreline[1] and 3,300 miles of Bay Shoreline, giving it the third longest coast in the United States.[2] The Texas coast experiences some of the highest erosion rates in the country, with parts of the coast having erosion rates of 55 feet per year.[3] On average, the Texas coastline is eroding at a rate of 4 feet per year.[4] As a result, Texas loses over 235 acres of land along the Gulf Coast, bays, and estuaries each year.[5] At the same time, development along the Texas coast in the last few decades has been extensive resulting in a "clash with the forces of erosion."[6] In its most recent report to the state legislature under the Coastal Erosion Response Planning Act ("CERPA"), the General Land Office ("GLO") noted that responding to these high rates of erosion is made more complicated because "the CEPRA program must address other challenges including relative sea level rise, impacts from tropical storms and hurricanes, and the *Severance v. Patterson* lawsuit."[7] The GLO went on to explain that Texas experiences higher rates of relative sea level rise than other parts of the country and that the *Severance v. Patterson* litiga-

---

1. Throughout this book Gulf Coast is used to describe the open ocean shoreline.
2. TEXAS GENERAL LAND OFFICE, COASTAL EROSION PLANNING AND RESPONSE ACT: REPORT TO THE 84TH TEXAS LEGISLATURE 1 (2015) [hereinafter GLO2015].
3. *Id.*
4. *Id.*
5. *Id.* at 6.
6. *See* TEXAS GENERAL LAND OFFICE, COASTAL EROSION PLANNING AND RESPONSE ACT: REPORT TO THE 81ST TEXAS LEGISLATURE 8 (2009).
7. GLO2015, *supra* note 2 at 2.

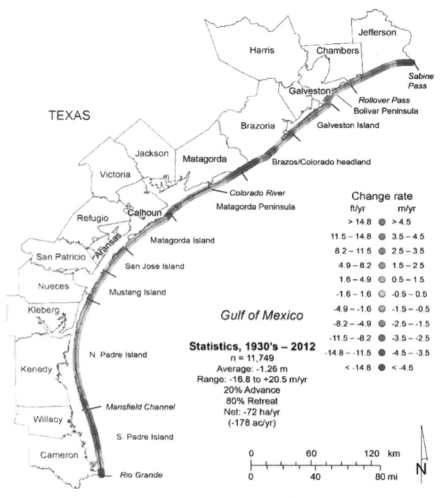

Figure 42: Map of Eroding Areas on the Texas Coast
Source: Texas General Land Office, Coastal Erosion Response & Planning Act: A Report to
the 84th Texas Legislature (2015), http://www.glo.texas.gov/coast/coastal-management/
forms/files/CEPRA-Report-2015.pdf

tion has created challenges through its redefinition of the public beach easement.[8]

---

8. *Id.*

This chapter focuses on the evolution of the public's right to access the beach as a result of the *Severance v. Patterson* litigation, and evaluates the impact that the resultant uncertainty has on Texas' options to respond to rising sea levels on the ocean coast. This chapter also contrasts the robust regulatory regime addressing Texas' 367 miles of ocean coastline with the relative lack of planning regulations that apply to the 3,300 miles of bay shoreline that are also at risk from the impacts of sea level rise.

In 1900, a major hurricane made landfall in Galveston, Texas, killing over 6,000 people.[9] To prevent inundation and further losses in future storms, the City of Galveston began a project to raise the city seventeen feet and construct the Galveston Seawall in 1902.[10] The vulnerability that the Galveston Seawall was designed to reduce was mostly human created, as many of the dunes in the Galveston area were leveled by developers in the late 1800s.[11] As a result, most of the City of Galveston is now protected by a ten-mile-long, seventeen-foot-high seawall.[12]

Until 2008, this seawall had been largely effective in protecting the city from inundation impacts of hurricanes. In September 2008, Hurricane Ike made landfall in Galveston. While only a category 2 hurricane, Ike produced extensive flooding along the Texas coast, including twenty feet of flooding in downtown Galveston.[13] Post-Ike repairs to the Galveston Seawall were reported to cost in excess of $10 million.[14] In assessing the damage from Ike the General Land Office's initial efforts were largely focused on restoring communities to their pre-storm condition. A GLO report to the Texas Legislature states that one of the few bright spots from Hurricane Ike was the Village of Surfside Beach, which was saved by a recently completed rock revetment.[15] In the wake of Hurricane Ike, Texas reflected classic natural disaster response, with an increased focus on restoring communities in their current location by building

---

9. GALVESTON BAY ESTUARY PROGRAM, THE STATE OF THE BAY 35 (2d ed. 2002) [hereinafter STATE OF THE BAY].

10. *Id.* at 35.

11. *Id.* at 34.

12. Ben Casselman, *Planning the "Ike Dike" Defense*, WALL ST. J., June 4, 2009, at A3; Kevin Moran, *City Has Raised Storm Preparedness to an Art*, HOUSTON CHRON., Sept. 9, 1990, at C1.

13. TEXAS HOUSE SELECT COMMITTEE ON HURRICANE IKE DEVASTATION TO THE TEXAS GULF COAST, INTERIM REPORT 1 (2008).

14. Matthew Tresaugue, *Damage from Hurricane Ike Threatens Seawall*, HOUSTON CHRON., Jan. 18, 2009, http://www.chron.com/neighborhood/baytown-news/article/Damage-from-Hurricane-Ike-threatens-Seawall-1727327.php.

15. TEXAS GENERAL LAND OFFICE, *supra* note 6, at ii.

The Great Galveston Hurricane of 1900

Throughout the 1800s Galveston was the major port city along the Texas coast and was a prominent commercial and cultural center. On September 8, 1900, a major hurricane made landfall in Galveston. The resulting storm surge was estimated to be over 15 feet, and the highest point on the island at the time was only 8.7 feet above sea level. The storm devastated the City and is estimated to have killed between 6,000 and 12,000 people.

Wanting to prevent future damage from storm surges, the City embarked upon the construction of the Galveston Seawall. Construction of the seawall began in 1902, and the original seawall was 3 miles long. Expansion of the seawall continued until the 1950s, with the current seawall stretching 10 miles. The seawall effectively protected the City from subsequent storm surges until Hurricane Ike made landfall in 2008. Hurricane Ike's storm surge of 15 to 20 feet flooded much of downtown Galveston.

back with better storm defenses. As explored at the end of this chapter, these dynamics only serve to encourage property owners to continue to overinvest in risk-prone coastal property because they correctly assume that the government will bail them out in the event of a natural disaster.

While Texas certainly faces significant challenges along the ocean coastline, it has nearly ten times as much estuarine shoreline that is also vulnerable to the impacts of sea level rise. Galveston Bay is one of the most important estuaries along the Gulf Coast, but it has experienced extensive wetland loss as a result of subsidence from ground water withdrawal.[16] The subsidence problem is exacerbated by the conversion of wetland habitat due to development, which not only reduces current wetland habitat but also limits the upland areas into which wetlands can migrate. By 1993, ten percent of the Bay shoreline had been bulkheaded or converted to docks or revetment, and coastal devel-

---

16. STATE OF THE BAY, *supra* note 9, at 2.

Surfside Beach

In 2008, Surfside Beach completed a rock revetment to protect coastal development from erosion. While the revetment successfully protected the homes on Surfside Beach from the storm surge in Hurricane Ike, the beach was washed out during the storm. As a result, a $4.4 million emergency beach nourishment project and a $1.7 million revetment repair project were required to continue to protect the development at Surfside Beach. 2011 Coastal Erosion and Response Planning Act Report.

In a 2008 report, the Surfside Beach revetment had been noted as one of the "bright spots" during Hurricane Ike, because it had successfully protected the homes in the village. However, restoration activities clearly demonstrate that the maintenance of such coastal defense structures in the future may prove costly and difficult.

Source: Texas General Land Office

opment has only increased since that time.[17] As a result, habitat loss is the number one threat to the continued functioning of the Bay as an ecosystem, and coastal development has been recognized as the most severe threat to the state's wetlands.[18] Further, the GLO has found that without comprehensive erosion response to counteract subsidence, large stretches of currently existing wetlands along the Galveston Intracoastal Waterway will revert to open water.[19]

---

17. *Id.* at 6.
18. *Id.* at 8; Texas Department of Parks and Wildlife, Wetlands Assistance Guide for Landowners 7 (2000).
19. Texas General Land Office, *supra* note 6, at ii.

The estuarine habitats along Galveston Bay are thus being squeezed in both directions and will be increasingly threatened by rising sea levels.

The Texas Ocean Coast

Overview of Legal Frameworks

In conducting a review after Hurricane Ike, the Texas House released a report stating "[t]he need for Texas to usher in improved laws to reduce the destructive damage of hurricanes is apparent and with an intelligent and thoughtful approach in this regard, Texans can become victorious over future disasters."[20] However, under the current state of the law not all parties with an interest in the coast can be "victorious" and state policy makers will have to choose between actions that benefit the public as a whole and the Texas Gulf Coast's tourism economy and actions that benefit private property owners. The policy framework in Texas has been substantially complicated by the outcome of the *Severance* litigation, which is discussed in detail below, and many questions remain regarding how Texas will continue to protect public access to its valuable beaches while accommodating sea level rise.

Coastal zone management in Texas is shaped by both the Open Beaches Act and the Dune Protection Act, which are administered by the Texas General Land Office.[21] Texas' regulations are focused on the protection of dune structures and the prevention of development that interferes with public access to the beach.[22] While being far more protective of public beach access than North Carolina's or California's coastal management provisions, Texas' management scheme does not have the explicit environmental protection measures seen in the other states' systems. For example, neither the Dune Protection Act nor the Open Beaches Act contains anything resembling provisions for ESHA or AECs.[23] Rather, the Acts maintain a singular focus on the protection of the public beach and dune system and eliminating or preventing structures that encroach upon the public beach.[24]

The focus of the Open Beaches Act on access is likely explained by the fact that it was a legislative response to a Texas Supreme Court decision. In 1958 the Texas Supreme Court issued its ruling in the *Luttes* case, holding that pri-

---

20. Texas House Select Committee, *supra* note 13, at 19.

21. Tex. Nat. Res. Code Chs. 61, 63.

22. *See id.*

23. *See supra* Chapters 5 and 6 for a discussion of California's ESHA provisions and North Carolina's use of AECs.

24. *See* Tex. Nat. Res. Code Ch. 61.

vate title extends over the dry sand beach down to the mark of mean higher high water.[25] Drawing upon the original Spanish and Mexican law, the Court traced the history of littoral property boundaries under the Texas common law and concluded that, translated into Anglo-American law, the correct boundary between private littoral property and state-owned submerged lands is the mean high tide line.[26] Because of its origin in Mexican law, there are two distinctions in the Texas common law of littoral boundaries that come from the *Luttes* decision. First, unlike the majority of coastal states, which draw the mean high tide line as the 18.6 year average of high tide, the *Luttes* decision suggests that the littoral boundary in Texas is properly drawn at the *present* location of the mean high tide line,[27] meaning that in cases of sea level rise or rapid erosion, the littoral property boundary in Texas will be more dynamic than it is in many coastal states. Second, the Texas Supreme Court found that Mexican common law restricted the uses to which the beach could be put because of the need for clear access to the beach for military purposes.[28] In light of the *Severance* decision, explained below, this latter finding of a common law right of the state to keep the beaches clear may be particularly significant in establishing a customary right of the public to access the beach in the future.

The *Luttes* decision raised public and legislative concern that absent a clear statement of the rights of the public, the dry sand beach in private hands would soon be fenced off by littoral owners, impeding meaningful public access to the beach.[29] In response to this concern, the legislature passed the Texas Open Beaches Act in 1959. The Open Beaches Act codifies what the legislature believed to be the Texas common law at the time by stating that the public has free and unrestricted access to the dry sand beach up to the first line of vegetation if the public has previously acquired the right of access through prescription, dedication, or customary use of the beach.[30] The Act protects public access by prohibiting construction of any obstruction, barrier, or restraint that interferes with the public's right to access the beach.[31] Further, the Act codified a policy of a rolling beach easement: any structure that comes to encroach

---

25. Luttes v. Texas, 324 S.W.2d 167 (Tex. 1958).

26. *Id.*

27. *Id.*

28. *Id.*

29. Interview with Member of the Texas Legislature (Nov. 20, 2009); Eddie R. Fisher & Angela L. Sunley, *A Line in the Sand: Balancing the Texas Open Beaches Act and Coastal Development*, Proceedings of Coastal Zone 07, July 22–26, 2007, in Portland, OR.

30. Tex. Nat. Res. Code §61.011. The details of how each of these access rights could be acquired are discussed in more detail in Chapter 4.

31. Tex. Nat. Res. Code §61.013.

upon the public beach as the result of a natural event is subject to removal.[32] Through this provision, the Texas Open Beaches Act was thought to codify common law inherited from Mexico that does not recognize the doctrine of avulsion and treats all erosive loss of beach in the same way in order to ensure that the mechanism of sediment loss cannot be used as a means to justify restricting public access.[33]

The Open Beaches Act further protects public access by limiting littoral development. Under the Open Beaches Act, permitting authority rests with local governments, similar to California's system of Local Coastal Plans, but the standards they must apply are set by the GLO through regulation.[34] The Act requires that all local governments create beach access plans that are consistent with GLO rules.[35] Beach access plans and their accompanying development regulations are jointly administered with Dune Protection Plans under the Dune Protection Act.

One of the most significant authorities granted to the state under the Open Beaches Act is the ability to judicially enforce the Act and its accompanying regulations. Under the Open Beaches Act, the Attorney General may seek a judicial order or injunction to remove improvements that violate the Open Beaches Act.[36] In such a lawsuit, the state may seek not only the removal of the illegal improvement but also penalties and costs of removing the obstruction.[37] Most importantly, the Attorney General has the authority to seek the removal of structures that were legally built but have come to lie on the public beach as a result of natural events.[38] This means that if a major hurricane moves the line of vegetation landward, homeowners who suddenly find their houses on the public beach may be subject to a suit in condemnation ordering them to remove the houses.[39] The Open Beaches Act does give the Commissioner of the General Land Office a limited ability to protect littoral owners in the wake of a storm: the Commissioner may initiate a three-year moratorium on enforcement of the Open Beaches Act after a natural disaster.[40] This moratorium then applies to all homes other than those that are below the mean high tide

---

32. *Id.* §61.018.

33. Note that the *Severance* decision appears to change this prevailing understanding of the Open Beaches Act and adopt a limited version of the doctrine of avulsion, which will be explained in more detail below.

34. 31 Tex. Admin. Code §15.3–.5.

35. Tex. Nat. Res. Code §61.015.

36. *Id.* §61.018.

37. *Id.* §61.0185.

38. *Id.*

39. *Id.*

40. *Id.* §61.0185.

line or more than 50% destroyed.[41] While a moratorium may provide some temporary protection to homeowners whose homes come to lie on the beach and are largely intact, the Act still subjects them to the potential of removal orders at the end of the three-year moratorium period.[42]

In order to ensure that homeowners are aware of the risk of losing their homes under the condemnation provisions of the Act, all purchasers of property seaward of the Intracoastal Waterway must sign a notice and disclosure provision when they sign the real estate contract to buy coastal property.[43] The disclosure makes it plain to property owners that they run the risk of being forced to move their homes from the public beach without receiving compensation stating:

STRUCTURES ERECTED SEAWARD OF THE VEGETATION LINE (OR OTHER APPLICABLE EASEMENT BOUNDARY) OR THAT BECOME SEAWARD OF THE VEGETATION LINE AS A RESULT OF NATURAL PROCESSES SUCH AS SHORELINE EROSION ARE SUBJECT TO A LAWSUIT BY THE STATE OF TEXAS TO REMOVE THE STRUCTURES.[44]

The language is quoted from a disclosure that must be recorded with the deed in order to make a conveyance of coastal property valid in Texas. In addition, in recent years, local groups have worked with the legislature to improve the required disclosure provisions.[45] Most significantly, the required disclosure had been presented only at real estate closing, but now it must be included when the initial land contract is executed.[46] Because of changes to the disclosure requirements, most realtors along the Texas Coast now give prospective buyer information about the Open Beaches Act at the time they first start looking at property.[47] Despite these warnings, there continues to be a brisk market for coastal property, and coastal property owners are increasingly demanding that the government help them protect their property. Thus, the GLO's role in preserving beach access and protecting coastal dunes will become increasingly important as Galveston County is caught between rising seas and increasing pressure from coastal property owners.

---

41. *Id.*
42. *Id.*
43. Interview with State Government Official (Nov. 19, 2009).
44. Tex. Nat. Res. Code §61.025 (emphasis in original); *see also* p. 216–17, *infra*, setting forth the full text of the required disclosure.
45. Interview with Nonprofit Organization Staff Member (Oct. 30, 2009).
46. Tex. Nat. Res. Code. §61.025.
47. Interview with Nonprofit Organization Staff Member (Oct. 30, 2009).

Disclosure Required under the Texas Open Beaches Act

The Texas Open Beaches Act requires that all sellers of property seaward of the intercoastal waterway provide a disclosure to buyers that the property may be subject to the restrictions of the Open Beaches Act. The text of the full form is as follows:

CONCERNING THE PROPERTY AT _____

DISCLOSURE NOTICE CONCERNING LEGAL AND ECONOMIC RISKS OF PURCHASING COASTAL REAL PROPERTY NEAR A BEACH

WARNING: THE FOLLOWING NOTICE OF POTENTIAL RISKS OF ECONOMIC LOSS TO YOU AS THE PURCHASER OF COASTAL REAL PROPERTY IS REQUIRED BY STATE LAW.

- READ THIS NOTICE CAREFULLY. DO NOT SIGN THIS CONTRACT UNTIL YOU FULLY UNDERSTAND THE RISKS YOU ARE ASSUMING.
- BY PURCHASING THIS PROPERTY, YOU MAY BE ASSUMING ECONOMIC RISKS OVER AND ABOVE THE RISKS INVOLVED IN PURCHASING INLAND REAL PROPERTY.
- IF YOU OWN A STRUCTURE LOCATED ON COASTAL REAL PROPERTY NEAR A GULF COAST BEACH, IT MAY COME TO BE LOCATED ON THE PUBLIC BEACH BECAUSE OF COASTAL EROSION AND STORM EVENTS.
- AS THE OWNER OF A STRUCTURE LOCATED ON THE PUBLIC BEACH, YOU COULD BE SUED BY THE STATE OF TEXAS AND ORDERED TO REMOVE THE STRUCTURE.
- THE COSTS OF REMOVING A STRUCTURE FROM THE PUBLIC BEACH AND ANY OTHER ECONOMIC LOSS INCURRED BECAUSE OF A REMOVAL ORDER WOULD BE SOLELY YOUR RESPONSIBILITY.

The real property described in this contract is located seaward of the Gulf Intracoastal Waterway to its southernmost point and then seaward of the longitudinal line also known as 97 degrees, 12', 19" which runs southerly to the international boundary from the intersection of the centerline of the Gulf Intracoastal Waterway and the Brownsville Ship Channel. If the property is in close proximity to a beach fronting the Gulf of Mexico, the purchaser is hereby advised that the public has acquired a right of use or easement to or over the area of any public beach by prescription, dedication, or presumption, or has retained a right by virtue of continuous right in the public since time immemorial, as recognized in law and custom.

(continued)

Disclosure Required under the Texas Open Beaches Act

(continued)

The extreme seaward boundary of natural vegetation that spreads continuously inland customarily marks the landward boundary of the public easement. If there is no clearly marked natural vegetation line, the landward boundary of the easement is as provided by Sections 61.016 and 61.017, Natural Resources Code.

Much of the Gulf of Mexico coastline is eroding at rates of more than five feet per year. Erosion rates for all Texas Gulf property subject to the open beaches act are available from the Texas General Land Office.

State law prohibits any obstruction, barrier, restraint, or interference with the use of the public easement, including the placement of structures seaward of the landward boundary of the easement. OWNERS OF STRUCTURES ERECTED SEAWARD OF THE VEGETATION LINE (OR OTHER APPLICABLE EASEMENT BOUNDARY) OR THAT BECOME SEAWARD OF THE VEGETATION LINE AS A RESULT OF PROCESSES SUCH AS SHORELINE EROSION ARE SUBJECT TO A LAWSUIT BY THE STATE OF TEXAS TO REMOVE THE STRUCTURES.

The purchaser is hereby notified that the purchaser should:

(1) determine the rate of shoreline erosion in the vicinity of the real property; and

(2) seek the advice of an attorney or other qualified person before executing this contract or instrument of conveyance as to the relevance of these statutes and facts to the value of the property the purchaser is hereby purchasing or contracting to purchase.

(b) If the statement is not included in the executory contract for conveyance or there is no executory contract for conveyance, the statement must be delivered to, and receipt thereof acknowledged by, the purchaser not later than 10 calendar days prior to closing the transaction.

(c) Failure to comply with Subsection (a) or (b), as applicable, shall be grounds for the purchaser to terminate the contract or agreement to convey, and upon termination any earnest money shall be returned to the party making the deposit.

(d) A seller commits a deceptive act under Section 17.46, Business & Commerce Code, if the seller fails to comply with Subsection (a) or Subsection (b), as applicable.

(e) This section, or the failure of a person to give or receive the notice in the manner required by this section, does not diminish or modify the beach access and use rights of the public acquired through statute or under common law.

The Dune Protection Act finds that ocean shoreline contains "a significant portion of the state's human, natural, and recreational resources" and that it is necessary to protect dunes "because stabilized, vegetated dunes offer the best natural defense against storms and are areas of significant biological diversity."[48] Pursuant to its authority under the Dune Protection Act, the GLO defines all dune areas within 1000 feet of mean high tide as critical dune areas that must be protected.[49] The GLO requires all local government authorities to adopt dune protection plans that govern these dune areas, which are subject to approval by the GLO.[50] The local governments are then responsible for issuing permits for construction in coastal areas. In issuing permits, there are a number of GLO standards that local governments must apply. These include the requirement that 1) any construction not lead to material weakening of the dune or material damage to dune vegetation, 2) construction not interfere with public access to the beach, and 3) erosion control structures within 200 feet of the vegetation line be prohibited.[51]

The GLO administers both the Dune Protection Act and the Open Beaches Act under the state's Beach and Dune Rules, which call upon local governments to prepare a combined Beach Access and Dune Protection Plan.[52] The rules explicitly recognize that local governments are best-positioned to handle beach management issues on a day-to-day basis and seek to provide tools and resources for effective coastal management.[53] The rules call for the local government to establish a Dune Protection Line that then defines the maximum extent of the geographic area covered by the plan, but in no case is this area to extend more than one thousand feet from the mean high tide line.[54] Once the Dune Protection Line has been established, it governs the extent of the plan that the local government must prepare. The joint plan must comply with the public access provisions of the Open Beaches Act and the protection measures called for in the Dune Protection Act. Once a local plan has been approved by the GLO, the local government is responsible for permitting, which includes both issuance of dune protection permits and beachfront construction certificates.[55] Under an approved Beach and Dune Plan, the following activities

---

48. Tex. Nat. Res. Code §63.001(1), (6).
49. 31 Tex. Admin. Code §15.3.
50. Tex. Nat. Res. Code §63.011–.012.
51. 31 Tex. Admin. Code §15.4–.6.
52. Id. §15.3.
53. Id.
54. Id.
55. Id.

are prohibited without permit: 1) activities that will destroy or remove a portion of a sand dune in a protected area; 2) activities that will kill or destroy sand dune vegetation in a protected area; and 3) construction adjacent to the public beach that affects or may affect the beach.[56] While permitting authority is vested in local governments with approved plans, the standards for permit issuance are set by the GLO in the Beach and Dune Rules.[57]

Texans voiced their support for protection of the public beach by passing Proposition 9 in the November 2009 general election. Proposition 9 incorporates the public's right to access the beach under the Open Beaches Act directly into the Texas Constitution.[58] As with all constitutional Amendments in Texas, Proposition 9 had to pass both houses of the state legislature as a House Joint Resolution before being placed on the ballot for voter approval. With the help of Commissioner Patterson advocating for the bill, it ultimately won passage in both houses with only three "no" votes.[59] With many state legislators, including more conservative members of the state body, encouraging their constituents to support the measure, Proposition 9 ultimately passed with 76.94% of the popular vote.[60] The success of Proposition 9 was due to a combination of factors, including the *Severance* case, discussed in more detail below, and State Representative Wayne Christensen's successful lobbying for an exemption from the Open Beaches Act for himself and his neighbors on the Bolivar Peninsula after Hurricane Ike.[61] One local paper advocated for Proposition 9 saying that if it passed "well-connected property owners could no longer bend or reshape the Open Beaches Act to fit their private purposes."[62]

Public beach access and private homes are also protected by the Coastal Erosion Planning and Response Act. CEPRA is a state-run program that encourages erosion response planning and provides funding for beach nourishment.

---

56. *Id.* § 15.3(s).

57. *See id.* §§ 15.4 (dune protection standards); 15.5 (beach construction certificate standards); 15.6 (standards for issuing or conditioning permits on the beach); 15.7 (standards for management of the public beach).

58. Texas House of Representatives House Research Organization, Focus Report: Amendments Proposed for November 2009 Ballot 21 (Aug. 20, 2009).

59. Interview with Nonprofit Organization Staff Member (Oct. 30, 2009).

60. Texas Office of the Secretary of State, Race Summary Report: 2009 Constitutional Amendment Election (Nov. 3, 2009), http://elections.sos.state.tx.us/elchist147_state.htm.

61. Mike Norman, *Private Interests Hungry to Seize Texas Public Beaches*, Star-Telegram, Oct. 2, 2009.

62. *Id.*

Proposition 9 and Public Beach Access in Texas

Proposition 9 in 2009 amended the Texas Constitution to read as follows:

Sec. 33. ACCESS AND USE OF PUBLIC BEACHES.

(a) In this section, "public beach" means a state-owned beach bordering on the seaward shore of the Gulf of Mexico, extending from mean low tide to the landward boundary of state-owned submerged land, and any larger area extending from the line of mean low tide to the line of vegetation bordering on the Gulf of Mexico to which the public has acquired a right of use or easement to or over the area by prescription or dedication or has established and retained a right by virtue of continuous right in the public under Texas common law.

(b) The public, individually and collectively, has an unrestricted right to use and a right of ingress to and egress from a public beach. The right granted by this subsection is dedicated as a permanent easement in favor of the public.

(c) The legislature may enact laws to protect the right of the public to access and use a public beach and to protect the public beach easement from interference and encroachments.

(d) This section does not create a private right of enforcement.

Proposition 9 passed with overwhelming support, and was widely viewed as Texans' way of expressing their displeasure with the *Severance* lawsuit and reasserting their widely held belief that the dry sand beach is a public resource that should be available to everyone.

According to the General Land Office, CEPRA helps to ensure the productivity of the coastal zone by, "reduc[ing] impacts to valuable coastal resources caused by erosion."[63] CEPRA allows the General Land Office to partner with local governments and the federal government to undertake eligible projects, which include beach nourishment, dune restoration, and the installation of shoreline stabilization structures.[64]

---

63. Texas General Land Office, *supra* note 6, at 1.
64. Tex. Nat. Res. Code § 33.603.

The Coastal Erosion Response Planning Act

Created in 1999, the Coastal Erosion Response Planning Act ("CEPRA") gives the General Land Office the ability to administer grants for coastal erosion response and related studies. CEPRA funds are obtained through competitive application to the GLO and can be used for a variety of projects including beach nourishment, shoreline stabilization, habitat restoration and protection, demonstration projects, and research.

In an effort to encourage better planning in the face of erosion, the Texas Legislature amended the Natural Resources Code in 2009 to require local governments to develop plans to reduce public expenditures for erosion and storm damage losses (through the development of erosion response plans), and granted county governments the authority to adopt erosion setbacks of up to sixty times the erosion rate.[65] Initially, Land Commissioner Patterson had proposed linking this new county authority to CEPRA by restricting CEPRA funding only to those counties that adopt a setback.[66] However, this proposal was abandoned after Hurricane Ike. Galveston's erosion response plan was adopted by the City Council in 2012, but conforming changes to the City Code were not made until 2015.[67] Galveston's Erosion Response Plan establishes a 25-foot setback for most construction by establishing the landward limit of the Dune Conservation Area as "the north toe of the existing dune or restored (man-made) dune plus a 25-foot landward offset."[68] The Erosion Response Plan also establishes an "enhanced construction zone" as the area behind the Dune Conservation area that has the potential to be impacted by long-term erosion.[69] The erosion response plan was formally adopted as a City Ordinance in 2015.[70]

---

65. *Id.* § 33.607.

66. Interview with Nonprofit Organization Staff Member (Oct. 30, 2009).

67. Kristopher Benson, *So What About the Erosion Response Plan,* Galveston County The Daily News, Nov. 28, 2014, http://www.galvnews.com/opinion/guest_columns/article_91593e28-76c5-11e4-a8cb-ff84eb72d6df.html.

68. City of Galveston, Erosion Response Plan 14 (2012), http://www.cityofgalveston.org/DocumentCenter/View/1712.

69. *Id.* at 13.

70. *See* City of Galveston Ordinance No. 15-071.

The Severance Case and Rebuilding after Hurricanes in Galveston

The *Severance* case has redefined the scope of public access rights to the beach in Texas. In so doing, it has created substantial uncertainty regarding the protection of the ocean shoreline from the combined impacts of erosion and sea level rise and significantly complicated the state's coastal management efforts. In order to fully understand the *Severance* case and its implications for sea level rise adaptation in Texas, a fulsome description of the case and its history is necessary. As described further in this section, the *Severance* litigation was a case between an out-of-state property owner and the Texas GLO that began in the federal courts, was considered twice by the Texas Supreme Court, and ultimately settled. While the settlement means that full judicial resolution of the case was never reached, the Texas Supreme Court's opinions, answering specific questions about the Open Beaches Act posed by the Fifth Circuit, fundamentally redefined Texas' law regarding public access. Furthermore, the interactions of this ruling with limitations in the Texas constitution regarding how public funds may be spent have significantly constrained the state's ability to respond to erosion and sea level rise in the future. While the *Severance* opinion may thus "protect" the rights of coastal property owners from a taking by the GLO through enforcement of the Open Beaches Act, it likely expedites the ultimate taking of these same properties due to the natural forces of erosion and sea level rise.

Downtown Galveston is protected by an extensive seawall running approximately forty blocks. Because of the tendency of seawalls to create passive erosion, the City uses a series of small groins and annual beach nourishment to maintain a sandy beach in front of the seawall.[71] The City attempts to preserve this beach both to provide public beach access and to protect the seawall from the impacts of storm surge.[72]

However, the continued high erosion rates make maintenance of the beach difficult. Figure 43 shows extensive groin construction and beach renourishment being carried out in fall 2009. Figure 44 shows the beach in front of the Galveston seawall after a 2016 restoration project.

While the seawall combined with nourishment provides protection for downtown Galveston, it does not protect the entire City. Over the years, the City of Galveston has expanded its borders through annexation, and it now controls all of Galveston Island except for the Town of Jamaica Beach.[73] Beyond the end

---

71. Interview with Local Government Official (Nov. 16, 2009).
72. *Id.*
73. *Id.*

Figure 43: Rebuilding a Groin in Front of the Galveston Seawall

of the seawall, the City has regulatory authority over miles of sandy beach that have been the site of extensive private home development in recent years. Because of the high average annual erosion rate and a series of significant storms between 2004 and 2009, many of these homes have come to interfere with the public beach. As a result, West Galveston Island provides an interesting exam-

Figure 44: Galveston Seawall in 2016
Babe's Beach in front of the Galveston Seawall in 2016 after beach nourishment. The nourishment project established a beach along this stretch of the seawall for the first time in nearly 20 years. Photo Credit: Ellis Pickett

ple of how the ideals of the Open Beaches Act clash with the political realities of storm response and the needs of oceanfront property owners.

As explained above, the GLO has the authority to condemn any homes that come to lie on the public beach as a result of natural events. For years, the GLO has struggled with how to use this authority to fulfill its duty to protect public beach access. After a particularly severe storm season in 2004, the GLO was confronted with the problem of trying to figure out what to do with a large number of houses that suddenly encroached upon the public beach. Wanting more time to figure out an appropriate option, the Land Commissioner invoked his statutory authority under the Open Beaches Act and instituted a two-year moratorium on enforcement in 2004.[74]

Background on the *Severance* Case

The *Severance* litigation has fundamentally redefined the nature of the public's right to access the beach in Texas. The litigation went through three key phases that are discussed below: 1) initial litigation in federal court, 2) hearing of certified questions by the Texas Supreme Court, and 3) rehearing in the Texas Supreme Court. After these three phases were over, what remained of the case was remanded to federal court, and the dispute was ultimately settled out of court.

In 2005 Carol Severance, a California attorney, purchased three of the West Galveston homes subject to this enforcement moratorium as investment properties.[75] Shortly after Severance purchased these homes, Hurricane Rita hit the Gulf Coast, causing her properties to further encroach upon the public beach. In 2006, the GLO enforcement moratorium expired. Because the GLO had yet to develop a new approach to dealing with the large number of homes on the public beach, it immediately reverted to its old rules requiring removal of all structures that encroach upon the beach.[76] As a result, the GLO sent Ms. Severance enforcement letters for two of her properties informing her that each house encroached upon the public beach and may be subject to suit for removal in the future.[77] In the enforcement letters, the GLO followed its stan-

---

74. Tex. Nat. Res. Code §61.0185; Press Release, Texas General Land Office, Patterson Takes Action to Enforce Open Beaches Act (June 8, 2004) (announcing a two-year enforcement moratorium for 116 homes located on the public beach).

75. Severance v. Patterson, 485 F. Supp. 2d 793 (S.D. Tex. 2007). Note that Carol Severance at one time owned four threatened homes in West Galveston, but only the two homes purchased in 2005 are relevant to her lawsuit.

76. Interview with State Government Official (Nov. 19, 2009).

77. Brief of Plaintiff-Appellant 4–5, Severance v. Patterson, No. 09-0387 (Tex. June 12, 2009).

Figure 45: The *Severance* Properties

dard practice and offered Ms. Severance $40,000 per home to assist her in re-
moving or relocating the structures in order to avoid a judicially ordered removal in the future.[78] The state asserted that Ms. Severance's homes fell under
its Open Beaches Act jurisdiction because it had obtained a judicial determination in 1975 of an easement over the dry sand beach in front of what was
now Ms. Severance's property.[79]

Believing that the General Land Office did not have the authority to constitutionally enforce the Open Beaches Act against her, Ms. Severance immediately filed a claim in federal District Court seeking an order to stop the GLO
from enforcing the Open Beaches Act on her properties.[80] In her complaint,
Ms. Severance alleged that the enforcement of the Open Beaches Act would result in: 1) a taking of her property without just compensation, 2) violation of
her due process rights, and 3) unreasonable seizure of her property.[81] The Court
ultimately dismissed her claims on the grounds that she had not yet been subject to GLO enforcement and therefore it was too early for a court to hear them.[82]

Between the time that Ms. Severance filed her initial claim in the District
Court and the issuance of the Court's opinion, the GLO promulgated new regulations under the Beach and Dune Rules to deal with the properties that had
been subject to the moratorium. These rules were intended to provide a means
for property owners in Ms. Severance's position to be legally able to restore util-

---

78. Jerry Patterson, *Open Beaches Act Worth Defending*, Galveston County Daily
News, Dec. 8, 2010. *But see* Joint Answering Brief for Defendants-Appellees 8–9, Severance v. Patterson, No. 09-0387 (Tex. Sept. 4, 2009) (stating Severance was offered $40,000
per home).

79. *Id.* at 27.

80. Severance v. Patterson, 485 F. Supp. 2d at 798.

81. *Id.* at 798.

82. *Id.* at 802, 805.

Understanding the Legal Claims in *Severance v. Patterson*

In her initial lawsuit in federal District Court, Carol Severance makes three legal claims: 1) the GLO has attempted to take her property without just compensation; 2) the GLO's actions violate her due process rights; and 3) the GLO has engaged in an unlawful seizure of her property. It is important to explain the legal grounds for each of these claims.

(1) Takings Liability

As explained in Chapter 4, the Fifth Amendment of the United States Constitution prohibits the taking of private property for public use without just compensation. That is, if the government were to condemn a private person's property, to physically occupy the property, or to so heavily regulate the use of the property that it no longer had a reasonable economic use, the property owner must be paid just compensation. While it can be adjusted to account for other factors, just compensation is usually set at the fair market value of the property.

In her lawsuit, Ms. Severance claimed that it would be a taking to apply the Open Beaches Act's rolling easement to her property because the state could not demonstrate that it had obtained an easement over the property by dedication and prescription. The District Court dismissed this claim because plaintiffs in takings cases are required to seek compensation from the state before they file lawsuits, and Ms. Severance had not asked the state of Texas to compensate her first.

(2) Violation of Due Process Rights

The concept of substantive due process is derived from the due process clause of the Fifth Amendment. As interpreted by the U.S. Supreme Court, substantive due process rights guarantee that the government may not take an individual's life, liberty, or property without appropriate governmental justification. Thus, substantive due process is a means to safeguard the fairness of the laws.

(continued)

Understanding the Legal Claims in *Severance v. Patterson*

(continued)

It appears that in alleging violations of substantive due process Ms. Severance attempted to claim that the imposition of the public beach easement on her property through the operation of the Open Beaches Act rolling easement is a government action that cannot be justified.

(3) Unlawful Seizure

The Fourth Amendment of the Constitution protects individuals from unlawful searches and seizures of their property. The Fourth Amendment thus establishes procedural safeguards that will be familiar to any reader, such as the requirement that the police obtain a warrant before searching someone's property.

Ms. Severance claimed that the application of the Open Beaches Act to her property constitutes an unlawful seizure. It is important to understand how different this is from a normal unlawful seizure claim, which usually involves a situation like the police taking someone's personal property to use as evidence without a proper warrant. The Fourth Amendment theory asserted by Ms. Severance has not been recognized by a court before, and if it is recognized in the future, it may make meaningless the requirement that plaintiffs in takings claims seek compensation before filing suit because those plaintiffs could instead proceed under the Fourth Amendment.

---

ity connections and take other measures to make their minimally damaged homes on the public beach habitable.[83] In promulgating these Rules, the GLO stated:

> The coastal destruction caused by Hurricane Ike in September 2008 demonstrates the need for long-term procedures that can be implemented when certain disaster conditions exist. These procedures will enable local governments and their citizens to better respond to coastal disasters and allow these areas to protect and rebuild in the most ef-

---

83. Interview with State Government Official (Nov. 17, 2009).

ficient and safe manner possible, while still protecting coastal areas and the public's right to use and access the public beach.[84]

The revised rules focus on disaster recovery and only apply to those homes that are located within an area subject to a disaster recovery order issued by the Commissioner.[85] Should the Commissioner issue a disaster recovery order under § 15.13, it would apply to all covered properties for a period of two years unless a shorter time period is specified in the order.[86] The rules permit repairs that would otherwise be forbidden under the Act and also permit certain types of shoreline restoration, such as the building of clay-core dunes (that would not otherwise be allowed) when the following findings are made: 1) the vegetation line has shifted as the result of a meteorological event; 2) the house was completely landward of the vegetation line before the event; 3) no portion of the house is seaward of the mean high tide line; 4) the house is less than 50% damaged; and 5) the house is not an imminent threat to public health or safety.[87]

The intent of the emergency rules was to permit littoral owners to remain in their homes as long as they did not pose a hazard to the public health and safety in accessing the beach. The emergency rules thus represent a compromise by GLO to try to maintain what it saw to be a fair balance between the interests of littoral owners and the rights of the public to access the beach. It should be noted that many littoral owners in Texas freely acknowledge the right of the public to access the dry sand beach and do not object to the public's presence. Therefore, permitting houses that do not threaten public health or safety to remain was not seen as a threat to public access because not only does the Open Beaches Act prohibit littoral owners from taking actions to impede public access but public access is also a core value that is shared by the majority of Texans.

Despite the fact that these new rules would have permitted Ms. Severance to rebuild the damaged portions of her homes and make them habitable, she decided to continue to pursue her legal challenge with an appeal to the Fifth Circuit Court of Appeals. This decision, combined with the fact that Ms. Severance, a California resident, received free legal representation from the Pacific Legal Foundation, a pro-property rights group in California, has led some

---

84. 34 Tex. Reg. 968 (Feb. 13, 2009).
85. 31 Tex. Admin. Code § 15.13.
86. *Id.*
87. *Id.*

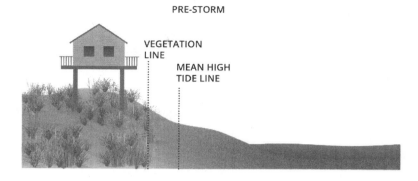

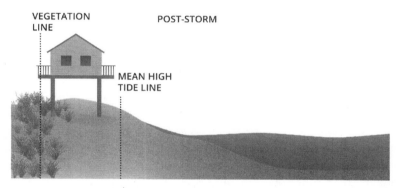

Figure 46: Rebuilding under Section 15.13 of the Beach and Dune Rules

Under Section 15.13 of the Beach and Dune Rules, a house that was landward of the mean high tide line pre-storm can undertake limited repairs post-storm if it is between the vegetation line and mean high tide line, is less than 50% destroyed, and is not an immediate danger to public health or safety.

observers in Texas to question whether Ms. Severance purchased the properties with the intent to attempt to judicially invalidate the Open Beaches Act.[88] As mentioned above, this speculation was certainly one of the factors that fueled the passage of Proposition 9 in the November 2010 election. Although not discussed in the California chapter, it is important here to understand that

88. Interview with Nonprofit Organization Staff Member (Oct. 30, 2009); Interview with State Government Official (Nov. 19, 2009).

some Southern California communities have a long history of litigation over public beach access in which littoral owners have fought to keep the public off of dry sand beaches, reflecting a value set that is not consistent with that expressed by an overwhelming majority of the people of Texas in their support for Proposition 9. In fact, as discussed later in this chapter, when asking the Supreme Court of Texas to consider rehearing the *Severance* case, Land Commissioner Patterson directly accused Ms. Severance and her attorneys of attempting to "Californize" the Texas coast.[89]

In a move that some characterized as hedging her bets, Ms. Severance applied for the FEMA buyout program for homes that are threatened by subsequent flood events.[90] FEMA buyouts were available along the Galveston coast as part of hazard mitigation after Hurricane Ike. Under the Voluntary Buyout and Elevation Program, a county government could nominate homes for buyouts under FEMA's hazard mitigation grant program and FEMA would cover 75% of the costs of the buyout.[91] GLO provided local governments with assistance in meeting their responsibility for the other 25% of the buyout costs: it paid directly to the homeowner accepting a buyout up to $65,000 to help meet the local government's matching responsibility.[92] Initially, there were over 200 homes that wanted to participate in the Hazard Mitigation Buyout program, but the County limited this number by restricting eligible homes to those seaward of the line at which the beach rises to 4.5 feet above sea level.[93] Using this narrowing criteria, the County approved the buyout of 62 homes in October 2009, including two of Ms. Severance's homes.[94] These buyouts are but one component of GLO's policy in practice, which is far more permissive of homes on the public beach than one might expect under the Open Beaches Act. Therefore, while her appeal was pending, Ms. Severance both had the choice between rebuilding under the revised Beach and Dune Rules or participating in a FEMA buyout.

---

89. Brief of Amicus Curiae Jerry Patterson in his Individual Capacity in Support of the Joint Motion for Rehearing Filed by Defendants-Appellees, Severance v. Patterson, No. 09-0387 (Tex. Jan. 14, 2011).

90. Note that entry into the buyout program does not appear to jeopardize Ms. Severance's standing to bring suit because she can withdraw from the buyout at any time until it is final. Interview with State Government Official (Nov. 19, 2009).

91. Beck Disaster Recovery, Property Owner Handbook: Voluntary Buyout and Elevation Program Galveston County, Texas 3 (2009).

92. Interview with State Government Official (Nov. 19, 2009).

93. Interview with Local Government Official (Nov. 15, 2009).

94. Leigh Jones, *Council Oks All Beach-Front Buyouts*, Daily News, Oct. 25, 2009.

FEMA's Hazard Mitigation Grant Program

The Hazard Mitigation Grant Program provides funds to state and local governments to implement long-term hazard reduction measures in the aftermath of a major disaster declaration. Hazard Mitigation Grant Program funds must be used to provide long-term solutions. Examples of projects that may be approved under the Hazard Mitigation Grant Program are the acquisition of property and elevation of flood-prone structures.

Under the program, the Federal Emergency Management Agency can provide up to 75% of the funds for a qualifying project if the state or local government applying for the Grant supplies the other 25%. States apply directly to FEMA for Hazard Mitigation Grant funds, and then the state or local government will be responsible for administering the grant program, including advertising the availability of hazard mitigation funds and determining who is eligible to participate in the program. Often, hazard mitigation grant funds are used to acquire flood-prone properties and remove the structures on them. Such programs are commonly referred to as FEMA buyouts. Any land that is purchased through a hazard mitigation program may only be used for open space, recreation, or wetlands management after the buyout.

The Initial Federal Court Challenges

Ms. Severance filed her initial challenge to the GLO's actions in federal court in the Southern District of Texas ("the District Court") in 2006.[95] The District Court issued its opinion in May of 2007, attempting to resolve Ms. Severance's claims against the GLO. Ms. Severance's suit against Land Commissioner Patterson alleged that the GLO's attempts to enforce the public's access rights were a violation of her constitutional property rights under the Fourth and Fifth Amendments. The District Court concluded that Severance's claims with respect to enforcement against her specific properties were not ripe for review.[96] However, the court suggested that a challenge to the con-

---

95. 485 F. Supp. 2d 793, 798 (S.D. Tex. 2007).
96. *Id.* at 802.

stitutionality of the Texas' rolling beach easement could proceed "[i]f her claim were meritorious."[97]

Turning to the issue of Texas' rolling beach easement, the District Court applied the Supreme Court's precedent in *Lucas* and concluded that Ms. Severance had no constitutionally protected property interest because her properties "are (and always have been) subject to the public's superior interest in its pre-existing easement."[98] Central to the District Court's conclusion was a finding that the Open Beaches Act was not attempting to create a new access easement over Severance's properties, which it concluded were subject to the rolling beach easement when she purchased them.[99]

Ms. Severance appealed the District Court's decision to the Fifth Circuit Court of Appeals. In the Fifth Circuit, Ms. Severance's appeals centered on two claims. First, she alleged that the Open Beaches Act effected an unconstitutional taking of her property in violation of the Fifth Amendment.[100] The Fifth Circuit found that this claim was not ripe for review because Ms. Severance failed to seek compensation through Texas' established system, and an attempt to seek such redress before bringing a takings claim is required by Supreme Court precedent.[101] Second she alleged that rolling easements, as codified under the Open Beaches Act, result in a seizure of her property in violation of the Fourth Amendment.[102] With regard to this claim, the Court decided that it did not have enough information about Texas common law to determine whether the rolling easements doctrine was created by the Open Beaches Act and resulted in an unconstitutional seizure of property.[103] The Court therefore certified three questions to the Texas Supreme Court, asking it to clarify the state of Texas law.

---

97. *Id.*

98. *Id.* at 803.

99. *Id.*

100. 566 F.3d 490, 494–95 (5th Cir. 2009) (*"Severance I"*). The Fifth Amendment of the United States Constitution establishes that private property shall not be taken for public use without just compensation. U.S. CONST. amend. V.

101. *Severance I*, 566 F.3d at 496; Williamson Cnty. Reg'l Planning Comm'n v. Hamilton Bank of Johnson City, 473 U.S. 172, 194 (1985).

102. *Severance I*, 566 F.3d at 494. The Fourth Amendment of the United States Constitution provides protection against unreasonable searches and seizures. U.S. CONST. amend. IV.

103. *Severance I*, 566 F.3d at 503–04.

How a Takings Claim Becomes Ripe for Review

Ripeness is a judicial doctrine which says that courts should wait until the facts of a case have developed sufficiently before ruling on a case. In the context of a takings claim, a central element of the claim is that the plaintiff was not provided with adequate compensation for the taking. In *Williamson County Regional Planning Commission v. Hamilton Bank of Johnson City*, the U.S. Supreme Court concluded that a takings claim is not ripe for review if a plaintiff has not first sought compensation from the state. 473 U.S. 172, 186 (1985). The Court reasoned that the actionable violation in a takings claim is the failure of the government to provide just compensation, and therefore, there is no claim at all until the plaintiff has sought compensation and been denied.

Like the plaintiffs in *Williamson County*, Ms. Severance sought to bring a takings claim without following the procedures that Texas provides to determine appropriate compensation for property owners who claim they have suffered takings. Because Ms. Severance did not attempt to obtain compensation from the state before filing her lawsuit, the Fifth Circuit found that it was too early to consider whether she had suffered a Fifth Amendment taking.

The three questions the Fifth Circuit certified to the Texas Supreme Court were:

1. Does Texas recognize a rolling beach easement?
2. If so, does that easement come from the common law or is it a creation of the legislature through the Open Beaches Act?
3. To what extent is a landowner entitled to compensation when a rolling easement limits the use of private property and no easement over the beach is found through prescription, dedication, or custom?[104]

The First *Severance* Decision in the Supreme Court of Texas

The Texas Supreme Court twice addressed the certified questions presented by the Fifth Circuit. The case was initially heard in 2009 and decided in November 2010. After the effects of the ruling were immediately felt, the

---

104. *Id.*

Texas Supreme Court granted rehearing of the *Severance* case. The rehearing took place in April 2011, with the Texas Supreme Court issuing its second (and final) opinion in March of 2012.[105] The Texas Supreme Court first heard arguments in the *Severance* litigation on November 19, 2009. Representing Ms. Severance, the Pacific Legal Foundation argued that rolling easements "seriously threaten[ ] the stability and viability of private property along the Texas shore."[106] Severance's attorneys further argued that there was no historical precedent for easements to move.[107] On the other side, the State argued that the rolling beach easement is a natural extension of well-established common-law principles and provided numerous examples of dynamic easements elsewhere.[108]

Surprising many observers, in November 2010, the Texas Supreme Court issued a ruling in the *Severance* case that significantly limited the reach of the Open Beaches Act.[109] Traditionally, Texas courts have read the definition of public beach expansively,[110] finding that it covers most of the Texas Gulf Coast. In particular, courts have relied on the long-standing use of the beach as a public highway in Texas to find public beaches exist based on the doctrine of custom.[111] Because of the Open Beaches Act's language stating that the public beach is defined by the vegetation line, regardless of where it moves as the result of natural events, Texas courts have found that the public beach easement under the Open Beaches Act will roll landward with the vegetation line.[112] As a result, Texas was widely understood to be the only state that had enacted a policy of rolling easements. Given this body of precedent, it was broadly expected that the Texas Supreme Court would answer the Fifth Circuit's first question in the

---

105. 370 S.W.3d 705.

106. Brief of Plaintiff-Appellant 3, Severance v. Patterson, No. 09-0387 (Tex. June 12, 2009).

107. Oral Argument, Severance v. Patterson, No. 09-0387, 2009 WL 4823928 (Tex. Nov. 19, 2009), http://www.supreme.courts.state.tx.us/oralarguments/2009.asp#09-0387.

108. *Id.*

109. Severance v. Patterson, 2010 WL 4371438 (Tex. Nov. 5, 2010), *republished* 2010 WL 8366839 (Nov. 5, 2010), *opinion withdrawn and superceded by* 370 S.W.3d 705 (2012).

110. Public beach is defined by the Texas Constitution as: a state-owned beach bordering on the seaward shore of the Gulf of Mexico, extending from mean low tide to the landward boundary of state-owned submerged land, and any larger area extending from the line of mean low tide to the line of vegetation bordering on the Gulf of Mexico to which the public has acquired a right of use or easement to or over the area by prescription or dedication or has established and retained a right by virtue of continuous right in the public under Texas common law. Tex. Const. art. I §33.

111. Matcha v. Mattox, 711 S.W.2d 95, 98–99 (Tex. Ct. App. 1986).

112. *Id.* at 100.

affirmative, finding that there is a rolling beach easement. Because of its roots in the common law, many observers also expected that the Court would answer the Fifth Circuit's second question by finding that the Open Beaches Act's rolling easement was merely a codification of the state's common law.

However, the *Severance* court upset this settled understanding of Texas property law, holding that there is no rolling easement.[113] According to the *Severance* court, public beach only exists where an easement can be proven over a specific property. Furthermore, unless public beach access was expressly reserved by the state in the initial land grant, the state may not rely upon custom to secure public access.[114] Because much of the Texas coast experiences very high erosion rates, often upwards of ten feet a year, many of the properties over which Open Beaches Act easements had been proven are now submerged and part of the public trust. As a result of the *Severance* holding, property that becomes littoral by virtue of erosion and loss of the original oceanfront lot will not be encumbered by the public beach easement, and public access to the dry sand beach along large sections of the Texas coast has effectively been eliminated.

In *Severance*, the Court, for the first time, recognized a form of the doctrine of avulsion in Texas.[115] The Court held that avulsion will operate to preserve the pre-storm vegetation line as the landward extent of the public's easement over the dry sand beach.[116] However, the Court also concluded that *Luttes*, which established the seaward limit of littoral property to be the current location of the mean high tide line, would still control to determine the boundary between private littoral property and public trust lands.[117] As a result of this significant shift in the application of the doctrine of avulsion, it will no longer be possible for homes to come to interfere with the public beach as the result of storm events. Instead, the GLO's condemnation power can only be exercised when (1) a littoral home comes to occupy submerged public trust lands or (2) erosion causes the vegetation line to migrate landward of the littoral home. Furthermore, the *Severance* decision appears to destroy the public's access right in many dry sand beaches.

---

113. Severance v. Patterson, 2010 WL 4371438, at *11 (Tex. Nov. 5, 2010).
114. *Id.* at *5, *11.
115. *Id.*
116. *Id.* at *10.
117. *Id.* at *11.

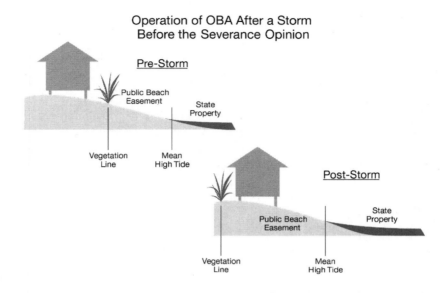

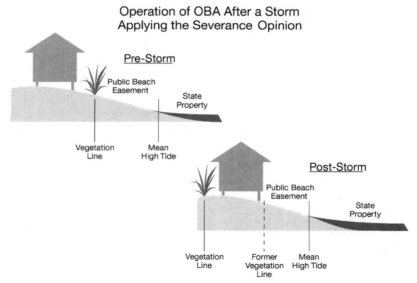

Figure 47: Application of the Doctrine of Avulsion after *Severance*

The Response to the Texas Supreme Court's First *Severance* Opinion

The impacts of the *Severance* decision were immediately felt. Under the Texas Constitution, the government may not spend taxpayer dollars to enhance the value of private property. Given that the *Severance* holding seemed to give littoral owners the right to exclude the public from the dry sand beach in front of their homes, the state raised questions about the legality of continuing to spend public funds on activities that inured to the benefit of dry sand beach that may be private under *Severance*. This led the GLO to halt a planned nourishment project at Galveston's West Beach and the City of Galveston to restrict beach cleaning services to recognized public beaches.

When the Texas Supreme Court's decision was announced, the GLO had equipment in place to conduct beach nourishment activities on Galveston's West Beach.[118] The GLO immediately halted the nourishment project citing concerns over the constitutionality of the project.[119] Because the creation of dry sand beach through nourishment would create new private property to which the public was not guaranteed access, the GLO determined that the project would amount to the spending of public funds to improve private property in violation of the Texas Constitution.

Shortly after the West Beach nourishment project was put on hold, littoral owners attempted to organize to dedicate easements to any beach created by nourishment.[120] While a group of property owners did ultimately offer to dedicate a static easement to that land subject to beach nourishment, the state rejected this offer, stating that only the dedication of a rolling easement would be sufficient for it to proceed with nourishment.[121] Thus, the littoral owners in West Beach, many of whom opposed Carol Severance's lawsuit, found their homes increasingly in jeopardy because of the state's inability to conduct nourishment.

The public also felt the immediate impacts of the *Severance* decision. Citing the same constitutional concerns, the Galveston Parks Department ceased using public funds to clean up private dry sand beach;[122] there was no trash

---

118. Ian White, *State Kills West Beach Restoration Project*, GALVESTON COUNTY DAILY NEWS, Nov. 16, 2010.

119. *Id.*

120. Ian White, *GLO Says "No" to Static Easements on West End*, GALVESTON COUNTY DAILY NEWS, Nov. 26, 2010.

121. *Id.*

122. Harvey Rice, *Galveston Cleans Private Beaches with Public Money*, HOUSTON CHRON., Mar. 25, 2011.

or seaweed removal on dry sand beach unless it was conducted by littoral owners.[123]

As a result of these immediate impacts and the extent to which the *Severance* decision was contrary to Texans' long-held expectations about the nature of the public beach, numerous groups called for a reconsideration of the Texas Supreme Court's *Severance* holding. The State Attorney General's office filed a petition for reconsideration emphasizing that the majority opinion in *Severance* was inconsistent with the established common law of Texas.[124] Supporting the Petition for Reconsideration, Land Commissioner Patterson filed a letter arguing that if the majority's opinion were allowed to stand, it would undermine Texas' tradition of public beach access and result in the "Californization" of the Texas coast.[125]

The Second Texas Supreme Court *Severance* Opinion

After the rehearing was granted and the second round of oral arguments in the case were held in April 2011, the Texas Supreme Court had to consider whether it still had jurisdiction over the *Severance* case. At some point during the Texas Supreme Court's reconsideration of the case, Ms. Severance took advantage of a FEMA buyout, selling the homes that were the subject of her case. On June 27, 2011, Ms. Severance filed a letter with the Texas Supreme Court notifying them that she had sold the last remaining home involved in the suit. In its subsequent supplemental brief, the Attorney General's office asked the Court to dismiss the case as moot. The Texas Supreme Court found that it must abate the case and send it back to the Fifth Circuit for a determination on mootness.[126] The Fifth Circuit concluded that the case was not moot because Ms. Severance still faced potential liability for past violations of the Open Beaches Act.[127] Therefore, the Texas Supreme Court lifted its abatement order on October 7, 2011, and issued a decision in March 2012.

The Texas Supreme Court's rehearing opinion is highly consistent with its original ruling. The Texas Supreme Court recognized the dynamic nature of

---

123. *Id.*

124. Joint Motion for Rehearing, Severance v. Patterson No. 09-0387 (Tex. Dec. 10, 2010).

125. Brief of Amicus Curiae Jerry Patterson in his Individual Capacity in Support of the Joint Motion for Rehearing Filed by Defendants-Appellees 3, Severance v. Patterson, No. 09-0387 (Tex. Jan. 14, 2011).

126. Opinion, Severance v. Patterson, No. 09-0387 (Tex. July 29, 2011).

127. *See* Harvey Rice, *Appeals Court Upholds Beach Act Challenge*, Houston Chron., Sept. 28, 2011.

What Are Judicial Takings?

The judicial takings theory has yet to be recognized by any court, but rests on the premise that the holding of a court could so dramatically depart from established law that the court's decision itself is a Constitutional taking. While judicial takings have been a popular subject of scholarship, courts are reluctant to address them because doing so would impair the ability of the courts to permit the common law (judge-made law) to evolve with the changing needs of society. Thus, a judicial takings doctrine would threaten to strip the common law of one of its most essential features.

The Supreme Court considered the possibility of judicial takings in *Stop the Beach Renourishment v. Florida Department of Environmental Protection*. 560 U.S. 702 (2010). Under Florida law, beaches created through nourishment belong to the state, and Plaintiffs alleged that in holding that a nourishment project that cut off their access to the water did not take their littoral rights, the Florida Supreme Court had affected a judicial taking. The Supreme Court concluded that plaintiffs had not stated a takings claim because the State had always had a right to fill submerged lands that was superior to the littoral owner's right of access, and thus, the owners had been deprived of no property right. However, the court was highly fractured as to whether judicial takings could ever exist, leaving the question unresolved.

the state's ocean coastline and explained that "[a]ccordingly, public easements that burden these properties along the sea are also dynamic."[128] However, the Texas Supreme Court concluded that in order for the Open Beaches Act's regime to protect dynamic beach access easements to apply, the state must first prove that an easement—acquired by prescription, dedication, or custom—exists over the specific property at issue.[129] As the Texas Supreme Court succinctly put it: "For an easement to roll, there must first be an easement."[130] As explained in the discussion of the first Texas Supreme Court opinion in *Severance*, this is a significant departure from Texas' previously established com-

---

128. Severance v. Patterson, 370 S.W.3d at 708.
129. *Id.* at 711, 714.
130. *Id.*

mon law, which understood the public to have acquired an easement by custom over the dry sand beaches in Texas.

As in its first opinion, the Supreme Court of Texas determined that a version of the doctrine of avulsion should apply to the public's easement over the dry sand beach in Texas. The court held that where the shoreline changes gradually and imperceptibly due to accretion or erosion, the public easement over the dry sand beach will follow these boundary shifts. However, "when changes occur suddenly and perceptibly to materially alter littoral boundaries, the land encumbered by the easement is lost to the public trust, along with the easement attached to that land."[131] Thus, when land is lost to avulsion in storm events, public access to the new dry sand beach will not exist unless the state can prove an easement over the new littoral property.

Resolution in the Fifth Circuit and Settlement of the *Severance* Case

After the Supreme Court of Texas issued its second opinion answering the Fifth Circuit's certified questions, the *Severance* case returned to the Fifth Circuit in the spring of 2012. The Fifth Circuit issued a short opinion in which it concluded that in light of the Supreme Court of Texas' opinion, Ms. Severance had a potential Fourth Amendment claim for unreasonable seizure of her property arising from the state's assertion of an easement over the dry sand beach shifted landward by Hurricane Rita.[132] As a result, the Fifth Circuit reversed the District Court and remanded the case to the District Court for further proceedings.[133] The Severance case was ultimately settled out of court.

The Future of the Open Beaches Act

In defining GLO's position on Open Beaches Act enforcement, Land Commissioner Patterson stated, "[a]s a Texan I honor the right to public property" and went on to note that he did not think that the goals of the Open Beaches Act and private property rights were incompatible.[134] After issuing a moratorium on enforcement for 116 homes slated for removal in 2004, Commissioner Patterson ultimately announced that the state would not seek re-

---

131. *Id.* at 724.
132. 682 F.3d 360 (5th Cir. 2012) (per curiam).
133. *Id.*
134. Texas General Land Office, Texas Land Commissioner Jerry Patterson's Plan for Texas Open Beaches 1 (2006).

moval of the homes noting that the legal costs to do so could rise to the tens of millions of dollars.[135] As the case of Surfside Beach shows, even where the GLO has been successful in winning judicial removal orders, gaining the actual removal of houses is practically impossible.[136] In acknowledgment of this fact, the GLO had already shifted its focus away from judicial removals before the *Severance* decision and promulgated the rules for limited repairs described above. The GLO seemed resigned to the fact that its judicial authority under the Open Beaches Act cannot be effectively used to force retreat. Instead, the GLO essentially adopted a policy to wait until littoral homes come to lie on submerged lands and use the public's title, rather than the easement the public holds over dry beach, as a stronger basis to force property owners to move. Even before the Texas Supreme Court issued its opinion in *Severance*, the GLO's policy had shifted to allow homes to remain on the public beach until they become a threat to public health and safety or encroach upon state submerged lands.

The greater challenge for Texas arises in how it will protect the state's valuable beach resources and preserve public access in light of the *Severance* decision. While the GLO has expressed a desire to maintain the beach through nourishment, the *Severance* case introduced a number of new legal hurdles to using nourishment to preserve the beach in place. When the Texas Supreme Court issued its first opinion in *Severance* in 2010, the state was about to begin a beach nourishment project on West Beach in Galveston.[137] The planned $40 million dollar project would have placed 1.8 million cubic feet of sand on West Galveston's beaches.[138] However, citing uncertainty over the legality of the project created by the *Severance* opinion, the state halted the nourishment project.[139] As a result of the *Severance* decision, the state concluded that it was unclear whether beach nourishment, which would now likely be an avulsive

---

135. *Id.* at 4.

136. *See* Brannan v. Texas, 365 S.W.3d 1 (Tex. Ct. App. 2010) (upholding the trial court's finding of an easement on Surfside Beach in the ongoing Open Beaches Act litigation where state's removal was initially upheld by a court in 2001).

137. Ian White, *West End Beach Work Set to Begin*, GALVESTON COUNTY DAILY NEWS, Nov. 15, 2010, at A1.

138. *Id.*

139. CHRIS O'SHEA ROPER & TOM LINTON, A NEW PARADIGM FOR TEXAS BEACHES: IMPLICATIONS OF THE SEVERANCE DECISION ON PUBLIC BEACH ACCESS (2013), http://www.tamug.edu/linton/New%20Series%20on%20Water%20Management%20Issues/WhitePaperANPFTB.pdf; Ian White, *Beach, Dune Project Halted*, GALVESTON COUNTY DAILY NEWS, Nov. 16, 2010, at A1.

change under Texas law would move the property boundary or expand the public beach. This legal uncertainty was not addressed in a meaningful way in the second Supreme Court of Texas opinion, creating significant challenges for future responses to sea level rise.

The Texas Constitution expressly forbids the use of state funds solely to increase the value of private property.[140] As a result, the GLO has concluded that it does not have the ability to spend public funds, including funds available under CEPRA, on nourishment projects in front of private property unless the property owner is willing to dedicate a public access easement.[141] Under Land Commissioner Patterson, the GLO established a policy that it would not consider beach nourishment in front of private properties unless the private property owners dedicated rolling access easements.[142]

In discussing the decision to halt the West Beach nourishment project, Land Commissioner Patterson noted that it was "ironic that a property rights group screwed a bunch of beach homeowners. It just goes to show you have to be careful what you ask for."[143] Prior to the *Severance* holding, the state was prepared to pursue a policy of holding the line through nourishment, protecting littoral property owners as a means to ensure continued public beach access. However, the *Severance* holding's limitation of public beach access has also denied property owners state-funded nourishment. Under the GLO's post-*Severance* policy, nourishment on West Beach will only proceed if rolling easements are dedicated by each of the littoral property owners who will benefit from the nourishment project.

Obtaining agreement from all littoral owners has been made more difficult by the fact that the GLO has rejected the dedication of static easements over the dry sand beach created by nourishment. According to the GLO, it will only restart the West Beach nourishment project if littoral owners will grant rolling easements that exist in perpetuity.[144] Because the West End property owners have not been able to come to a consensus on the dedication of

---

140. The Texas Constitution states "All free men, when they form a social compact, have equal rights, and no man, or set of men, is entitled to exclusive separate public emoluments, or privileges, but in consideration of public services." Tex. Const. art. 1, § 3.

141. GLO2015, *supra* note 2, at 2.

142. Texas General Land Office, *Severance v. Patterson* Frequently Asked Questions, http://www.galvestonparkboard.org/beachmaintenance/FAQ_severance.pdf.

143. White, *supra* note 137, at A8.

144. Ian White, *GLO Says No to "Static" Easements on West End*, Galveston County Daily News, Nov. 26, 2010.

rolling beach easements, direct nourishment in front of these properties has yet to proceed. However, West Beach is likely to benefit — through along-shore littoral transport — from a significant beach nourishment project along the west end of the Galveston seawall that was completed in 2015.[145] This project reportedly included privately owned beach in front of the Seascape Condominiums, and the GLO determined that the nourishment project could proceed because the condominium owners dedicated a static easement over the dry sand beach and contributed funds to pay for the nourishment project.[146] In addition, GLO, the Army Corps, and the Park Board have also collaborated to conduct extensive nourishment along the beaches in front of the Galveston seawall.[147] Because of the pattern of flow along the beach in Galveston, it is expected that these nourishment projects will ultimately benefit the West End through the littoral transport of sand and that continual nourishment in connection with regular maintenance dredging of the Houston ship channel could help to restore the beaches along the entire Galveston coast.

In addition to the overwhelming political pressures to hold the line, which manifest themselves in the new sections of the Beach and Dune Rules, the example of West Beach in Galveston and the *Severance* case demonstrate the ability of litigation to frustrate not only state adaption policies but also undermine the wishes of property owners. One of the most interesting aspects of Carol Severance's story is that she is not from Texas. Many littoral property owners in Texas were dismayed by her lawsuit and the Texas Supreme Court's ultimate decision. While Severance and her attorneys claimed to be defending the rights of all littoral property owners, many beachfront owners in Texas actually embrace the long tradition of public beach access in Texas. Furthermore, the Texas Constitutional resolution shows that, as a whole, Texans place a strong cultural value on continuous access to the ocean coastline. What's more, when given the choice, the vast majority of littoral owners would prefer to have state

---

145. Harvey Rice, *Galveston Begins Building 20 New Blocks of Beach*, Houston Chron., Aug. 13, 2015.

146. John Wayne Ferguson, *Megadune Project Will Soon Rise West of Galveston's Seawall*, Galveston County The Daily News, Sept. 27, 2014, http://www.galvnews.com/news/free/article_4c07b9e8-46c9-11e4-aacd-0017a43b2370.html.

147. Press Release, Texas General Land Office, USACE, Texas GLO and Galveston Parks Board Celebrate Completion of Beach Renourishment Project (Nov. 20, 2015), http://www.glo.texas.gov/the-glo/news/press-releases/2015/november/usace-texas-glo-and-galveston-parks-board-celebrate-completion-of-beach-renourishment-project.html.

support to maintain a dry sand beach to which the public has access rather than risk losing their homes to Galveston's high erosion rates and sea level rise. Thus, Texas appears to have struck a unique cultural balance between the rights of private property owners on the coast, which have always been limited by the Open Beaches Act, and the public's paramount right to access the coast. However, in the aftermath of the *Severance* decision this balance has been upset and the future of public beach access and beach maintenance along Texas' ocean coastline remains uncertain.

Opportunities for Adaptation along Texas' Estuaries

Overview of Legal Framework

Unlike the other states examined in detail in this book, Texas neither extends the laws protecting its ocean coastline to its extensive estuarine shoreline nor has an independent legal regime designed to govern development along the estuaries. Instead, the only significant limitations on upland construction along the estuarine coastline are those imposed by local building regulations, FEMA regulations for flood hazard mitigation, and federal Clean Water Act restrictions if the development will impact wetlands. While the Army Corps' section 404 authority will keep some development from directly interfering with wetlands,[148] there is no one other than the local government who has the authority to mandate setbacks from the wetland edge. While the Corps does attempt to work with local governments to create wetland setbacks for water quality protection and future wetland migration, there are many developments with which the Corps never interacts because the development itself does not disturb a wetland or other water of the United States, and there is nothing that the Corps can do to keep developers from building right up to the edge of the wetland.[149] Therefore, as development increases along Texas' estuarine shoreline, FEMA's flood elevation regulations coupled with restrictions imposed by local governments will be the most significant means of reducing vulnerability to sea level rise.

---

148. Interview with Army Corps of Engineers Staff Member (Nov. 17, 2009).
149. *Id.*

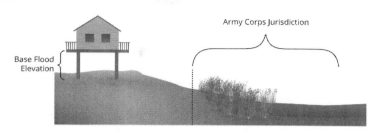

Regulatory requirement for elevation
of structures in the flood plain

Developers will set back from wetlands to
avoid Army Corps jurisdiction.

**Figure 48: Role of Base Flood Elevation and Army Corps
Jurisdiction in Shaping Development**

Harborwalk

The Harborwalk site lies in the town of Hitchcock, Texas, on the mainland
side of Galveston Bay. The project site was originally purchased by Houston
oilman John Mecom, who had plans for extensive development at the site, including hundreds of acres of canal subdivisions and several golf courses.[150] In
the 1960s, Mecom's group began to develop the site, digging canals and using
the spoil to build up the lots.[151] At that time, most of the existing main canals
and fingers were dug and five thousand linear feet of bulkheads were installed
along the canals.[152] The initial site development also included the formation
of a municipal utility district ("MUD"); installation of a water system, roads,
and streetlights; and the construction of five homes for the MUD directors.[153]
The project developer then went bankrupt and the property sat idle for over
forty years, passing through several owners as part of a larger 6,000-acre tract.[154]
The larger property was ultimately split up at auction and Watkins Properties
purchased an 800-acre tract that included the initial canal development site.[155]
The property was attractive to Watkins because most of the major environmental impacts associated with development had occurred over 40 years ago,
and because of the heavy clay nature of the soils, the canals were still largely
intact.[156]

---

150. Interview with Harborwalk Official (Nov. 17, 2009).
151. Interview with Army Corps of Engineers Staff Member (Nov. 17, 2009).
152. Interview with Harborwalk Official (Nov. 17, 2009).
153. *Id.*
154. *Id.*
155. *Id.*
156. *Id.*

John Mecom's Flamingo Isles

Houston Oilman John Mecom assembled a site over 3,000 acres in the 1960s and made his plans for Flamingo Isles—a community that was to accommodate between 30,000 and 100,000 people. Mecom's original plan included 20 miles of slips to accommodate 5,000 boats as well as an 18-hole golf course and a private jet airport. BRUCE WEBB, SHORE THING (2004), http://offcite.org/wp-content/uploads/sites/3/2010/03/ShoreThing_Webb_Cite59.pdf.

Construction of Flamingo Isles began in 1966 with the dredging of canals. Mecom also installed roads and lighting and established a municipal utility district. In 1969, Mecom halted development in the face of mounting costs, and the site remained untouched until purchased by Watkins Properties for development as Harborwalk.

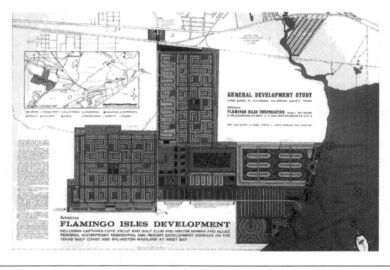

The Harborwalk project is a dredged canal community with over 350 home sites. Watkins Properties handled the permitting and construction associated with restoration of the canals and installation of a new 500-slip marina and yacht club. Individual lots are now sold to private owners for development. Individual owners are then responsible for getting their own building permits from the City of Hitchcock, which enforces the International Building Code

Requirements and FEMA flood elevations.[157] In Hitchcock, the minimum FEMA flood elevation is fourteen feet.[158] In addition to obtaining permits from the City of Hitchcock, homebuilders must have their plans approved by Harborwalk's Development Review Committee.[159] Most of the Development Review Committee's restrictions involve preserving the aesthetics of the community, but they also cover aspects of the development plan that may impact flood risk and water quality, including amount of lot coverage, landscaping, and height of driveways relative to the connecting roads.[160] One of the requirements unique to Harborwalk is that it imposes a setback requirement on all homes constructed in the community. In most canal subdivisions, property owners may build right up to the edge of the bulkhead, but in Harborwalk, homebuilders must adhere to a fifteen-foot setback.[161]

Watkins Properties, the developer of Harborwalk, freely acknowledged that the site is very flat, and that there is little they can do to protect the property from the impacts of storm surge.[162] However, Watkins Properties did observe that compliance with FEMA flood elevation requirements was a key determinant of how homes fared during Hurricane Ike, and therefore felt it is very important that the City of Hitchcock enforce these regulations.[163] The Texas Commission on Environmental Quality also noted that the flat nature of the site could lead to increased runoff and water quality impacts. For this reason, it has recommended sloping the lots towards the collector roads. However, the Texas Commission on Environmental Quality acknowledges that while they often suggest such land-side measures, they have no authority to enforce them.[164]

The Harborwalk project site does include two innovative wetland mitigation projects in order to meet its obligations under section 404 of the Clean Water Act.[165] While the developers did consider adopting a living shorelines approach, they ultimately determined that this was infeasible due to the pre-existing canal structure.[166] According to Watkins Properties, the canal lots in

---

157. Hitchcock, Texas Code of Ordinances tit. XV.

158. FEMA, *RiskMAP6: Flood Information Portal: Galveston County, TX,* http://maps.riskmap6.com/TX/Galveston/.

159. Interview with Harborwalk Official (Nov. 17, 2009).

160. *Id.*

161. *Id.*; Interview with Army Corps of Engineers Staff Member (Nov. 17, 2009) (stating that much estuarine development goes right up to the waters' edge).

162. Interview with Watkins Properties Official (Nov. 17, 2009).

163. *Id.*

164. Interview with State Government Official (Nov. 20, 2009).

165. Interview with Army Corps of Engineers Staff Member (Nov. 17, 2009).

166. Interview with Harborwalk Official (Nov. 17, 2009).

Figure 49: Overview of Harborwalk Showing Infeasibility of Living Shore-lines Given the Existing Canal and Lot Structure
© 2016 Google

Harborwalk are already very narrow by today's standards, and as a result, there was not enough space to provide both a marketable lot and leave space for living shorelines.[167]

Harborwalk has since changed owners and it continues to build out the development.[168] As with the homes that are already in place, these future homes will be constrained only by the requirements of the City of Hitchcock, FEMA flood elevations, and Harborwalk's fifteen-foot setback. As Figure 50 shows, there is already extensive bulkheading throughout the community. The tops of these bulkheads are level with the height of the lots, and normal high tide comes within one foot of the tops of these bulkheads. This means that even small amounts of sea level rise combined with storm surge events could pose serious problems for the community. While the houses themselves must be elevated, there are still ground-level structures that will be threatened. Most notable among these are the roads and water infrastructure for the community.

---

167. *Id.*

168. *See* Brochure, Coastal Cottages by Trendmaker Homes: Harborwalk, http://harbor walk.com/homes/coastal-cottages/.

Figure 50: Bulkheads at Harborwalk

The Harborwalk case does not stand alone. While the Army Corps has expressed the opinion that canal subdivisions on this scale would be difficult to permit in the future, the Texas Commission on Environmental Quality reports that it has continued to receive applications for canal subdivisions along other parts of the coast.[169] Furthermore, there are other canal subdivisions that have already been built, and many of these include homes and other structures that extend right up to the water line. This style of intensive development on the coastal edge of low-lying areas that are prone to storm surges is, in part, the result of a lack of comprehensive land use planning. In this context, FEMA's flood elevation requirements become a particularly important means of reducing vulnerability to sea level rise. However, these elevation requirements can only save the homes themselves and not the necessary infrastructure, which continues to be at ground level.

Comparing Opportunities for Adaptation on the Texas Gulf and Estuarine Coasts

What is most striking in comparing the coastal and estuarine case studies in Texas is that despite vastly different regulatory structures, the development

---

169. Interview with Army Corps of Engineers Staff Member (Nov. 17, 2009); Interview with State Government Official (Nov. 20, 2009).

outcomes on the ground are very similar. Looking only at the Open Beaches Act, one would expect Texas' ocean coastline to look quite different. Given the pre-*Severance* understanding and enforcement of the Open Beaches Act, one would expect that Texas' ocean coast would observe significant setbacks and give way to the advance of eroding beaches, particularly in the wake of major storms. However, reality shows quite the opposite: In West Galveston, there is political lock-in and entrenchment of interests leading to preservation of the status quo. Judicial enforcement has proven difficult, and will be more so in the wake of *Severance*, reducing the reach of the Open Beaches Act.

While the Open Beaches Act stands significantly weakened, implementation of carefully developed Beach Access Plans could still help to reduce vulnerability. However, to date it is not clear that Beach Access Plans are written such that they will reduce coastal vulnerability and can be integrated with broader coastal land use planning. In addition, the GLO cannot mandate specific setbacks, therefore the Beach Access Plan is not necessarily an effective tool in reducing community vulnerability. Furthermore, only 7% of the undeveloped Texas coast remains available for development, meaning that in many places most future development opportunities will be either infill or redevelopment opportunities.[170] The fact that much of the future development of the coast will be redevelopment is significant in its relationship to disaster recovery. Both GLO's disaster recovery rules and FEMA's relief programs are designed to restore communities to the way they were *before* the storm happened. As a result, disaster recovery rebuilding fuels entrenchment of coastal property owners who are allowed to build back without measured consideration of whether, as a matter of public policy, vulnerable development really should be replaced. It is these dynamics of disaster relief, discussed further below, combined with the inability of the GLO to enforce the Open Beaches Act that have led two very different regulatory frameworks on the ocean and estuarine coasts to produce very similar development outcomes.

Were it not for extensive stretches of ocean and estuarine coastline held as public parks, the ability of Texas' general public to gain meaningful access to the shoreline in the future would be in serious doubt. Given the political impossibility of mandating, or even discussing, the type of land use planning that could lead to meaningful retreat, it is difficult to see what options other than nourishment are left for Texas. This singular adaptation pathway is particularly significant in light of the fact that state-funded nourishment is now limited by the impacts of the *Severance* opinion.

---

170. Fisher & Sunley, *supra* note 29, at 3.

Figure 51: Coastal Development That Is a Danger to Public Health and Safety

This search for answers becomes particularly urgent when one considers the public's right to access the beach under the Texas Constitution. Under *Severance*, the GLO will only be able to rely upon the submerged lands doctrine to move people out of hazard zones on the beach at some indeterminate time in the future. This limitation of the state's authority will collide head-on with the public's constitutional right to have an unobstructed dry sand beach. Submerged land cases will likely be as difficult to litigate as Open Beaches Act removal cases, at least until the entire house is on submerged lands, and by that point the public's access has been effectively cut off by the danger of swimming near a stilted or partially destroyed house. Should the GLO be limited to only removing houses that are a danger to public health or safety on the public beach or that are on submerged lands, it will soon be faced with the challenge of articulating precisely what it means to be a danger to public health or safety, as it is likely that houses will be removable on these grounds long before they can be successfully judicially removed for encroachment upon submerged lands.

Underlying all of this, it is important to remember that the Land Commissioner and Attorney General are elected officials in Texas. Therefore, both decisions regarding general GLO policy and Open Beaches Act rules as well as judicial enforcement of the Open Beaches Act will be influenced by a change in officeholder. With the passage of Proposition 9, it is clear that there is a strong political majority that cares, at least in the abstract, about their ability to access the beaches. However, given that this is just one small part of what the Land Commissioner or Attorney General does, it is difficult to believe that a future election will turn solely on a willingness to defend the public's interest in the beach. Thus, it appears likely that for the foreseeable future, the lack of comprehensive land use planning in the Texas coastal zone will only serve to intensify the challenges in responding to erosion and sea level rise.

Chapter 8

Lessons for Policy Makers

This Chapter draws upon the case studies presented in Chapters 5 through 7 to distill a series of lessons for policy makers. The primary intent of this chapter is to provide a comparative analysis of the coastal governance features in the case study states that tend to aid or impair efforts to adapt to sea level rise. As with the case studies, the chapter emphasizes the important role of political, rather than legal, challenges in implementing measures to adapt to sea level rise. This chapter then turns to examine the lessons and opportunities that exist in facilitating adaption to sea level rise in coastal communities.

Comparison of Substantive Features of Governance Structures in the Case Study States

Table 1 summarizes and compares the key substantive features of coastal governance in California, Texas, and North Carolina. Below, I discuss some of these factors and the results that differences in state policies may lead to with respect to climate change adaptation.

Observance of the Doctrine of Avulsion

As explained in Chapter 6, the doctrine of avulsion plays a key role in North Carolina and other states engaged in extensive beach nourishment in expanding the scope of dry sand beach subject to the public trust. The doctrine of avulsion is conversely significant to littoral owners in the event of shoreline changes resulting from storms. Because the doctrine of avulsion does not change the line between public and private property, the advance of the shore-

Table 1: Comparison of Substantive Governance Features

	California	North Carolina	Texas
Extent of Public Trust	Mean High Tide (common law)	Mean High Tide is the property line (common law), public has an easement over dry sand beach.	First Line of Vegetation, where public easement has been established (Open Beaches Act, codifies common law)
Source of Legal Protection of Public Access	Prescription, California Coastal Act	Prescription, avulsion in areas of beach nourishment, Coastal Area Management Act ("CAMA")	Open Beaches Act ("OBA"), where easements have been proven through common law mechanisms
Public Access Requirements	Coastal Act requires that the public be provided with maximum access that is consistent with the rights of private property owners. Development may not interfere with access, and new development must provide public access from the nearest public roadway.	Development may not interfere with public beach access. There are specific requirements for the number of access points in particular types of areas.	OBA forbids construction of structures on the public beach or that impede access to the public beach. OBA provides for judicial removal of structures that come to lie on the public beach. The Beach and Dune Rules also contain provisions requiring the creation of beach access plans.
Observance of Doctrine of Avulsion?	Yes	Probably—CAMA exemptions may be sought to replace beach lost in avulsive event.	Yes, but only with respect to public access easements. *Severance* establishes that avulsion submerging property acts to transfer title from the littoral owner to the state, but that public access easements do not follow avulsive movements of the shoreline or first line of vegetation.

	California	North Carolina	Texas
Observance of Doctrine of Accretion?	Yes	Yes	Yes, but the public may maintain an easement over all dry sand to the first line of vegetation.
Comprehensive Land Use Planning?	Yes—CCA requires local governments to have approved Local Coastal Plans ("LCP"). Plans should be updated every five years, but the California Coastal Commission ("CCC") has no authority to require updates. There is no requirement for comprehensive land use planning in estuaries.	Yes—CAMA requires that Local Governments have Certified Land Use Plans. Land Use Plans must be updated within six years of every update to the CAMA rules. This applies to both ocean coastline and estuaries.	No, but the erosion response planning process can be implemented by local governments to provide for enhanced evaluation of construction in Dune Protection areas and immediately adjacent areas.
Special Rules for Beach Nourishment and Title?	Accretion only applies to "natural events," with no specific rules for beach nourishment.	Yes—beach created through nourishment activities belongs to the local government.	No
Extent of Zone for Coastal Permitting?	Coastal Act designates and varies from a few hundred feet in coastal urban areas to several miles in rural areas.	CAMA applies to all coastal counties, permits are required in any AEC, and setbacks apply in Ocean Hazard Areas, which are areas that are highly vulnerable to erosion and flooding and so designated by the Coastal Resources Commission ("CRC").	OBA and Dune Protection Act designate as the farther of 1000 feet from vegetation line or nearest parallel road.

	California	North Carolina	Texas
Right of Littoral Owner to Build a Seawall on the Ocean Coast?	Coastal Act says that owners can defend property when necessary to protect coastal-dependent uses or existing structures as long as the structure is designed to eliminate or mitigate adverse impacts on local shoreline sand supply. Note the potential inconsistency between Coastal Act and common law. Even if an area is delegated under an LCP, the CCC retains permitting authority over seawalls.	Depends—The State has a no oceanfront hardening policy, but permission may be sought to install temporary erosion control structures.	Depends—OBA forbids building of seawalls. Maintenance or repair of an existing seawall may be authorized only when a lack of seawall presents an unreasonable hazard to a public facility.
Setback Requirements?	There is no legislated distance. This is determined on a case-by-case basis in LCPs based on expected erosion rates. There is a requirement that Coastal Management Policies assure stability and not cause or contribute to erosion. Current setback calculations do not explicitly take sea level rise into account.	In Ocean Hazard Areas development must be behind primary dunes (if they exist) or 30 times the annual erosion rate behind the vegetation line.	No building may be permitted in dune areas within 1000 feet of mean high tide line. Counties may adopt a setback of up to 60 times the annual erosion rate.

	California	North Carolina	Texas
Concern Over Takings Claims?	Yes—Coastal Act prohibits condemnation by the CCC.	Setback requirements are designed to avoid takings claims. There has been litigation around takings and mandated removal of temporary erosion control structures, but removal orders have been upheld.	Yes—a background principle and therefore there is no taking, but *Severance* raises concerns about the extent of OBA's applicability
Coastal Barrier Resources Act ("CBRA") Applies?	No—CBRA doesn't cover the West Coast, where coastal barrier islands are uncommon.	Yes—This applies to selected communities along the Outer Banks.	Yes—This applies to Galveston and surrounding communities.

line due to acute storm-driven erosion does not give the state title over this newly submerged land. Rather, the private property owner retains title to property lost in avulsive events.[1] This is most clearly illustrated by the provisions of the North Carolina Administrative Code dealing with property loss due to avulsion. Under North Carolina regulations, a property owner who loses his shorefront property in a storm may seek permission from the Coastal Resources Commission ("CRC") to rebuild his beach at his own expense.[2] The only limitation upon the littoral owner's right to rebuild his beach is that the application must be made in a reasonable amount of time after the storm event.[3]

In contrast to this approach, the Texas Open Beaches Act ("OBA") makes explicit that the state does not recognize the doctrine of avulsion with respect to shifts in the mean high tide line that create newly submerged lands.[4] As a result, when coastal homes end up on the public beach after major storm events, the private property owner has no right to restore his lost beach. In fact, not only does the property owner have no right to rebuild the beach, but he may also be subject to a suit in condemnation to force him to remove his home and other structures on the submerged property that now belongs to the state.[5] Given the difficulties in enforcement of the OBA when homes come to lie on the dry public beach, the lack of a doctrine of avulsion with respect to the boundary between private and state public trust lands in Texas is likely to become more significant because it means that mean high tide can move landward after storm events, meaning that the state will be able to apply the submerged lands doctrine in a relatively speedier manner than those states that follow avulsion.

The consequences of continued adherence to the doctrine of avulsion thus have significant ramifications for the state's legal ability to prevent rebuilding in vulnerable areas after storm events. States may always enforce their setback requirements to the extent that they do not result in a total taking of the littoral property, but in states such as North Carolina where property owners can rebuild their beach, storm events may not lead to coastal retreat because property owners will be able to rebuild their beach and then rebuild their homes consistent with setback requirements. Note, however, that in North Carolina the setback requirement is enforced from the line of vegetation, so if a storm led to permanent loss of vegetation that did not recover, the state may be able

---

1. For a more thorough explanation of the doctrine of avulsion, *see* Chapter 4 Figure 17 and accompanying text.

2. N.C. GEN. STAT. § 146-6.

3. *Id.*

4. *See* TEX. NAT. RES. CODE §61.0183.

5. *Id.*

to move a house further back when it rebuilds. However, the state's general policy has been to enforce a setback requirement once and allow subsequent rebuilding within the same footprint.[6] This right to restore the beach and rebuild can lead to entrenchment of the interests of coastal property owners, which is discussed in more detail below.

In contrast, the Open Beaches Act gives Texas the ability to come in after storm events and prohibit rebuilding in certain coastal areas. While Texas does have a unique legal tool that is unavailable to other states, political circumstances do not allow the state to exercise this authority in the wake of a disaster. I will explore this issue in more detail below by evaluating the State's actions in the aftermath of Hurricane Ike (in the context of disaster response literature) to further explain the conclusion, presented above, that the political factors—particularly when combined with uncertainty regarding the reach of the OBA after *Severance*—have rendered the Open Beaches Act largely ineffective.

Use of a Comprehensive Land Use Planning System

Perhaps the most significant factor in differentiating the ability of coastal states to successfully prepare for and adapt to sea level rise is the extent to which their coastal zone management laws require regularly updated, comprehensive land use plans. As the previous chapters have made clear, the battle lines have currently been drawn in the sand over the first row of homes. Over time, states will lose their battle to keep up with sea level rise through beach nourishment, and will be forced to consider more permanent solutions, including retreat. If retreat is to be a viable option, state and local governments need to be planning now for what will happen when the second row of houses becomes promoted to littoral property. This means that the current focus primarily on littoral owners is unlikely to produce successful adaptation results; rather, states need to have comprehensive and long-term policies that consider appropriate land uses not just today, but in future years as coastal property becomes inundated by rising seas and the erosion rate also increases.

In order for states to be able to successfully promote this kind of planning for adaptation, they must have comprehensive land use planning systems that require periodic updates such that the plan remains relevant and includes the most current information regarding climate change impacts. The California Coastal Commission's *Sea Level Rise Policy Guidance* is an admirable attempt

---

6. Interview with Local Government Official (Dec. 4, 2009).

to incorporate sea level rise risks into local land use planning, but it is likely to be limited by the fact that the CCC has no legal authority to mandate up-dates to local coastal plans. States must also retain some degree of control over local land use planning, whether it be through the issuance of direct standards for enforcement, such as what the Texas General Land Office ("GLO") does with the Beach and Dune Rules, or a more comprehensive and meaningful re-view of consistency of land use plans.

Along this dimension, it is clear that North Carolina's legal structure would be most readily able to require local jurisdictions to plan for the impacts of sea level rise, because CAMA requires that land use plans be updated in response to changes in CAMA rules. At a fundamental level, the CAMA Land Use Plans and the California Coastal Act's Local Coastal Plans should not differ dramatically. However, in substance, the results of these programs could be quite different, largely due to the fact that the California Coastal Commission has no authority to require updates to Local Coastal Plans. As explained in Chapter 5, many Local Coastal Plans have not been updated since their initial approval over 30 years ago, and have thus become obsolete and irrelevant planning documents. In con-trast, CAMA Land Use Plans must be updated within six years of each update to the CAMA rules, so as long as the Division of Coastal Management ("DCM") and the CRC remain active in amending the CAMA rules to respond to chang-ing conditions, Land Use Plans will be constantly updated. This is particularly important with respect to sea level rise because the CRC will not only have the ability to adjust its rules as it obtains better information about the impacts of sea level rise, but also to require that local governments incorporate and respond to this new information in a timely fashion. However, as Chapter 6 highlights, the CRC's ability to respond to new information has been limited by the North Carolina legislature, and continued legislative actions to limit planning for sea level rise could substantially hinder the CRC's efforts to encourage the same.

The other significant and unique feature of CAMA is that it applies to both ocean and estuarine shorelines. In this regard, North Carolina is well ahead of both Texas and California in its ability to facilitate planning for sea level rise. Development of cities in California is governed by general plans, and there is a requirement that these plans be updated once every ten years.[7] While these plans do give cities along the San Francisco Bay some authority and responsi-bility with respect to land use planning, they do not have the particular focus on the coastal zone that a CAMA Land Use Plan provides along the estuaries in North Carolina. The CAMA Plan is an extra overlay on top of normal city

---

7. Interview with Local Government Official (Oct. 13, 2009).

planning requirements that is absent in both California and Texas. Given that over \$62 billion of real estate is at risk from sea level rise in the San Francisco Bay, it would seem that California would want to follow North Carolina's model and require some sort of comprehensive coastal land use planning along the San Francisco Bay.[8] However, such an outcome is unlikely for two reasons. First, with the exception of the Redwood City Saltworks Site, the Bay shoreline is almost completely built out. Second, there is no way to require comprehensive coastal land use planning with review along the Bay shoreline without dramatically expanding the San Francisco Bay Conservation and Development Commission's ("BCDC") authority.

States that don't have comprehensive land use planning with periodic updates may not have sufficient political will to pass the necessary legislative reform to create a system that is both comprehensive and forward looking. Even in states where such legal regimes do exist, North Carolina's example shows that legislative priorities may, in fact, run counter to forward-looking land use planning that accounts for rising sea levels. In the absence of legislation to require regularly updated land use planning that accounts for climate impacts, states will do best to follow the lead of DCM and BCDC as they have envisioned their role as facilitators. Both of these agencies understand the importance of empowering local governments by providing information on both the expected impacts of climate change and policy options to address it. This information, particularly if combined with a facilitation role to promote coordination between state agencies and local agencies, can help to provide local governments with the resources that they need to undertake their own adaptation efforts. Should states choose this option of leadership and facilitation, they are likely to still need some legislation or major state policy to guide local action. In the absence of overarching state mandates, states run the risk of chilling local adaptation behavior because local governments will fear that the efficacy of their actions may be undermined by the inaction of neighboring jurisdictions.

In sum, the states that are best positioned to adapt to sea level rise are those that are able to engage in comprehensive land use planning that is periodically updated and applies to all potentially impacted areas. Short of this broad land use planning authority, states can increase their adaptive capacity by adopting overarching strategies to guide local action coupled with resources to help local governments undertake this planning. While this latter option will not be as

---

8. Will Travis & Joseph LaClair, Draft Staff Report and Revised Preliminary Recommendation for Proposed Bay Plan Amendment 1-08 Concerning Climate Change 2 (Oct. 1, 2009).

effective as the former, local officials in coastal communities reveal that their actions are frequently shaped by the availability of state or federal funding to augment municipal budgets.[9] Therefore, the proper combination of information, guidelines, and incentives should encourage some adaptation planning by local governments.

Geographic Extent of the Coastal Zone for Permitting

The extent of the coastal zone for permitting purposes varies both within and among states. This variation may be significant in shaping the scope of a state's authority to limit vulnerability-increasing development. While the takings doctrine may limit the ability of coastal management agencies to forbid development outright, coastal permitting authorities do have a number of tools at their disposal that allow them to reduce vulnerability to climate change.

The most significant among these tools are building code standards and setback requirements. In the coastal zone there are a number of building code standards that can reduce property damage in the event of inundation or storms, including the requirement that houses be elevated on pilings. While these measures will prevent damage to individual properties, they are largely ineffective in protecting the public's ability to access the beach in the face of sea level rise because they make homes more structurally robust to sea level rise and therefore more likely to remain in place. Of more significance to preserving public access to the beach are setback requirements for coastal development. However, as discussed in more detail in Chapter 4, setback requirements are of only limited utility because the potential of a takings claim will generally lead a local permitting authority to grant a variance. Under *Lucas v. South Carolina Coastal Council*, the denial of a variance would constitute a *per se* taking in the absence of a background principle in property law that would produce the same result.[10]

Right of the Littoral Owner to Defend Property

If littoral owners have a vested right to defend their property from erosion and rising sea levels, this right will significantly impair the ability of coastal states to adapt to rising sea levels in a manner that preserves public access to

---

9. Interview with Local Government Official (Dec. 3, 2009); Interview with Local Government Official (Dec. 4, 2009); Interview with State Government Official (Dec. 1, 2009).

10. *See generally* Lucas v. S. Carolina Coastal Council, 505 U.S. 1003 (1992). *But see* Margaret Peloso & Margaret Caldwell, *Dynamic Property Rights: The Public Trust Doctrine and Takings in a Changing Climate*, 30 STAN. ENVTL. L.J. 51, 62–63, 67–76 (2011), for a discussion of the extent to which the public trust doctrine is a *Lucas* background principle.

the beach. In Texas, littoral owners have no right to defend their property and are actually subject to losing it when threatened by sea level rise and erosion. The Open Beaches Act requires that all persons purchasing littoral property file with the transfer of title a signed document, laid out in the Act, that acknowledges that the rights of the littoral property owner are subject to a lack of interference with the public beach and that they may be sued by the state in condemnation if as a result of changing shorelines their home encroaches upon the public beach.[11] In addition, the regulations of the General Land Office forbid the installation of erosion control structures within 200 feet landward of the first line of vegetation.[12]

In contrast, the California Coastal Act explicitly recognizes the right of coastal property owners to defend their property under prescribed circumstances.[13] In its recent *Sea Level Rise Policy Guidance*, the Coastal Commission has suggested that the correct interpretation of these provisions is that they only apply to pre-Coastal Act structures, but this approach seems to represent a change in Coastal Commission policy. Over the last two decades, the Commission has written provisions into littoral development permits stating that the coastal landowner will not have the right to armor his property in the future and that in the event erosion or sea level rise threatens the property, the agency reserves the right to require relocation of the structure. The "no future seawall" provision must also be recorded as a deed restriction and therefore operates against all successors in interest.[14] Also important is that even when coastal permitting has been delegated through a Local Coastal Plan, the Coastal Commission retains authority over seawall permitting.[15] However, neither these permit provisions nor the Coastal Commission's approach outlined in the *Sea Level Rise Policy Guidance* completely resolves the internal inconsistency of the Coastal Act.

North Carolina embodies a third approach to defining the rights of littoral owners. The CRC has adopted a no coastal hardening policy, which prohibits the construction of seawalls along the state's ocean beaches.[16] Significantly, the no coastal hardening policy does not apply to the state's extensive estuarine shoreline, which is also vulnerable to inundation from sea level rise.[17] Additionally, the CRC has the authority to allow the placement of temporary ero-

---

11. TEX. NAT. RES. CODE Ch. 61.

12. 31 TEX. ADMIN. CODE § 15.6(c).

13. CAL. PUB. RES. CODE § 30235.

14. Meg Caldwell & Graig Holt Segall, *No Day at the Beach: Sea Level Rise, Ecosystem Loss, and Public Access Along the California Coast*, 34 ECOLOGY L.Q. 533, 565 (2009).

15. CAL PUB. RES. CODE § 30235.

16. 15A N.C. ADMIN. CODE § 07M.0202.

17. *Id.*

sion control structures, and as the Riggings case study[18] illustrates, it does not appear that it will be politically possible to order the removal of these structures in the face of rising sea levels.[19] The political drivers to allow additional "temporary" hardening of the North Carolina coast are further underscored by recent legislation and conforming changes to the CAMA rules that expand the circumstances under which temporary erosion control structures may be used.

Without well-defined limitations on the rights of littoral owners, it appears that coastal permitting authorities will have difficulty in preventing coastal property owners from attempting to defend their homes. This is clear from both the sandbag conflicts in North Carolina, and the continued demands for seawalls to protect threatened structures in California. However, as the *Severance* case and GLO policies along the Texas coast demonstrate, a clear limitation on the rights of littoral owners is not sufficient in and of itself to promote retreat.

Because of its historical interpretations of the Coastal Act's armoring provisions, California may be in a more difficult legal position when it comes to telling littoral owners that they may not protect their homes, though it is attempting to justify a modified interpretation of the Coastal Act in its new *Sea Level Rise Policy Guidance*. In addition, California may actually be in a stronger position vis-a-vis owners who recorded deed restrictions limiting their right to armor as a condition of a coastal development permit than enforcement officials in many other states. In general, there is no common law right to defend one's home from the threat of erosion. However, any state attempting to adopt a policy of retreat is nearly certain to face challenges from littoral owners on the grounds that they have a right to defend their property. Considering the universe of potential landowners who might bring this claim, those in the weakest position would be property owners who have knowingly and intelligently waived their right to defend their property from erosion or expressly acknowledged that this is a right they do not have. Specifically, this category of owners would include both Texas littoral owners, who sign required notices of the GLO's right to enforce under the Open Beaches Act, and littoral owners in California with deed restrictions waiving the right to armor.

Many states, like North Carolina, will be caught somewhere in between and will likely be faced with extensive litigation to define the right of the littoral

---

18. *See supra* Chapter 6: North Carolina.

19. *See* Gareth McGrath, *Commission Refuses to Alter Sandbag Rules*, STAR NEWS ONLINE, May 22, 2008, http://www.starnewsonline.com/article/20080522/ARTICLE/805220342 (last visited Feb. 26, 2016).

owner to defend his property from erosion. Under the standard common law doctrine of erosion, discussed in more detail in Chapter 4, the right to halt natural forces and defend littoral property is a right that the property owner simply did not buy. However, as Texas clearly shows, even a knowing acknowledgement that a buyer is not purchasing the right to defend property is often insufficient to properly shape property owners' expectations and the amount that they will pay for littoral property. Littoral owners will understandably be reluctant to simply let their investments wash away, and in the case of the ignorant owner, this may well appeal to regulators' or judges' sense of fairness and implicate the equitable doctrines that underlie property law.[20]

Therefore, all coastal states will benefit by clarifying their own understandings of the rights that littoral owners may or may not have to defend their properties. Coastal states should also consider notice provisions similar to those employed in Texas. While these notice provisions have not had the intended effect of causing property purchasers to properly factor the risky nature of coastal property into their investment decisions, they do put the state on better footing in the event of a future challenge by a littoral property owner. If states require explicit acknowledgement that the owner has no right to defend his property as a matter of course, they will ultimately be spared future litigation as to whether a littoral owner has the right to defend his property and, if so, what the extent of the right is. In addition, over time as the general public becomes more aware of the erosion and inundation risks associated with sea level rise, such waiver provisions may come to have their intended effect of communicating the risk of purchasing coastal property.

Political Pressures to Defend the Coast

In the wake of Hurricane Ike, footage coming out of Galveston revealed the extent of coastal damage from the storm and that many homes came to lie upon the public beach. While this appeared to be a prime opportunity for Texas to reduce coastal vulnerability by exercising its authority under the Open

---

20. For example, one CRC member told me of a variance case in which a retired property owner from out of state had purchased her dream retirement home on the coast sight unseen. She later came before the CRC because the house was washing away and she had not been aware at the time of purchase that the house had already been sandbagged and therefore she could not take action to protect it in the future. The Commissioner noted that those types of cases just appeal to your sense of fairness, and it is difficult to deny those variance applications. Interview with Coastal Resource Commission Member (Nov. 23, 2009).

Beaches Act, then-Governor Perry pledged that Galveston would be rebuilt.[21] The response to Hurricane Ike, detailed in Chapter 7 and conducted pursuant to the GLO's disaster order rules, demonstrates that even coastal governance structures that are best positioned to reduce coastal vulnerability may be unable to do so because of political pressures. This section explores another aspect of this conclusion by reviewing the literature on disaster response and examining whether governance structure in the coastal zone matters at all in the context of intense political-economic pressures to defend the coast and rebuild damaged communities.

Underlying all coastal development in the modern era is the Safe Development Paradox.[22] According to the Safe Development Paradox, rather than asking if some areas are simply too risky to build in, governments have generally adopted the position that all areas can be made safe for profitable development. This dynamic has led to such phenomena as the extensive development of levee systems to hold back floodwaters and allowing construction in areas that should be unbuildable due to frequent flooding. The development of the levee system in the San Francisco Bay-Delta Region, which has more than 1700 kilometers of privately owned and maintained levees, is a prime example.[23] Mount and Twiss note that the extensive levee system maintains dry land in the delta in areas that are as much as eight meters below sea level as a result of island subsidence and sea level rise.[24]

In fact, Kunreuther and Pauly demonstrate the extent to which the public expects that government will make areas safe for development. They show that if members of the public are given freedom to build where they choose, they will elect to build in floodplains.[25] The decision of members of the public to place their homes in floodplains is predicated upon the assumption that if they

---

21. Governor Perry Remarks Touring Hurricane Ike Impact Zone, Sept. 18, 2008, http://www.lrl.state.tx.us/legeLeaders/governors/searchProc.cfm?docSearch=Search&beginGovDocDate=&docAuthor=44&docSession=none&endGovDocDate=&govDocCaption=&govDocType=none&textInput=.

22. Raymond J. Burby, *Hurricane Katrina and the Paradoxes of Government Disaster Policy: Bringing About Wise Governmental Decisions for Hazardous Areas*, 604 ANNALS AM. ACAD. POL. & SOC. SCIENCE 171, 172 (2006).

23. Jeffery Mount & Robert Twiss, *Subsidence, Sea Level Rise, and Seismicity in the Sacramento-San Joaquin Delta*, 3 SAN FRANCISCO ESTUARY & WATERSHED SCIENCE Article 5 (2005).

24. *Id.*

25. Howard Kunreuther & Mark Pauly, *Rules Rather Than Discretion: Lessons from Hurricane Katrina*, 33 J. RISK & UNCERTAINTY 101 (2006); *see also* John M. Gowdy, *Behavioral Economics and Climate Change Policy*, 68 J. ECON. BEHAVIOR & ORG. 632 (2008).

build in these areas, the government will then be forced to respond to the moral hazard created under a scheme of permissive development and build flood protection structures. Kunreuther and Pauly argue that because of these expectations, homeowners in floodplains will not want to move in response to threats and that it is more efficient to forbid initial development in vulnerable areas.[26] Unfortunately, we are well past this point for much of the coast.

Coupled with the history of the Safe Development Paradox, vulnerability of coastal areas is exacerbated by what Kunreuther calls Natural Disaster Syndrome.[27] Under the Natural Disaster Syndrome, individuals in hazard prone areas tend not to adopt even cost-effective hazard mitigation measures prior to natural disasters.[28] Rather, they simply wait for the government to bail them out.[29] This behavior is partially explained by the historical experience of governments intervening to protect disaster victims and also by the empirical finding that most people tend to severely underestimate their risk exposure.

Thus, coastal state governments have a number of important factors working against them: the historically based belief of property owners that they can transfer the cost of risks from development in hazard areas to the government; the belief that even if they do experience a hazard, coastal property owners can count on the government to bail them out; and the inability of property owners to fully comprehend their risk exposure.[30]

Against this backdrop, coastal states are faced with the challenge of limiting development in the coastal zone that will increase societal exposure to the risks of inundation and storms and ultimately make the implementation of rolling easements more difficult. While coastal permitting agencies are likely to have the authority to forbid the construction of seawalls, they are also likely to face intense political pressures when affected property owners come before them seeking to keep their homes from falling into the sea.

Nowhere is this dynamic more apparent than in the GLO's policies under the Open Beaches Act and their application to post-hurricane rebuilding. After the storm, the Texas General Land Office had announced that it may take over a year to decide which homeowners would be allowed to rebuild.[31] In the mean-

---

26. *Id.*

27. Howard Kunreuther, *Disaster Mitigation and Insurance: Learning from Katrina*, 604 ANNALS AM. ACAD. POL. & SOC. SCIENCE 208 (2006).

28. *Id.*

29. *Id.*

30. WHARTON RISK MANAGEMENT & DECISION PROCESSES CENTER, MANAGING LARGE-SCALE RISKS IN A NEW ERA OF CATASTROPHES (2008).

31. Interview with State Government Official (Nov. 19, 2009).

time, the Commissioner issued Beach and Dune Rules to allow for disaster recovery and limited rebuilding and repair of those same homes, which may render future condemnation infeasible, even if it remained possible after the *Severance* decision. While the General Land Office has twice revised the location of the vegetation line since Hurricane Ike, thereby affecting what homes are on the public beach,[32] it has operated in an atmosphere of intense political pressure to rebuild. This example, particularly the promulgation of GLO's disaster recovery rules, not only demonstrates that short-term political pressures will prevail in the face of disasters but also that if the government is to make changes, it needs to have disaster response plans in place prior to the event.

A further challenge will arise in the more drawn-out process of responding to sea level rise. Property owners have historically been a group that possesses and wields a large amount of political power. Therefore, over the longer term, it is possible that littoral owners will band together in an attempt to defend their property. This campaign could either take the form of pressuring coastal permitting bodies to issue variances allowing for coastal defense or attempts to change the law so as to ensure that coastal property is defended. Examples of these behaviors and the ultimate influence of political-economic factors on the coastal permitting process are readily observed in the Riggings and Capitola case studies.[33]

Neither of these solutions is desirable, and if state and local governments wish to pursue the implementation of rolling easements, they need to create permitting systems based upon legal mandates that will immunize permitting bodies against political pressures to allow for coastal defense. In this context the challenge is to design coastal governance systems that are robust to vulnerability-enhancing political pressures. This challenge is particularly daunting when one considers that permitting decisions made today may not interact with sea level rise to create harmful impacts until well after current decision makers are out of office.

---

32. The initial line was set at the line of 4.5' elevation above sea level pursuant to Texas Natural Resource Code §61. Since that time, it has been revised to be 200' from mean high water, the rule under the Open Beaches Act for areas in which the vegetation line cannot be readily determined. *Id.* §61.016.

33. *See* Chapter 6 (Riggings case study) and Chapter 5 (Capitola case study).

Opportunities for Adaptation

Coastal states face a variety of challenges in promoting adaptation to climate change. Differences in coastal states' legal structures will lead to different adaptive capacities. States that have legal structures that clearly define the rights of littoral property owners and promote comprehensive, long-range land use planning will likely have higher adaptive capacities, as they will be better able to face the challenges of sea level rise. Regardless of the legal structure that is in place, all coastal states will be challenged to implement their laws to promote actual retreat. These pressures will manifest both in the form of disaster response and longer-term discussions regarding how to respond to sea level rise.

Over time, unless states elect to construct expensive and elaborate levee and seawall systems, they will likely reach a point at which nourishment and other attempts to hold the line simply cannot keep up with the combined effects of sea level rise and erosion. Therefore, even states that currently employ policies of maintaining their shoreline location should take steps today to prepare them for the possibility of future retreat. These steps should include an assessment of coastal vulnerabilities, with a particular emphasis on critical infrastructure and disaster response capacity; clarification of the state's common law doctrines for dynamic littoral boundaries; creation of notice provisions to ensure that purchasers of coastal property are aware of the limited scope of their rights; and promotion of coordination of local government efforts either through comprehensive land use plans approved by a state regulatory body or the adoption of an overarching policy and incentives to encourage proactive planning by local governments.

The general policy of states at this time is to hold the line with soft measures, such as beach nourishment. This result is not surprising because it is a no-regrets option: nourishment provides substantial economic benefits to coastal communities and, if properly done, helps to rebuild dune protection systems. However, over time increased erosion rates driven by rising sea levels and increasing storms will result in a situation where coastal communities simply cannot maintain the current position of the shoreline through nourishment alone. As explained in earlier chapters, rolling easements or some other form of managed realignment will be necessary if communities want to promote both social and ecological resilience. However, there are numerous challenges in building the political support necessary for managed realignment.

Fortunately, sea levels are unlikely to change dramatically overnight, and therefore governments can take steps today to increase their adaptive capacity in anticipation of sea level rise. Even if state and local governments are not prepared to adopt managed retreat policies, they can begin to reduce their vulnerability to sea level rise with a number of policy and public education measures. Below, I explain some of the measures that states can take today to reduce their future vulnerability to sea level rise.

Education

One of the major determinants of a society's adaptive capacity is the ability to choose between available adaptation options. Therefore, measures that increase understanding of the impacts of sea level rise, the various adaptation options available, and the impacts of those options on vulnerability and valued resources will decrease vulnerability to sea level rise. The three major groups that need to be engaged in education efforts are the public, policy makers, and private property owners. Each of these groups has different educational needs that will increase their ability to meaningfully engage in adaptation measures.

The Public

If governments are to successfully adopt adaptation policies that include anything other than no-regrets adaptation strategies, they will have to impose costs on the general public today for future benefits that cannot yet be precisely quantified. Imposing such costs on constituents will prove a challenge if they are not engaged in the issue of climate change adaptation. Therefore, local governments face a serious challenge in garnering public support for climate change adaptation measures. Gaining public support has the potential to be a particularly difficult task if the governments' managed retreat policy is opposed by local property owners with whom the public is sympathetic.

This reveals that there are three major dimensions along which public education should proceed: 1) education on the impacts of climate change anticipated locally; 2) education regarding the public's right to access the beach; and 3) education as to the amount of tax dollars spent to protect local coastal property owners. While survey work on climate change adaptation shows strong public support for planning for the impacts of sea level rise, it is not clear how these results manifest themselves at the community level where individuals will be asked to make specific tradeoffs to respond to the threat of sea level rise.[34] Having a grasp of climate change only as a general challenge does not create the type of public engagement that is necessary to create momentum for policy making nor does it allow the public to participate in a mean-

---

34. STANFORD WOODS INSTITUTE FOR THE ENVIRONMENT, EXECUTIVE SUMMARY: SURVEY RESULTS: U.S. VIEWS ON CLIMATE ADAPTATION (2013), https://woods.stanford.edu/sites/default/files/documents/Climate_Survey_Exec_Summ_US.pdf.

ingful way in larger social decisions about the future structure of the coast. Therefore, the public must be informed of the expected impacts of sea level rise at a locally relevant scale before politically difficult adaptation measures can proceed.

Education on the impacts of sea level rise will help to engage those members of the public who live along the coast. However, it may not be sufficient to capture the attention of residents of coastal counties living further inland and is not likely to engage residents of inland counties. If these citizens are unconcerned about the future of the coast, then the state is left alone to defend the public trust while also facing pressure from the vocal minority at the coast to sacrifice public access to allow for the defense of littoral properties. To the extent that the general public is not engaged, there is a risk that public trust rights will be sacrificed because of a failure of collective action.

Therefore, governments wanting to build political support for managed retreat must be sure that the general public is aware not only of its right to access the beach but also how that right is impacted by the sea level rise and coastal development squeeze. The general public should be made aware of the impacts on future public access to the shoreline generated by coastal engineering or allowing homes to remain on the public beach. As the passage of Proposition 9 in Texas shows, in states where open access to the beaches is the norm, members of the general public tend to view the beach as a public park and expect it to remain open for their access. Therefore, governments should be able to gain public support for retreat strategies, such as rolling easements, that are designed to protect the public trust.

Finally, governments should educate the general public as to the amount of taxpayer dollars spent on coastal communities. The most significant expenditures in this category are disaster relief, including flood insurance, and expenditures on beach nourishment. It is important for all taxpayers to be aware of the extent to which their tax dollars are spent holding the line as they participate in the public process of deciding the future of the coast. While coastal communities are large contributors to the tax base, they are also the recipient of large public expenditures. Over time, as sea levels rise and more frequent beach nourishment is required, public expenditures on nourishment could rise to a level that inland residents do not wish to support. While it is in fact the case that many coastal communities are looking for local ways to support nourishment, these means alone will not be enough, and continued nourishment activities will require state or federal assistance.

Educating the public as to the expenditures on nourishment in combination with their right of access will be particularly important for governments that wish to reduce vulnerability by pursuing retreat. For members of the general public who are only concerned with beach access, nourishment may well be an acceptable adaptation option so long as the nourishment is frequent enough that it maintains an attractive beach. However, if these same members of the public are aware that they can access the beach wherever it happens to migrate and that beach nourishment to hold the line is a costly proposition, they may be more likely to support policies of retreat. Either way, the public's ability to choose among adaptation options is enhanced by having full information about their rights and the costs (economic, environmental, and social) of various adaptation options.

Policy Makers

Policy makers appear to be generally aware of the potential for sea level rise, but there are significant knowledge gaps as to the timing and scale of impacts, particularly at the local level. In order to frame policy options for adaptation, policy makers must have a concrete idea of the impacts they are dealing with and the time horizons over which they will occur. This challenge is one of education and in some places, appropriate research to scale down climate change projections. Many states are in the process of conducting this education at the state level, but it is essential that it is also passed on to local government officials. Because they control land use decision making and permitting, local government officials are best positioned to take actions today that make the physical structure of a community less vulnerable to the impacts of sea level rise. However, they are also the least equipped to do so, and without reliable, geographically relevant information as to the projected impacts of climate change, local government officials have no incentive to act to reduce vulnerability.

Another key dimension of educating policy makers is making them aware of the range of adaptation options that are available. Governments that present state and local officials with information about the significant impacts of sea level rise but no potential solutions run the risk of inducing institutional paralysis. This is particularly true at the local level: City officials shown sea level rise maps reflecting that they will be completely underwater will be rightly concerned, but they are likely to have no idea where to begin with respect to adaptation policies. Therefore, particularly at the local government level, policy makers should be presented with information regarding impacts and adaptation options at the same time.

The final dimension of policy-maker education relates to those officials who have significant responsibilities in implementing state coastal laws and protecting the public trust. The interviews I conducted with state-level officials revealed that many of them remain a bit unclear as to the state of the common law or the full extent of their agency's authority to promote adaptation under the law. This is certainly understandable, as in some cases the law is simply not well defined. However, in order to allay fears about potential takings claims or other lawsuits, policy makers should be educated as to the specific parameters of the common and statutory law governing the coast so that they are better equipped to decide what policy innovations the law may permit.

Property Owners

At least in some states, littoral property owners in general seem to understand that sea level rise is happening.[35] However, many of them either expect that they will not experience the impacts of sea level rise hazards or that the government will defend them against rising seas. One of the largest misconceptions among coastal property owners is that they have a right to defend their property against erosion, and ultimately sea level rise. As Chapter 4 explained, the common law has always defined littoral property as having three fixed borders platted on a map and a final boundary line set by the natural movement of the shoreline. Because the right that a littoral property owner has is to a piece of land with a dynamic boundary, he does not have a vested right to protect that property from erosion. However, many coastal property owners buy their property with the belief that they have the right to maintain it as it is, and this may increase property values above what they otherwise would be. Ultimately, a property owner's erroneous belief about his right to defend his property makes some adaptation measures more difficult to adopt because the state will be faced with the additional costs of litigating the rights of the littoral owner or paying compensation to an owner for a right he does not have.

The other important aspect of property owner education is to teach property owners about the coastal hazards to which they are exposed and how these will change over time. As discussed in Chapter 3, property owners tend to believe that natural hazards will not impact them and this makes them both less likely to engage in private adaptation and more reliant on government-sponsored disaster relief programs. These property owners increase societal vulnerability because they are less likely to purchase insurance, making them individually less resilient; they are more dependent on government financial

---

35. Interviews with Coastal Property Owners (Oct. 1, 2009, Oct. 2, 2009); NORTH CAROLINA DIVISION OF COASTAL MANAGEMENT, SEA LEVEL RISE SCOPING SURVEY FINAL REPORT 9 (2010) (reporting that 51% of coastal property owners in North Carolina believe that they will be affected by sea level rise).

relief, increasing the exposure of all taxpayers to hazards. Local government officials report that it is difficult to achieve community participation in flood hazard mitigation because property owners do not perceive it as a problem. Therefore, property owner education regarding the potential impacts of climate change is an essential first step in promoting measures that will mitigate future damages from inundation.

Begin a Public Discussion about Retreat

Adaptive capacity is the ability of a society to choose among various adaptation options and act in a way that will reduce their vulnerability to climate change. In addition to education about climate change, it is important that governments begin to engage in meaningful discussions about the possibility of retreat in the future. Even if governments are not in a political position to adopt current measures for retreat, they must acknowledge that any process of planned retreat will be a lengthy one. Therefore, all coastal governments would benefit from an assessment of their current coastal vulnerability to climate change and initiating a discussion about retreat.

Given the attachment that people have to places and the large amounts of capital invested in coastal infrastructure, it is unrealistic to think that any coastal retreat policy will involve a wholesale move from the coast until all other options have been exhausted. While it may ultimately be necessary to move some large population centers, in many cases decision making will likely focus on selective retreat. The first step in any hybrid adaptation strategy is to determine which places are vulnerable and which ones we as a society are unwilling to give up. This discussion implicates our social values and will require that some communities reimagine their futures on the coasts. For such a process to be meaningful, it must be given the time and attention it deserves to fully understand the implications of retreat from both ecological and sociological perspectives. Therefore, if they have not already done so, coastal states should begin conducting assessments of their own vulnerability and initiate community conversations about what their constituents value and how to preserve those values in the face of rising seas.

Clarify the Legal Landscape

As mentioned above in the discussion on education, coastal policy makers often do not have a clear grasp of the metes and bounds of the laws they are charged with implementing. This is particularly true for institutional actors that are charged with upholding the public trust and policy makers who may face takings claims.

While this authority exists on paper, coastal governments have yet to exercise it. This is certainly in part due to the political factors reviewed earlier in Chapter 3. However, interviews with coastal agency decision makers also reveal that oftentimes they are unaware of the scope of their own authority under the common law. In order to empower coastal states to make decisions about adaption, including consideration of coastal retreat, states must take steps to clarify their own legal doctrines. This clarification may take the form of education, state statutes codifying the common law, or test cases in state courts. The two points of law on which clarification is most needed are the state's observance of the doctrine of avulsion and the rights that the littoral property owner may have to block coastal retreat.

Doctrine of Avulsion

As explained in Chapter 4, the doctrine of avulsion is a common law doctrine under which sudden changes in the mean high water line do not result in a change in title. From a coastal dynamics perspective, it simply does not make sense to differentiate between erosion (a gradual, imperceptible change in the property boundary) and avulsion (sudden erosion, usually in a storm event). Even the Supreme Court struggled to determine where to draw the line between a change that is sudden enough to be avulsive and a change that is merely erosion.[36]

While geologic timing does not make a difference in the configuration of the coast, from a property rights perspective it is everything. If there is a sudden loss of property through an avulsive event, then the property owner may have the right to restore his beach. For a government that wants to adopt a policy of retreat, the existence of the doctrine of avulsion is problematic, as it negates the effect of sudden erosive events for the purposes of retreat.

The Supreme Court has recognized the doctrine of avulsion as part of the common law of the coasts inherited from England.[37] While numerous general sources on water law and Supreme Court jurisprudence indicate that the doctrine of avulsion is observed by all states that follow the common law,[38] this is not necessarily the case because many state courts have not yet had the op-

---

36. *See* Trans. of Oral Argument, Stop the Beach Renourishment v. Florida, No. 08-1151(S. Ct. Dec. 2, 2009).

37. *See* Arkansas v. Tennessee, 246 U.S. 158 (1918).

38. *See, e.g.,* THOMPSON ON REAL PROPERTY §90.03.

portunity to consider the doctrine of avulsion. There is no such thing as federal common law with respect to state law issues, including dynamic shoreline boundaries.[39] Therefore, recognition by the Supreme Court that the doctrine of avulsion is in the common law of one state does not mean that it applies to all states. What's more, there are surprisingly few cases that even discussed the doctrine of avulsion. Therefore, it is possible that many coastal states have never explicitly recognized the doctrine.

Coastal states that do not have direct common law precedents defining the existence of the doctrine of avulsion would benefit from clarifying the doctrine's status in their states. For states where most erosive loss is in avulsive events, the ability of the state to pursue retreat through rolling easements is almost completely eliminated by the doctrine of avulsion. Therefore, states that wish to preserve meaningful public access to dry sand beach must understand whether, because of the doctrine of avulsion, the only means of doing so is through extensive beach nourishment. Further, to the extent that the doctrine of avulsion is not codified in the common law of a particular state, the state will benefit from the passage of a statutory provision declaring that the state does not recognize the doctrine of avulsion.

Property Owner Rights

The case studies in the preceding Chapters reveal that neither property owners nor many state policy makers understand the extent of a littoral owner's rights, particularly with respect to coastal defense. As explained earlier, under the common law a littoral owner usually does not own the right to defend his property, but many believe they do. What is more limiting from an adaptation perspective is that it appears many state policy makers share the belief that a property owner may have some right to defend his littoral property against rising seas. Believing that a property owner has the right to defend his property, coastal policy makers may refuse to act out of fear that they may face subsequent takings claims.

The extent to which the fear of takings claims influences decision making in the coastal zone is unclear. Coastal policy makers often raise takings as a concern, but some observers feel that this is more of an excuse for inaction than a genuine concern. Regardless of whether they are actually concerned about facing lawsuits, it is clear that coastal policy makers are reluctant to step on the toes of littoral owners. Therefore, to the extent that the rights of lit-

---

39. Erie R.R. Co. v. Tompkins, 304 U.S. 64 (1938).

toral owners are unclear, coastal permitting authorities are likely to err on the side of issuing permits.

So long as coastal policy makers are haunted by the lingering belief that coastal property owners have a right to defend their homes, this will be the backstop to all decision making and will severely constrain the range of adaptation options that policy makers are willing to consider. Therefore, it is important that states clarify the extent of the rights of the littoral owner to defend his or her property. In the absence of a statutory right, the doctrine of erosion and the public trust should control. States must therefore help policy makers to feel comfortable articulating the idea that there is no taking in the denial of the right to defend littoral property because it is not a right the littoral owner had when he first took title. It is likely that in some states, the articulation of the full contours of littoral rights to defend will require additional litigation, as has already been the case in Texas and Washington.[40]

Adopt Policies that Promote Long-Range Planning

Finally, states should adopt policies that promote long-range planning.[41] Conducting planning on time horizons that are sufficient to include at least some of the impacts of sea level rise will help states to ensure that future development is resilient to its impacts. For example, states could require that all new infrastructure projects examine the potential for sea level rise impacts over the projected lifetime of the infrastructure and that they be designed to withstand those impacts. Such a policy would be consistent with the recommendations of the Council on Environmental Quality's Climate Change Guidance for implementing the National Environmental Policy Act, which is discussed in more detail in Chapter 9.

States can also take measures to facilitate long-range planning by local governments and private individuals. Local government's planning capacity is often constrained by the availability of personnel and funding, and state grants can be an essential element driving plans to completion. Therefore,

---

40. *See* Severance v. Patterson, 370 S.W.3d 705 (Tex. 2012); United States v. Milner, 583 F.3d 1174 (9th Cir. 2009).

41. *See* NATIONAL RESEARCH COUNCIL, INFORMING DECISIONS IN A CHANGING CLIMATE 16 (2009) (encouraging the adoption of longer time horizons for decision making and finding "[t]he need for a longer perspective is especially acute for decisions that are hard to readjust in the future, such as those about development policy [and] long-lived infrastructure....").

states should offer grant money for long-term planning or condition the receipt of state grant funds for projects in vulnerable areas on the showing that the project can withstand projected impacts. Finally, states can encourage long-range planning at all levels by amending state environmental policy acts to require that all environmental analyses include an evaluation of the long-term exposure of the project to climate change impacts and a plan to adapt to those impacts.

In sum, there are a number of important measures that states can take today to facilitate adaptation to sea level rise in the future. The impacts of sea level rise are real and felt today, and they will only increase in the future. However, political constraints are likely to keep most states from adopting broad-based policies of retreat. This does not mean that states should sit idly by and wait for the impacts of climate change to be experienced. Rather, states should engage in the measures outlined above to enhance their adaptive capacity so that when the political tides turn they are well positioned to take definitive action.

All discussions of retreat must be conducted with an awareness that for political, economic, and social reasons there are some places we simply will not abandon. Therefore, the aim of any plan to adapt to sea level rise should be to identify the key vulnerabilities in the system and figure out how to reduce them. In some cases, society will certainly tolerate higher risk exposure than would otherwise be optimal because of attachment to place or inability to move other valuable assets. Because of the need to balance social values, it should not be the goal of adaptation policy to reduce hazard exposure to near-zero. Rather, policies of adaptation to sea level rise should seek to articulate what it is that society as a whole values and how to best protect it. Where this process concludes that the value of natural assets, such as the beach and estuaries, outweigh pre-existing capital investments, retreat will be appropriate. However, retreat is only one piece of the large puzzle of reconfiguring our relationship with the coast to accommodate rising seas. Because the redefinition of this relationship will be a long and complex process, governments should act now to begin taking actions that will increase their future adaptive capacity.

Chapter 9

Challenges for Corporations in Adapting to Sea Level Rise

All businesses function within the nation's legal and regulatory framework, comprised of the rule of common law established through cases, legislatively enacted statutory mandates, constraints as interpreted through administrative rulemaking and agency guidance, and private contracts enforceable through the courts. This chapter evaluates several of the discrete legal issues that will confront businesses as they contend with the physical impacts of sea level rise and suggests that over time the impacts of increased storm surge areas and gradual inundation due to sea level rise will force private corporations—particularly those with coastal-dependent activities—to fundamentally rethink how they manage their operations in order to ensure business continuity and manage future environmental liabilities.

Common Law Climate Change Claims

The first area in which private corporations faced legal exposure for climate change was through the pursuit of common law climate change claims. While the Supreme Court's holding in *American Electric Power Co.* ("*AEP*") *v. Connecticut* now forecloses these claims at the federal level,[1] a brief overview is provided here because many of the early climate change tort claims were based on the types of coastal hazards on which this book is focused. For example, *Native Village of Kivalina* focused on claims that climate change was increasing coastal erosion rates that in turn lead to a need to relocate the village, and

---

1. 564 U.S. 410 (2011).

Comer v. Murphy Oil alleged that defendants greenhouse gas ("GHG") emissions were an important contributor to the strength of Hurricane Katrina.[2] Understanding these cases is also important because they provide needed context for the discussion of insurance litigation at the end of this chapter and because similar common law claims in state courts may not be foreclosed.

Filed in 2004, *Connecticut v. American Electric Power* was the first of the major common law climate change claims.[3] In this case, eight states and three land trusts alleged that the American Electric Power Service Corporation and four other power companies contributed to the public nuisance of global warming through their emission of greenhouse gases as a result of power generation activities.[4] The plaintiffs asked the court to determine that the power company defendants were jointly and severally liable for their contributions to global climate change and requested that the court impose a cap on the power companies' GHG emissions.[5] Before reaching the merits of the plaintiffs' claims, the Southern District of New York determined that it must decide whether the case posed a nonjusticiable political question, meaning that the court had to first decide whether the case was asking the court to make policy when neither Congress nor the executive branch had spoken. The court determined that at the time, in 2005, there was no national policy on climate change in the U.S. and that the political question doctrine precluded it from deciding the case.[6] Plaintiffs then appealed to the Second Circuit, which reversed the decision of the Southern District of New York.[7] In 2009, the Second Circuit concluded that resolution of the plaintiffs' claims did not require a court to make a broad political decision regarding climate change policy and determined that the plaintiffs' nuisance claim could be heard in court.[8]

The case was then appealed to the United States Supreme Court under the name *American Electric Power v. Connecticut*.[9] The Supreme Court heard and decided the case in 2011. Between 2009 and 2011, EPA had taken initial actions to regulate GHG emissions by issuing the Endangerment Finding—a finding under the Clean Air Act that greenhouse gases are harmful to public

---

2. Native Village of Kivalina v. ExxonMobil Corp., 696 F.3d 849 (9th Cir. 2012); Comer v. Murphy Oil, 585 F.3d 855 (5th Cir. 2009).

3. 406 F. Supp. 2d 265 (S.D.N.Y. 2005).

4. *Id.* at 267.

5. *Id.* at 270.

6. *Id.* at 274.

7. 582 F.3d 309 (2d Cir. 2009).

8. *Id.*

9. 564 U.S. 410 (2011).

health and welfare—and taking initial steps to regulate greenhouse gases from both motor vehicles and large stationary sources.[10] Because of EPA's intervening actions to regulate GHG emissions, the Supreme Court held "the Clean Air Act and EPA actions it authorizes displace any federal common law right to seek abatement of carbon-dioxide emissions from fossil-fuel fired power plants."[11] The Supreme Court's decision thus forecloses common law nuisance claims for climate change harms under federal law—including future claims such as those in the other cases discussed in this Part—but leaves open the possibility that climate change plaintiffs could pursue tort claims under state law in state courts.[12]

In *Native Village of Kivalina v. ExxonMobil* an Inupiat Eskimo village on the Alaska coast alleged that climate change was resulting in the later formation of sea ice adjacent to their village and early melting of the ice in the spring.[13] According to the plaintiffs, the shortening of the ice season resulted in increased rates of coastal erosion that would ultimately necessitate the relocation of the entire village.[14] The plaintiffs sought damages from several oil, energy, and power companies, alleging that they contributed to the public and private nuisances of global warming. Specifically, the plaintiffs sought to have defendants pay for the relocation of the entire village to be safe from increased erosion, which they estimated would cost between $95 million and $400 million.[15] Like the Southern District of New York in *Connecticut v. AEP*, the Northern District of California found that the *Kivalina* plaintiffs' federal public nuisance claim required it to resolve a political question and therefore could not be adjudicated.[16] The court also raised concerns about whether plaintiffs had standing to bring their claims because it concluded that plaintiffs could not establish that defendants' GHG emissions caused the reduction in sea ice that led to their injuries.[17]

Kivalina was appealed to the Ninth Circuit, which did not issue a final decision in the case until 2012, which was after the Supreme Court issued its decision in *AEP v. Connecticut*.[18] The Ninth Circuit concluded that under the Supreme Court's precedent in *AEP v. Connecticut*, federal common law claims

---

10. 74 Fed. Reg. 66,496 (Dec. 15, 2009) (Endangerment Finding); 75 Fed. Reg. 25,324 (May 7, 2010) (regulating GHG emissions from cars); 75 Fed. Reg. 31,520 (June 3, 2010) (phasing in regulations of GHGs from major stationary sources).
11. 564 U.S. 410 (2011).
12. *Id.* at 429.
13. 663 F. Supp. 2d 863, 868, 869 (N.D. Cal. 2009).
14. *Id.*
15. *Id.* at 869.
16. *Id.* at 876–77.
17. *Id.* at 883.
18. 696 F.3d 849 (9th Cir. 2012).

What Are Tort Claims?

Torts are a type of civil (as opposed to criminal) liability that is recognized in the U.S. legal system. Generally, successful tort claimants must show that the defendant owed them a duty, that the duty was breached, and that this breach of duty (the tortious conduct) caused their injury. Torts are civil wrongs that the common law recognizes can be remedied by awarding the injured party damages—typically in the form of financial compensation or by ordering the tortfeasor to undertake a specific action to remediate the injury suffered by the harmed party. In the context of climate change claims, the following are important types of potential tort claims:

Public nuisance is an "unreasonable interference with a right common to the general public," Restatement (Second) of Torts §821B, and can include any activity that interferes with public health, safety, convenience, or comfort that is not otherwise permitted by law.

Private nuisance is an invasion in a private person's use and enjoyment of his land that does not constitute a trespass. Restatement (Second) of Torts §821D. Claims for private nuisance are distinguished from those for public nuisance in that the land owner claiming nuisance must demonstrate that he suffered a specific harm that is distinct from that suffered by the general public.

Trespass is the unauthorized entry onto the land of another. A party can be liable for trespass if he enters another person's land without permission or causes an invasion of the land. An example of the latter category of trespass would occur when one person causes the flooding of the land of another. In this instance, the trespass results from the unauthorized entry of water onto the property.

Negligence is a cause of action that arises when one person owes a duty of care to another, he unintentionally fails to live up to that duty, and the other party is injured as a result. Restatement (Second) of Torts §281. Negligence claims can arise from a variety of actions including failure to exercise reasonable care, failure to warn of a danger, lack of competence, or misrepresentation of information. *Id.* §§298–304.

What Is Standing?

Article III of the Constitution limits the jurisdiction of the courts such that a court may only hear an actual case or controversy. Over time, judicial opinions have elaborated on the requirements a plaintiff must meet to qualify to have its claims heard in court. To establish constitutional standing, a plaintiff must show the following:

1. The plaintiff has suffered an "injury in fact," meaning that the injury is actual and not merely future or speculative;

2. The injury is "fairly traceable" to the defendant's action, meaning that the plaintiff can demonstrate that the defendant's actions are a cause of the injury; and

3. The injury is likely to be addressed by a favorable decision, meaning that there is some remedy a court can order that will redress the injury plaintiff claims.

---

were precluded for harms from greenhouse gases that are subject to regulation under the Clean Air Act.[19]

In *Comer v. Murphy Oil Company*, landowners along the Mississippi Gulf Coast brought claims against a group of energy companies alleging that their contributions to GHG emissions caused climate change that worsened the impacts of Hurricane Katrina and the resultant damage to plaintiffs' properties.[20] Specifically, plaintiffs claimed that defendants' GHG emissions contributed to global sea level rise, which increased the extent of flood damage during the storm.[21] The plaintiffs also claimed that the resultant storm surge "caused saltwater, debris, sediment, hazardous substances, and other materials to enter, remain on, and damage plaintiffs' property," constituting a trespass.[22] In its initial decision, a panel of the Fifth Circuit overturned the Southern District of Mississippi and found that the plaintiffs' claims for public and private nuisance, trespass, and negligence could be heard in court.[23] However, the whole

---

19. *Id.* at 857–58.
20. 585 F.3d 855 (5th Cir. 2009).
21. *Id.* at 861.
22. *Id.*
23. *Id.* at 879.

Fifth Circuit later decided to hear the case in what is called an *en banc* proceeding (where all of the judges instead of a panel of just three hear the case), and through a complicated series of procedural rulings later determined they could not actually hear the case.[24] This decision had the effect of overturning the initial Fifth Circuit decision that plaintiffs' claims could be heard in court, and such claims are now effectively precluded by the Supreme Court's later decision in *AEP v. Connecticut.*

Overall, EPA's continued regulation of greenhouse gases under the federal Clean Air Act will effectively preclude future climate change tort claims in federal court in instances where plaintiffs would seek damages for harms caused by greenhouse gas emissions that contribute to global climate change. However, it is not necessarily the case that all climate change tort claims are effectively foreclosed. In theory, plaintiffs could continue to seek tort relief through claims filed in state courts. While there appears to be little activity along these lines to date, the potential for future state tort liability is something that private corporations may need to carefully evaluate in the future. Like the federal claims outlined above, plaintiffs in state tort claims would face an uphill battle in proving a causal connection between GHG emissions and the harms that they allege that is sufficient to establish tort liability.[25] While this may be a significant barrier to ultimate findings of liability, it does not necessarily relieve potential defendants from the need to defend themselves against state tort claims in court.

CERCLA Liability

The Comprehensive Environmental Response, Cleanup, and Liability Act ("CERCLA") was passed by Congress in 1980 to address the problem of legacy hazardous waste sites in the United States. CERCLA applies to sites that are no longer in operation where hazardous wastes have come to be located, and applies retroactive joint and several liability to entities that bear responsibility for the wastes located at the CERCLA site (the "potentially responsible parties" or "PRPs"). CERCLA defines hazardous substances by reference to the other major environmental statutes, but explicitly excludes petroleum and crude

---

24. 607 F.3d 1049 (5th Cir. 2010).

25. *See* Kevin A. Gaynor, Benjamin S. Lippard, & Margaret E. Peloso, *Challenges Plaintiffs Face in Litigating Federal Common Law Climate Change Claims*, 40 Envtl. L. Rep. News & Analysis 10845 (2010).

CERCLA's Key Terms

CERCLA uses a number of key terms that help to define who is liable for releases of hazardous substances into the environment. Some of the key definitions from the statute include:

Disposal: "means the discharge, deposit, injection, dumping, spilling, leaking, or placing of any solid waste or hazardous waste into or on any land or water so that such solid waste or hazardous waste or any constituent thereof may enter the environment or be emitted into the air or discharged into any waters, including ground waters." 42 U.S.C. §§ 6903(3); 9601(29).

Facility: "(A) any building, structure, installation, equipment, pipe or pipeline…, well, pit, pond, lagoon, impoundment, ditch, landfill, storage container, motor vehicle, rolling stock, or aircraft, or (B) any site or area where a hazardous substance has been deposited, stored, disposed of, or placed, or otherwise come to be located…." 42 U.S.C. § 9601(9).

Release: "means any spilling, leaking, pumping, pouring, emitting, emptying, discharging, injecting, escaping, leaching, dumping, or disposing into the environment…." *Id.* § 9601(22).

---

oil.[26] The EPA Administrator also has the authority to designate substances as hazardous by regulation.[27] CERCLA recognizes four classes of potentially responsible parties:

1. Current owners of the CERCLA site or entities that owned the site at the time of hazardous waste disposal;
2. Current operators of the CERCLA site or entities who operated the site at the time of hazardous waste disposal;
3. Entities who arranged for the disposal of hazardous waste at a CERCLA site; and
4. Entities who transported waste to a CERCLA site selected by the transporter.[28]

---

26. 42 U.S.C. § 9601(14).
27. *Id.* § 9602.
28. *Id.* § 9607(a).

CERCLA's statutory scheme provides for two kinds of actions: removal actions and remedial actions.[29] Removal actions are actions to be undertaken before a final cleanup decision is made for a site to mitigate a release or threatened release of a hazardous substance.[30] Removal activities are any activities to remove hazardous substances from the environment to mitigate a release or threatened release of hazardous substances, and can include both actual removal of environmental media (e.g., soils or sediments) as well as measures to limit public access or exposure, such as the installation of fencing.[31] In contrast, remedial actions are designed to be taken instead of or in addition to removal actions, and are defined to be actions consistent with a permanent remedy, including cleanup of hazardous substances, dredging or excavations, onsite treatment or incineration, provision of alternative water supplies, and "any monitoring reasonably required to assure that such actions protect the public health and welfare and the environment."[32] For both removal and remedial actions, CERCLA grants EPA the authority to either undertake actions on its own or order the potentially responsible parties to undertake a removal or remedial action.[33] Typically, EPA will use its authority to enter into an administrative order on consent ("AOC") with potentially responsible parties as a way to facilitate private-party investigations or a consent decree to facilitate private-party cleanups of CERCLA sites.[34] However, if a PRP is unwilling to negotiate with EPA or later decides not to comply with the terms of an AOC or consent decree, EPA also has the authority to issue a unilateral administrative order requiring a party to conduct or participate in a cleanup.[35]

The implementation of CERCLA is governed by the National Contingency Plan ("NCP").[36] The NCP establishes several criteria that EPA is to evaluate when selecting a remedy and issuing a record of decision ("ROD") to implement that remedy. Among the criteria that EPA must consider in the selec-

---

29. *Id.* § 9604.

30. *Id.* § 9604 (a)(2).

31. *Id.* § 9601(23).

32. *Id.* § 9601(24).

33. *Id.* § 9604(a)(1).

34. EPA has issued both a model administrative order on consent for the RI/FS process and a model consent decree for the RD/RA process. *See* http://www.epa.gov/sites/production/files/2013-10/documents/rev-aoc-rifs-mod-04-mem.pdf.

35. 42 U.S.C. § 9606(a). For EPA's sample UAO language *see* http://www.epa.gov/enforcement/guidance-2015-cercla-rdra-uao-and-sow (last visited Feb. 27, 2016).

36. 40 C.F.R. § 300.400 et seq.

How Does a Superfund Site Get Cleaned Up?

The first step in the cleanup of a Superfund site is the Remedial Investigation/Feasibility Study ("RI/FS"). The Remedial Investigation is a process in which data is collected to characterize the site and types of waste present, evaluate potential risks to human health and the environment, and evaluate potential treatment technologies. The Feasibility Study is prepared using the data from the Remedial Investigation, and is used to evaluate various options for site cleanup. After completion of the RI/FS, EPA will issue a Record of Decision ("ROD") adopting a particular remedial strategy outlined in the Feasibility Study as the preferred remedy for the Superfund Site.

After the ROD issues, the next phase in the cleanup process is preparation of the Remedial Design ("RD"), which sets forth the technical specifications to execute the cleanup alternative selected in the ROD. This is followed by the Remedial Action ("RA") during which actual construction and implementation of the remedy for the site occurs.

---

tion of a final remedy is the long-term effectiveness and permanence of the remedy.[37]

When thinking about adaptation to rising sea levels and increased storminess, CERCLA raises two major questions. First, how will climate change affect CERCLA sites that have already been subject to remediation? With respect to this question EPA has two possible legal tools to revisit already remediated sites: the ability to reopen consent decrees under CERCLA and the five-year review process. Second, how will climate change and adaptation responses to sea level rise shape future remedial activities under CERCLA? It is important to note that while there are many examples of CERCLA sites along low-lying coastal and estuarine areas, there is not a comprehensive listing of the number of closed and active CERCLA sites that are vulnerable to rising sea levels and increased storm surges at this time. As a result, it is difficult to articulate the extent of the threat posed by sea level rise at CERCLA sites. However, given that site remediation costs can rise into the billions of dollars for individual

---

37. *Id.* §300.430(f)(i)(B).

sediment sites, it is likely that many corporations with legacy environmental liabilities could face significant potential exposures as the result of climate change impacts at CERCLA sites.

CERCLA Tools to Reopen Remedies to Account for the Impacts of Sea Level Rise

EPA has two important tools under CERCLA that may enable it to modify remedies to account for sea level rise: the five-year review process for RODs and reopener provisions in consent decrees. As discussed below, each of these tools gives EPA the authority to require additional action at a closed CERCLA site if warranted by significant changes. In some circumstances, sea level rise and the threat of increased storm surges may qualify as the types of changes that can serve as the basis for EPA to require additional remedial action. However, given the limited development of the law in this area, it is not yet clear exactly what EPA must show to reopen a CERCLA remedy due to projected changes in sea level or increased storm surges. While these are certainly risks that companies with assets in the coastal zone may wish to carefully consider, it is not clear at this time that EPA possesses data at a fine enough spatial and temporal scale to successfully use the five-year review process or reopener provisions to require additional cleanup of CERCLA sites. However, as the impacts of sea level rise and increased storm surges are actually experienced in the future, climate change considerations are likely to become more relevant to assessing the ongoing adequacy of CERCLA remedies.

The Five-Year Review Process

Any time EPA selects a remedial action that will leave hazardous substances onsite, CERCLA requires that EPA review the remedial action at least once every five years.[38] The five-year review must ensure that the remedial action remains protective of public health and the environment.[39] If EPA determines in a five-year review that additional remedial action is needed, EPA is authorized to either take additional action itself or require the PRPs to take additional remedial actions.[40] EPA's regulations in the National Contingency Plan ("NCP") clarify this requirement stating:

---

38. 42 U.S.C. § 9621(c).
39. *Id.*
40. *Id.*

If a remedial action is selected that results in hazardous substances, pollutants, or contaminants remaining at the site above levels that allow for unlimited use and unrestricted exposure, the lead agency shall review such action no less often than every five years after initiation of the selected remedial action.[41]

EPA's 2001 Comprehensive Five-Year Review Guidance gives examples of the types of remedies for which five-year reviews are required, and these include waste stabilization, institutional controls, and sediment capping.[42] The Guidance directs that five-year reviews should continue until hazardous substances are no longer present at levels that require restricted access or use.[43] The end point of the five-year review process is a protectiveness determination where EPA must determine whether the remedy remains protective of human health and the environment.[44] According to the Guidance the three key questions that must be addressed in the protectiveness determination are: (1) is the remedy functioning as the decision documents intended; (2) are the exposure assumptions used at the time of the ROD still valid; and (3) has any other information come to light that would call into question the protectiveness of the remedy?[45] The Guidance gives specific examples of information that may call into question the protectiveness of the remedy, which include that the area has been or could be subject to a 100-year flood.[46]

If the five-year review determines that the remedy is no longer protective at the site, it is to include recommendations for follow-up action.[47] In the event that follow-up response actions are needed, they should be recommended in the five-year report. EPA can then use its authority under sections 104 and 106 of CERCLA to undertake additional remedial action or require the PRPs to do so. It is important to note that the five-year review process can be applied to closed CERCLA sites that have received no further action letters. EPA's guidance on five-year reviews states "Regions should conduct a five-year review for a remedy where a no action or no further action ROD leaves hazardous substances, pollutants, or contaminants on sites above levels that allow for unlimited use and unrestricted exposure."[48]

---

41. 40 C.F.R. §300.430(f)(4)(ii).
42. OSWER No. 9355.7-03B-P at 1–3.
43. *Id.* at 1–4.
44. *Id.* at 4–1.
45. *Id.*
46. *Id.* at 4–2.
47. *Id.* at 4–10.
48. *Id.* at 1–8.

CAD CELL

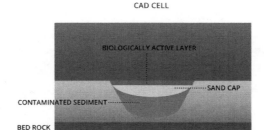

CONFINED DISPOSAL

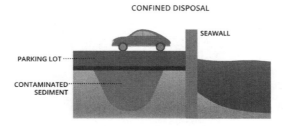

GROUNDWATER PUMP AND TREAT

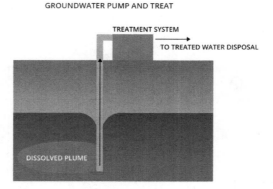

Figure 52: CERCLA Remedies That May Be Subject to Five-Year Reviews

Sea level rise may interact with the five-year review provisions of CERCLA in two important ways. First, rising sea levels will increase the intensity of storm surges when they occur, which will increase the spatial extent and intensity of flooding. Thus, it is possible that sea level rise will cause flooding at a site that was previously thought to lie outside of the floodplain. Second, sea level rise will result in the inundation of low-lying coastal areas, turning these areas from dry lands into submerged lands that are part of the adjacent coastal system. In coastal areas where Superfund sites have adopted remedies that include capping, institutional controls, or other methods to isolate contaminants, these remedies may not be designed to withstand flood impacts, much less permanent inundation. As a result, a five-year review that incorporates consideration of the effects of sea level rise may find that additional remedial actions are required to ensure that the remedy remains protective in the face of more frequent flooding or ultimate inundation of a site.

For example, after Hurricanes Katrina and Rita in 2005, EPA conducted sampling at Superfund sites located along the Texas Gulf coast and in Louisiana to assess the impacts that the storms may have had on completed remedies at those sites.[49] In addition EPA conducted assessments of 55 Superfund sites across four states.[50] EPA's post-storm site assessment activities included sampling both at sites where remedial action was ongoing and sites where cleanups were complete.[51] In addition, after Superstorm Sandy, local residents became concerned that Superfund sites such as Newtown Creek and the Gowanus Canal were impacted by the storm causing stormwater to contribute contaminated sediments from the sites.[52] EPA's response noted that it had "secured contaminated sites in the federal Superfund program" in advance of the storm to prevent damage.[53] While EPA noted it did not believe that any sites were impacted in a way that would threaten public health, it conducted additional sampling at several Superfund sites, including the Gowanus Canal, Newtown Creek, and Raritan Bay.[54] In this instance, the Occupational Safety and Health Administration announced that testing did identify higher levels of potential toxins in the areas impacted by Sandy, but that the amounts were not above established

---

49. *Response to 2005 Hurricanes, Superfund National Priority List* Sites, UNITED STATES ENVIRONMENTAL PROTECTION AGENCY, http://www.epa.gov/katrina/testresults/index.html#Superfund (last visited Feb. 27, 2016).

50. *See Response to 2005 Hurricanes, Summary of Assessments at Superfund National Priority List Sites,* UNITED STATES ENVIRONMENTAL PROTECTION AGENCY, http://www.epa.gov/katrina/superfund.html (last visited Feb. 27, 2016).

51. *Id.*

52. Emma Bryce, *Getting the Dirt on Hurricane Sandy,* N.Y. Times, Dec. 26, 2012, http://green.blogs.nytimes.com/2012/12/26/getting-the-dirt-on-sandy/ (last visited Feb. 26, 2016).

53. *EPA Home: Hurricane Sandy Response: Historical Information About the Response,* UNITED STATES ENVIRONMENTAL PROTECTION AGENCY, http://archive.epa.gov/region02/sandy/web/html/history.html.

54. *Id.*

exposure limits.[55] While no additional remedial action was found to be necessary in this immediate post-storm review, consideration of the potential for future major storm events in the five-year review process could lead to the conclusion that additional remedial actions are necessary.

If EPA were to use the five-year review process to require additional cleanup actions at a site, it would first need to reach the conclusion that the existing remedy at the site was no longer protective of public health and the environment. While EPA can use its five-year reviews to recommend additional cleanup activities at a CERCLA site, these activities are generally focused on the continued progress to meet remedial goals that have yet to be met for a site.[56] While the Five-Year Review Guidance clearly leaves open the possibility that flooding of areas previously thought to be outside the 100-year floodplain could be the basis for a recommendation for additional remedial action, there does not yet appear to be a CERCLA site where a flooding event during the five-year review period served as the basis for EPA to recommend additional remedial actions. To do so may in fact be quite complicated. By using the 100-year floodplain as the relevant metric in CERCLA processes, EPA has implicitly accepted that CERCLA remedies may have a 1% chance of failure in any given year.[57] As such, a determination that the remedy is no longer sufficiently protective of human health and the environment would likely require a showing that sea level rise and increased storminess result in an annual probability of flooding that is significantly greater than 1% and that this flooding materially impacts the effectiveness of the implemented remedy. While such a showing may ultimately become straightforward in areas that are subject to regular inundation at high tide (or ultimately permanent inundation due to rising sea levels), it is not currently clear that EPA possesses or the five-year review process could generate data of sufficient precision to demonstrate a materially increased flood risk that renders a remedy in the coastal zone insufficiently protective of human health and the environment. Thus, while sea level rise and increased storm surges are likely to be an important consideration over the medium to

---

55. Jeremy P. Jacobs, *Superstorm Sandy: Federal Tests Find Higher Toxin Levels at Cleanup Sites, But Within Limits*, Greenwire (Jan. 10, 2013), http://www.eenews.net/greenwire/2013/01/10/stories/1059974600.

56. *See, e.g.*, United States Environmental Protection Agency Region V, Five-Year Review Report for Sheboygan Harbor and River Superfund Site (2014) (explaining the need for continued monitoring and institutional controls because PCB tissue concentrations in fish were still higher than the remedial goals despite implementation of the remedy), http://www.epa.gov/region5/cleanup/sheboygan/pdfs/sheboygan-fyr-2014.pdf.

57. *See* Katrina Kuh, *Climate Change and CERCLA Remedies: Adaptation Strategies for Contaminated Sediment Sites*, 2 Seattle J. Envtl. L. 61, 79 (2012).

long term, it is not clear yet that those conditions provide a tool for EPA to order additional remedial activities under the five-year review process. However, if a significant storm event that is shown to compromise the physical integrity of a remedy such that there may be a release or threat of release of hazardous substances to the environment, the five-year review process could likely be used to require additional remedial action.

Consent Decree Reopeners

Section 122 of CERCLA encourages EPA to enter into consent decrees with PRPs to conduct CERCLA cleanups.[58] By statute, EPA is permitted to provide settling PRPs with a release from future liability and a covenant not to sue.[59] Generally, these provisions act as a release from liability once EPA determines that no further remedial action is required at a site. However, CERCLA requires that any covenant not to sue contain a provision that allows EPA to sue a settling PRP when there is a release or threatened release of hazardous substances that "arises out of conditions which are unknown at the time the President certifies ... that remedial action has been completed at the facility concerned."[60]

The case law on the reopening of consent decrees is extraordinarily limited and focuses on whether courts can approve consent decrees that do not contain reopener provisions.[61] In addition, there do not appear to be examples of CERCLA consent decrees that have been reopened due to changes in environmental conditions that were not foreseen at the time of the consent decree's entry. Therefore, it is difficult to assess how a reviewing court may approach an attempt by EPA to reopen a CERCLA cleanup after a consent decree is issued to require additional remedial actions due to changes that result from sea level rise and storm surge events. Were EPA to seek reopening of a consent decree it would have to make two key showings: (1) that the impacts of sea level rise or storm surge on the site could result in a release or threatened release of hazardous substances and (2) that the threat arises from conditions that were unknown at the time the consent decree was entered.

With respect to the first element, EPA would need to demonstrate that sea level rise or storm surges would lead to the failure or risk of failure of a CERCLA remedy. In defending against such a claim, the CERCLA PRPs could pres-

---

58. 42 U.S.C. §9622(a) ("the President shall act to facilitate agreements under this section that are in the public interest....").

59. *Id.* §9622(f).

60. *Id.* §9622(f)(6)(A).

61. United States v. BASF-Inmont Corp., 819 F. Supp. 601, 611 (E.D. Mich. 1993); In re Acushnet River, 712 F. Supp. 1019, 1036 (D. Mass. 1989).

ent evidence of any risk of failure that was implicitly accepted in the original remedy approved by EPA under the consent decree (e.g., allowing onsite capping and containment in the 100-year floodplain implicitly accepts a 1% chance that the site will flood each year), and EPA would be required to show that the risk of failure from sea level rise or increased storm surge events is materially greater than it was at the time of remedy approval. Because there is no case law on the topic, it is difficult to assess the standard that a reviewing court would apply to determine whether there is a materially greater risk of a release or threatened release than there was at the time of approval of the remedy. However, it seems likely that a reviewing court would, at minimum, require EPA to make a showing of how much more often it expects a site to be subject to flooding due to sea level rise and increased storm events, how this recurrence of flooding relates to any engineering assumptions made in the remedy design and selection process, and the likelihood that increased flooding risk would cause the remedy to fail resulting in a release or threatened release of hazardous substances.

Even if EPA could make all of these showings, it still could not reopen a consent decree based on sea level rise impacts unless it could prove that sea level rise was a condition that was unknown at the time that the consent decree was entered. While the science explaining the causes and likely amounts of sea level rise has improved substantially in recent years,[62] the threat of at least two feet of sea level rise by 2100 has been well documented at least since the IPCC issued its First Assessment Report in 1990.[63] Thus, the ability to reopen CERCLA consent decrees due to the unforeseeability of sea level rise at the time of consent decree entry likely depends on when the consent decree was entered. For those consent decrees entered before 1990, EPA may be able to make a showing that the science of sea level rise was not yet sufficiently established for it to be a known potentially adverse condition when the consent decree was entered. If EPA can make the showing for earlier-entered CERCLA consent decrees that the impacts of global climate change on sea level rise and storm surge events were not yet known, EPA may have arguments that these consent decrees could be reopened to require additional remedial action to account for sea level rise. More challenging are those consent decrees entered in the 1990s and more recently—when the risks of sea level rise were understood in the scientific community, but have become better defined over time. The plain language of CERCLA's consent decree reopener provision requires that

---

62. *See generally* Chapter 1.

63. Intergovernmental Panel on Climate Change, Climate Change: The IPCC Scientific Assessment 52 (J.T. Houghton, G.J. Jenkins & J.J. Ephraums eds. 1990).

the condition be *unknown* at the time of consent decree entry, not merely that more is known about the condition now or that the Agency didn't expressly consider it in the initial remedial design. Thus, it will not be sufficient for EPA to allege that a consent decree can now be reopened due to its failure to consider climate change impacts in the remedy design.

However, there remains a possibility that later-in-time consent decrees could be reopened if EPA could demonstrate that the risks of sea level rise are now understood to be so much greater than they were at the time of consent decree entry that they now present a risk that could not have been foreseen at the time. For example, predictions of the amount of sea level rise that will occur by 2100 have increased significantly both due to advances in the science characterizing sea level rise and increases in atmospheric GHG concentrations, which increase the amount of warming that the scientific community predicts the planet will experience. In addition, advances in the science have made it possible to better understand regional variations in sea level rise and make region-specific predictions of the rate of future sea level rise over the coming decades. This increased precision of information and larger magnitude of projected impacts may provide EPA with an argument that even if sea level rise as a broad concept was known at the time of consent decree entry, the specific impacts that result in the release or threatened release of a hazardous substance were unknown. If EPA could make such an argument, it could be successful in reopening a CERCLA consent decree due to sea level rise impacts. Furthermore, it is important to note that a consent decree reopening would likely only be needed at a site where hazardous substances are allowed to remain in place, and these sites would also be subject to the five-year review process under CERCLA. As a result, it may not be necessary for EPA to avail itself of the consent decree reopener provision under CERCLA to obtain additional remedial action to respond to the threat of sea level rise.

The Impact of Sea Level Rise on Current CERCLA Remedies

Future sea level rise and storm surges are also relevant considerations in CERCLA remedies that are currently under development and that will be developed in the future. For current and future CERCLA remedies, the threats of sea level rise and storm surge are certainly known conditions, and therefore they arguably should be considered in evaluating the feasibility of various engineering remedies as part of the remedy selection process. There are two principal ways that sea level rise and storm surge impacts can be factored into current and future CERCLA remedies. First, in locations that may be susceptible to future sea level rise and storm surges, EPA and PRPs may wish to undertake activities in the initial remedial action that ensure the remedy will remain adequately protective of human health and the environment in the event that the site later becomes submerged. Second, other actions taken by federal, state, and local governments to respond to sea level rise—such as constructing physical barriers to protect areas near CERCLA sites from storm surge impacts—may impact CERCLA remedies in the coastal zone.

For future feasibility studies and remedial design processes in the coastal zone, sea level rise and storm surge are likely to be relevant considerations. For example, a feasibility study assessing the effectiveness of a remedy that would isolate contaminated soils along a waterway from the environment by using a seawall and a surface cap would likely need to consider whether such a remedy could be engineered to sustain repeated flooding in storm surge events. In addition, were the remedy under evaluation in an area that was so low-lying as to be subject to long-term inundation, the feasibility study may need to evaluate whether the cap could be designed in a way that it could also function as a confined aquatic disposal facility ("CAD") if the site were to become submerged in the long run. These considerations would also be relevant in the remedial design process where EPA and the PRPs detail the engineering specifications for and technical details of a remedial activity. In this process, it may be necessary to adjust engineering specifications to ensure that any on-site construction is designed to withstand flooding from storm surge and potentially ultimate inundation due to sea level rise.

In addition to considering sea level rise in the context of evaluating the suitability of particular CERCLA remedies, it is important to evaluate how actions that state and local governments may take to adapt to rising sea levels could themselves impact the effectiveness of a CERCLA remedy. For example, in the aftermath of both Hurricane Ike and Superstorm Sandy, local governments considered the construction of tidal barriers. In effect, these barriers would be closed in anticipation of a storm and act as a giant dam to protect inland areas from storm surge. The proposed "Ike Dike" in Texas would close the mouth of Galveston Bay during storm events to protect Houston from the impacts of storm surge.[64] Similarly, after Superstorm Sandy a series of tidal barriers were proposed to protect Manhattan from storm surge.[65] The impact of such tidal

---

64. *Ike Dike*, TEXAS A&M UNIVERSITY GALVESTON, http://www.tamug.edu/ikedike/ (last visited Feb. 27, 2016).

65. Mark Garrison, *NY Debates Expensive Storm Surge Barrier*, MARKETPLACE (Jan. 10, 2013), http://www.marketplace.org/topics/life/weather-economy/ny-debates-expensive-storm-surge-barrier.

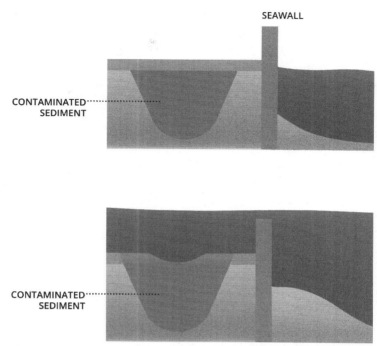

Figure 53: Submergence of an Upland Cap Due to Sea Level Rise

Over time, sea levels will rise and may cause upland remedies to become more submerged. For example, an upland cap to contain soils on tidal waterways can become submerged and may not be able to withstand those physical stresses.

barriers on CERCLA sites would depend on where they are located. While the tidal barrier theoretically protects those behind it from storm impacts, the wave energy creating the storm surge is deflected and will cause flooding to worsen in those areas that lie outside the tidal barrier. For example in the case of New York, a tidal barrier to protect Manhattan from a future Sandy-like event would increase storm surge impacts on Staten Island and portions of Long Island. There are thus two potentially relevant considerations for CERCLA sites. First, for sites outside of any coastal protection structures that may be installed, the PRPs will need to be prepared to address the possibility that adaptation actions taken by government entities could worsen the impacts of sea level rise and storm surge at their CERCLA sites. Second, for sites that lie inside coastal protection structures, the existence of such structures could change flow and circulation patterns, which may have particular significance for sediment sites where capping and monitored natural recovery are part of the CERCLA remedy.

In addition, EPA and PRPs may need to consider whether state and local adaptation planning measures could constitute applicable or relevant and appropriate regulations ("ARARs") under CERCLA. Section 121(d) of CERCLA requires that remedial actions meet any "standard, requirement, criteria, or limitation [of] any Federal environmental law" or "any promulgated standard, requirement, criteria, or limitation under a State environmental or facility siting law that is more stringent than any Federal" equivalent when such laws are "legally *applicable* to the hazardous substance or pollutant or contaminant concerned or [are] *relevant and appropriate* under the circumstances of the release or threatened release...."[66] However, not all state programs will rise to the level of being ARARs that EPA must consider under CERCLA. EPA guidance defines "applicable" and "relevant and appropriate" requirements as follows:

> *Applicable requirements* are those cleanup standards, standards of control, and other substantive environmental protection requirements, criteria, or limitations promulgated under Federal or State law that specifically address a hazardous substance, pollutant, contaminant, remedial action, location, or other circumstance at a CERCLA site.

> *Relevant and appropriate requirements* are those ... substantive environmental protection requirements ... promulgated under Federal or State law that, while not "applicable" ... address problems or situations sufficiently similar to those encountered at the CERCLA site that their use is well suited to the particular site.[67]

Notably, both "applicable" and "relevant and appropriate" requirements must be "promulgated." Thus, in order to be an ARAR, such requirements must be both "legally enforceable" and "generally applicable."[68] In order to be legally enforceable, state statutes or regulations may either "(1) have their own specific enforcement provisions written into them; or (2) be enforced through the State's general legal authority."[69] To be generally applicable, state requirements "must apply to a broader universe than Superfund sites."[70] Thus, state policies

---

66. 42 U.S.C. § 9621(d) (emphasis added).

67. See United States Environmental Protection Agency, EPA/540/G-89/006, CERCLA Compliance with Other Laws Manual xiii (1988) (emphasis in original).

68. United States Environmental Protection Agency, Pub. No. 9234.2-05/FS, CERCLA Compliance with State Requirements 3 (Dec. 1989).

69. *Id.*

70. *Id.*

that are not codified as enforceable laws are not considered ARARs under CER-CLA. Therefore, unless states develop and implement adaptation policies as a matter of state law, EPA would not be required to consider them as part of the design of a CERCLA remedy.

NEPA

On August 1, 2016, the Council on Environmental Quality ("CEQ") issued guidance for the consideration of climate change in analyses under the National Environmental Policy Act ("NEPA").[71] While this guidance has since been withdrawn,[72] it is discussed in detail here because project developers and Federal Agencies will still have to grapple with the incorporation of sea level rise impacts in NEPA analyses and Federal Agencies or reviewing courts may look to the now-withdrawn guidance as a roadmap for considering those impacts. NEPA requires the consideration of environmental impacts and evaluation of alternatives for each "major Federal action[ ] significantly affecting the quality of the human environment."[73] Importantly, NEPA does not mandate particular environmental outcomes, but rather mandates a process in which federal agencies must consider the environmental impacts of their proposed project and project alternatives.[74] However, the sufficiency of NEPA analyses can be judicially challenged, meaning that NEPA analyses can be a significant source of litigation risk for both federal agencies and the private parties seeking permits from them. Particularly in recent years, there has been an increase in the amount of NEPA litigation challenging the sufficiency of climate change analyses in the NEPA process,[75] suggesting that NEPA may be an increasing focus of litigation efforts in coming years.

---

71. Notice of Availability of Final Guidance for Federal Departments and Agencies on Consideration of Greenhouse Gas Emissions and the Effects of Climate Change in National Environmental Policy Act Reviews, 81 Fed. Reg. 51,866 (Aug. 5, 2016).

72. 82 Fed. Reg. 16,576 (Apr. 5, 2017).

73. 42 U.S.C. §4332(2)(C); 40 C.F.R. §1508.5.

74. Vermont Yankee Nuclear Power Corp. v. Nat. Res. Def. Council, 435 U.S. 519, 558 (1978).

75. For a comprehensive overview of NEPA climate change challenges see: *Climate Change Litigation in the U.S.*

When Is a NEPA Analysis Required?

NEPA analysis is required for "major Federal actions significantly affecting the quality of the human environment." 42 U.S.C. §4332(2)(C). Federal actions under NEPA can include projects actually carried out by government agencies as well as projects requiring government approval or receiving government funding.

Under NEPA, there are two levels of environmental evaluation that an agency may choose to conduct. First, an agency may choose to conduct an environmental assessment ("EA"), which is defined as a concise document that provides enough information to determine whether an agency can issue a finding of no significant impact ("FONSI") or if a full environmental impact statement ("EIS") is required.[76] If the environmental impacts of a project are likely to be significant enough that an EA does not provide sufficient information, the agency must prepare an EIS.[77] An EIS must contain a detailed discussion of the environmental impact of the proposed action, any avoidable adverse environmental impacts, alternatives to the proposed action, the relationship between local short-term uses of the environment and the maintenance and enhancement of long-term productivity in the project area, and any irreversible or irretrievable commitments of resources that would be associated with the proposed project.[78]

Whether an EA or an EIS is required will depend on the significance of the project, which is determined by the project's environmental impacts.[79] In determining the environmental impacts of a project, the reviewing agency must evaluate both the significant impacts that result from the project itself as well as any cumulative impacts. Cumulative impacts are defined to be impacts on the environment "result[ing] from the incremental impact of the action when added to other past, present, and reasonably foreseeable future actions regardless of what agency ... or person undertakes such other actions."[80] According to the CEQ's NEPA regulations, the assessment of cumulative impacts is an essential part of the NEPA analysis because "[c]umulative impacts can

---

76. 40 C.F.R. §1508.9.
77. *Id.*
78. 42 U.S.C. §4332(2)(C).
79. 40 C.F.R. §1506.1.
80. 40 C.F.R. §1508.7.

result from individually minor but collectively significant actions taking place over a period of time."[81]

Under the CEQ's NEPA regulations, agencies are to initiate the NEPA process "at the earliest possible time,"[82] and until the Agency has issued a decision under NEPA, it may not take actions that have an adverse environmental impact or limit the choice among alternatives.[83] An important early step in the NEPA analysis is the scoping of the assessment to be conducted.

While NEPA requires an assessment of all potentially significant environmental impacts of a project, there has recently been an increasing focus on the extent to which a NEPA analysis requires an express consideration of climate change. The CEQ first issued guidance on the consideration of climate change impacts under NEPA in 2010.[84] The 2010 Draft Guidance was never finalized, and CEQ instead proposed a revised draft guidance document in December 2014 that ultimately became the 2016 NEPA Climate Change Guidance ("the Guidance").

On August 7, 2014, the CEQ formally denied a petition for rulemaking that asked it to amend the NEPA regulations to expressly include considerations of climate change.[85] Specifically, the environmental petitioners had asked the CEQ to revise the regulatory definitions of direct and indirect effects to include specific reference to climate change and also include climate change as an explicit factor in the regulatory definition of "effects" under NEPA.[86] The petition also requested that the CEQ issue guidance on how agencies should incorporate climate considerations into the NEPA process.[87] In denying the petition the CEQ concluded that "revisions [to the NEPA regulations] are unnecessary because NEPA and its implementing regulations already require Federal agencies to evaluate the reasonably foreseeable environmental impacts of their actions, including foreseeable GHG and climate change implications."[88]

---

81. *Id.*

82. 40 C.F.R. § 1501.2.

83. *Id.* § 1506.1(a).

84. Memorandum from Nancy H. Sutley, Chair, CEQ, to Heads of Federal Departments and Agencies (Feb. 18, 2010), https://www.whitehouse.gov/sites/default/files/microsites/ceq/20100218-nepa-consideration-effects-ghg-draft-guidance.pdf.

85. Letter from Michael J. Boots, Acting Chair, CEQ, to Joseph Mendelson et al. (Aug. 7, 2014), http://energy.gov/sites/prod/files/2014/08/f18/CEQPetition_InclusionofClimateChangeAnalysisinNEPA_2014.pdf.

86. *Id.* at 3.

87. *Id.* at 4.

88. *Id.* at 6.

The 2016 NEPA Climate Change Guidance provided guidance on both the consideration of climate change impacts caused by a potential project and the physical impacts that climate changes may have on project design.[89] The Guidance began by evaluating the difficulties that are associated with addressing the climate change impacts of individual projects, and it then took several notable positions that seem to redefine the nature of NEPA analysis for GHG emissions.

The Guidance rejected the currently common practice of limiting the discussion of climate change in a NEPA analysis on the grounds that the GHG emissions from a particular project are insignificant (as compared to global GHG emissions) and therefore are not of consequence to global climate change on their own. The Guidance asserted that this type of statement "is essentially a statement about the nature of the climate change challenge" and thus is "not an appropriate basis for deciding whether or to what extent to consider climate change impacts under NEPA."[90] Instead, the Guidance recommended that agencies use greenhouse gas emissions as a proxy for climate change impacts in a NEPA assessment.[91]

The Guidance recommended further that agencies quantify both the direct and indirect GHG emissions from a proposed project.[92] In the event that an agency determined that quantitative analysis of GHG emissions was not appropriate the Guidance directed that "the agency should provide a qualitative analysis and its rationale for determining that the quantitative analysis is not warranted."[93] Notably, the Guidance declined to set an emissions threshold below which GHG emissions do not need to be considered in a NEPA analysis.

In addressing the scope of an action for the consideration of GHG emissions under NEPA, the Guidance explained that connected actions that have "a reasonably close causal relationship" to the proposed action should be considered in the NEPA analysis.[94] In providing examples of the types of actions that may be connected, the Guidance noted that "NEPA reviews for proposed resource extraction typically include reasonably foreseeable effects of various

---

89. Memorandum from Christina Goldfuss, Council on Environmental Quality, to Heads of Federal Departments and Agencies (Aug. 1, 2016) [hereinafter Guidance], https://www.whitehouse.gov/sites/whitehouse.gov/files/documents/nepa_final_ghg_guidance.pdf.

90. *Id.* at 11.

91. *Id.* at 10.

92. *Id.* at 11.

93. *Id.* at 13.

94. *Id.*

phases in the project, such as ... extraction, transport, refining, processing, [and] using the resource...."[95] The Guidance advised that determining which of these activities may be within the scope of a given NEPA analysis is something that should be determined by the reviewing agency to "use the analytical scope that best informs their decision making."[96]

The Guidance's proposed approach to considering projects that emit GHGs contained a number of legal deficiencies that demonstrate the challenge of evaluating the impacts of an individual project on global climate change under NEPA. First, NEPA itself requires the analysis of environmental impacts caused by a project.[97] However, the Guidance called on agencies to use GHG emissions as a proxy measure for climate change impacts rather than directly examining the incremental amount of climate change that may be caused by any individual project.[98] The Guidance directed that "[c]onsistent with NEPA, Federal agencies should consider the extent to which a proposed action and its reasonable alternatives would contribute to climate change[ ] through GHG emissions...."[99] The Guidance concluded that reliance on GHG emissions as a proxy for climate impacts is appropriate to "assess[] proposed actions' potential effects on climate change in NEPA analysis."[100] While the Guidance's reliance on GHG emissions as a proxy for climate impacts may be reasonable as a technical matter, it demanded an assessment of the direct and indirect impacts of proposed projects that is broader than what the Supreme Court has concluded NEPA requires. In *Department of Transportation v. Public Citizen*, the Supreme Court concluded that "NEPA requires a 'reasonably close causal relationship' between the environmental effect and the alleged cause" in order for consideration of a particular environmental effect to be a required component of the NEPA analysis.[101] As the Guidance itself acknowledged, "the totality of climate change impacts is not attributable to any single action,"[102] and thus seems to admit that the "reasonably close causal relationship" necessary before an effect must be analyzed under NEPA will not exist for the GHG emissions resulting from proposed projects. Thus, under the

---

95. *Id.* at 14.

96. *Id.*

97. 42 U.S.C. §4332(2)(C).

98. Guidance, *supra* note 89, at 10.

99. *Id.* at 9.

100. *Id.* at 10.

101. Department of Transp. v. Public Citizen, 541 U.S. 752, 767 (2004) (quoting Metropolitan Edison Co. v. People Against Nuclear Energy, 460 U.S. 766, 774 (1983)).

102. Guidance, *supra* note 89, at 11.

logic of the Supreme Court's decision in *Public Citizen*, it is unlikely that individual projects will ever have a level of greenhouse gas emissions that would be significant enough to require the analysis of climate change as a significant affect under NEPA.[103]

This is not to suggest that there is no place at all for the analysis of GHG emissions from an individual project under NEPA. GHG emissions from a project can be analyzed as part of a cumulative impacts analysis. In conducting a cumulative impacts analysis under NEPA, the reviewing agency must determine whether the incremental additional GHG emissions resulting from a particular proposed action, when combined with other past, present, and reasonably foreseeable future relevant actions, are significant and warrant analysis. In the Guidance, EPA departed from this approach by concluding that direct and indirect GHG emissions should be quantified in the analysis of the project's impacts. In fact, the Guidance recognized that this approach "is essentially a cumulative effects analysis that is subsumed within the general analysis and discussion of climate change impacts.... and a separate cumulative effects analysis for GHG emissions is not needed."[104]

The second area where the Guidance was limited by the scope of legal authority under NEPA is in its discussion of mitigation. The Guidance encouraged agencies to consider reasonable mitigation measures and alternatives to lower the level of the potential GHG emissions.[105] According to the Guidance these measures should include "enhanced energy efficiency, lower GHG-emitting technology, carbon capture, carbon sequestration..., sustainable land management practices, and capturing or beneficially using GHG emissions such as methane."[106] In *Robertson v. Methow Valley Citizens Council*, the Supreme Court concluded that NEPA's requirement that mitigation measures be considered extends only to those mitigation measures that are within the control of the agency conducting the NEPA analysis.[107] Thus, any consideration of mitigation of climate change impacts under NEPA would be limited to those actions for which there is an independent source of legal authority on which the agency can rely to curtail the project's GHG emissions.

---

103. Note that this stands in contrast to federal regulations potentially subject to NEPA analysis which might be able to produce GHG emissions changes that are large enough to warrant analysis on an individual basis under NEPA.

104. Guidance, *supra* note 89, at 17.

105. *Id.* at 18.

106. *Id.* at 19.

107. 490 U.S. 332, 359 (1989).

Of particular importance in the context of sea level rise adaptation is the potential use of NEPA to evaluate the impacts of a project in the context of both current and future environmental conditions. In establishing the baseline conditions against which the project is to be evaluated, the Guidance expressly directed agencies to consider both current environmental conditions and reasonably foreseeable future environmental conditions.[108] This means that in evaluating the impacts of a project, an agency should integrate data on expected changes in climate, including projected changes in rainfall patterns, increases in sea level, and increases in storminess. The Guidance suggested that when considering future changes in climate, agencies should consider two types of impacts. First, the Guidance directed agencies to consider whether climate change will cause the environmental impacts of a project itself to change over time.[109] For example, if a proposed project will use substantial amounts of water in a region where increasing droughts are anticipated in the future, an agency would need to consider the environmental impacts of the project's water withdrawals in a drier future climate.[110] This consideration of future climatic conditions would theoretically be applied to consideration of each of the project alternatives and could influence an agency's conclusions regarding which project alternative is preferred or what types of mitigation measures may be required.

Second, the Guidance stated that when a project is to be located in an area that is particularly susceptible to the physical impacts of climate change, the agency should consider how these physical impacts could affect the functioning of the project itself.[111] In this discussion the Guidance gave two specific examples of the consideration of sea level rise impacts. The Guidance stated that an agency considering a transportation project on a coastal barrier island should consider the "consequences of rebuilding where sea level rise and more intense storms will shorten the projected life of the project and change its effects on the environment."[112] The Guidance also noted that "chemical facilities located near the coastline could have increased risk of spills or leakages due to sea level rise or increased storm surges, …"[113] However, the Guidance, like NEPA itself, did not mandate that an agency make a particular decision or choose a project that avoids or lessens physical exposure to climate change. Rather, the most

---

108. Guidance, *supra* note 89, at 20.
109. *Id.* at 21.
110. *See id.*
111. *Id.* at 24.
112. *Id.*
113. *Id.* at 25.

that NEPA and the Guidance could have required was that agencies evaluate particular types of information before making their decisions.

Furthermore, the ultimate impact of the Guidance remains to be seen. The Guidance was withdrawn by President Trump's Council on Environmental Quality on April 5, 2017.

Even if the Guidance had not been withdrawn, it would not have been binding on Federal agencies.[114] The withdrawal of the Guidance substantially decreased the likelihood that agencies will choose to follow it in their NEPA analyses. However, the Guidance may still be significant as courts review legal challenges to NEPA analyses and look to contribute standards for the evaluation of climate change impacts.

NEPA climate change challenges are likely to continue for the foreseeable future. To date, most NEPA climate change challenges have focused upon whether an agency has adequately considered the impacts of greenhouse gas emissions expected to result from a particular project.[115] However, in November 2014, the Sabin Center on Climate Change Law submitted letters to the Federal Energy Regulatory Commission ("FERC") arguing that the physical impacts of sea level rise and storminess should be considered in FERC's NEPA evaluation of proposed natural gas facilities in Louisiana and Maine.[116] The comments on both projects addressed the scoping analysis conducted by FERC as an initial step in determining what environmental impacts should be considered in the NEPA analysis.[117] The letters state that pursuant to FERC's obligations under NEPA "the Commission must consider sea level rise and related coastal processes as reasonably foreseeable significant adverse impacts."[118] The letters continue that "[t]he Commission also must consider sea level rise and storm surge as future baseline environmental conditions" that should be considered in a NEPA analysis.[119] In response to the letter submitted regarding Louisiana LNG Energy, FERC has reportedly ordered the

---

114. *Id.* at 3 (noting that "Agencies have discretion in how they tailor their individual NEPA reviews" to incorporate climate change).

115. *Climate Change Litigation in the U.S., supra* note 75.

116. Letter from Jennifer M. Klein to Kimberly D. Bose, Secretary, Federal Energy Regulatory Commission, regarding Louisiana LNG Energy LLC (Oct. 27, 2014), http://www.eenews.net/assets/2014/10/30/document_gw_09.pdf; Letter from Jennifer M. Klein to Kimberly D. Bose, Secretary, Federal Energy Regulatory Commission, regarding Downeast Liquefaction LLC (Oct. 27, 2014), http://www.eenews.net/assets/2014/10/30/document_gw_10.pdf.

117. *Id.*

118. *Id.* at 1.

119. *Id.* at 2.

company to submit information regarding the potential impacts of climate change on the proposed facility.[120]

This is likely only the first in a series of actions that will require increasing scrutiny of the impacts of sea level rise and storminess on new projects in the coastal zone that are being evaluated under NEPA. An increase in the rigor of evaluation of climate change impacts in the coastal zone under NEPA is potentially significant for two reasons. First, it may lead to alternatives analyses that provide for a more explicit consideration of sea level rise and storminess conditions and lead to the selection of projects that will be more resilient to the physical impacts of climate change. The incorporation of such alternatives in a NEPA analysis has the potential to benefit both the project proponent and the coastal environment by ensuring that new developments are constructed in a manner that can accommodate sea level rise and its attendant impacts. Second, there is a likelihood that there will be an increase in NEPA litigation regarding the adequacy of any consideration of the physical impacts of climate change on a new project. While NEPA cannot force an agency to select a particular project alternative, agency analyses are frequently subject to challenge on the grounds that they failed to adequately consider particular environmental impacts, and sea level rise and increased storm surge events could certainly pose significant environmental impacts in the future. Thus, it is possible that new projects in the coastal zone could face significant delays due to the potential for protracted NEPA litigation if they fail to adequately account for the impacts of sea level rise and storm surge events.

Force Majeure and Climate Change

Increasing and increasingly foreseeable inundation events that accompany sea level rise and climate change have the potential to profoundly reshape the contractual liability of businesses under force majeure clauses. Businesses have traditionally relied on force majeure or "Act of God" provisions in their contracts to excuse performance or avoid liability when an unforeseen or unanticipated event prevents the business from performing its contractual

---

120. Jennifer M. Klein, *FERC Directs LNG Facility Applicant to Disclose Climate Change Impacts, as Urged by Sabin Center*, Climate Law Blog (Nov. 26th, 2014), http://blogs.law.columbia.edu/climatechange/2014/11/26/ferc-directs-lng-facility-applicant-to-disclose-climate-change-impacts-as-urged-by-sabin-center/.

obligations. In general, a force majeure provision in a contract will allow a party to either affirmatively seek to excuse its performance of a contractual obligation or to defend against a claim for a breach of contract when it can show (1) the event that caused the non-performance of a contractual obligation was not foreseeable at the time the contract was drafted and (2) the event was beyond the party's control.[121] Climate change potentially impacts the ability of businesses to rely on force majeure clauses in two significant ways. First, as the impacts of sea level rise, increased storminess, and other climate-driven changes become more frequent and severe, it is less likely that they will be defined as "unforeseeable" events either as a matter of contract law or by a reviewing court that is trying to determine whether a particular incident qualifies as a force majeure event. Second, in examining whether the harms of an event were beyond a party's control, courts will tend to evaluate what, if anything, a party did to mitigate the harms that resulted from its breach of the contract.[122] This has potentially profound implications as a driver of corporate climate change adaptation if courts begin to find that the duty to mitigate contractual damages from climate-driven events is far-reaching.

A typical force majeure provision covers "acts of God" (e.g., fires, floods, earthquakes, tsunamis, storms, hurricanes, or other natural disasters), war, terrorism or acts of the public enemy.[123] For example, consider a hypothetical power plant located in the coastal zone that supplies power to an industrial facility under a power purchase agreement. Typically, the power purchase agreement would require the power company to deliver to the purchasing facility as much power as it requires, up to a certain amount specified in the contract. However, the agreement would likely provide that a force majeure event would excuse the power plant from meeting its obligation to supply power. Such a provision might be structured as follows:

> For the purposes of this Agreement, a "Force Majeure Event" as to a Party means any occurrence, nonoccurrence or set of circumstances that is beyond the reasonable control of such Party and is not caused by such Party's negligence, lack of due diligence, or failure to follow Prudent Industry Practices.

---

121. *See* FORCE-MAJEURE CLAUSE, Black's Law Dictionary (10th ed. 2014).

122. *See* 30 Williston on Contracts §77:31 (4th ed.) ("An express force majeure clause in a contract must be accompanied by proof that the failure to perform was proximately caused by a contingency and that, in spite of skill, diligence, and good faith on the promisor's part, performance remains impossible or unreasonably expensive.").

123. *See generally* 84 A.L.R. 2d 12; 30 Williston on Contracts §77:31 (4th ed.).

When such a force majeure event happens and the power plant cannot run, the power company would then be excused from its obligation to supply power. For example, if the power plant were to be located along the coast and experiences flooding due to a storm surge event associated with a hurricane, the power plant could be excused from its contractual obligation to deliver power if the flooding made it impossible to safely run the plant.

Force majeure may also excuse performance based on the failure of third parties (e.g., suppliers and subcontractors) to perform their obligations to the contracting party. Following the above example of a power purchase agreement, assume that the hypothetical power plant depended upon a natural gas pipeline for its fuel source and that the pipeline was damaged during the hurricane and storm surge event. As a result of the damage, the power plant cannot obtain enough natural gas to generate the power required by its contract with the industrial facility. In this case, the failure of the natural gas pipeline company to provide adequate natural gas could provide a force majeure excuse negating the power plant's contractual obligation to supply power to the industrial facility. However, force majeure is not intended to excuse a party if the failure to perform could have been reasonably avoided by that party.[124] This distinction was explained by the Third Circuit in *Gulf Oil Company v. FERC*.[125] The case arose from Gulf Oil's failure to deliver natural gas under a supply contract with Texas Eastern Transmission Corporation. Under the contract between Gulf Oil and Texas Eastern and the accompanying certificate issued by FERC under the Natural Gas Act, Gulf Oil was required to deliver natural gas to Texas Eastern within a specified quantity range, but Gulf Oil was permitted to supply less gas under the contract during a force majeure event. That is, if a force majeure event prevented Gulf Oil from producing or delivering the required quantity of gas, Gulf Oil would not be liable for a breach of the contract. The Third Circuit explained that in order to use a force majeure clause to excuse Gulf Oil's failure to deliver the required quantities of natural gas "the [force majeure] event must have been beyond the party's control and without its fault or negligence."[126] In determining whether Gulf Oil's failure to deliver natural gas due to pipeline integrity issues qualified as a force majeure event, the Court distinguished between those events that could qualify as force majeure and those that could not stating:

---

124. Black's Law Dictionary 645 (6th ed. 1990).
125. 706 F.2d 444 (3d Cir. 1983).
126. *Id.* at 452.

> For example, the occurrence of a hurricane is a *force majeure* event. The resultant unavailability of gas follows from the occurrence of the event and carries with it the same amount of uncertainty. However, the effect of the event on the delivery of gas, the actual damage to the pipes, is not inferred from the event and thus does not carry the presumption of uncertainty. It is incumbent on Gulf to establish that the pipe damage and mechanical breakdowns in issue would not have occurred if there had not been a hurricane. Pipe damage occurs because of normal wear and tear and therefore can be anticipated. If the *force majeure* event causes the inability to deliver the gas rather than the inability to obtain the gas, the supplying party has the burden of proving that the inability to deliver was not caused by routine maintenance.[127]

Thus, *Gulf Oil* illustrates the concept that even when a force majeure event occurs, a party can only be excused from performance if it can show that the non-performance was a direct result of the force majeure event. The Court in *Gulf Oil* went on to explain that some events that may be initially unforeseeable could become foreseeable over time, concluding "[f]urthermore, it is possible to accurately describe an event at its initial occurrence as unforeseeable and later because of the regularity with which it occurs, to find that such a description is no longer applicable."[128] This latter conclusion is particularly significant in the context of a changing climate because it suggests that climate-driven events, such as inundation due to sea level rise and increased storm surge events, could be force majeure events when they first occur, but that their increased frequency over time could cause them to become foreseeable events that no longer qualify as force majeure.

When contracting parties define the scope of force majeure in their agreement, the contractual language will *usually* dictate the interpretation, application, and effect of the provision.[129] While force majeure provisions vary contract-to-contract, common elements include notice and mitigation requirements. A notice requirement typically requires a party asserting force majeure to give the other party to the contract prompt, written notice of its intention to assert force majeure to excuse non-performance. In addition, force majeure clauses customarily require the party asserting the defense to

---

127. *Id.* at 453.
128. *Id.*
129. *See, e.g.*, Sun Operating Ltd. P'ship v. Holt, 984 S.W.2d 277, 283 (Tex. Ct. App. 1998).

take reasonable steps to minimize the delay or damages resulting from its default in performance and to perform all other possible obligations under the contract.

When a contract does not contain an express force majeure provision, applicable law may excuse a party's contractual performance in much the same way that a force majeure clause would. For example, the United Nations Convention on Contracts for the International Sale of Goods ("CISG") provides:

> A party is not liable for a failure to perform any of his obligations if he proves that the failure was due to an impediment beyond his control and that he could not reasonably be expected to have taken the impediment into account at the time of the conclusion of the contract or to have avoided or overcome it, or its consequences.[130]

In addition to the CISG, many jurisdictions provide a force majeure defense in contracts that do not include an explicit force majeure provision, provided that the parties do not expressly indicate that force majeure does not apply.[131] Whether a force majeure defense exists, however, is only the beginning of the analysis to determine whether, and to what extent, force majeure excuses a contracting party's performance under a contract. The governing law, contract language, and facts and circumstances of the matter require additional consideration.

Some jurisdictions require that a force majeure provision be interpreted consistent with a judicially created force majeure doctrine ("doctrinal jurisdiction").[132] The doctrine usually requires such provisions be interpreted narrowly and strictly to relieve a party of liability only when (1) performance is prevented or delayed due to an extreme and unforeseeable event (2) that is beyond the party's control and occurs without the fault or negligence of the party claiming the defense.[133]

---

130. U.N. CONVENTION ON CONTRACTS FOR THE INT'L SALE OF GOODS, Art. 79(1), U.N. SALES NO. E.10.V.14 (2010). The CISG is a treaty that applies to contracts for the sale of goods between parties in different states when both states have ratified the CISG, or when the rules of private international law lead to the application of the law of a state that has ratified the CISG. *Id.* Art. 1(1).

131. *See, e.g.,* CODE CIVIL Art. 1148 (Fr.); U.C.C. §2-615.

132. *See, e.g.,* Watson Labs., Inc. v. Rhone-Poulenc Rorer, Inc., 178 F. Supp. 2d 1099, 1110 (C.D. Cal. 2001) (reading the common law force majeure elements of unforeseeability and lack of control into force majeure provision of a contract irrespective of the contract language).

133. *See id.*

Other jurisdictions use a "non-doctrinal" approach, allowing parties to freely assign risk of nonperformance as they see fit under their contracts ("non-doctrinal jurisdictions").[134] If the contracting parties agreed to a force majeure clause that does not require the event to be unforeseeable at the time of contracting, the court will not impose such a requirement. Texas is one example of a non-doctrinal jurisdiction. Indeed, some Texas courts have suggested that interpreting force majeure provisions under the doctrinal approach is unreasonable because imposing a requirement that specified events be unforeseeable to justify excusing performance would be contrary to the parties' intent.[135] Thus, contracting parties in these jurisdictions can create extremely broad force majeure provisions. The only real limitation would be to ensure that the provision does not allow the party's performance to be excused for conditions that existed at the time of contracting, or for an event that the party affirmatively caused because, then, the bargained-for promise would be illusory.[136] These limitations, and the unforeseeability and control requirements in doctrinal jurisdictions, create issues when asserting force majeure in response to climate change impacts.

Because climate change is predicted to increase sea levels (and associated flood events) and may increase storminess,[137] which are precisely the types of events that may have qualified for force majeure defenses in the past, it is arguable that the utility of the force majeure defense for weather events linked to climate change is decreasing, especially in doctrinal jurisdictions.[138] Indeed, it is increasingly recognized in the legal field that climate-driven shifts in weather patterns may present significant challenges to the application of the force majeure defense and require new approaches to contracting in the future if parties wish to protect themselves from liability for certain types of natural disasters.[139]

---

134. *See, e.g.*, *Sun Operating Ltd. P'ship*, 984 S.W.2d at 283 (stating that reviewing courts are not at liberty to rewrite the contract or interpret it in a manner which the parties never intended).

135. *Id.* at 288 n.4 ("[T]o imply an unforeseeability requirement into a force majeure clause would be unreasonable[,] ... because in naming specific force majeure events in the clause the parties undoubtedly foresaw the possibility that they could occur, and that is why they enumerated them to begin with.").

136. *See, e.g.*, Home Devco/Tivoli Isles LLC v. Silver, 26 So.3d 718, 722 (Fla. Dist. Ct. App. 2010) (finding that as long as the force majeure clause limits exclusions to events beyond the parties' control and not within their discretion, the contract is not illusory).

137. *See* Chapter 1 pp. 7–10.

138. *See* Kenneth T. Kristl, *Diminishing the Divine: Climate Change and the Act of God Defense*, 15 WIDENER L. REV. 325, 354 (2010) (discussing the bleak future of the "act of God" defense in tort law, admiralty law, and environmental law due to climate change and advances in meteorological technology).

139. *See generally* Jocelyn L. Knoll & Shannon L. Bjorkland, *Force Majeure and Climate Change: What is the New Normal?* 8 AM. COLL. CONSTRUCTION LAWYERS J. 29 (2014); Wm.

In fact, in doctrinal jurisdictions, where unforeseeability and lack of control tests are read into force majeure provisions, the force majeure defense will be measured against a shifting baseline of sea level rise and storm surge events, making the scope of its protections less predictable. As climate change-induced "acts of God" become more frequent and severe and scientists' ability to link particular events to climate change improves, it will be more difficult for parties to meet the unforeseeability test imposed by courts.[140] As a result, parties claiming force majeure may face increasing difficulties in proving that the event was unexpected or unanticipated, and, as more intense storms occur, it will be more difficult to support conclusions that the event was unusual or somehow exceptional.[141]

For non-doctrinal jurisdictions like Texas, the growing amount of research on climate change impacts and weather trends will make it more difficult to prove that force majeure events did not already exist at the time of contracting. In fact, as discussed in Chapter 1, the National Climate Assessment now projects that incremental annual damage to capital assets in the coastal zone along the Gulf Coast caused by climate change could reach $2.7 to $4.6 billion per year by 2030 and $8.3 to $13.2 billion per year by 2050.[142] When the damages—resulting from sea level rise, storm surges, and other climate-driven events—are realized, parties may face challenges arguing that they were unforeseeable at the time of entry into a contract.

The issue of climate-driven shifts in weather events may be particularly problematic for parties who find themselves in litigation over the scope of force majeure clauses. In determining whether a weather event is unusually severe and would qualify as a force majeure event, both contracting parties and courts tend to look to historical weather patterns.[143] However, as the impacts of climate change are increasingly experienced, these historical baselines may cease to provide an accurate indicator of what types of events are expected and which events are truly unforeseeable. To account for these shifts in weather patterns, several approaches have been suggested, each of which may fundamentally

---

Cary Wright, *Force Majeure Clauses and the Insurability of Force Majeure Risks*, 23 Construction Lawyer 16 (2003).

140. Knoll & Bjorkland, *supra* note 139.

141. *See id.*

142. United States Global Change Research Program, Climate Change Impacts in the United States: The Third National Climate Assessment 589 (2014).

143. Knoll & Bjorkland, *supra* note 139.

alter the reliability of the force majeure defense.[144] First, the historical data examined to determine whether an event is extraordinary could be limited to data from the last 10 to 20 years.[145] This approach theoretically provides the benefit of incorporating any shifts in baseline weather conditions into what is expected. However, there are several reasons that this approach may be unattractive to contracting parties. As discussed in Chapter 1, larger, multi-decadal weather phenomena contribute to both the rate of sea level rise in particular regions and the likelihood that hurricanes will form and make landfall.[146] Thus, the selection of a shorter historical time period as the baseline against which to evaluate potential force majeure weather events may miss these important longer-term phenomena and improperly alter the scope of events that are determined to be foreseeable. The second potential approach is to attempt to adjust historical data to account for changing weather patterns.[147] An example of this approach would be to take an area like the Northeast United States, where total amounts of rainfall are projected to increase only slightly but rainfall events are expected to be more intense when they do occur, and attempt to adjust historical data on maximum rainfall events to reflect this projected shift in weather patterns. While a potentially promising approach, it is not clear that data at the appropriate local and regional scales are available to make these kinds of adjustments in a manner that would be legally significant. Recall that the key question in evaluating a force majeure weather event is whether the event was reasonably foreseeable; because all future projections of climate change are subject to deviations from actual future conditions due to assumptions in the modeling and limitations in data, it would be challenging to use projections of future conditions to define foreseeability for the purposes of force majeure. However, as shifts in weather patterns are actually experienced, there may be some possibility of attempting to adjust historical data to form a new baseline. A third approach that has been suggested to factor climate-driven shifts in weather patterns into force majeure clauses is to explicitly incorporate future assumptions about the weather into the contract.[148] This is an approach that may be particularly attractive in non-doctrinal jurisdictions where the parties have broad latitude to define the scope of events that will be considered force majeure. In these jurisdictions, parties could agree on a baseline meteorological dataset or

---

144. *Id.*
145. *Id.*
146. *See* Chapter 1 pp. 8–10.
147. Knoll & Bjorkland, *supra* note 139.
148. *Id.*

set of conditions against which events that may happen during the contract period would be assessed to determine if they are force majeure events.

Parties seeking to assert force majeure also bear the burden of demonstrating that the damages at issue were beyond their control. The control requirement is typically understood to have two distinct elements. First, the party must show that it did not cause the alleged force majeure event. Second, parties are generally required to show that they took all reasonable measures to mitigate the damages caused by the event. Each of these issues may pose unique challenges when climate-driven events are considered under force majeure clauses.

With respect to the first prong, there is a potential issue arising from a party's contribution to global climate change in the form of greenhouse gas emissions. In doctrinal jurisdictions, courts require the unforeseeable event to be beyond the party's control and occur without the fault or negligence of the party claiming the defense.[149] In non-doctrinal jurisdictions, the party's performance may not be excused for an event that the party affirmatively caused.[150] To the extent that a party seeking to claim force majeure is a significant emitter of GHGs, it may find itself facing arguments that it contributed to climate change and therefore was a cause of the alleged force majeure event. However, such arguments are likely to be unsuccessful because, as discussed above, it would be extremely difficult if not impossible to demonstrate that a particular entity's GHG emissions were a legally proximate cause of a specific amount of climate change or could be tied to a particular weather event.

Of more significance is the second prong, which requires parties to show that they have mitigated against the damages caused by a particular event. The Third Circuit has already stated, albeit in dicta, that although an event might initially be unforeseeable, subsequent and frequent recurrences might make the event foreseeable.[151] Thus, a frequent and almost predictable occurrence removes an event from the realm of force majeure.[152] In addition, other courts have concluded that even when disruptions to contract performance are caused by weather events, the party claiming force majeure still has a duty to minimize the damages that will result from the weather events.[153] Therefore, as climate change increases the foreseeability of particular events, including coastal storms and flooding, contracting parties may

---

149. *See, e.g., Watson Labs.*, 178 F. Supp. 2d at 1110.
150. *See, e.g., Home Devco/Tivoli Isles*, 26 So.3d at 722.
151. *Gulf Oil*, 706 F.2d at 453–54.
152. *Id.*
153. *See* McDevitt & Street Co. v. Marriott Corp., 713 F. Supp. 906, 915 (E.D. Va. 1989).

be required to take precautions to protect against their facilities and supply chains from these foreseeable effects before they will be able to successfully assert a force majeure defense.[154] Thus, the future ability to assert force majeure defenses could become an important driver of corporate actions to adapt to climate change. For example, facilities with onsite power generation that is critical to their operation may find it advantageous to relocate key infrastructure to higher ground so that it is less likely to be disrupted by flood events. Corporations may also find it desirable to build redundancies into their supply chains or keep larger inventories of key supplies onsite during times of year when flooding or storm events may be more likely to cause disruptions.

To ensure sufficient protection from true force majeure events, businesses should draft contracts carefully to adequately allocate liability for unpredictable impacts resulting from climate events. Due to the increased foreseeability of climate change impacts and severe weather events, it would be prudent for businesses in non-doctrinal jurisdictions to expressly eliminate the notion of foreseeability in a force majeure clause and avoid the potential for court inquiry altogether.[155] In doctrinal jurisdictions, however, businesses may wish to attempt to broaden the potential applicability of a force majeure provision by focusing the clause "on the effects of a disruptive event, rather than specifically enumerating all potential [qualifying] events."[156] Contracting parties should anticipate the possible effects of increasingly severe storms on contracted activities and review the force majeure language closely in light of those effects. For instance, parties could draft a force majeure clause to focus on the unavailability of raw materials (as an effect of a hurricane) rather than on the event causing the material shortage specifically.[157] In these instances, courts may be inclined to focus more on the unforeseeability of the specific effects of the event, even if the event was foreseeable.[158]

Parties can further attempt to protect themselves by including broadening language in any force majeure clause such as "or other causes similar to those enumerated," to help cover events similar to those listed but that defy exact definition. Parties are free to define the risks of nonperformance as long as the

---

154. Kristl, *supra* note 138, at 357.

155. Wm. Cary Wright, *Force Majeure Delays*, 26 CONSTRUCTION LAWYER 33, 33 (2006) (citing P.J.M. Declercq, *Modern Analysis of the Legal Effect of Force Majeure Clauses in Situations of Commercial Impracticability*, 15 J.L. & COM. 213, 237 (Fall 1995)).

156. *Id.* at 34.

157. *Id.*

158. *Id.*

standards are not "manifestly unreasonable."[159] The "manifestly unreasonable" standard will determine whether a party's [causing an event], either affirmatively or negligently, may preclude a legitimate claim for [force majeure]."[160] These drafting concepts are especially important for companies in sectors where weather and climate are an integral part of production (e.g., agriculture and construction), and industries that rely heavily on transport and other infrastructure in their supply and demand chains.

Insurance Litigation

Another important concern for the private sector is the potential for increasing insurance coverage litigation arising from climate change. At this time, climate-related insurance litigation has been relatively limited. As a result, the goal of this section is to simply highlight the issues that have arisen in litigation so far and note additional areas of potential development that could be of concern in the coming years rather than attempting to provide a comprehensive overview of climate change and insurance issues.

The first significant piece of climate change insurance litigation was a coverage case that was ultimately heard by the Supreme Court of Virginia. In *AES v. Steadfast Insurance Company*, AES—one of the power company defendants in the *Kivalina* case discussed above—sought to require Steadfast, its insurer, to defend it in the *Kivalina* litigation.[161] AES had purchased a commercial general liability policy from Steadfast. These policies typically provide coverage for the insured against legal claims for bodily injury or property damage. When a company that has purchased a commercial general liability policy receives a claim that is covered by the policy, it may tender the claim to its insurer. The insurer then provides a legal defense to the insured company and the policy will typically cover any award against the insured party up to a contractually specified amount. In *AES v. Steadfast*, AES attempted to tender the *Kivalina* plaintiffs' claim to Steadfast as a claim for property damage under its insurance policy.[162] Steadfast asserted that it did not have an obligation to provide AES with a defense and coverage because AES's policy only provided coverage for property damage resulting from "an occurrence," which was a term specifically

---

159. U.C.C. § 1-302(b) (2001).
160. Wright, *supra* note 155, at 34.
161. 725 S.E.2d 532 (Va. 2012).
162. *Id.* at 533.

defined in the contract.[163] The insurance policy itself defined an "occurrence" as "an accident, including continuous or repeated exposure to substantially the same general harmful condition."[164] Upon review, the Supreme Court of Virginia concluded that because of the contract's definition of an occurrence and the state's case law finding that "occurrence" and "accident" are generally synonymous in the insurance coverage context, the *Kivalina* claims would only be a covered occurrence if the plaintiffs' complaint could be read to allege that the Village's injuries "resulted from unforeseen consequences that were not natural or probable consequences of AES's deliberate act of emitting carbon dioxide and greenhouse gases."[165] Turning to the facts of the case, the Court concluded that AES's acts resulting in greenhouse gas emissions were intentional and that the consequences for the Village of Kivalina were "natural and probable."[166] As a result, the Court concluded that the *Kivalina* claim was not an "occurrence" for which Steadfast was required to provide insurance coverage to AES.[167]

AES v. Steadfast is significant for at least two reasons. First, it provides some insight into how courts may choose to interpret the foreseeability of climate change impacts in the future. Importantly, the Virginia Supreme Court did not determine that AES itself actually knew at the time the GHGs were emitted that they would cause the climate-driven changes of which the *Kivalina* plaintiffs complained. Rather, the court concluded that such consequences were not so unforeseeable as to constitute an accident under Virginia law that fell within the scope of AES's insurance policy.[168] Second, the case suggests that some private parties may find themselves under-insured when the impacts of sea-level rise and increased storminess are actually felt, particularly if these events result in increased litigation. In the context of liability insurance, two principal situations could arise in which parties may find their insurance to be lacking. The first would be claims along the lines of those made by plaintiffs in *Kivalina* and *Comer* that allege that the defendants contributed to the climate impacts that caused their injuries. Second, there is a possibility that facilities in the coastal zone may face risks of physical damage resulting from sea level rise or storm surge and that the physical damage may cause the release of pollutants into the environment. To the extent that commercial general liability policies or pollu-

---

163. *Id.*
164. *Id.* at 534.
165. *Id.* at 536.
166. *Id.* at 537–38.
167. *Id.* at 538.
168. *Id.*

tion liability policies limit their coverage to "accidents" that are unforeseeable, facilities that have taken inadequate measures to make themselves resilient to storm surge and flooding exposure may find their insurance coverage lacking.

The second significant piece of litigation to arise in the context of climate change and insurance litigation was the *Illinois Farmers* case, filed in the Spring of 2014. The *Illinois Farmers* case was filed in a federal district court and was voluntarily dismissed by the plaintiffs before trial.[169] However, it highlights a new species of potential insurance litigation that could be significant in the future. The *Illinois Farmers* case was brought by a division of Farmers Insurance Company against a number of municipalities in the greater Chicago area. The insurance company had paid property insurance claims to homeowners who had experienced flooding after a severe rain event. In its complaint, the insurance company sought to recover from the defendant municipalities the money it had paid to its insured policy owners, alleging that payments on the policies were only necessary because the municipalities had not taken adequate measures to accommodate anticipated stormwater flows.[170] The complaint alleged that the municipal defendants knew or should have known that climate change will cause greater stormwater volumes requiring management, that the storm in question would fall within the climate-adjusted 100-year return period, and that the flooding event at issue would not have occurred if the municipalities had adopted adequate stormwater management practices.[171] While the case did not go to trial, it is potentially significant because it is the first instance of plaintiffs alleging that a local government had a duty to anticipate and plan for the flooding impacts of climate change. Were such a legal duty to be recognized by a reviewing court, it could lead to significant future climate change litigation against municipalities.

The final area of potential future insurance litigation where there has been recent activity related to climate change is directors and officers ("D&O") liability. D&O coverage is a type of insurance that provides protection to corporate officers and directors for the decisions they make within the scope of their duties running a company.[172] In May of 2014, Greenpeace, the Center for In-

---

169. Notice of Dismissal, Ill. Farmers Ins. Co. v. Metro. Water Reclamation Dist. of Greater Chi., No. 1:2014cv3251 (N.D. Ill. May 2, 2014), ECF No. 62.

170. Complaint, Ill. Farmers Ins. Co. v. Metro. Water Reclamation Dist. of Greater Chi., No. 1:2014cv3251 (N.D. Ill. Apr. 17, 2014), ECF No. 1.

171. *Id.* ¶¶ 50, 60.1, 61.

172. *See* ALLIANZ GLOBAL CORPORATE AND SPECIALTY, INTRODUCTION TO D&O INSURANCE (2010), http://www.agcs.allianz.com/assets/PDFs/risk%20insights/AGCS-DO-infopaper.pdf.

ternational Environmental Law, and the World Wildlife Fund sent letters to 36 large companies involved in the energy industry and their insurers raising questions about their D&O policies.[173] The letter sent directly to the companies claims that "aiming to obstruct action on climate change, coupled with the development, sponsorship or dissemination of false, misleading or intentionally incomplete information about the climate risks associated with fossil fuel products and services to regulators, shareholders, and insurers could pose a risk to directors and officers personally."[174] The letter asks that each officer and director who receives it respond to an attached series of questions that seek information on whether the recipient company has "implemented a clear and specific policy to make sure it is not involved in distorting the public's, investors', regulators', insurers' or policymakers' understanding of the severity of the risks of climate change and the consequential liability risks to your company."[175] The letter also asks questions about the extent to which the respondents believe that their current D&O policies would provide liability protection.[176] The letter to insurers makes similar contentions and poses a suite of questions about the scope of D&O coverage that are designed to suggest that the insured companies at issue are intentionally misleading investors regarding climate change risks.[177] As described in more detail in the following section, the nature of Greenpeace's underlying claims about energy companies intentionally misleading investors on climate change is highly suspect, as there are explicit federal legal requirements that demand the disclosure of material climate change risks to investors. Thus, the tactic taken in the letters themselves is questionable and the underlying logic appears to be unsound. However, the letters in and of themselves are significant because they suggest

---

173. For a complete list of the insurers and companies that received these letters, *see* http://www.greenpeace.org/international/Global/international/briefings/climate/2014/climate-denialism/Insurers-and-Companies-List.pdf.

174. *See* Letter from Greenpeace International to Andrew MacKenzie, BHP Billiton Limited (May 28, 2014), http://www.greenpeace.org/international/Global/international/briefings/climate/2014/climate-denialism/Companies-letter-example.pdf.

175. Letter from Greenpeace International to Andrew MacKenzie, BHP Billiton Limited, Annex C Questions for Fossil Fuel Company Directors and Officers (May 28, 2014), http://www.greenpeace.org/international/Global/international/briefings/climate/2014/climate-denialism/Annex-C.pdf.

176. *Id.*

177. *See* Letter from Greenpeace International to Andrew MacKenzie, BHP Billiton Limited, Annex D Questions for Senior Executives of Writers of D&O Liability Insurance Policies (May 28, 2014), http://www.greenpeace.org/international/Global/international/briefings/climate/2014/climate-denialism/Annex-D.pdf.

that groups may increasingly seek to target directors and officers of individual companies with claims related to climate change impacts.

SEC Reporting Requirements

In 2010, the Securities and Exchange Commission ("SEC") released a document interpreting how its corporate disclosure rules should be applied to climate change.[178] The guidance identifies four key areas of required reporting under the SEC rules where disclosures related to climate change may be relevant: (1) a description of the business making the filing, particularly with respect to disclosures related to environmental compliance costs; (2) legal proceedings in which the party is involved; (3) risk factors; and (4) management's discussion and analysis.[179] Specifically addressing how these required disclosures interact with climate change, the SEC guidance instructs that companies should evaluate the impacts on their businesses of new and emerging legal regimes that address climate change.[180] Turning to the physical impacts of climate change, the SEC guidance notes "[s]ignificant physical effects of climate change, such as effects on the severity of weather (for example, floods or hurricanes), sea levels, the arability of farmland, and water availability and quality, have the potential to affect a registrant's operations and results."[181] The guidance lists the following specific examples of physical disruptions due to climate change that could lead to impacts on a company's operations: property damage and disruption to operations for companies with operations concentrated on coastlines; indirect financial and operational impacts resulting from disruptions to major customers or suppliers due to severe weather events such as major hurricanes or floods; increased insurance claims and increased liabilities for insurance companies; and increased insurance premiums and decreased availability of coverage for companies with plants and operations in areas subject to severe weather.[182]

Importantly, the SEC's climate change guidance only requires a company to disclose those climate risks it considers to be "material." The Supreme Court has interpreted a material risk requiring disclosure to be one that there is a

---

178. Commission Guidance Regarding Disclosure Related to Climate Change, Release Nos. 33-9106, 34-61469, FR-82, 75 Fed. Reg. 6290 (Feb. 8, 2010).
179. *Id.* at 6293–94.
180. *Id.* at 6295–96.
181. *Id.* at 6296.
182. *Id.* at 6297.

substantial likelihood a reasonable investor would consider important in making his decision whether to invest in a company.[183] Many companies engage in reporting on climate change risks that is independent of SEC reporting through forums such as the Carbon Disclosure Project. Comparison of the voluntary reports that companies file and their SEC disclosures reveals that most companies tend to disclose substantially more climate risks in their voluntary filings than in SEC disclosure statements.[184] This suggests that while many companies have begun to acknowledge the risks of climate change, they do not yet assess these risks as being sufficiently material to warrant disclosure in their SEC filings.

However, this is a trend that may be changing, particularly for public companies with assets in the coastal zone that are potentially exposed to the impacts of sea level rise and increased storminess. Shareholder proposals continue to encourage companies to increase their disclosure of climate change risks and such resolutions are starting to win significant votes.[185] While to date, many of these proposals have focused on disclosures related to greenhouse gas emissions themselves or risks that climate change regulation may limit companies' ability to exploit their fossil fuel reserves, similar actions focused on physical exposure to climate change are likely to follow. As such, businesses with assets concentrated in the coastal zone may find that more robust disclosures on the potential impacts of sea level rise and climate change are necessary to respond to shareholder demands in the future.

Conclusions

This chapter has provided several examples of how the physical impacts of sea level rise and increased storminess may already require consideration under traditional environmental legal frameworks. There are numerous other traditional environmental laws and broader legal frameworks that will undoubtedly be implicated as the physical impacts of climate change are increasingly felt. It

---

183. Basic Inc. v. Levinson, 485 U.S. 224, 231–32 (1988).

184. *See* Center for Climate & Energy Solutions, Weathering the Next Storm: A Closer Look at Business Resilience (2015).

185. In the 2017 Proxy season, several major energy companies received significant votes in favor of proposals to complete reports on operating in a manner consistent with a 2 Degree Celsius Secession. See PPL Corporation, Current Report (Form 8-K) (May 18, 2017) (reporting over 50% of shareholder votes for the 2 degrees celsius proposal); FirstEnergy Corp., Current Report (Form 8-K) (May 17, 2017) (reporting a 43% vote for the 2 degree celsius proposal).

is important to recall that all modern environmental law and nearly all of the key legal concepts governing business operations were developed over a long period of relatively stable climatic conditions. As such, these laws are all underpinned by basic assumptions that the external environment will remain largely the same or that, except in highly unusual cases, it will not impact business operations as they have typically been carried out. As the impacts of climate change continue to be felt, these assumptions may be rendered invalid, suggesting that climate change issues will ultimately permeate through many facets of our legal system and fundamentally impact how companies do business.

Index